Luminaries

Luminaries

Princeton Faculty Remembered

EDITED BY Patricia H. Marks

ASSOCIATION OF PRINCETON GRADUATE ALUMNI
PRINCETON, NEW JERSEY
1996

Photograph Credits

Fabian Bachrach: GERALD EADES BENTLEY

Berko, Aspen, Colorado: CYRIL E. BLACK

Blackstone: GREGORY VLASTOS

Martin, Baltimore: SOLOMON LEFSCHETZ

Robert P. Matthews: SIR WILLIAM ARTHUR LEWIS, WILLIAM F. SHELLMAN, JR.

Elizabeth G.C. Menzies: DONALD R. HAMILTON

Alan W. Richards: E. HARRIS HARBISON, WHITNEY J. OATES, R. PAUL RAMSEY, HENRY DEWOLF SMYTH

Lucien Rorelle, Paris: LUIGI CROCCO

Naomi Savage: MELVIN TUMIN

John W.H. Simpson: CARLOS HEARD BAKER, FRITZ MACHLUP, HENRY DEWOLF SMYTH

Ulli Steltzer: ERIC F. GOLDMAN

Orren Jack Turner: NINA BERBEROVA, WESLEY FRANK CRAVEN, GEORGE E. DUCKWORTH, DONALD DREW EGBERT, LEON LAPIDUS, OSKAR MORGENSTERN, DURANT W. ROBERTSON, JR., OLIVER STRUNK, HUGH STOTT TAYLOR, RICHARD H. WILHELM

ISBN 0691-01167-2

Published as part of the celebration of the 250th anniversary of the founding of Princeton University.

DESIGNED BY Judith Martin Waterman of Martin-Waterman Associates, Ltd.

Printed in the United States of America
by Princeton Academic Press
at Lawrenceville, New Jersey

▼ CONTENTS ▼

▼ ACKNOWLEDGMENTS ▼

The Association of Princeton Graduate Alumni (APGA) has made this book possible. Since its founding in 1948 by Dean Hugh Stott Taylor and a small group of alumni, APGA's mission has been to support graduate study at Princeton and to facilitate the development of a community of scholars among alumni of the Graduate School. APGA pays special attention to the future of the professoriat by funding the annual "Teaching Awards" for graduate students who have excelled in their roles as preceptors and laboratory supervisors in undergraduate courses, and "Travel and Research Grants" for graduate students who need to consult archives or attend conferences away from Princeton. Since 1973, APGA has awarded the James Madison Medal honoring graduate alumni who have distinguished themselves by their work both within and outside of academe. Among the earliest recipients of the Madison Medal were John Bardeen, who twice won the Nobel Prize; playwright and novelist Thornton Wilder; and William O. Baker, president of the Bell Telephone Laboratories. More recently, the Medal has been awarded to classicist Robert F. Goheen, Princeton's president from 1957 to 1972; to Nobel physicist Steven Weinberg; Admiral William J. Crowe, Jr., political scientist and former chairman of the Joint Chiefs of Staff; and to religious philosopher Cornell R. West, whose books about race relations in the United States have enabled us to grapple more humanely with a continuing problem.

The achievements of the men and women who have contributed essays to this volume are themselves worthy of note, and are described too briefly in the "Contributors" chapter. I am grateful for their unfailing generosity and cooperation; their tributes to their mentors and friends make for interesting and moving reading.

The work of the Advisory Committee has been essential. I imposed on them constantly, and was rewarded with good advice. They were instrumental in developing the list of subjects for these essays and identifying those who should write about them. They also read the essays and provided suggestions for editing them.

Princeton University Archivist Ben Primer, Assistant Archivists Nanci A. Young and Daniel J. Linke, and their staff were unfailingly efficient, helpful, and cheerful as the photographs and research for the book were gathered together. Tributes to them abound in the many books based upon research conducted in the Archives and in the Public Policy Papers (both collections are housed in the Seeley G. Mudd Manuscript Library), and I am happy to add yet another encomium.

John Blazejewski did the reproduction photography for the book; his work is always of the highest quality, and I am pleased and grateful that he could undertake the work for this project.

Dorothy L. Bedford, Executive Director of Princeton's 250th Anniversary, and MaryMargaret Halsey of the Graduate School's Alumni Relations Office have been patient and helpful with a long string of queries. Their many suggestions have made this a better book.

Finally, my husband, Russell E. Marks, Jr., Class of 1954, was the soul of patience as work on the book proceeded to occupy evenings and weekends, seemingly without end. To him I owe special thanks.

P.H.M.

▼ ADVISORY COMMITTEE ▼

▼ INTRODUCTION ▼

From its earliest days as a center of "New Light" Presbyterianism, the College of New Jersey aspired to educate young people who would become leaders of church and state. The institution acquired deep roots in the Scottish Enlightenment, particularly that form of the intellectual tradition espoused by two Presbyterian clergymen, John Witherspoon (1723–1794) and James McCosh (1811–1894). Each became president of the College of New Jersey — Witherspoon in 1768 and McCosh in 1868, exactly one century later. Both men changed the small college profoundly, but it fell to McCosh, with his reform of the curriculum and hiring of new faculty, to prepare the way for a small institution set in rural New Jersey to become Princeton University.[1]

From the beginning of his presidency, McCosh went about laying the foundations of the University, which, he believed, should be firmly grounded in an excellent college where students were encouraged to develop the full range of their intellectual, moral,

[1] The bibliography on Princeton's history is lengthy and growing apace. Two essential sources are Thomas J. Wertenbaker, *Princeton 1746–1896* (Princeton: Princeton University Press, 1946), and Alexander Leitch, *A Princeton Companion* (Princeton: Princeton University Press, 1968). For a portrait of the College of New Jersey fifteen years before McCosh arrived, see James Buchanan Henry and Christian Henry Scharff, *College As It Is; or, The Collegian's Manual in 1853*, ed. J. Jefferson Looney (Princeton: Princeton University Libraries, 1996). On McCosh and his reforms, see the fine biography by J. David Hoeveler, Jr., *James McCosh and the Scottish Intellectual Tradition, from Glasgow to Princeton* (Princeton: Princeton University Press, 1981); Hoeveler's book includes a complete bibliography of McCosh's writing. See also *Princeton: From College to University*, edited by Anthony C. Grafton and John M. Murrin, comprising the 1996–1997 lectures on Princeton's history, which will be published in 1997 as part of the celebration of the University's 250th anniversary.

and physical capacities. Like most educators of his time (Charles W. Eliot of Harvard was the great exception), he subscribed fully to the notion that "there are branches [of learning] which are necessary to the full development of the mind, which every educated man ought to know. No one, I think, should be a graduate of a college who does not know mathematics and classics, the one to solidify the reasoning powers, and the other to refine the taste." He insisted that students must be carefully grounded in "the fundamental principles of the branch which they are studying," and thus should not be allowed to elect at random their course of study. But McCosh was no purblind clergyman, intent upon limiting the studies of his boys to narrow realms of knowledge, the courses in Greek, Latin, mathematics, religion, and a sprinkling of natural science accepted by long tradition as essential to the education of Christian gentlemen. On the contrary, he was an ardent advocate of broadening the curriculum to include "new and attractive branches of science," including contemporary literature, economics, and history as well as the new sciences of evolution and "physiological psychology," courses that would be taught by a faculty that was itself committed to the expansion of knowledge. When he retired in 1888, he was justly proud of his success in bringing to Princeton just such a professoriat:

> Our professors have not only been attending to their work in the college as instructors, but have been widening the field of knowledge, each in his own department. I at one time thought of printing a list of the books, pamphlets, and articles published by our professors since I came here, but I found that it would take sixty pages to do it.[2]

McCosh early recognized that, if his dream of making Princeton a university were to become reality, a different kind of man was needed to instruct students. The young tutors, many of them students of divinity, whom he found at Princeton when he arrived would need to be aided and eventually replaced by mature scholars

[2] William Milligan Sloane, ed., *The Life of James McCosh: A Record Chiefly Autobiographical* (New York: Charles Scribner's Sons, 1896), pp. 198, 199, 204, 208; Hoeveler, *James McCosh*, pp. 215–271.

— not all of them clergymen — who were leaders in their fields of study. Professors who taught primarily by rote and drill should give way to men dedicated to the task of lively teaching that would inspire students with a love of learning. Thus it was that he assigned senior professors even to freshman and sophomore classes, and began seeking the kind of man he wanted wherever he could be found (he was not above raiding the faculties of other institutions, when that served his purpose). True to his principle of building on the strengths of the College of New Jersey, he began a program to identify promising young scholars and give them opportunities to pursue advanced studies both at Princeton and in Europe:

> From an early period of my presidency, we have had post-graduate students. We have always thrown open our doors to them. We encourage them because it is out of them we hope to make scholars. . . . [W]hen students come up to us after graduation, and take up earnestly one or two departments, we can carry them on to very high attainments, and it may be prepare them to be professors. The number of our graduate students has been gradually increasing; this last year [1887] we have had seventy-eight. I have commonly had upwards of forty, most of them students from the seminary, studying the higher questions to of philosophy. These graduate classes will force us on to become a university.[3]

By the day of his eightieth birthday on April 1, 1891, no fewer than 115 of his former students had become professors, and some of them had been brought back to teach at Princeton by McCosh himself.[4] They became the first generation of teacher-scholars who, imbued with McCosh's evangelical concern for the welfare of students, led Princeton to nationwide acclaim as one of the country's premier educational institutions. McCosh died in 1894, just two years before the College of New Jersey became Princeton

[3] Sloane, *Life of James McCosh*, pp. 210–211.

[4] Sloane, *Life of James McCosh*, pp. 262–263; Hoeveler, *James McCosh*, pp. 284–291.

University and six years before the Graduate School was officially founded.[5]

That McCosh could not himself effect the change from college to university was, perhaps, the greatest disappointment of his long tenure (1868–1888) as president. The change in name represented, to him, the public and national recognition of all that he had achieved at Princeton, and he proposed it to the trustees in June 1885. The trustees, however, voted against him; as McCosh's biographer explains, "Hardened clerical interests especially sensed a threat to the religious character and identity of the college. Others probably resented any endorsing of the liberal academic changes of the past two decades."[6] Having greatly enlarged and modernized the course of study and elevated the standards of scholarship among students and faculty alike, McCosh wrote in his final report to the trustees in 1888:

> I meant all along that these new and varied studies, with their groupings and combinations, should lead to the formation of a *Studium Generale*, which was supposed in the Middle Ages to constitute a university. At one time I cherished a hope that I might be honored to introduce such a measure. From my intimate acquaintance with the systems of Princeton and other colleges, I was so vain as to think that out of our available materials I could have constructed a university of a high order. I would have embraced in it all that is good in our college; in particular, I would have seen that it was pervaded with religion, as the college is. . . . The college has been brought to the very borders, and I leave it to another to carry it over into the land of promise.[7]

Like Moses, McCosh did not live to see his promised land, and would not have defined it in all respects as we would today. Princeton's trek from conservative sectarian college to inclusive

[5] See Willard Thorp, Jeremiah Finch, and Minor Myers, Jr., *The Princeton Graduate School: A History* (Princeton: Princeton University Press, 1972). The book, now out of print, will be updated and republished as part of the 250th anniversary of Princeton's founding and the coming centennial of the Graduate School in 2000.

[6] Hoeveler, *James McCosh*, pp. 326–328.

[7] Sloane, *Life of James McCosh*, pp. 213–214.

modern research university took more than the forty years that the Children of Israel spent in the wilderness. The kind of opposition to changes in the undergraduate curriculum voiced even by one of McCosh's favorite pupils, Andrew Fleming West, gradually subsided. (West argued passionately against a system of electives which, he believed, would lead to abandoning the classics and with them the ability to reason correctly. Greek, he wrote, was "the mother tongue of pure thought, the perfect instrument of human reason," and as such should continue to be required of undergraduates; the amount of time spent on mathematics and physical science should be reduced in order to make time for it.[8]) After it was officially founded in 1900, the Graduate School matured rapidly, attracting first-rate young scholars who went on to become leading members of the professoriat and contributors to the advancement of knowledge in many fields both within and outside of academe. They were trained by a group of men (they were almost always white men) who fulfilled McCosh's dream of establishing a *Studium Generale* at Princeton but who were not themselves representative of the diversity of humankind.

This book is a record — inevitably incomplete and idiosyncratic — of the achievement of a generation of Princeton faculty, the "Luminaries," givers of light and enlightenment who, like McCosh, changed Princeton forever. They, too, created a new institution, one that is far more open to the world's diversity of peoples and knowledge and cultures than the nineteenth-century clergyman-philosopher could have imagined possible. They brought to Princeton many kinds of brilliance in many fields unimagined and uninvented in McCosh's time, but they also carried into the present McCosh's vision of a student-centered

[8] Andrew Fleming West, "Must the Classics Go?"and "What is Academic Freedom?" in David N. Portman, ed., *Early Reform in American Higher Education* (Chicago: Nelson-Hall Co., 1972), pp. 47–75, esp. pp. 49, 56–57, 69. These two essays, which first appeared in the *North American Review*, vol. 138, no. 327 (February 1884) and vol. 140, no. 342 (May 1885) respectively, were part of the debate with Harvard's Charles W. Eliot over the reform of the curriculum that captured the attention of the literate public during the last years of the century.

research university, one where faculty devotion to teaching would remain as important as commitment to advancing knowledge. As Walter Murphy reminds us in these pages, Alpheus T. Mason was openly disdainful of faculty "ornaments" who did not take teaching seriously, and Mason was not alone in this attitude. Time and again the graduate students who studied with these men (and one woman) or the younger colleagues who worked with them remark upon the attention paid to students by a faculty member who had gained a worldwide reputation for distinguished scholarship in his field.

Each of the scholars profiled here was pivotal in the development of a field of study. Without Willard Thorp, for example, the study of American literature would have been both delayed and diminished. Without Henry Norris Russell's spectrographic research, we would be unable to analyze the elements that make up the distant planets, made visible in images beamed to earth by cameras on board the latest generation of rocket-propelled vehicles pioneered by Luigi Crocco. Absent Eric Goldman or Melvin Tumin, we would know too little about contemporary America, and if Kurt Weitzmann had not devoted his life to the study of Byzantine art, we would be ignorant of all but the remote existence of a richly endowed civilization.

In some cases, of course, developments in a field moved so fast that the subjects of these memoirs have already been relegated to positions of honored but ancient history. In the case of physicist Henry DeWolf Smyth, it happened in his lifetime. He himself told the story of taking pleasure in leaving his office door open so that he could overhear his younger colleagues discussing their work, even though he did not always understand what they were talking about. In English, Gerald Eades Bentley has been characterized as "the last of the Victorian encyclopedists." In the social sciences, the same phenomenon occurs. Oleg Grabar tells us that some of the work of Middle Eastern historian Philip K. Hitti has not stood the test of time very well, but that his books, especially his *History of the Arabs from the Earliest Times to the Present*, are still worth reading. Stanley Stein conveys the antique feeling to much of the work of Latin American historian Dana Gardner Munro. Marius Jansen notes that William Lockwood did not bring the analytical tools expected of political economists to bear on his still-relevant studies of Japan's economic growth. But all three were critically important in enlarging the study of history at Princeton, which had until then focused almost exclusively on European history.

The authors of these memoirs knew their mentors and colleagues well, and bring to their essays a profound appreciation for their research and teaching talents. As should be expected, these essays are as diverse as their authors and the interests of the professors they are writing about. Some of the memoirs are short, personal glimpses of a relationship between a senior scholar and his apprentice. Others are more concerned with scholarly careers. And one — Daniel J. Kevles' long essay about Eric Goldman — is more like an intellectual biography of a man who spent his life not only in Princeton's contemplative environs but also in New York's television studios and, briefly, at the very center of national power during a time of significant political and social change.

Those changes, of course, have been mirrored by changes that took place in the University in the wake of the Depression, World War II, and the Vietnam War. Once cloistered in an idyllic setting, Princeton and its faculty were suddenly involved in war work and economic advising on the national and international stage. The Woodrow Wilson School of Public and International Affairs and the Center of International Studies were established; the curriculum was expanded to include courses like Cyril Black's on Russian history, intended to prepare students for the changed role of the United States in world affairs.

Throughout the University, old subjects were taught in new ways, even in the Classics Department, where Whitney J. Oates' magisterial introduction to English translations of Greek drama introduced generations of twentieth-century students to the heritage that had been a part of Princeton since its beginnings. Interdisciplinary approaches gained respectability, not only in the

Woodrow Wilson School, where professors from the Departments of History, Politics, and Economics taught, but also in other disciplines representing modern incarnations of the "groupings and combinations" introduced to Princeton by President McCosh. New departments were added — Sociology, Comparative Literature, Anthropology, Computer Science, and Molecular Biology — and most of the faculty who have taught their courses are, happily, alive today and therefore ineligible for inclusion in this book.

Some of Princeton's most distinguished and best known professors are absent, however, even though they were active contributors to their fields in the period since the founding of the Graduate School. Art historians Rensselear Lee and Alan Marquand are missing because almost everyone who studied with them is also deceased. Economist E. W. Kemmerer, the "money doctor" who travelled extensively to developing countries, has been the subject of books by those who did not work with him, but he had no graduate students who could write a personal memoir of him. To leave out political scientist Edward S. Corwin, whose 1920 book *The Constitution and What it Means Today* is still studied, is also a great loss, but a new biography of him, written by Professor of Politics Gerald Garvey, has just been published. The list goes on, and suggests that this book could have been much longer than it is. Indeed, there are few members of Princeton's faculty active since 1900 who do not merit inclusion.

Had the editorial committee decided to include living members of the faculty, active or emeritus, the book would have grown to unmanageable proportions, but it would have provided more portraits of Princeton professors who are not white men. Women especially would have been more prominent, but their presence is nevertheless notable in these essays: faculty wives are often mentioned, not only as hostesses (though that was important to the nurture of impecunious and chronically exhausted graduate students) but also as research assistants, colleagues, and participants in the conversations that helped to educate their husbands' disciples. Margaret Sprout was even recognized as the co-author of her husband's books.

It is doubtful, however, that the women and minorities who have joined Princeton's white male faculty during the most recent decades are much different in character from those portrayed here. Like them, today's faculty members are committed to the highest standards of scholarship; like them, they are making significant contributions to the sum of human knowledge in old and new fields of study. They, too, take teaching seriously, and are the kind of teachers who make Princeton all but unique among the great research universities of America. Their undergraduate and graduate students could testify as readily to the care and attention they receive as have those who wrote these memoirs about an earlier generation of Princeton faculty.

Daniel Coit Gilman, the first president of the Johns Hopkins University, may have been belaboring the obvious when he wrote that "the power of the University will depend upon the character of its resident staff of permanent professors."[9] And yet, it is the obvious that often escapes our attention, that is taken so much for granted that we fail to recognize its importance. These memoirs, written by people who are themselves distinguished members of the professoriat, will perhaps remind us of Princeton's special character and the exhilarating hard work that has made it one of the nation's essential institutions.

Patricia H. Marks
Princeton, New Jersey
August 9, 1996

[9] Daniel Coit Gilman, "Fundamental Principles," in his *The Launching of a University* (New York: Dodd, Merad & Co., 1906), p. 42.

Luminaries

Carlos Heard Baker

Department of English

BY A. WALTON LITZ

Those of us who attended the 1977 commencement, where Carlos Baker received an honorary degree, will never forget the standing ovation he received. His long career at Princeton coincided with the transformation of this place from a college with a small but highly effective graduate program into a large research university, and Carlos was an essential link between the two Princetons. At the time of his death a decade later he was working on a study of Ralph Waldo Emerson, who believed that the American scholar should "unlock" the connections between literature and life. Carlos was the embodiment of Emerson's ideal. As he once said in an interview, "You want to project not your own superior knowledge but your enthusiasm for the material, for . . . the buried notions beneath the lines."

When I was an undergraduate at Princeton from 1947 to 1951,

I never had Carlos as a teacher, although my secret interest lay in the modern (then contemporary) writers — Joyce, Eliot, Pound, Hemingway, Faulkner. At that time these writers were not taught in the department, but an unofficial course was given by a young instructor, John Hite, whose career was predictably short-lived. Yet this must have been precisely the time when Carlos was moving out of the Romantic period and forming his interest in Hemingway; we would have had a great deal to talk about.

After graduate education at Oxford and a stint in the United States Army, I returned to the Princeton English Department as an instructor in 1956, and it was then that Carlos and I became both colleagues and friends. He was chairman of the department — one never forgot this — but he treated all his colleagues as equals, and within two years we were "team-teaching" a popular course in modern literature that Carlos had initiated in the early 1950s. We alternated lectures (Carlos always attended mine, no matter how trite the subject), and I learned a vast amount about teaching from his quiet comments. What impressed me most was his respect for student opinions and his openness to new writing. Each year we devoted the final week of English 206 (Modern Literature) to a recently-published work, and although some of the choices may look bizarre from the perspective of 1996 (James Gould Cozzens' *By Love Possessed* leaps to mind) that does not affect the central issue: Carlos was asking the students to engage themselves with the writing of their own time.

A native of Maine, Carlos Baker (1909–1987) graduated from Dartmouth in 1932, where he won high scholastic honors and participated in extracurricular activities ranging from the presidency of his fraternity to manager of the hockey team. After earning an M.A. at Harvard, he taught for three years at the Nichols School in Buffalo, and then came to Princeton in 1937 as a graduate student and instructor. He received his Ph.D. in 1940, and moved through the ranks to full professor in 1951.

Carlos led a distinguished scholarly life. He was a member of Phi Beta Kappa and the American Philosophical Society. He frequently taught in the summers at Middlebury's Bread Loaf School of English, where he could combine his devotion to teaching with outdoor life in the New England he loved. He served on the editorial boards of Princeton University Press and the Modern Language Association, and was also a member of the juries for the Pulitzer Prize and the National Book Award. As a Fulbright scholar he lectured widely in Europe and England, and taught for a year at Oxford. He received honorary degrees from Dartmouth and the University of Maine.

But the honor that Carlos cherished most was the 1976 Howard T. Behrman Award for Distinguished Achievement in the Humanities, of which he was one of the first recipients. Although Carlos was a highly effective graduate teacher who supervised a number of important dissertations, I think it is fair to say that his great strength lay in undergraduate teaching. He took the undergraduates seriously at a time when that was very difficult for scholars of his generation, and I shall always be grateful to him for that example.

In addition to his many scholarly publications, Carlos was the author of three novels, a collection of short stories, and a volume of poetry — the poetry revealing a sensitive, elegiac temperament that casual acquaintances rarely discovered. His 1958 novel *A Friend in Power* was a highly fictionalized account of the search for Princeton's new president, in which Carlos played a key role.

Carlos's understanding of how a writer thinks and feels informed all of his scholarship, and led to a critical style that was lucid, flexible, and totally free of fashionable jargon. He began his scholarly life as a student of the great Romantic poets — his first book was *Shelley's Major Poetry: The Fabric of a Vision* — and the relationship between the Romantics and the great modern writers of our century became his lifelong interest. His last book, *The Echoing Green*, traces the Romantic inheritance of writers such as Yeats, Pound, Eliot, Frost, Stevens, and Auden.

Carlos was probably best known for his work on Ernest Hemingway. *Hemingway: The Writer as Artist* (1952) initiated the serious study of Hemingway's fiction; the book was twice revised, and translated into a number of other languages. After Hemingway's death in 1961 Carlos was invited by Charles Scribner, Jr., to write the authorized biography, which appeared in 1969 and has been translated into fourteen foreign languages. One reviewer described it as the bedrock upon which all subsequent Hemingway criticism would be founded, and this has proved to be true.

A great scholar, Carlos Baker was first of all a great teacher, and generations of Princeton students, both undergraduate and graduate, have testified that their lives were changed by his example.

READING LIST

Shelley's Major Poetry: The Fabric of a Vision (Princeton: Princeton University Press, 1948)

Editor: *Shelley: Selected Poetry and Prose* (New York: Modern Library, 1951)

Hemingway: The Writer as Artist (Princeton: Princeton University Press, 1952)

A Friend in Power (New York: Charles Scribner's Sons, 1958)

The Land of Rumbelow (New York: Charles Scribner's Sons, 1963)

A Year and a Day (Nashville: Vanderbilt University Press, 1963)

Ernest Hemingway: A Life Story (New York: Charles Scribner's Sons, 1969)

The Gay Head Conspiracy (New York: Charles Scribner's Sons, 1973)

The Talisman and Other Stories (New York: Charles Scribner's Sons, 1976)

Editor: *Ernest Hemingway: Selected Letters* (New York: Charles Scribner's Sons, 1981)

The Echoing Green: Romanticism, Modernism, and the Phenomena of Transference in Poetry (Princeton: Princeton University Press, 1984)

Gerald Eades Bentley

Department of English

BY SUZANNE GOSSETT

Sometime just before classes started in the fall of 1964 I met Gerald Eades Bentley. It was a significant moment for me: I had come to Princeton from Oxford the year before to study Jacobean drama, and to study it with Bentley, but when I arrived Ged, as he was universally known, was on leave. Being in the first group of a dozen women graduate students admitted to Princeton in 1963 had not proven easy; all of us, even married ones like myself, were subject to constant insinuations that our only reason for coming to Princeton was to search for husbands, and we had to demonstrate our right to everything from fellowships to summer library cards. I was eager to start working with the material I cared most about and to forget the hostility I had encountered. Finally I was going to take classes in my chosen field, determine a dissertation topic, and be exposed to someone from the line of great scholars of English Renaissance drama.

Bentley's classes were wonderful, but profoundly unfamiliar in style. Almost all of us had been trained as undergraduates by teachers from the school of New Criticism. Close reading of text was our primary skill and had been especially well drilled into Smith graduates like myself. Even at Oxford my tutors had expected intensely analytical essays. Bentley, with rare exceptions, taught theatrical context and historical and biographical fact, adding an occasional class on the development of a dramatic form like revenge tragedy. (In the Preface to the third volume of *The Jacobean and Caroline Stage* he actually apologized because "I have tried to suppress my comments on literary and dramatic values in the plays — not always successfully.")[1] As students we could only intuit his enthusiasm for those aesthetic qualities most of us assumed formed the central interest of works of literature and implicitly justified our discipline.

But of theatrical facts and contexts he had absolute control. He accepted no traditional wisdom without verification, which had led to one of his early books, *Shakespeare and Jonson: Their Reputations in the Seventeenth Century Compared*, where he demolished long-accepted views about the comparative early esteem of the two playwrights by using references gathered during the course of his research for *The Jacobean and Caroline Stage*. We knew that anything he taught us was based on the latest scholarship, often his own. Week after week the splendid lectures rolled on, from "The Antecedents of the Elizabethan Drama" to the "Inns of Court Drama," from "The Regulation of the Theatres" through the semester break to "Play Publishing," from "Tragedy" to a grand May finale in "The Masque." This last — about which I still write — prompted Bentley in a rare moment of Renais-

[1] Gerald Eades Bentley, *The Jacobean and Caroline Stage*, 7 vols. (Oxford: Oxford University Press, 1941–1968), vol. 3, pp. ix–x.

sance boosterism to tell us that there was nothing done in the theatre now which couldn't have been done in 1610 unless it required electric power, like focused lighting. Then he added, smiling, that with lots of men and candles almost all of that could be and was done, too.

Meanwhile we were receiving a training unique in my experience at Princeton. Bentley was determined that his students would be accurate scholars, knowledgeable investigators, and teachers worthy of him. The first week he taught us what he called the "tools" of our trade, such as the major bibliographical sources, and noted which ones were lacking, such as a reliable survey of the drama of the period. He enunciated the rules governing the class reports that are what everyone from his classes of that era remembers best: we were encouraged to be critical of the books we reported on (it was not uncommon to learn that a standard work had "more reputation than worth"), to compare reviews by major scholars, to expect grading based on presentation as well as content. Furthermore, we would have to adhere to the number of minutes he set on the egg timer that he invariably produced as one began. By the end of the semester we were each to give a thirty-minute lecture for which he carefully established our audience ("college seniors," my old notes say).

The following year, when I was gone, Bentley went further in trying to prepare teachers. Since Princeton English graduate students did not teach in those days, he substituted for his regular Shakespeare course a seminar on teaching the subject, involving all of the students as informal assistants in his freshman Shakespeare class. This was not done to save him time: he observed each student lecture and then had an individual conference to work on the improvement of the student's pedagogical technique. These discussions, he believed, were as important as the individual conferences that invariably followed his reading and analysis of a student's term paper.

Accuracy was a primary goal. In 1964 Bentley was working on

the last two of the seven volumes of *The Jacobean and Caroline Stage*, which he had begun as a doctoral student in London in 1929. This massive, still-standard reference work, which I had pounced on in Blackwell's bookstore long before imagining I could study with its author, provides in Volumes I and II all the surviving information on the dramatic companies and players of the period; in Volumes III, IV, and V similar information on roughly 1,200 plays and all known playwrights, including Anon.; in Volume VI information on all the English theatres; and in Volume VII, along with a magisterial index, annals of Jacobean and Caroline theatrical events from 1616 (when Sir E. K. Chambers' *The Elizabethan Stage* cuts off) to 1642. Quite typical of the work is a note in the preface to the first volume. There Bentley announces that in the section on players he has departed from the methods of earlier scholars. They had offered biographical summaries; he, instead, for each actor quotes "every scrap of biographical evidence in chronological order." Such primary evidence gathering, done longhand on note cards in record offices and libraries all over Britain and in American collections over a period of almost forty years, is close to inconceivable to my own students, raised on the Xerox machine and computer; for us it set a terrifyingly high standard. Bentley started training us right away, however: we were required to hand in our papers in two copies, one to him and one to a partner, each of whom would then proceed to check every single reference, quote, and footnote. We could hardly complain: every word of *The Jacobean and Caroline Stage* had been read aloud, some say letter by letter and some say letter by letter backward, to insure its accuracy.[2]

[2] Professor Emeritus Mark Ashin of the University of Chicago has told me that as a student at that institution he was hired by Bentley on money from the National Youth Administration to work on checking the early volumes; Ashin and Mrs. Bentley read aloud to each other. Professor Charles Crupi of Albion College remembers that in the 1960s a graduate student was hired to proofread out loud every letter and symbol of the final volumes, but Professor George Bornstein of the University of Michigan recalls that the requirement was that the volumes be read aloud backward. Bentley was the kind of professor who generated graduate student legends.

Furthermore, we were permitted to cite only the most authentic texts, usually first editions. Therefore, for the first time I found myself in Firestone Library's Department of Rare Books and Special Collections, searching through Massinger quartos and other rare books. I was astonished at the library's riches in the field of Elizabethan and Jacobean drama. Oh, someone explained, Bentley came from Chicago to Princeton in 1945, and after the war ended the University sent him to England to buy books, then plentiful and painfully cheap. Hence Firestone's large collection of play quartos from the early period. It is perhaps understandable that after Bentley's retirement in 1970 he was prevailed upon to serve as Assistant University Librarian for Rare Books and Special Collections for three years.

Sadly for me, despite the gallantry toward women which led Bentley to bring handfuls of roses cut from his own bushes when invited to dinner, despite the respect he manifested towards his wife's contributions to *The Jacobean and Caroline Stage*, and despite his own education in coeducational institutions such as DePauw (opened to women in 1867) and the Universities of Illinois and London, Bentley was opposed to the admission of women to Princeton and specifically to the graduate English program. He explained to me that the female students he had had at the University of Chicago from 1929 until 1945, though good, had not remained in the profession. More aware than he of how times had changed, deeply committed to my subject, and perhaps profoundly stubborn, I avoided the obvious response and altered neither topic nor dissertation director. All went smoothly enough — my work gained his consistent approval and his suggestions for improvement were invaluable. Then, with a degree expected the following June (1968), I made it clear that, like all the other members of my class, I was looking for a job. The depth of our differences about women's professional and scholarly potential became clear. In an era when a phone call from the right person routinely netted Princeton graduate students interviews and even jobs, he took no active role in assisting me. Unlike my male peers, I was thrown on my own resources. Meeting me in June on

Nassau Street, Bentley sounded as much surprised as pleased when he said, "I hear you got a job."

As I persevered through the always difficult first years, during which I produced children along with the qualifications for tenure, one major incentive was to demonstrate to Princeton and to Ged that their investment of time and scholarly resources had been worthwhile. He had taught me a good deal of what I knew, and like my classmates I proceeded to build on that foundation both in the classroom and in the world of scholarship. To this day much of my work is closely tied to that early course on Elizabethan and Jacobean drama, and to the standards it set. For example, Bentley's research established the theatrical context for the plays of the great flowering of Jacobean drama; let loose in the archives of the English College in Rome, I worked (on note cards, longhand) to establish a history of the theatre and conditions of performance there, based on sixteenth- and seventeenth-century records and manuscript sources. Or again, Bentley urged us to join the Malone Society, the premiere scholarly publisher of English Renaissance drama, which he would go on to serve as president from 1971 to 1989. A dutiful student, I joined. Later, when my English College work led me to edit the manuscript of an unknown Jacobean academic play, I sent it to the Society for publication, and I continued to work with them on other projects thereafter.

For a while the work that Bentley did was deeply respected but rather unfashionable, used but taken for granted by many scholars who would not themselves have considered expanding it. Even Thomas P. Roche, Jr., now the incumbent of the Murray Chair that Bentley himself held, called him the last of the Victorian encyclopedists.[3] The profession I entered in the fall of 1968, only two years before Bentley's retirement in 1970, was soon sub-

[3] See the memorial by Thomas P. Roche, Jr., in *Princeton University Library Chronicle* 56, no. 2 (Winter 1995): 318–321. Professor Bentley's own papers are available for scholarly study in the Manuscripts Division, Rare Books and Special Collections, Princeton University Library.

ject to almost as much revolution as Chicago, the city to which we moved, was encountering in its streets. Certainly Bentley was not sympathetic to feminist criticism, and both structuralism and deconstruction would have left him cold. But his work on the relationship between dramatic literature, its occasion, and its environment was a precursor to the New Historicism. Bentley had fought such oversimplifications as bardolatry by demonstrating factually how all dramatists of Shakespeare's period were affected if not determined by the conditions of their companies and stages, as well as by external factors such as plagues and politics.[4] And the much-discussed "death of the author" has created new attention to and respect for artistic collaboration, which Bentley showed was a constant in every aspect of the Elizabethan stage. At conferences and in articles on the subject his books, *The Profession of Dramatist in Shakespeare's Time* and *The Profession of Player in Shakespeare's Time*, are constantly mentioned and cited, and his comments on the theatre as a collaborative art have become almost a mantra.

A mentor, like a parent, can be simultaneously a taskmaster, a deeply-internalized model, and an inspiration. Bentley was all of these, as well as a central figure in the Princeton English Department and in the world of literary and dramatic scholarship from the end of the Second World War until long past his retirement. Though he was born almost a century ago, his students are still teaching and his books are in constant circulation. In my mind he is a link in the line of great scholars of English Renaissance drama, reaching back not only to E. K. Chambers (1866–1954), whose *Elizabethan Stage* he continued, but all the way to Edmond Malone (1741–1812), the first great scholarly editor of Shakespeare and the man whose name W. W. Greg and R. B. McKerrow took for their Society.

[4] One very influential example was his article on "Shakespeare and the Blackfriars Theatre," *Shakespeare Survey* 1 (1948): 41–46, which iconoclastically argued that Shakespeare had learned how to write plays for the King's Men's new theatre by imitating the young but successful upstarts Beaumont and Fletcher.

READING LIST

The Jacobean and Caroline Stage, 7 vols. (Oxford: Oxford University Press, 1941–1968)

Shakespeare and Jonson: Their Reputations in the Seventeenth Century Compared (Chicago and London: University of Chicago Press, 1945)

The Profession of Dramatist and Player in Shakespeare's Time, 1590–1642 (Princeton: Princeton University Press, 1986), incorporating *The Profession of Dramatist in Shakespeare's Time* (Princeton: Princeton University Press, 1971), and *The Profession of Player in Shakespeare's Time* (Princeton: Princeton University Press, 1984)

Nina Berberova

Department of Slavic Languages and Literatures

BY ELLEN CHANCES

I do not remember exactly when, during those early days of graduate school, I met Nina Nikolaevna Berberova for the first time. I had known about her from my mother, Natasha Chances, and grandfather, Samson Soloveitchik, who, in turn, had known her in Paris, where they were all part of the Russian émigré community in the 1920s and 1930s. Nina Berberova and my grandparents moved in different circles of the intelligentsia and were affiliated with different émigré political/literary journals. Nevertheless, the circles did sometimes intersect on the pages of a journal or at a social event. Berberova recalled, for example, a social gathering at her country home, where my mother, as a teenager, had been surrounded by admiring men. During the spring before I entered graduate school, Berberova and my grandfather had been featured speakers at a Russian Studies symposium convened by Fred Warner Neal, professor of international relations at Claremont Graduate School.

Nina Berberova started teaching at Princeton in 1963.[1] She had arrived in the United States from France in 1950 and had then, in 1958, begun to teach Russian, as a lecturer, in the Department of Slavic Languages and Literatures at Yale University, where she stayed until she moved to Princeton. She came to Princeton because Richard Burgi, chairman of Princeton's Department of Slavic Languages and Literatures in 1963, invited her and another Russian-language lecturer, Veronica Dolenko, to follow him when he moved from Yale to Princeton. At the time, at age sixty-two, she had already led an extraordinarily full life. She would continue to lead an exciting life, far beyond the confines of an academic life, in the two decades that followed her retirement from Princeton in 1971 until her death, in Philadelphia, in 1993.

As a young woman, Berberova had been a part of the cultural "scene" of Russia. She remembered attending the funeral of one of Russia's great Symbolist poets, Alexander Blok, in 1921, the year before she left Russia for good. She lived, for years, with one of Russia's foremost émigré poets, Vladislav Khodasevich, until his death in 1939. As a member of the Russian émigré community in Paris in the 1920s, 1930s, and 1940s, and later, too, in the United States, she herself wrote prose and poetry, autobiography and biography, literary criticism and drama.

She brought to her teaching a sense of the vitality of the cultural happenings of Russian émigré life. Her love of poetry she infused into her courses on Russian poetry. When we graduate students walked into her classes, always taught in Russian, we were absorbing something other than a scholar's analysis of a poem.

[1] Some of the material in this memoir is based on my articles, "Nina Nikolaevna Berberova," *Dictionary of Russian Women Writers*, ed. Marina Ledkovsky, Charlotte Rosenthal, Mary Zirin, (Westport, Connecticut, and London: Greenwood Press, 1994), pp.77–79, and "Berberova Imbued with Joie de Vivre," *Trenton Sunday Times*, May 22, 1994.

We were actually experiencing, actually tasting the flavor of Russian Symbolist poetry, whose peak was 1890–1910, from someone, a poet, who had known the Russian Symbolists about whom she spoke. As a writer herself, she could analyze a poem with a poet's intuitive grasp of how it is shaped. As a writer and member of the intelligentsia, she spoke a beautiful pre-revolutionary Russian that has, with few exceptions, all but disappeared.

Berberova both analyzed and, in her reading aloud of the poetry, reproduced the musicality of Alexander Blok's poems and the disjunctures contained within the lines of Innokenty Annensky's verses. She mimicked perfectly the stinging, tart, acerbic stabs of jealousy enfolded in Marina Tsvetaeva's line, addressed to her former lover, "How is Life with Another?"

Berberova's courses, filled with *explications de texte* analyses of the poems, were also filled with anecdotes about the love lives of the poets and the cultural gossip of the period, as if these juicy tidbits were about incidents that had happened here and now and just around the corner. It was clear that the personalities of these literary figures were evoked by someone who had spent a great deal of time in their presence.

When Berberova read the poetry, she performed — just as Russian poets who give poetry readings today expect that they will be public, certainly *not* understated, events. She explained that when we listened to her read the poetry of Khodasevich, or of Acmeist poet Osip Mandelstam, we were participating in a piece of Russian cultural history that extended back to the nineteenth century, back to the so-called "father of Russian literature," Alexander Pushkin. She told us that Khodasevich had explained that he reads in the style of Russian poetry-reading to which Pushkin and later "Petersburg poets" adhered. This way of reading poetry has continued to the present in the poetry-reading manner of the recently deceased Joseph Brodsky, also a part of the Petersburg tradition.

Berberova also explained that there was another way of reading poetry, very different from the Pushkin style. This was a declamatory mode, one favored by the early twentieth-century poet Vladimir Mayakovsky and later poets. This tradition, too, lives on, in the reading style of poets like contemporary Russian poet Yevgeny Yevtushenko.

Thus, when Berberova taught poetry, it was not dead-on-the-page material to be yawned at and struggled through. Rather, here was someone who herself was intimately involved, in life and art, with Russian poetry and Russian poets. Poetry mattered, the way that food and water mattered — and this, too, was a part of the Russian tradition of literature that was conveyed to us, consciously and unconsciously, in every seminar and every office-hour discussion of literature.

Berberova's courses on late nineteenth-century and early twentieth-century Russian prose, as well as her courses on poetry, reflected her own literary tastes. In her reading performances, she often leaned toward the modernists. For instance, she translated four T. S. Eliot poems into Russian; the translations appeared in *Novyi zhurnal* (New Journal), an émigré journal, in 1962. While she loved and primarily taught the modernists, the structure and style of her own prose, surprisingly, fit more into the tradition of nineteenth-century realists.

Among Russian writers, she held in particularly high esteem Vladimir Nabokov's fiction and Andrei Bely's poetry and prose. An early champion of Andrei Bely, she directed many doctoral dissertations on this Russian Symbolist's works, and thus contributed greatly to scholarly interest in Bely among Russian literature specialists in this country. Among her star students, for example, was John Malmstad, a Harvard University professor of Russian poetry and one of the country's leading Russian poetry experts.

Berberova gave generously of her knowledge and her time to students and non-students alike. When the eminent Russian émigré linguist Roman Jakobson came to Princeton to deliver the Gauss lectures, she invited graduate students to attend. At the time, the Gauss lecture series was open by invitation only to a small number of faculty. Berberova told the story of Jakobson's asking her, since she, like him, now exceeded the age of sixty, whether she still stood or whether she now sat when she taught. She stood, she informed him. He, five years her senior, announced to her that he had "sat down."

Berberova invited students to lunch in the faculty club or at her apartment. Every year, she hosted a small Thanksgiving dinner for a few students and former students. We would gather in Berberova's small rented apartment in University housing on Stanworth Lane, among the memorabilia of Russian culture — photographs and art works of Russian writers. At one point during those years, a caricature of Nabokov with a butterfly net in his hand popped up on the wall near her front door. The latest books, journals, and newspapers, in Russian, French, and English, would always be stacked on the coffee table in her living room, as if waiting to be included in the conversation.

Berberova's celebration of Thanksgiving, a custom of her new country, was indicative of her personality. She lived passionately in the moment. She was proud to adopt the favored mode of transportation of her new country: she was proud that she had learned to drive. She was proud to adopt the language of her new country and spoke often, and disdainfully, of those émigrés who refused to learn English and who refused to throw themselves into American life.

Berberova had strong opinions about everything — people, literature, politics, the gossip of literary politics of the Russian émigré cultural community, social policy, the Soviet Union, American presidential elections, current events, the places to get the best bargains on sophisticated, elegant clothes with a Parisian flair, the latest films, the latest art exhibits, the latest books, the latest articles in the *New York Review of Books.* She hated provincialism. She hated conventionality. She detested the bourgeoisie. She detested sentimentality. She detested the dead, glazed eyes of anyone who retreated from the energy of a profound engagement with life. She was friendly to all sorts of people from all sorts of walks of life. She was intensely interested in life.

I am not the only person to have conjectured that the title of Berberova's 1981 book, *The Iron Woman*, about Moura Budberg (Baroness Maria Ignatievna Benkendorf-Budberg), referred not only to Budberg, but also to Berberova herself. Berberova was a tough, hardy survivor of not one, but two emigrations, first from Russia and then from France. The traumas of emigration are etched into the lines of some of her most compelling poetry. The first three lines of her poem "Separation," composed in 1945, are stark and blunt in their characterization of the life of an exile: "Separation resembles a terrible story:/ It begins at night,/ And it has no end." Another poem, untitled (part of the cycle, "Five Poems," published in 1956), is a chilling, sobering reminder of the rootlessness of émigrés in general, and in particular, of the special qualities of rootlessness of Russian émigrés, whose paths back to their homeland had been blocked because they were now personae non grata in the Soviet Union. Here is an excerpt from that poem:

> The cashier asked: Round-trip ticket?
> "— Only one-way. Irrevocable journey" . . .
> "Would you like to go back?
> "Where? I have no place to go."

Had Berberova's role been confined to her contributions up to the time of her retirement, she would have left behind a legacy of which to be proud. She trained several generations of students of Russian literature. She recorded her version of Russian cultural life in her memoirs, *The Italics Are Mine*, which came out first in English in this country, in 1969, and then, three years later in Russian, in West Germany.

She was the author of short stories, such as "Billancourt Holidays"[2] and of an anthology of short stories, *The Easing of One's*

[2] Paris, 1937–1938.

Fate.[3] She was the author of novels, such as *The Last and the First*[4] and *Without Sunset.*[5] Her play, *Madame*, was staged in Paris in 1938. She wrote three biographies, *Tchaikovsky*, *Borodin*, and *Alexandre Blok et son temps.*[6]

In the United States, she continued to publish her own prose and poetry in émigré journals. Her literary analyses and book reviews appeared both in émigré journals and in American professional academic journals devoted to Russian literature. She edited and contributed commentary to a collected edition of Khodasevich's works: *Collected Poems of Vladislav Khodasevich.*[7] After retirement, she continued to write, publish, and reissue her works.

Increasingly, as members of her generation died off, Berberova acted as a source for Soviet, European, and American visitors interested in the pre-revolutionary and émigré period of Russian literature. She had a steady flow of visitors and letters with inquiries, from around the world, about the Russian and émigré life with which she was so familiar.

In the years after retirement, the convergence of three forces gave new life to Berberova's writings and to her place in Russian cultural history. First was the women's movement in the West, which increased interest in women's creative accomplishments. Second, there was *glasnost*, which meant that in the Soviet Union, and then, in post-Soviet Russia, people, works, and cultural movements once banned by Soviet authorities were now welcomed, invited, published, and celebrated. Finally, by the late 1980s, Berberova was one of the last living representatives of the Russian émigré period. Thus, in the USSR and in the West, there was a real interest in Berberova both as a writer and as a person.

Extensive articles and writings in literary journals and newspapers by and about Berberova began to appear in the Soviet Union and abroad. A collection, *Poems (1921–1983)*, came out in Russian

[3] Paris, 1948.
[4] Paris, 1930.
[5] Paris, 1938.
[6] Paris, 1937; Paris, 1938; Paris, 1948.
[7] Munich, 1960.

in 1984. Her fiction, translated into French and English (including *The Accompanist* and *The Tattered Cloak and Other Novels*), has been highly praised in Europe and the United States as well as in Russia, where it has appeared in the original. I have seen her works on the shelves of bookstores in Moscow, Paris, New York, and Chartres. Near the end of her life, she herself returned to Russia for the first and only time since the 1920s. The visit was a triumph. Russians squeezed into packed halls to see her and to hear her speak.

And here in Princeton, a few months after her death, a French movie, "The Accompanist," based on her fiction, was playing in the Montgomery movie theater, where Berberova had so often seen European art films.

Nina Berberova lives on in her writings, in the knowledge of and love of Russian literature that she transmitted to her students, in her capacity to make Petersburg and Paris culture come alive, in her fierce and passionate dedication to the preservation of Russian culture.

READING LIST

Tchaikovsky (Paris: Egloff, 1948)

Alexandre Blok et son temps (Paris: Éditions du Chène, 1947)

Poems. Selections (New York: Russica, 1987)

The Accompanist, trans. Marian Schwartz (London: Collins, 1987)

The Tattered Cloak and Other Novels, trans. Marian Schwartz (New York: Alfred A. Knopf, 1991)

The Italics Are Mine, trans. Philippe Radley (London: Chatto & Windus, 1991)

Cyril Edwin Black

Department of History

BY MARIUS B. JANSEN

In the years after World War II, institutions of higher learning in the United States reoriented themselves to prepare their students for challenges posed by the country's new global role. A curriculum that had always focused on Classical and Western civilization needed now to take account of the rest of the world without sacrificing the strengths it had developed during the previous two centuries of Princeton's existence. There was dramatic growth in resources. Foundations and the federal government needed help in developing policies at a time when student bodies were growing in number and diversity; curricula were broadening, and new language programs required the addition of library collections and the staff to serve them. At Princeton, Professor Cyril E. Black emerged as a principal architect of these developments under the administration of President Robert F.

Goheen, who saw the internationalization of the University as one of the major needs of his time.

Cy Black was uniquely prepared to carry out this task. His long tenure guaranteed extraordinary continuity. He was first appointed to the faculty in the Department of History in 1939, and retired as Professor of European History in 1986, a span of almost fifty years that stands as one of the longest in the annals of the Princeton faculty. He first offered his course on Russian history in 1946. It became a staple of the undergraduate experience, and by the time of his retirement, as John Waterbury, his student and later professor of Politics and International Affairs puts it, the contingent of those who took it "must surely number in the thousands." He made Princeton a center for the study of Russian history and trained thirty-five graduate students. When the American Association for the Advancement of Slavic Studies honored him in 1985, its citation noted that the number of specialists who had studied under him was "surpassed only by that of others whom you have helped and advised as a friend and colleague."

Everything in Cy Black's background came together to prepare him for a career of intellectual adventure and academic leadership. Born in North Carolina in 1915, he spent six years in Turkey and grew to manhood in Bulgaria. His mother was Bulgarian — a granddaughter was to carry on her name — and his father was president first of the American College in Sofia and then of Robert College in Istanbul. His very name, his colleague Charles Issawi remarked, evoked memories of St. Cyril, the ninth-century "Apostle to the Slavs."

Black's early education was in Turkey and Bulgaria, followed by studies in Vienna, Berlin, and France, before he completed his A.B. at Duke University in 1936. His graduate degrees were from Harvard, which was then the center of Russian studies in the United States. His dissertation harked back to his background to discuss the establishment of constitutional government in Bulgaria; it appeared as a book in 1943.

During World War II someone with Cy's breadth of experience and interests was sure to be sought out by the United States government. After the German defeat he was involved in efforts to reestablish representative government in Eastern Europe, serving as advisor to the American representative on the Allied Control Commission in Bulgaria and to the Ethridge Mission sent to investigate the implementation of the Yalta agreements in Eastern Europe. Cy also served in a United Nations investigation of Greek frontier incidents and the treatment of minorities. Then, after Eastern Europe fell under the control of the Soviet Union, he was for a time consultant to the CIA Board of National Estimates. (Subsequently the Communist government of Bulgaria honored him with the charge of espionage, an accusation he dismissed scornfully as "a complete fabrication.") Cy Black was in fact remarkably unideological in his analysis of international politics, and his clear-eyed and even-handed approach to issues kept him in demand at institutions like the Council on Foreign Relations in New York.

In 1958 Cy was asked to serve as a member of the U.S. Delegation to Observe Elections to the USSR Supreme Soviet. This experience, and others like it, provided humor and self-deprecating anecdotes with which he could sharpen his points in lecture and preceptorial. Thus he sometimes drew on a discussion with then-Premier Nikita Khrushchev about the future of the world, in which Khrushchev had calmly predicted the victory of communism over capitalism, with the warning "Some of you may have heard this Khrushchev story before, but it's the only one I have." He was not, in any case, inclined to take such predictions very seriously; as he wrote in 1986, "the Soviet victory of communism, as defined by their theories, is no more of a threat than if they said the world were flat, and they were going to push us off the edge."

Cy's background and experience were calculated to make him aware of what United States universities, and Princeton in particular, needed with respect to international studies. Major foundations sought his advice in building programs to support area studies. He was central to the establishment of the IREX program, which began academic exchanges with Russia and Eastern Europe, and toward the end of his career he was active in arranging exchanges with China. Out of all this came an awareness of the problems other campuses had encountered with the development of international and area studies, and a sensitivity to the way things should be done at Princeton. With the exception of work in Near Eastern Studies, where Professor Philip K. Hitti tried to work out coverage of the contemporary period, Cy's course in Russian history was almost a pioneering effort to deal with the non-Western world.

In the late 1950s and early 1960s Cy showed himself to be an academic statesman of the first order. He served as chair of Princeton's Committee on Foreign and International Affairs from its formation in 1961 to 1968, and recruited resources and faculty for programs of study in Russian, East Asian, Near Eastern, and Latin American studies. These served as coordinating and not as competing or degree-giving units, so that candidates for faculty positions had to satisfy the scrutiny of their respective departments. Growth at Princeton was consequently less disruptive and more enduring than that on many campuses, where sudden infusions of support produced strains between "area" and "discipline." Cy played a central role in all of this. He also chaired the group that supervised the development of work in anthropology.

The new developments in international studies served to broaden the University's social makeup as well as its curriculum. When they were first begun, the new programs in languages were under-utilized, and in 1963 a Cooperative Undergraduate Program for Critical Languages was established to bring to the campus students whose institutions did not offer more than elementary courses in Russian, East Asian, and Near Eastern languages. For several years that small community at Princeton included women as well as men, and since they attended other courses as well as the language courses for which they had come, their presence helped to bridge Princeton's move to coeducation in 1968.

In addition to all this, Cy was, of course, carrying on his teaching and his writing on Russian history. His lectures were remarkable for the clarity with which he could convey complex material in concise terms. As Professor Richard Wortman, now of Columbia University, put it, Cy "had an extraordinary ability to question, to unsettle established views, and to do so with pithy and direct statements that made everyone sit up and realize how the standard interpretations of Russia's past cannot hold for the modern world." At the same time he had no patience for those who wrote as if Russia's history had begun with the Bolshevik Revolution. He always insisted that the two Russias, pre-Soviet and Soviet, should be studied in their changing interrelationship. That was the purpose of a major scholarly conference that he conceived and organized in 1958. In his contribution to the book that emerged, *The Transformation of Russian Society*, he wrote that such an approach was "controversial because it involves seeking out continuities between the Tsarist and Soviet eras which the adherents of both find odious."

That comment, economically phrased for the weight it carries, tells something about Cy's refusal to be limited by neat boundaries of time and space or by evasion. S. Frederick Starr, who went on to the presidency of Oberlin, recently recalled that Cy had little patience for anyone who "was not coming straight to the point or drawing the Big Conclusion and instead getting lost in elegant expression, footnoted details, or circumlocution. . . . Cy was a person of very broad sympathies and few prejudices, but it seemed to me that he always retained a dose of old-style decisiveness. At bottom, he believed that things have real meaning and messages and that it was his job to discover them." James H. Billington, Librarian of Congress, agreed. "Cy was a preceptor to us all," he said, "a person who made us feel there was something to say and something to learn from every human encounter — a person anxious to move towards a better conclusion even if someone else got to make the point or get the credit." He ranged widely and he encouraged his students to do so too. The best of them had something of his breadth: Starr, whose focus extended from

Russian local government to architecture, and Billington, whose epic treatment of Russian culture was followed by a study of theorists of revolution.

Once the institutions were in place at Princeton, Cy turned his interests to the coordination of research. He was director of the University's Center of International Studies from 1968 to 1985. He was warned that the Center, which began as a group of research scholars, was full of prima donnas, but, as Corrine Black, his wife, recalls, "whatever turbulence he encountered was handled by his gift for diplomacy, his genial presence, and his wit and humor." In addition to editing the Center's distinguished journal, *World Politics*, he secured funding to increase the number of visiting fellows and coordinate programs of research. His interests seemed to broaden constantly. When a new survey course in East Asian history was established, he volunteered to offer preceptorials in order to educate himself. Because he was always learning, he could organize and lead without dominating. Together with his wife, herself an anthropologist, he would seek out visiting foreign fellows to the Center to learn about their societies, and in turn encouraged them to report on their research at informal Center luncheons. By doing what he could to facilitate their studies, he was quietly using them to broaden the Center's intellectual community.

This breadth of interest led also to a remarkable program of seminars and publications on the development of the modern world. Cy staked out this interest in an ambitious set of lectures, published in 1963 as *The Dynamics of Modernization: A Study in Comparative History*. This slim volume, which was soon translated into seven languages, looked for commonalities in comparable categories in modern world history. "I wanted to clarify my own thinking about the way in which societies change," he later recalled, "what is common to modernizing societies, and in what ways each is distinctive, and with what problems of policy these developments confront a country like ours." It was a search with pattern. He believed that in every country, as in the Russia he knew best, history had left its legacy, and that the sweeping changes of our times could not be understood without full attention to historical continuity.

This interest in the process of modernization began with the case of Russia in an essay Black had written in 1958 on the modernization of Russian society. It seemed to him that the forces usually credited with motive power in world history — for Marxists, class struggle; for Western liberals, political freedom; for world-systems theorists, economic dependency — were less important and universal than the advancement of knowledge and the scientific and technological revolutions. It was there, he felt, that the real locomotive of historical change was to be found. To argue otherwise was to substitute ideology for process. Cy used the word "modernization" as a useful generalization under which to group such changes. He considered it ideologically neutral and as nearly value-free as possible. The process did not necessarily work for freedom, for the mobilization and participation that marked "modernized" societies had proved as possible under technologically-armed police states as they had under systems that permitted choice. He did not equate the two by any means, but he wanted to find ways to relate them.

What followed was a series of seminars in which Princeton and outside specialists participated to trace commonalities and differences in the ares of change experienced in different parts of the world. Unlike most such efforts, each study began with careful consideration of the pre-modern tradition. Out of this came *The Modernization of Japan and Russia*, published in 1975, *The Modernization of China*, published in 1981, and similar coverage of the Near East and of Central Asia in books that were completed and published after his death. These undertakings were personal as well as intellectual achievements, for throughout the process Cy's presence, his humor, unflappable calm, and academic statesmanship served to make him the core, or perhaps the fulcrum, of interdepartmental and interdisciplinary effort.

It is small wonder that so many organizations asked Cy Black for help over the years. A full list of his contributions would burden this essay. In work with his students, his colleagues at Princeton and other institutions, in service as board member of Princeton University Press, as counselor to government, to foundations and universities, and to organizations like the Kennan Institute of the Woodrow Wilson Center for Visiting Scholars in Washington, his academic statesmanship, intellectual curiosity, and rigor and honesty showed the way for others. It is fitting that the seminar room of the Center of International Studies, formerly Room 012 in Bendheim Hall, was renamed Cyril Black Seminar Room in 1995.

READING LIST

The Establishment of Constitutional Government in Bulgaria (Princeton: Princeton University Press, 1943)

Editor: *The Transformation of Russian Society* (Cambridge, Massachusetts: Harvard University Press, 1960)

Rewriting Russian History: Soviet Interpretations of Russia's Past, 2d ed. (New York: Vintage Books, 1962)

The Dynamics of Modernization: A Study in Comparative History (New York: Harper, 1966)

Editor: *The Modernization of Japan and Russia: A Comparative Study* (New York: The Free Press, 1975)

Richard Palmer Blackmur

Department of English

BY EDMUND L. KEELEY

As is often true of celebrated writers, the image of R. P. Blackmur that has survived him continues to be part myth and part down-to-earth reality. The myth holds him to have been a portrait of contradictions: essentially uneducated yet inaccessibly erudite, a brilliant conversationalist yet largely incomprehensible, a loner walking the green pathways of his own mind yet persistently in need of an audience. And as is the case with much mythology, even here an element of truth inhabits the essential fantasy that makes myths entertaining. Blackmur did in fact fail to earn a high school diploma, let alone attend a university, but this rejection of formal schooling freed him to educate himself more broadly than many of his bright contemporaries through intensive reading as his passion for literature dictated, especially while working for some years in one or another bookstore in Cambridge, Massachusetts, within easy reach of Harvard's Widener Library. He had to learn early to nourish his creativity out of his own resources and was forced for a long time to live on the margins financially, but far from being a recluse, he was generally available to those who shared his commitment to a discriminating literary life. And his talk was usually of a quality that engendered all the audience one could want, whether he was conversing at home with friends or in the lecture hall or at the Gauss Seminars, where his dialogue with the invited speaker, rather than the speaker's presentation, often became the seminar's stimulating center.

The reality both inside and outside the myth is what made R. P. Blackmur an exceptional member of the Princeton community from 1940 until his death at sixty-one in 1965, and my remarks here will focus on this period of his life. Blackmur was already firmly established as a poet and literary critic by the time he arrived in Princeton, having published by then a well-received first volume of poems, *From Jordan's Delight*, and two important volumes of essays, *The Double Agent* and *The Expense of Greatness.* The latter confirmed his position as a leading figure in the New Criticism, the "school" that was to dominate the reading and study of Anglo-American literature during the postwar years. His first position at the University was as associate to Allen Tate in the young Creative Arts Program. World War II put that program on hold, but in 1943 Blackmur was appointed the first Alfred Hodder Memorial Fellow, a fellowship that still brings a writer or translator to the Princeton campus for a year of creative enterprise without other obligations. He then spent two years at the Institute for Advanced Study as Fellow of the School of Economics and Politics, and in 1946 began his long association with the Princeton English Department, first as Resident Fellow in Creative Writing, in due course as an associate professor, and finally, in 1951, as a tenured full professor. Blackmur was thus crucial in opening Princeton — and by example, the academy more generally — to creative artists, especially writers, and it is his legacy that prepared the way for the abundant gathering of tenured writers now at Princeton: the novelists Joyce Carol Oates, Toni Morrison, and Russell Banks, the poets James Richardson and Paul Muldoon.

The full acceptance of writers in the academy took time, and in Blackmur's case it was not complete. Though an eminent member of the English Department for eighteen years, and though recognized by most of his colleagues and certainly most departmental graduate students as an increasingly influential figure in American literary studies, he was among the very few professors of English in the Princeton of his day never to hold a chair. On that score, he deserved better. But despite further mythology to the contrary, his years on the faculty were unusually rewarding for him, for those colleagues who knew him best, and for a number of either talented or adventurous students.

There were some early admirers who felt that his having left the rugged natural life of the Maine coast for the well-kept lawns of Princeton deprived him of certain resources that his poetic sensibility needed, which explained his abandonment of his poetic muse after his 1942 and 1947 volumes, *The Second World* and *The Good European.* But the fact is that Blackmur remained highly productive in other ways central to the literary life, publishing a number of volumes of criticism during his Princeton years, among them, *Language as Gesture*, *The Lion and the Honeycomb*, and *Anni Mirabiles.* These, if sometimes abstruse and in his late style even vatic, almost always glowed with a poet's heightened sensitivity to language and image, his eloquence sharpened by acutely original perceptions and an increasingly judicious insight not only into the nature of poetry but into the relation between literature and the larger culture. A sense of the Blackmur mode is conveyed by an early yet typical illumination of his in a book review that apparently served to initiate a long friendship with the poet John Berryman, as is suggested by the poem "Olympus" in Berryman s 1971 volume, *Love and Fame*:

In my serpentine researches
I came on a book review in *Poetry*
which began, with sublime assurance,
A comprehensive air of majesty,

"The art of poetry
is amply distinguished from the manufacture of verse
by the animating presence in the poetry
of a fresh idiom: language

so twisted & posed in a form
that it not only expresses the matter in hand
but adds to the stock of available reality."
I was never altogether the same man after *that* . . .

What was perhaps least visible but nevertheless immensely productive about Blackmur's Princeton years was his influence on students and younger colleagues. There is ample testimony by former students to his remarkable qualities as a teacher in the commemorative section of the *Princeton Alumni Weekly* published May, 1965. Among the shared themes there is Blackmur's insistence on treating his students as though they were as intelligent as he was when both he and they knew all too well that they weren't. This refusal to condescend to them inevitably had the effect of making them want to be better than they were. His passionate commitment to the high seriousness of literature, his insistence on its necessary value for both the unfolding individual mind and the growth of a civilized society, not only created disciples but opened the possibility of faith in those who had none and sustained the faith of those given to doubt. And this was so even when his way of revealing what was essential about literature stretched the capacity of his students to absorb obscure analogy, attenuated logic, and subtle playfulness. As someone once said of his friend Robert Lowell, Blackmur's priceless gift to his writing students was his ability to inspire in them a sense of artistic perfectionism whatever their limitations. His commitment to the highest forms of expression in art was thus moral as much as it was aesthetic.

The passion that nourished Blackmur's faith in literature was most apparent in the sweet lingering over word or image that he brought to the reading of lines of verse that he recited for their beauty or wisdom. Something of the same unhurried pleasure, a hovering delight, came into the testing of his own suddenly brilliant formulations as he worked his way into a poem or novel, seemingly by improvisation. Though few of his students could pretend that they understood at first hearing the full richness of what he gradually laid out before them, many testified to its sustained aftereffects, the access it provided in time to the possibilities of crafted expression and relished insight. For most of those who eventually entered the profession of letters, Blackmur appears to have remained the ideal audience they hoped to please as writers and thinkers.

Some of those students who confessed to finding his mind so formidable as to be rather terrifying at moments also spoke of his unfailing personal kindness and sympathy. In his writing tutorials, he had the wit and generosity of spirit to measure out his judgement in a way that served the occasion diplomatically yet without compromising his aesthetic perfectionism. To this I can testify by a personal example. When, at the beginning of my senior year as an English major, I was audacious enough to go to Blackmur's office, uninvited and unannounced, to ask him for an opinion regarding my future prospects after my first efforts at writing poetry — nature poetry inspired by a grand tour of national parks the previous summer — Professor Blackmur received this "Mr. Keeley" (we were all more formal in those days) without complaint or evasion, read my poems slowly in front of me, looked up from my thin manuscript and said, "Mr. Keeley, may I ask how old you are?" "Twenty," I said. "Going on twenty-one." "Well, let me say this," Professor Blackmur said. "Keats at eighteen did not write as well as this." I took my manuscript from him, smiling broadly, though for the life of me I couldn't remember anything Keats at written at eighteen — who could? The smile died in the corridor outside when my heady brain began to remember what Keats was capable of writing at twenty going on twenty-one: his most famous sonnet, the one on reading Chapman's Homer, and his lines about burning to see "Beauties of deeper glance, and hear them singing, /and float with them about the summer waters," not to mention the remarkable odes written only two years later — and then his death two years after that. From this painful if quick English-major review of literary history outside Blackmur's office emerged my decision — still in effect almost fifty years later — to give poetry a break and try my hand at writing fiction instead. Justly or not, that is what I took to be the professor's unstated message, though I didn't have the courage to show him what my fiction was up to until I was safely a professor myself.

An exceptionally rewarding hospitality that mixed fine food for the mind with ample bourbon for the spirit is what R. P. Blackmur — called "Richard" rather than "Dick" by his closest Princeton friends — provided those young colleagues, and a few older ones, who became part of the literary salon that prospered for some years in Blackmur's living room first on Princeton Avenue and then on McCosh Circle. The gathering in these places, especially following the Gauss Seminars on Thursday evenings, would often bring together some visiting celebrity from the United States or abroad and those of Blackmur's associates — graduate students sometimes, colleagues from various departments, friends from New York — who had qualified, by their cunning or persistence or their capacity for exalted talk and free-flowing whiskey, as members of the salon. Blackmur's tolerance of eccentricity among the talented provided for some exasperating behavior on the part of his guests and even his invited speakers, and he allowed those few who chose to come and go of an evening the right to do so, though there was inevitably a core group of the faithful who attended regularly and went home late. Those evenings were almost always exhilarating if sometimes punishing occasions, the weak at heart at moments overwhelmed by the bourbon or the relentlessly elevated dialogue or the host's loquacious good humor. But for those devoted to letters, it was without doubt the most stimulating classroom in town.

And Blacknur was the writer's only resident oracle in town, present for advice whatever the hour. If an aspiring novelist, for example, suffering from the insomnia that comes out of an excess of unrealized ambition, might take to wandering the streets of Princeton at three or four in the morning and happen to see the light on at Blackmur's — as it often was that late — he would have no reason to be ashamed of his impulse to ring the front doorbell. And if he actually did so, he could count on R. P. B. to look up from his work desk, cigarette held between the third and fourth fingers of his writing hand (some thought to make it possible for him to turn the page he was reading or to add a marginal note in his tight script without changing the definitive angle of his cigarette and its long ash), his tiny mouth now slightly pursed not so much in surprise at the sound of the bell as in resigned expectation, and after waiting for the slow rise and soundless walk to the door on miniature feet, his night visitor would find the mouth curled up into a little smile, the eyebrows raised, the eyes gently narrowed by a hint of irony. "So it's you. Abandoned by the muse again? Maybe we can try to warm her wavering heart with a touch of bourbon on the rocks even at this hour. Come on in."

Whatever Blackmur may have left behind him in Maine, what he brought to Princeton enriched a generation of students in ways no other literary figure on the scene could have, and for many of those who came to know him personally, he made the life of letters seem divinely charged. In a summary evaluation, the London *Economist* wrote of the density of meaning and resonance in Blackmur's style but also of the mystery in it: the kind that excites the mind and compels it to better work —"and that is the gift of a great critic." It is also the gift of a great teacher. But one suspects it was the poet in the critic and teacher that provided the mystery's source, and I conclude with a poem by Blackmur from his Maine years that best makes the case:

Mirage

The wind was in another country, and
the day had gathered to its heart of noon
the sum of silence, heat, and stricken time.
Not a ripple spread. The sea mirrored
perfectly all the nothing in the sky.
We had to walk about to keep our eyes
from seeing nothing, and our hearts from stopping
at nothing. Then most suddenly we saw
horizon on horizon lifting up
out of the sea's edge a shining mountain
sun-yellow and seagreen; against it surf
flung spray and spume into the miles of sky.
Somebody said mirage, and it was gone,
but there I have been living ever since.

READING LIST

The Double Agent: Essays in Craft and Elucidation (New York: Arrow Editions, 1935)

From Jordan's Delight (New York: Arrow Editions, 1937)

The Expense of Greatness (New York: Arrow Editions, 1940)

The Second World (Cummington, Massachusetts: Cummington Press, 1942)

Language as Gesture: Essays in Poetry (New York: Harcourt, 1952)

The Lion and the Honeycomb: Essays in Solicitude and Critique (New York: Harcourt, 1955)

The Good European and Other Poems (Cummington, Massachusetts: Cummington Press, 1977)

Américo Castro

Department of Romance Languages and Literatures

BY EDMUND L. KING

"How did you ever get to be a member of the Princeton faculty?" I was asked by a young historian spending, as was I, the academic year 1953–1954 in Madrid. I confessed that I often felt some wonderment myself over fortune's kindness. There was nothing to it, I explained.

In 1946, with World War II just over, universities were being overrun with students, and there was a sudden demand to refill the depleted ranks of junior faculty, a demand so compelling that I, an erstwhile graduate student in Spanish, was given an instructorship in English at the University of Texas in Austin. With no warning at all, my friend and mentor there, Ramón Martínez López, told me one day that Américo Castro had written to say that Princeton too was hungry for teachers and that he, in particular, needed an instructor in Spanish, preferably an American.

Would I like to go to Princeton and teach with Américo Castro? Could I make up my mind on the spur of the moment? Yes, I said. I can make up my mind. And a day or so later, with the exchange of two telegrams, I had the job. (O tempora, o mores!) I arrived in Princeton in September of 1946 and have been here ever since.

Because of the close relationship that eventually developed between us, it is generally assumed by those who take an interest in such matters that I was Don Américo's student, his *discípulo.* The fact is, I completed my formal studies for the doctorate far from the reach of Castro's shadow. To the extent possible out in the wilderness, I was self-taught in the doctrine of the then "New Criticism," and five years of teaching in Mississippi before World War II and almost five years of military service in that war had given the common clay I was made of not a shape of arresting lines but nonetheless whatever distinctive configuration it was capable of taking on. This is not to suggest that I had nothing, or thought I had nothing, to learn from Américo Castro. Indeed, what knowledge and understanding I brought with me of literature in general and particularly of Spanish literature was as nothing compared with what I acquired through the years of association with the person we all, those of us who knew him at Princeton, thought of quite simply as a great man. Let me try to put some life into that abstract characterization.

Elsewhere I have described Castro as an intellectual activist. He was possessed of a nervous and nervy mind. Even in the fairly conventional philological studies of his early maturity one notices a certain jerkiness, a disposition to insert surprising observations, an impatience with the obligations of linear exposition, an inclination to attack the subject from an unprepared point of view. Above all, one feels the presence of immensely energetic thought. All this intellectual energy was, from the establishment in Madrid of the Centro de Estudios Históricos in 1910 to the Spanish Civil War (1936–1939), expended in teaching and writing about Spanish philology in the amplest sense of the term and taking a hyperactive role in the intellectual life of the Hispanic world — lectures and seminars at the University of Madrid (he held the chair of the History of the Spanish Language) and elsewhere, articles in the scholarly journals, columns, at times weekly, in the Hispanic press, editions and monographic volumes that are now classics. It was this Castro — the translator of Meyer-Lübke's *Einführung...* (with emendations and many added notes), the editor of *Fueros leoneses* (with Onis) and of works by the Golden Age playwrights, the author of a life of Lope de Vega (superseding Rennert's), the author, this time of surpassing originality, of *El pensamiento de Cervantes* — it was this Castro who was invited to occupy Princeton's Emory L. Ford Chair of Spanish in 1940. But this Castro, unquestionably the most eminent philologist and particularly the most original and prolific literary scholar in the Republican diaspora following the Spanish war, was precisely at that juncture evolving into a thinker and writer of a very different stripe, an evolution consummated, so to speak, with the publication in 1948 of the great work for which he became generally known, perhaps the work that confirmed his eligibility for inclusion in this gallery of portraits. I remember a cold autumn afternoon when the young Cuban editor José ("Pepito") Rodriguez Feo came by my apartment to tell me, with irrepressible excitement, that he was reading Don Américo's new book, "un libro *ma-ra-vi-llo-so.*" The book was *España en su historia*, eventually to appear, much revised, in English as *The Structure of Spanish History*, of which more, presently.

Castro had no sooner settled into life and teaching at Princeton than the nation got into World War II. Only a small number of undergraduate and graduate students were to benefit from his tutelage before they were dispersed into military service. When normal University life resumed in 1946, it was possible to observe, in Castro's seminars, an unusual academic phenomenon. Students who had come to Princeton to study with the author of *El pensamiento de Cervantes* found themselves studying with the author who was devoting all his intellectual energy to finishing

España en su historia. Although I was not, as I have explained, a student, I attended the seminars along with other junior faculty members, and so I can say that we, only partially aware of what was going on, hardly knew what to make of the Castro who all but repudiated *El pensamiento de Cervantes,* the Castro who would quote something he had written years before and which seemed beyond refutation, only to break off and say, "When I wrote that. . . . Well, it's not all wrong, but it's not the right way to think about it. Now I understand. . . ." A currently fashionable word fits to perfection: aporia, aporia in the flesh. (Self-revision even in the middle of sentences was a characteristic of Castro's oral style. Richard Blackmur once remarked to me that while he was always engaged by what Castro had to say and would not dare to devote, as he would like to do, one of his semi-public lecture series to *Don Quixote* as long as Castro was around, he did wish "Américo would for once say a whole complete paragraph coherent from beginning to end.")

The subjects of the seminars were the standard ones, mostly pertaining to the Golden Age, but the treatment was utterly idiosyncratic. I clearly remember one evening (we met from seven to ten) when it occurred to Don Américo to contrast Lucan (one of the Roman writers Castro considered it ridiculous to call Spanish merely because he was born in Córdoba) with whichever writer was being studied. He went into the stacks and brought back a copy of the *Pharsalia* in Latin. He translated a page or two without so much as a pause along the way, as if he were reading from a written-out text. We did not applaud but we were astonished.

The seminars went on in this jerky way, filled with factual clarifications where earlier scholars had not had the wit to see problems, dazzling insights, and just plain delightful *explication de texte,* as Castro shuttled back and forth between his old, fairly conventional but immensely learned philology and his new existential historicism, working its way before our eyes into *España en su historia* and its sequels — in a peculiarly literal sense, history in the making.

I do not wish to get bogged down in a discussion of whether *España en su historia* is, as I have perhaps too glibly insinuated, history. It will not help much to call it diachronic existential cultural anthropology, but I do think Castro might have accepted and even been pleased by such a description. Whatever its genre, in due course I became more than a mere observer of the dialectic from which it emerged.

One night in October of 1949 Don Américo telephoned me. Princeton University Press wanted to publish an English version of *España en su historia.* Would I be willing to translate it? He would pay me . . . . (This is not the place for the financial details. I believe, implausible as it may seem, that the most poorly compensated and the most richly rewarding work I have ever done in my life was to be paid for with money from Castro's own pocket.) Quite innocently, I said yes. Looking back on the project, I realize that without Don Américo's constant help I would not have been able to see it through. Rumor had it that four, five, maybe six persons had made a stab at it without finishing a whole chapter. (Considerable lore built up around the book, began to do so, in fact, when it first became known that Castro was writing it.) In truth, I had no idea that the task I had taken on was going to be so difficult. I went to work.

It turned out that the book I was translating was not really the *España en su historia* of 1948, but a new work, to be entitled in Spanish *La realidad histórica de España*, made up of large chunks of the earlier one much rewritten and greatly recast, intermingled with a number of new chapters, some complementing the existing ones, some replacing chapters to be discarded not always before they had been translated. Don Américo would telephone. What page had I got to? I never knew whether he was going to be disappointed that I had done so little or relieved to learn that I had not translated pages he now wanted to replace. I got quite accustomed to seeing good stretches of translation go into the wastebasket.

Things went on this way through 1950, 1951, and 1952, as Castro

Américo Castro (right) with Anthony Kerrigan (left) and Edmund L. King in Mallorca, 1960s.

made and re-made his text and I made and re-made the translation. Castro himself had composed one of his small early books in French, but he had never undergone the torture of having an important work of his translated before his very eyes. The fact is that although Don Américo was unwilling to write anything other than personal letters in English, he knew the language quite well and was perfectly competent to point out errors and infelicities in my translation — as he did — and to suggest improvements. As everyone who has given any attention to the matter knows, there is no more severe test of the comprehensibility of a text than translating it into another language, and a consequence of this for Castro was that he was constantly weighing and reweighing his words. *The Structure of Spanish History* was the title given by the Princeton University Press editors to the English translation, almost as much the work of the author himself as of the translator named on the title page. Readers of the Spanish version, *La realidad histórica de España,* are likely to think they have the original before them, but such is not strictly speaking the case. Much of that text would not be as it is if it had not been translated into English. A kind of reciprocal osmosis had gone on between our two languages.

It is not easy to estimate Américo Castro's legacy to those who may plausibly be called his heirs, partly because it was so manifold, partly because we ourselves are so various. He himself thought he was imparting a method, but it would be difficult if not impossible to say what that method was, as one might do, say, with an Auerbach or a Panofsky. What he gave us was his example of utter seriousness and dedication to the task at hand. "I want priests who believe in their religion," I once heard him say. And he did not have in mind the Church of Laodicea. When our faith faltered, it was an immense satisfaction to have it fortified by his example. But of course the example had substance. Nothing of a "hard gem-like flame." Rather, a problem-ridden, troubled attention, through the study of literary and other cultural artifacts, to the drama played out by Iberian Christians, Moors, and Jews as they created the Spanish way of thinking, feeling, and acting, and then to the projection of these created values, detached, so to speak, from their generators, down to the Spain that is still vulgarly called "different" at the end of the twentieth century. One can think of this content of Castro's thought either as a usable set of structuring concerns — points of departure for further study — or simply as "the truth." Don Américo wanted me to pick up where he had left off, to write about his work, to show how right he was, as several of his most convinced disciples had done — I think of Stephen Gilman, Juan Marichal, Samuel Armistead, Joseph Silverman, Francisco Márquez Villanueva, Albert Sicroff, Pedro Laín Entralgo. But except for one little note explaining an enigmatic sentence in *El Licenciado Vidriera,* I have refrained from trying to explore and extend Castro's views. Lacking the philology and detailed historical knowledge to do so with critical competence and authority, I am content to accept the force of Castro's arguments and to believe that he is right, and to let his truths show through as they may in my own work, work that included, in the decade 1972–1982, an undergraduate course entitled "The Problem of Spain." Everything I understand about this problem, I said regularly in the first lecture, I learned from Américo Castro; go to him if you want to read more on the subject. The fact is, many literary and historical scholars working today do not realize the debt they owe Castro for opening up a field of study that a generation or two ago was scarcely thought to exist.

Don Américo himself never regarded his work as something finished. No doubt, when he delivered the manuscript of *The Structure of Spanish History* to the University Press in 1952, he was thinking about how it should be redone. Indeed, he did re-argue and re-make it in book after book. How to dissect Spain's historical body without taking away its life was the aporetic task which he would never abandon. Surely he was turning it over in his mind as he took his last, fatal swim in the Mediterranean on the Feast of St. James the Great, Santiago de España, in 1972.

READING LIST

El pensamiento de Cervantes (Madrid: Hernando, 1925)

The Structure of Spanish History (Princeton: Princeton University Press, 1954)

An Idea of History: Selected Essays of Américo Castro, translated and edited by Stephen Gilman and Edmund L. King (Columbus: Ohio State University Press, 1977)

Américo Castro: The Impact of His Thought. Essays to Mark the Centenary of His Birth, ed. Ronald E. Surtz, Jaime Ferrán, and Daniel P. Testa (Madison: Hispanic Seminary of Medieval Studies, 1988)

Kenneth Hamilton Condit

Department of Civil and Mechanical Engineering

BY DAVID P. BILLINGTON

Arriving for the first time on the Princeton campus in the late summer of 1946, I went straight to the office of the dean of the Engineering School. Kenneth Condit was the first faculty member I met, and he would change my life in three ways as decidedly as he would change the Engineering School.

Dean Condit had received the degree of mechanical engineer in 1908 from the Stevens Institute of Technology in Hoboken, New Jersey, and after working in industry he entered Princeton, graduating with the class of 1913 as a civil engineer. One of his Stevens classmates, a close friend of my father, had urged me to discuss my career dilemma with the dean before classes began. I was nervous and a bit in awe of the position, but found Dean

Condit both welcoming and low key. Later I would interpret his demeanor as shyness, but at the time he gave me the advice I needed: enroll in engineering not, as I had intended, in liberal arts (I had wanted to major in physics). It was far easier to switch to liberal arts rather than into engineering, he explained, and that first influential change in direction made me an engineer. The second change came more slowly, but served to keep me from wandering too far from engineering.

Dean Condit himself had taught civil engineering at Princeton as an instructor for four years after graduation, then during World War I he taught airplane engine fundamentals. Following demobilization he joined the editorial staff of the *American Machinist*, becoming its editor for seventeen years. In 1940 he was appointed the second dean of the Engineering School (founded in 1921). In a 1939 letter to President Harold W. Dodds outlining new directions for the school, Condit had referred first to the basic engineering curriculum, which he was to direct during his tenure as dean and into which he encouraged me to come. As president of the Princeton Engineering Association and organizer of committees to get industry engineers as advisors to the school, he was instrumental in inaugurating the Basic Engineering Program in 1938. By 1946 this amorphous program included courses in all engineering departments plus some improbable extras such as organic and inorganic chemistry (taught by two stars of the chemistry department, Hugh Stott Taylor and Everett Wallis), as well as the popular Harvard Business School-type courses taught by Condit's assistant dean, Howard Menand. One major virtue of Basic Engineering for me was its freedom of electives, which allowed me to take many humanities courses — art history, literature, music, and the special humanities courses.

Being in the program gave me continual contact with the dean, who was my course advisor, and eventually I was to meet with him once a week as an unofficial engineering school correspondent for the *Daily Princetonian*. Although the news hardly made headlines, the conferences let me in to a small extent on the dean's world.

He had some difficulty conversing with students; he was not skilled at small talk, and he felt himself not to be a good teacher. He was giving a course on industrial development that I did not fully appreciate at the time, but which I have since tried to duplicate. The dean was unfailingly kind and soon we had a good rapport. Our meetings persisted despite the lack of dazzling news (one article that the hungry *Prince* published described the refurbished offices in chemical engineering, just painted turquoise) and it was clear to me that I was serving him as much as he was advising me. Yet I would not learn what was really on his mind until two decades later.

He advised me for my senior thesis on highway traffic planning, and then I came to him with the request for a different type of advice. My classmate-brother had just won a Rhodes Scholarship, and that stimulated me to search for a way to go overseas to study as well. The Fulbright Fellowship program was then in its first year, and I discussed this with the dean. Since competition for fellowships to Britain or to France (I knew a little French) was stiff, the dean recommended Belgium and suggested that I talk to Arthur Bigelow, a graphics professor, who had studied there and was honorary bellmaster to the University of Louvain. Dean Condit helped me construct a proposal related to my thesis and wrote a letter of recommendation for my successful application. He had not only directed my undergraduate program; his second major influence was to set me on a postgraduate course that would fix me decidedly into civil engineering and at the same time allow me to meet a fellow Fulbright student to Belgium, who would soon become my wife. Unlike Cecil Rhodes, William Fulbright included women in his plans from the start.

As an undergraduate I knew little about how the Engineering School was changing under Dean Condit's direction, but I did know that for the program in basic engineering, he supplied us with extraordinary teachers: Walter Johnson in Electrical Engineering, Daniel Sayre in Aeronautical Engineering, Ernest Johnson in Chemical Engineering, and Howard Menand. What I did not realize then was the extraordinary changes that the dean made. He increased the faculty from eighteen in 1940 to seventy-three when he retired. Although there were no masters or doctors degrees in 1940, the graduate program was far advanced and research already well established when he completed his fourteen-year tenure.

Returning to his 1939 letter to President Dodds, one can see Kenneth Condit's vision for engineering at Princeton. He listed eight major suggestions: the centrality of basic engineering for undergraduate engineers, the development of graduate education, the closer connection to engineering practice, the need for all students to work summers in practice, the necessity for faculty to have close contact with practice, the importance of getting industry to set up endowments for the Engineering School, the possibilities for close cooperation with other schools and departments at Princeton, and the potential for developing courses in engineering for non-engineering students. These ideas, as alive in 1996 as they were over half a century ago, resulted from Condit's career as an editor reflecting on engineering practice, and as an alumnus active in Princeton affairs ever since his graduation. I like to think that these sorts of thoughts played some small role in his last and most formative influence on my life.

Sometime in the middle 1950s, he came to Norman Sollenberger, then professor of civil engineering and soon to become chairman of the department. Dean Condit urged Sollenberger to look me up and see if he could get me to come to Princeton as a faculty member. Apparently he had read a technical article of mine and was reminded of his former student and advisee. Sollenberger followed the lead, inviting me to give a course while I still worked full-time as an engineer in New York.

Thus began two years of nighttime teaching, during which I discovered that I was a better teacher than practitioner. In 1960 I

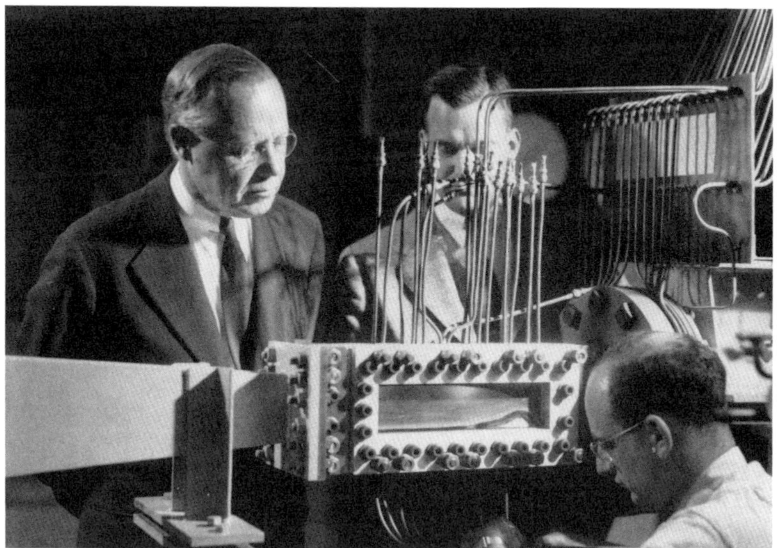

Kenneth H. Condit supervising work in his laboratory.

joined the faculty full time, thanks in no small part to the advice and foresight of Dean Kenneth Condit. He had meantime retired as dean in 1954 because of ill health, and then retired as chairman of mechanical engineering in 1956 to become a professor emeritus.

In 1957 Condit's successor, Joseph C. Elgin, "started a relentless campaign to persuade me to write a history of engineering at Princeton," as Condit wrote. "After two years of resistance," he continued, "I accepted the assignment." The 136-page book appeared in 1962 and gave a clear, documentary account of events from 1875 to 1955. In 1963 his wife died and he moved to Lawrence, Kansas, where he lived until moving to Denver in 1974, where he died on December 15, 1974, at the age of eighty-six. He had been an effective dean, turning the Engineering School into a modern institution focused on both teaching and research. Condit himself was not a researcher, nor was he a natural teacher, but he was an outstanding leader at Princeton. He was right for his time, and the health of the school today owes a great debt to his quiet direction.

In 1931, at the age of forty-two, Kenneth Condit took up painting, and by 1953 had created about 150 summer landscapes. An artist friend advised him not to take lessons because "if you don't take any you might be lucky enough to develop a style." That was Dean Condit. He learned the academic world as a dean and he developed real style.

READING LIST

A History of the Engineering School of Princeton University (Princeton?, 1962)

Cyrus Fogg Brackett (1833–1915) of Princeton, Pioneer in Electrical Engineering (New York: Newcomen Society in North America, 1952)

Lewis Buckley Stillwell, 1863–1941: A Biographical Memoir (New York: Published for the National Academy of Sciences of the United States, 1960)

Edwin Grant Conklin

Department of Biology

BY JOHN TYLER BONNER

Professor Edwin Grant Conklin was primarily responsible for making Princeton University an internationally important center of biology. Already a successful and distinguished biologist at the University of Pennsylvania, he was brought to Princeton in 1908 by Woodrow Wilson to lead a new biology department which was to be housed with geology in a modern laboratory. Guyot Hall was completed in 1910; it and Dr. Conklin's appointment mark the transition for biology at Princeton from that of a small teaching college to that of a research university.

At the time many wondered why Dr. Conklin, who was already recognized as one of the leading embryologists in this country, if not the world, would leave a prestigious position at the University of Pennsylvania and move to a place that still seemed to be living in the distant past as far as modern science was concerned. There were many theories at the time, varying from escaping the politics at Pennsylvania, where he was chairman, to a presumed increase in salary at Princeton. The real answer was undoubtedly the one Dr. Conklin himself gave: he was captivated by Woodrow Wilson, who had a vision for the future of biology at Princeton that was shared by Conklin. Wilson's enthusiasm was contagious enough so that when Wilson left in 1911, Conklin stayed on and carried out his mission without the direct support of his admired friend.

Edwin Grant Conklin was born in 1863 in Ohio, the same year (as he often pointed out) that Abraham Lincoln delivered the Gettysburg address. He did his undergraduate work at Ohio Wesleyan and his Ph.D. at the Johns Hopkins University. He did not go directly on to graduate work, but taught for three years at a missionary college for black students, an experience that undoubtedly reinforced his interest and increased his skill in teaching. It is noteworthy that at an early age he showed his breadth by giving courses in Latin, Greek, English, and a variety of sciences.

The work on his doctoral thesis, done in his late twenties, was to make him world-famous: it was his big scientific achievement, and his later biological research was an extension of that early work in embryology. Initially, for his thesis, he showed that in the development of the mollusc *Crepidula* there was a set pattern of cleavage: the lineage of each cell could be followed through a series of cleavages indicating that their pattern of development was rigid and fixed. Later he showed a similar phenomenon in the ascidian *Cynthia* where the cells are more clearly marked. The fixity of their fate was later proved by him and others by removing particular cells, and the resulting embryos lacked a specific part. Each region of the embryo was laid out at the earliest stage and development consisted of the successive partitioning of those "organ forming substances," as they were called. Conklin was a leader of these studies of "mosaic" development, a major part of the revolution in embryology that occurred at the turn of the century.

A few days before Dr. Conklin died in 1952, just before his ninetieth birthday, two colleagues from the Biology Department brought an old wire recorder to his bedroom and asked if he would like to record some of his reminiscences. He loved to tell those tales and he was still full of vigor. Fortunately that recording has been preserved, and in it he describes the early work for his doctoral thesis. The recording gives a clear picture of what he was like and how he talked in his strong, measured sentences. Professor W. K. Brooks was his thesis advisor in the days when one's professor was the absolute monarch. Here are Dr. Conklin's words after he describes his work on *Crepidula*:

> Well, I thought that was important, and so did the graduate students. But Brooks didn't. Brooks looked at it, and well, he brought the thesis back. I'd written it out at great labor. This was my last year at Johns Hopkins. I was married, Mrs. Conklin was my amanuensis, and she wrote it all out for me as I dictated it. And I submitted it all to Brooks with the plates — I had eight or ten plates made with pen and ink — and Brooks took it home with him, kept it for several days, brought it back. "Well," he said, "Conklin, I don't know what to say about this." He said, "I don't know where in the world you can ever print this. I don't know if it's worth printing." He said, "There is no morphological significance in it." That was his thesis. Well, the result was that he came back to see me after several interviews in which there were always half a dozen students in the room. We didn't have individual rooms, we were all thrown together, our graduate students, and finally he came back and he said, "Well, Conklin, I've decided that this University has given doctors' degrees for counting words in ancient languages. I don't know why they might not give one for counting cells."

Once Guyot Hall was finished in 1910, Dr. Conklin began in earnest to build an important and modern biology department. This was not easy, for he had great difficulty persuading prominent biologists to move to the uncertainties of a new department, but with persistence he finally gathered a core, some of junior people, that slowly emerged into a strong research-university department. He was chairman for twenty-five years until he retired in 1933, and during that period he wrought great changes for Princeton.

One day I asked him how he could have done the administrative work of a chairman for so long. He said that in the early days it was no great burden — he borrowed the Dean of the Faculty's secretary one afternoon a week and did all the departmental business. He had other stories showing the difference in the pace of those early days. One professor, I forget in which department, refused to have a telephone, and the only way to reach him was by sending a messenger with a note. He also described how the whole department, after lunch on pleasant days, would take a walk around Lake Carnegie, across the Washington Road and Harrison Street bridges. Those definitely were the days!

From the very beginning Dr. Conklin taught the basic course in general biology. He was a great teacher and the course became enormously popular. He talked and lectured like a seasoned preacher; at one time early in his career he had considered going into the ministry. In his lectures and in conversation each word was clear and distinct as he declaimed, rather than spoke. His voice would rise and fall with considerable drama, and when he emphasized a point, he positively boomed. He used to give a lecture every summer in the embryology course at the Marine Biological Laboratory in Woods Hole, Massachusetts, which I remember well, especially the ending: he would trail off with great pathos saying, in an uncharacteristically weak and wavering voice, "This may well be my swan song." Since he lived to a ripe old age, there were many of those splendid annual swan songs.

There is a verbatim transcript of his general biology course in the archives of the University. Apparently he was considering writing a textbook and had a stenographer take down his words and type them out. I looked at this manuscript some years ago and found that its main interest was the topics he covered for the freshmen and sophomores. Years later I went on to teach the same course, and the comparison showed the enormous extent to which biology had changed during the course of this century.

When I came to Princeton as an assistant professor in 1947, Dr. Conklin had been retired for fourteen years. Like all biologists I had great admiration for him and was eager to make his acquaintance. This turned out to be very easy to do because he was most approachable and seemed especially to enjoy the company of younger people. He loved to talk, and we all loved to listen to him. He was always full of tales. I wish I had recorded them all at the time.

By then he was a widower; Mrs. Conklin had died some years earlier. He still lived in his old Broadmead house which had welcomed him in 1908. The inside and the furniture were appropriately old-fashioned — the stairs and doors were yellow oak, and everything seemed sturdy and ancient. I can remember being there one evening for coffee, and he began to talk. He asked where I had been during World War II, and I explained that I had been in the Air Force in Dayton, Ohio. He knew Dayton; he had been through it on a "century run," a hundred-mile race on those bicycles with a huge wheel under the seat, and a smaller one behind (or in front). He had found the streets of Dayton shocking: they were all dirt roads and full of ruts. I assured him the streets were now paved.

One spring he came to me and said that he had heard I wanted to spend the summer at the Marine Biological Laboratory, and that I needed work space there. Would I be willing to share his room, which had been bequeathed to him in perpetuity as one of the founding fathers of the Laboratory? I was absolutely delighted, and I got to know him very much better that summer.

Every morning when I arrived at about nine o'clock, he would be there at his desk. The first thing he usually said, with considerable firmness, was that he had been there since seven o'clock, and I would express my admiration. There never seemed any irritation in his remark — it was just a fact. I never tried to see if I could beat him there, because I knew I would lose. But I had a problem: Dr. Conklin's love for talking. I was trying to write a book. It was not just anyone talking, however, it was Dr. Conklin, someone with really interesting things to say, so I would do much of my work in the library and ration my good times with him.

The most interesting subject for me was what he had to say about many of the biologists whom he knew from the previous century. Some he liked and admired enormously; some he despised. In the latter cases he poured scorn on their work and their characters in a wonderfully slanderous fashion. As a youngster I was agog. Here was not only someone who knew all those characters, who for me were mythical, but was high enough on Mt. Olympus to spread Jovian scorn when it was deserved. The one person who interested me most was Hans Dreisch, who discovered that some kinds of embryos were not mosaic, as the American school, and Dr. Conklin in particular, had discovered, but could be cut in two, and each half became a complete miniature larva. It all depended on what kind of invertebrate was tested. At the time of their respective discoveries the results seemed so diametrically opposed that the field divided between those who championed "mosaic" development, and those who championed "regulative" development, as the other was called. By 1950, the summer I was in Dr. Conklin's laboratory, it had been generally agreed for some time that not only did both kinds of development exist, but all animals had different degrees of both. However, Dr. Conklin had grave reservations about Hans Dreisch. He said he was a charming person, but fundamentally unsound. Since Driesch had been a hero of mine (I thought his experimental work was brilliant), I kept pushing for more, trying to find out why Dr. Conklin felt as he did. Initially I thought it was because Dreisch had become a philosopher and a vitalist later in life. I had always thought he had given up science because he felt living phenomena were too mysterious to be explained by the kind of simple mechanistic explanation scientists seek. While Dr. Conklin agreed with me in this, it was clear that was only one of the strikes against

Dreisch; I think the old wounds of the early mosaic-regulative development struggle had never completely healed.

Besides his embryological work, Dr. Conklin was to publish two books and give many lectures on science, philosophy, and social issues. He was an ardent supporter of Darwinism, that is, evolution as the result of natural selection. This was not just a struggle against doubters among fellow scientists, but also against laymen, and especially those who imagined a conflict between religion and evolution. From the very beginning of his career he attacked Lamarckian inheritance of acquired characters, and is quoted in an article about him in a 1939 *Time* magazine as saying, "Wooden legs are not inherited — but wooden heads may be."

This remark is typical of his forceful way of putting things. I can remember an occasion when he was being introduced by an old but slightly absent-minded friend and fellow scientist at a large gathering in New York. The introducer wanted to say something complimentary and started off in a rambling fashion, saying that some years ago Dr. Conklin had said to his son . . . and then there was a horrible pause. Clearly he could not remember what had been said. In desperation he turned to Dr. Conklin: "What did you say to my son?" at which Dr. Conklin, quick as lightning, replied in a deafening roar, "GOOD GOD, how should I know?" Needless to say, this brought down the house, and despite the fact that he was then in his mid-eighties, Dr. Conklin gave an inspired lecture.

Besides his laboratory science and his writing and public speaking, Conklin spent his life filling administrative posts of various sorts, even well into his retirement. He was twice elected president of the American Philosophical Society during his emeritus years. He carried out all these activities effectively and with great dignity. Once he described what he considered should be the duties and the vision of a scientist by saying, "Our strongest social instincts are for service; the joy of life is in progress; the desire of all men is for immortality through their work." His own words exactly describe the person he was and his splendid career.

READING LIST

"Problems of Evolution and Present Methods of Attacking Them," *The American Naturalist* 46 (March 1912): 121–128

Heredity and Environment in the Development of Men (Princeton: Princeton University Press, 1915, and later editions)

Has Human Evolution Come to an End? (Princeton: Princeton University Press, 1920)

The Direction of Human Evolution (New York: Charles Scribner's Sons, 1921)

A Synopsis of the General Morphology of Animals (Princeton: Princeton University Press, 1927)

Principles and Possibilities of Human Evolution (Philadelphia: Lippincott, 1930)

Man Real and Ideal: Observations and Reflections on Man's Nature, Development, and Destiny (New York: Charles Scribner's Sons, 1943)

Wesley Frank Craven

Department of History

BY GARY B. NASH

Forty-two years ago, daydreaming in a class on Colonial American History, my attention was captured by a remarkable statement issued from the lectern. "Boys," said Wesley Frank Craven in his measured way, "very nearly the most important problem the colonists had to face was the Indian problem." "Boys," he called us because at Princeton in the 1950s there were no women other than the office secretaries and the kitchen workers at the Prospect Street eating clubs. And "boys" because Frank Craven was the gentlest of paternalists, a man to whom the vocabulary of family and community came naturally.

Seven years after my initial encounter with Professor Craven, I sat again in one of his classes, this time a graduate seminar. As a late-blooming Ph.D. aspirant in 1961, I heard again about the "Indian problem." This time the words resonated differently, for

I was becoming active in the civil rights movement of the early 1960s and was beginning to see the connections between the distant colonial past and the turbulent present. I might have known better than cheerfully to accept Frank Craven's suggestion, in my first graduate seminar in American history, that I give an oral report on Cotton Mather's *Magnalia Christi Americana.* My shaky Latin suggested to me that it was about Christ in America, presumably in Puritan New England since even a novice knew that Mather was a towering Puritan minister.

Lugging the 800-page double-columned volume home, I soon saw that the "Swamp Fox," as graduate students called Frank, had dispatched me deep into the heart of the seventeenth-century Puritan mind — an intellectual terrain that was far beyond my ken at that point in my studies. How could I possibly give a ten-minute, brass-tacks summary of this dense and erudite jeremiad on how three generations of Puritans in New England had brought their "errand in the wilderness," by the late seventeenth century, to its perilous condition? With leftover time, I was to relate the book to the assigned reading on early New England history. Clearly, Professor Craven had meant to separate the goats from the sheep. Could I read Latin? Understand the Puritan mentality? Cut to the chase?

Frank Craven always set his intellectual traps for graduate students carefully — and with a special touch that all of us who studied with him would come to treasure. He made sure we dirtied our hands in primary documents; he wanted nobody wasting seminar time on any but the most important books; and he was a cagey intellectual matchmaker, always on the lookout for a dissertation topic that might bring out the best in each of his "boys."

Whatever I said in my allotted ten minutes to capture the essence of Mather's *Magnalia* was apparently good enough for Craven to encourage me to take a few more steps toward a commitment for a dissertation in early American history. Heaven knows, I hadn't digested more that a puny fraction of Mather's work. My salvation was probably in finding my way to the sections of this seven-chambered book where Mather pronounced on the Pequot War of 1637 and King Philip's War of 1676–1677, the fierce bloodlettings that pitted Puritans against Pequots, Wampanoags, Narragansetts, and other Algonkian peoples. My thirst for understanding the peculiar roots of American race relations was getting the better of me. In reading *Magnalia Christi Americana*, I was fascinated with Mather's very first sentence: "I WRITE the *Wonders* of the CHRISTIAN RELIGION, flying from the Depravations of *Europe*, to the *American Strand*." But then I blanched at Mather's reflection on the Puritans' burning of the Pequot fort near Mystic River, where hundreds of Pequots, mostly women and children, were incinerated: "In a little more than *one* hour, five or six hundred of these barbarians were dismissed from a world that was *burdened* with them." Turning to his history of King Philip's War, I read that Mount Hope "was the seat where Philip was kennell'd with the rest of these horrid savages" and that an English commander drove "the beasts of Prey back to their dens after he first sacrificed many scores of them unto the divine vengeance."

Whatever else I passed over in *Magnalia*, which was most of it, I apparently showed zest for the topic while remarking on the resonance of Mather's *Magnalia* at a time when the American Indian Movement was becoming part of the Civil Rights era. It seemed to convince Craven that I might make a decent historian, though perhaps he worried about this incipient activist in his seminar room.

I never heard that Frank was involved in the movement himself, but his graduate students thought his heart was surely in the cause. After all, graduate students knew that among his earliest publications was a probing essay on "Indian Policy in Early Virginia," a seminal article in which Craven attempted to see native Americans as something more than "savages" standing in the way of visionary European colonizers. We knew also of his book on early Bermuda, where slave labor became the foundation of the economy. In the 1950s and early 1960s, the scholarly literature on race was very thin, and undergraduates still learned early American history with only passing references to African and Indian aspects of the colonial experience.

Frank Craven came to Princeton in the fall of 1950, appointed as Edwards Professor of American History, the department's oldest endowed professorship. Born in Conway, North Carolina, in 1905, the son of a North Carolina Methodist minister, Craven had studied at Trinity College (later to become Duke University) and then took the uncustomary step of traveling far north to study English constitutional history at Cornell. There he completed his Ph.D. degree in 1930 at the remarkable age of twenty-five. Craven studied with Wallace Notestein and Charles Hull in English history and was also influenced by the titan of Cornell's history department, Carl Becker, who at the time had emerged as a pillar of the Progressive historians. Craven was the first southerner to receive a Ph.D. in history at Cornell.

If a precocious young man from rural North Carolina had acquired sophistication at Cornell, he quickly acquired urbanity in New York City when he accepted an appointment at New York University in 1930. That is where he spent the Great Depression years. After his marriage in 1932 to Helen McDaniel, the daughter of a Baptist missionary in China, Craven became the father of two girls. The young Craven family would spend the World War II years in Washington, D.C., where Frank served as a historian of the U.S. Army Air Force and as co-editor of the seven-volume *The Army Air Force in World War II.*[1]

The appointment of Craven to Princeton's faculty in 1950 brought him to a history department that was transforming itself from a collection of dazzling undergraduate lecturers to a remarkable cluster of path-breaking scholars and Graduate School Ph.D. mentors. In the 1950s, Princeton's History Department, long known for its vibrant undergraduate program, rose to the pinnacle of graduate training in history, a position it has not surrendered since.

[1] Wesley Frank Craven and James Lea Cate, eds., *The Army Air Force in World War II*, 7 vols. (Chicago: University of Chicago Press, 1948–1958).

Craven's appointment was a key part of this rise of the History Department. His predecessor at Princeton for thirty-seven years was Thomas Jefferson Wertenbaker, the leading historian of colonial Virginia before World War II and a man who, like Craven, was born and bred in the South. Like Wertenbaker, Craven was a cautious subscriber to the Progressive School of history. But Wertenbaker's forte was narrative history, and he was known as an unreconstructed southern apologist whose agenda had little room for race. Craven was more analytic, his range was broader, and nobody mistook him for a descendant of the southern aristocracy. In the 1960s, he was quietly leading his students into considerations of the centrality of race in the way American culture, in its first century, took form. It was no coincidence that in delivering the James W. Richard Lectures at the University of Virginia, he chose the title "White, Red, and Black: The Seventeenth-Century Virginian." When published in 1971, these lectures brought readers abreast of the growing scholarship on the tri-racial relationships that sank bone-deep in the developing American society of the pre-Revolutionary era.

Craven's impact on the historical profession grew as his interests broadened after coming to Princeton in 1950. All of his early work in the first half of his career was centered on southern history, capped by his magisterial *The Southern Colonies in the Seventeenth Century.* At Princeton his work took shape on a much larger canvas. His *Legend of the Founding Fathers* was his first foray into cultural history. Widely read for its perceptive and often wry study of popular conceptions and celebrations of our national origins, it has a special resonance today in the midst of acrid controversies over American national identity, history, and defining values, as portrayed in museums and textbooks. For some time, historians have regarded Craven's *The Colonies in Transition, 1660–1713,* a lively synthesis of politics and society that took its place in the New American Nation series, as his crowning achievement. But rereading his work from the vantage point of the mid-1990s, I believe his *Legend of the Founding Fathers* was his most original and enduring work, at least in terms of its interest to the general public. Four decades after its publication, it reads wonderfully well today. It is the only book he wrote about the character of modern American society and how it has changed — and he did it with humor and rapier-like thrusts at what he believed was the fileopietism and super-patriotism that served a democratic society poorly. Though he said not a word about McCarthyism, it is apparent that it was much on his mind as he wrote a series of stunning lectures, to be delivered at New York University, on the way the writing of history had changed and the way the public commemorated its past. At the end of the book, Craven talked about the Rockefellers' romantic restoration of Colonial Williamsburg. "We tend to preserve or restore," he wrote, "only that which by some artistic or other standard seems worth preserving, and so the picture can be distorted. Who among us can wander down the streets of Williamsburg, with promptings on every side to remember Washington and Jefferson, and still remember that it all rested originally on the back of a Negro?"

Craven was training a number of doctoral students as he was writing this book, and many chose topics focused on northern rather than southern colonies, as well as in English history. His catholic taste, on the one hand, and his distaste for discipleship on the other, always gave students who chose to work with him free rein to explore topics of almost any kind. Craven was not reticent to nudge doctoral students toward topics he found interesting, but he also knew that intellectual independence was nearly the most important quality to be cultivated. When it came time to home in on a dissertation topic, I nimbly sidestepped Frank's first suggestion for a doctoral thesis. He thought I was good with numbers — perhaps because of my work as graduate student loan officer when I was the assistant to the dean of the Graduate School. Pulling on his pipe and in his typical musing tone of voice, he told me "Gary, we don't know very much about taxation in the colonies, and, after all, the Revolution began in a protest against taxes." That dissertation still awaits its researcher. But with the civil rights movement in full flood, I was looking for a topic with much more drama and poignancy. Craven didn't object. Having lobbed one suggestion, he was content to leave the ball in my court. When I came up with a topic — how the persecuted Quakers wrestled with governing themselves in Pennsylvania, 3,000 miles from their tormentors — Frank gave his blessing.

If I had told Craven that the topic was partially inspired by seeing how the new Israeli nation found certain benefits to the tormentors that surrounded it, Frank would have warned me against "presentism" — applying contemporary concerns and perspectives to the past. But it was always a joy to receive penciled criticisms in the margins on draft chapters because they were always supportive, always informed, and always shrewd. Even when he had to disabuse a student with a half-baked idea, he did so with gentle comments about the need to rethink or consider alternative explanations.

Eventually, graduate students value their mentor for intellectual inspiration, a sure hand as a critic of seminar papers and dissertation chapters, and the ability to help the newly minted Ph.D. find a first job. Most mentors in Princeton's Department of

Wesley Frank Craven (right) perusing a small portion of the bibliography.

History were very good at all these things, but their style in playing the mentor's role varied sharply. Fear and intellectual intimidation were not uncommon in the tactics used by mentors. "So what?" one of Craven's colleagues was fond of saying after a much perspired-over presentation had been nervously delivered by a graduate student. "Your metaphysics stink," another is alleged to have said in response to a much redrafted dissertation chapter. "You're not smart enough to do intellectual history," shot back another after reading a seminar paper. But this was not Frank Craven's style. He knew that Princeton admitted very selectively to the Ph.D. programs, so dullards need not be ferreted out or spurred on like balky horses. He believed that a love of history was enough to motivate anyone. He was a shepherd and a samaritan, a universalist, nudging gently, always open to new ideas, steering his students to other books and other interpretations, and helping them polish their prose while honing their arguments. He was himself a felicitous writer and a voracious reader of journal articles and new books, always abreast of scholarship in English, American, and West Indies history. "Get on top of the bibliography," was about as far as he would go toward prodding his students. But in the hands of this wonderfully warm-hearted, wry, and orderly mentor, the dawn of our historical consciousness broke by stages.

READING LIST

The Legend of the Founding Fathers (New York: New York University Press, 1956)

The Colonies in Transition, 1660–1713 (New York: Harper and Row, 1967)

New Jersey and the English Colonization of North America (Princeton: Van Nostrand, 1964)

The Southern Colonies in the Seventeenth Century, 1607–1689, 2d. ed. (Baton Rouge: Louisiana State University Press, 1970)

Red, White, and Black: The Seventeenth-Century Virginian (Charlottesville: University Press of Virginia, 1971)

Luigi Crocco

Department of Aeronautical Engineering

BY IRVIN GLASSMAN

In 1949, Harry Guggenheim, philanthropist and patron of aeronautical research, through the Guggenheim Foundation, endowed a Daniel and Florence Guggenheim Jet Propulsion Laboratory at both Princeton University and the California Institute of Technology. This endowment established the Robert H. Goddard Professorships and graduate fellowships at both institutions. Mr. Guggenheim asked his advisor on aeronautical matters, the world's leading aerodynamicist Theodore von Karman, to recommend to both institutions candidates for the Goddard Professorships. Von Karman's recommendation to Princeton was a young 39-year-old Italian, Luigi Crocco. Who was this brilliant young aerodynamicist and rocket engineer who was to become the intellectual leader of Princeton's Guggenheim Jet Propulsion Laboratory? As a younger colleague and friend, I watched him lead Princeton's fledgling Department of Aeronautical Engineering to national and international prominence within a decade of his arrival.

Luigi Crocco had many engineering talents, and I would rank him equal to the best engineering scientists of all time. His insight coupled with his excellent mathematical ability put him, in my opinion, in a class with Ludwig Prandtl. He graduated as a mechanical engineer from the University of Rome in 1931, but from the time he entered the university he was involved in rocketry research with his father, the well-known Italian pioneer of aeronautics and astronautics, G. Arturo Crocco, then a professor in the newly created School of Aeronautical Engineering at the University of Rome. As early as 1927, when his father was becoming more and more involved with government and the military, Luigi Crocco began to assume full responsibility for this rocket research. Looking back now, it is remarkable that at this early date Crocco was devoting his studies to developing double-base powders as solid propellants for rockets. Both experimentally and theoretically, Crocco determined many of the known combustion laws governing these powders, but these laws did not become generally known until much later because they were classified military secrets. Beginning in 1929, Crocco's research focused on liquid propellants, and in 1930 he successfully ran a small regeneratively cooled rocket motor for ten minutes with the storable bipropellant combination of gasoline and nitrogen tetroxide. (Regenerative cooling is the process of cooling the rocket with one of its propellants during actual firing.) But once again, his work was not generally known: in the late 1940s investigators in the United States were still debating the feasibility of regeneratively cooling liquid-propellant rocket motors. With reason, Crocco often expressed his frustration at not being allowed to publish his rocket work.

In 1933 Crocco became interested in monopropellants, and he was one of the first to consider nitromethane, a solvent that could be very unstable under certain conditions. Nitromethane decomposes quite exothermically, and it appeared to Crocco to be ideal not only for monopropellant rockets, but also in other types of motors not requiring the use of air as an oxidizer. He performed the theoretical performance calculations of nitromethane and also carried out the experimental operations, even machining the rocket chambers himself. Unfortunately, as is characteristic of rockets, they blow up: during a test Crocco was seriously wounded, acquiring an enormous scar where a piece of shrapnel had pierced his arm. He temporarily suspended his rocket research in 1937 when he was appointed assistant professor of aviation engines at Rome.

Crocco would always tell colleagues that his natural bent was to be a theoretician. Nevertheless I can readily recall the time he entered the control room of our rocket laboratories and found a technician trying to determine why a particular piece of electronic instrumentation was not working. He said, "Mike, I do not think that is the proper tube." (We didn't have transistors in those days.)

But during all his years of experimental research, Crocco never gave up his theoretical efforts, particularly with high-speed aerodynamics. His first publication, in 1931, was on high-speed boundary layers; the approach in this paper led to what later became known as the "Crocco Energy Integral." In 1935 he produced a fundamental theoretical study on the relative merits of supersonic wind tunnels. (Von Karman referred to this study as the "bible" of supersonic wind tunnels.) His other major contributions during this period were the "Crocco Vorticity Law" and his seminal study of compressibility effects of laminar boundary layers. In 1939 he was made a full professor in the School of Aeronautical Engineering at Rome. It is not surprising, then, that he was invited to become the first Robert H. Goddard Professor of Jet Propulsion at Princeton in 1949.

When he arrived at Princeton, Crocco found an ongoing program on ram rockets in which the exhaust of fuel-rich rockets or monopropellants was afterburned in a flowing airstream. This device could in some ways be thought of as a self-accelerating ramjet. One of the significant research problems related to this device was whether it was feasible rapidly to mix and burn the supersonic exhaust of the rocket and the air. With a colleague, Lester Lees, Crocco produced a seminal paper on the subject which became known as the "Crocco-Lees Theory of High Speed Turbulent Mixing." It was through this paper that I had my first contact with Luigi Crocco.

I arrived in Princeton near the end of 1950 to begin what I believed to be post-doctoral research in fluid mechanics. I was assigned to undertake experimental work in supersonic mixing and given the Crocco-Lees paper to read. Although I was very inexperienced in the field, I thought I detected an error in the paper. Not knowing the reputation of either of the authors, I approached Crocco and told him of my concerns. He said he would be pleased to see where the error was and as we reviewed the paper he gently lead me through my misunderstanding of certain aspects of fluid mechanics. In no way did he attempt to humiliate me, and instead he thanked me for coming to see him. This was a marvelous trait, one that he used regularly in dealing with everyone, particularly his students.

Shortly thereafter Crocco became deeply involved in and led a theoretical and experimental program on combustion instability in liquid-propellant rocket motors. Instabilities in rocket motors plagued the American rocket industry during the early years and threatened to hold up the United States' space program. Crocco's work provided the first explanation of high-frequency rocket instability, its prediction and control, and was instrumental in assisting industry in the development of the F-1 rocket that was to power the Saturn primary stage that put the first man on the moon. His first theoretical paper on the subject was submitted for publication in 1951 to the *Journal of the American Rocket Society*. I had volunteered to be an assistant editor of this journal, and had the good fortune to have been assigned to oversee the review of Crocco's paper.

Crocco was an exceptional man who had the highest standards for himself and expected the same from others. He spoke five languages in addition to English, but if he were to speak and write English he wanted it to be perfect. The reviews of his article on high-frequency rocket instability were very positive, but I noticed that the paper's English could be improved, so I offered to make grammatical and punctuation modifications, if Crocco wished. He couldn't imagine that I would be willing to undertake such a task and couldn't thank me enough, but said that I must explain each rule for each change. That effort sealed a lifelong friendship, and Professor Luigi Crocco became Gino to me, as he was affectionately called by his friends. More importantly, I had found a mentor.

Crocco's impact on the rocket and aeronautics field is legendary, as is his teaching. He moved quickly with the times. His course on jet propulsion become aerospace propulsion and included not only rockets, but also the more exotic types of space propulsion. He created a new course on space flight and devoted it not only to boosting and reentry problems, but also to the flight mechanics of thrusted space vehicles, developed on the basis of celestial mechanics. His courses attracted practically every graduate student in the Department of Aerospace Engineering and many undergraduates. Students marveled at his lectures. Much of the material in his courses was analytical and he would write numerous equations on the chalkboard, yet he had no notes in front of him. Coming out of one of his lectures, I commented that it was incredible that he could walk into a class and give such a intricate lecture extemporaneously. He looked at me and said, "Are you kidding, Irv?" He pulled a large package of file cards from his coat pocket, with his lecture completely written out on them, but he never looked at them during the lecture. His graduate students revered him. They did their best to emulate him, becoming leaders in academia and industry.

Unfortunately, illness overtook Crocco and his wife, Simone, whom he adored. Thus in his later years, when he was not in class or attending meetings, he would meet with his students and his younger colleagues at home in the Mediterranean villa the Croccos had built on Fitzrandolph Road. Sitting with him in his den discussing research was an experience everyone cherished. After he resigned his position at Princeton to seek special treatment for his illness in Europe, I had occasion to visit him frequently. He always wanted to know all about my current research. I would enthusiastically tell him what we had accomplished in the last year or so and, in a few minutes, he would grasp the fundamental points and make pertinent suggestions: still my mentor.

To think of Gino Crocco simply as a scientist and engineer would do him a great injustice. He was a devoutly religious man and had one of the finest intellects that I have ever known. You could talk to him about any subject: religion, art, music, history, and even food. He seemed to be knowledgeable about everything. I still smile to myself as I recall when he came to see me after my return from my first trip abroad. My wife and I had sailed on the *Île-de-France,* and I described the marvelous meals, in particular the baked apples. It turned out that baked apples were one of his favorite foods, and we spent close to an hour discussing how the ship's apples were prepared and other ways of making this delicious dish.

There was nothing that did not interest Luigi Crocco. In my opinion, he was an aristocrat in the most complimentary meaning of the word. He was humane. He would converse frequently with his friend, the world-renowned philosopher Jacques Maritain, and he always had time to chat with the laboratory technicians. He was truly a legend to his students and colleagues. To this day my own students hear my many tales of this legendary figure.

READING LIST

With Lester Lees: "A Mixing Theory for the Interaction between Dissipative Flows and Nearly Isentropic Streams," *Journal of the Aeronautical Sciences* 19, no. 10 (October 1952)

With S. I. Cheng: "Theory of Combustion Instability in Liquid Propellant Rocket Motors," *AGARDograph* No. 8, Butterworth, 1955

With J. Grey and R. Monti: "Verification of Nozzle Admittance Theory by Direct Measurement of the Admittance Parameter," *Journal of the American Rocket Society* 31, no. 6 (June 1961): 771–775

With R. A. Dobbins and I. Glassman: "Measurement of Mean Particle Sizes of Sprays from Diffractively Scattered Light," *AIAA Journal* 1, no. 8 (August 1963): 1882–1886

"Transformations of the Compressible Turbulent Boundary Layer with Heat Exchange," *AIAA Journal* 1, no. 12 (December 1963): 2723–27331

With B. T. Zinn: "The Nozzle Boundary Condition in the Nonlinear Rocket Instability Problem," *Astronautica Acta* 13 (1968): 489–496

"Coordinate Perturbation and Multiple Scales in Gasdynamics," *Philosophical Transactions of the Royal Society of London*, June 1972

George Eckel Duckworth

Department of Classics

BY KARL GALINSKY

In Book 10 of the *Aeneid*, there are two lines where Vergil, with typical economy of language (a quality seldom emulated by Vergilian scholars) and suggestiveness, defines an existential issue about which whole libraries have been written:

> sua cuique exorsa laborem
> fortunamque ferent. rex Iuppiter omnibus idem.
> fata viam invenient. (lines 111–113)

> To each their own undertakings will bring toil
> and fortune. King Jupiter is the same to all.
> The fates will find their way.

If this is an appropriate formulation for the fate of individuals and nations, it is certainly an apt summary of the graduate experience of many of us at Princeton and, I suspect, not just in Classics. Jupiter, too, can always be given a suitable modern identity.

I did not go to Princeton because of George Duckworth. As a senior in college, I did not spend my days researching — let alone perusing — the publications of the senior professors in the graduate programs to which I was applying. Why take the trouble? Those were the early 1960s, Camelot not only in politics but in the academic job market, too. My professors at Bowdoin thought I should apply to Harvard, Princeton, and Stanford, and so I did. Besides, the point of the exercise for me was simply to be able to continue to stay in America — the sentimental goal of many Europeans of my generation, even some (academic) Marxists — and if Classics was going to be the means to that end, why not? *Fata viam invenient*: when the final decision had to be made, Stanford was just a bit too far away, Harvard didn't offer enough money, but Princeton did. And I was told the people there were very decent.

I had always liked the Romans. The Greeks really never got their act together, it seemed, unless they were threatened by an armada or participated in one under duress; so I looked forward to some Roman courses at Princeton. The first meeting with the graduate adviser — John Fine, a Greek historian — produced a quick denouement. I asked how many seminars were required per semester. The answer was three. That seemed reasonable; how many, then, were being offered in the fall semester of 1963? The answer again was three, and the implications were somewhat more than mathematical. Also, the course offerings all happened to be on Greek topics. There were alternatives to broaden the menu: Sanskrit, Greek philosophy, and a proseminar in ancient art and archaeology. I opted for the latter along with two of the Greek seminars, a choice that really turned out to be momentous for my future work.

For the Romans, however, I had to wait. George Duckworth was going to offer his Vergil seminar in the spring, and peers and faculty alike had only one recommendation: "Take it. A must." I don't remember exactly when I actually met George Duckworth (as distinct from seeing him around in Firestone Library), but it was before the spring term. The fact that I don't recall our first meeting and conversation in any detail is more typical of his personality and the way he worked with graduate students than of my mnemonic limitations. There was no epiphany and no defining moment resplendent with a charismatic aureole. Few working relationships between professors and future professors start out that way. Instead, they are the result of many unspectacular encounters which, however, add up to depth, substance, a true sharing of interests, genuine influence and, in the best cases, mutuality. (For similar reasons, psychologists, child psychologists in particular, have debunked the myth of Disneylandish "quality time.") I know that Duckworth and I talked at some time in the fall in his office. Yes, it was nicely panelled and book-lined, and he looked like the senior professor from central Princeton casting: white hair, dark-rimmed reading glasses, tweed jacket, pipe, and papers spilling all over his desk or desks. My principal recollection is not in terms of specifics, but of his general disposition: friendly encouragement and interest, a good listener who would always proceed from some point I had made instead of engaging in haughty didacticism (a note struck all too often by some of the German and English practitioners of Classics and their American wannabes) — the clear realization, then, that this was a great scholar who didn't have to be condescending. I parted by saying that I looked forward to taking his course, and he said he was looking forward to having me in that class — what a blessing it was that I could read German without a dictionary at my side; besides, there were a lot of interesting things going on in Vergilian scholarship.

By that time, of course, I had made a fairly thorough effort to familiarize myself with the professor's writings. They focused on pivotal authors: Plautus, Vergil, and Horace. I am certain that this model influenced my orientation, too, but, as in the case of all good models, by unconscious imitation rather than explicit reasoning (which can always be supplied after the fact). Why bother to write textual notes on Vibius Sequester when some substantive contributions still can be made to the understanding of major works of literature? Not surprisingly, Duckworth's first major publication, his dissertation, had this kind of breadth. It was on *Foreshadowing and Suspense in the Epics of Homer, Apollonius, and Vergil.* These topics are essential to epic and are still being discussed today, though mostly with isolated reference to one of the three poets. Compartmentalization in the humanities has come a long way. Today, Duckworth's book could be repackaged as a great piece of intertextual and comparative scholarship. *Plus ça change* . . . It is still a reliable, untrendy introduction to this important aspect of Greco-Roman epic.

All this, and more, is even truer of his big book, *The Nature of Roman Comedy.* It is still the standard introduction to the subject today, though many of the topics have been refined by the scholarship of the past four decades. Specialized scholarship, that is — a similarly synoptic work has not yet emerged. Like other fundamental books, *The Nature of Roman Comedy* was janiform in the best Roman tradition: it marked the conclusion of a longstanding, previous trend of scholarship and provided a road map for future work. Since the later nineteenth century, classical scholars had used Roman comedy as a prime exhibit for the reconstruction of lost Greek originals (if these originals were so terrific, how come no one bothered making copies of them?) through their debased Roman adaptations. The humor and brio of comedy were just about ruined amidst the resulting, and often mindless, philological *querelles.* It was hard for the modern reader or scholar to understand why Plautus' comedies packed in an actual audience.

Duckworth's book changed all that. It was typical of him (and of Princeton, and of his time) not to trumpet a manifesto in the preface, let alone in the text. Instead of hype, there were a wealth of information, fairness in stating different viewpoints, sound judgment, and the constant, if implied, invitation to the readers to test the findings and models on other texts of their choice. Far from being dogmatic, the really good scholars give their students that kind of freedom.

Latinists outside of Princeton in the first pentad of the 1960s might have had their doubts. To them, George had gotten carried away with "the most exciting discovery in Vergilian criticism" (so the book jacket of *Structural Patterns and Proportions in Vergil's Aeneid*): Vergil's poetry was based on the Golden Mean ratio, .618. His enthusiasm and determination in pursuing this find were unshakable. Seek and ye shall find, and the ratio just seemed to pop up everywhere in Latin poetry, from Lucretius to Manilius.

"Altertumswissenschaft — .618" even was emblazoned on the T-shirts of Princeton's Classics graduate students in the late 1960s; a free specimen was sent to me in Texas, fitting my not-so-golden mean less and less as the years went by. How could the proud discoverer of this outlandish idea be expected to teach an even-handed course on Vergil? Wouldn't he try to proselytize? Wouldn't he demand a validation of the scheme in every dissertation he supervised, short of asking that the dissertation itself be based on that ratio?

Reality, like George Duckworth, was much more gentle. The Vergil seminar he taught was one of the high points of my Princeton course work. It was a superb introduction to Vergil's poetry and the variety of approaches that had been applied to it. Not a glimmer of pressure to conform to or even discuss the professor's latest theses. Instead, there was incredible encouragement to find our own way and define worthwhile topics. It was exciting. The result was some truly superior reports by the members of the seminar, combining thorough research and bibliographical mastery with some new contributions of their own. That is what mattered to George Duckworth. He would share in our excitement in his paternal way and provide further guidance. Had I seen this Italian article in the *Atti* of some Accademia? Yes, the publication series could be found in the bowels of Firestone Library. Had I looked at another use of a similar phrase by Vergil and tried to make the connection? And so on. I don't remember anyone giving a report on the Golden Section; instead, he encouraged me to expand my paper into an article for the *American*

Journal of Philology, to whose editor he was going to write in my behalf. The article was accepted and became my first publication; of course I would completely rewrite it today.

More fundamentally, the seminar was a paradigm of the Princeton Ph.D. program in Classics at the time. Two years of course work, capped by the general examinations (all at once in one week from Hades), and the dissertation year — the underlying purpose was to provide students not with a vast knowledge of the discipline, but to show them how one gets at a given subject and how one opens up new fields for oneself. One of many corollaries is that the Ph.D. is just a passport to the profession, and the real work lies ahead — lifelong. I consider myself fortunate to have entered a program shaped by that mentality. It was, like so much in life, an accident (*fortuna*) of time and place, and what an individual makes of it (*labor*) — here comes that Vergilian maxim again. I tell our graduate students that stays in grad school are just like stays in hospitals: you don't get well in either. The sooner you get out, the better. The reactions are decidedly mixed; after all, the average length of graduate study in the humanities ballooned to ten years in the 1980s. I would not have gone into this profession had I been born in 1962 instead of 1942.

After spring 1964, however, there was no question that I was going to write my dissertation on something connected with Vergil and that George Duckworth would be one of the two principal readers. Concomitantly with his Vergil seminar, I was taking another seminar from Erik Sjöqvist, this one on Roman art, resulting in a paper (and then article) on the Altar of Augustan Peace. Princeton's program facilitated this sort of interdisciplinary work; again this was done without any shouting. It worked because of the presence of cooperative faculty who had a larger perspective than their egos. Duckworth critiqued that paper, too, and I could not have asked for a better working relationship with anyone for my next two years at Princeton.

Over the past two decades, "mentoring" has become a modish concept in the writings of the consulting industry that feeds on

American business. George Duckworth's mentoring had nothing to do with this kind of psychobabble. He was not a buddy who would take the students out for a beer or socialize heavily. He was there when you needed him: professional, friendly, always helpful. He gave you your own space, and he respected people's privacy just as he wanted them to respect his. We never talked much about family. The garden party he and his wife Dorothy gave at their house in the spring was the epitome of Princeton graciousness and class. Graduate students' psyches are endemically labile; to be under his humane aegis was a source of affirmation and strength. He combined, to use some Latin phrases, *auctoritas*, *humanitas*, and *magnitudo animi*.

I could go on with the narrative and detail his help with my dissertation (subsequently published by the Princeton University Press). There are more important aspects of his legacy, however. One is his generosity of spirit: the department offered me an instructorship during my third year, with a dissertation fellowship for the year after. I enjoyed the teaching and precepting (all sixteen hours of it per week, plus supervision of several senior theses), started my dissertation anyway and finished it in the following summer. I never took up the dissertation fellowship, but I was eager to move on, despite an offer from the department to join its faculty. Besides my own adventurousness, the moving force was William Arrowsmith (a Princeton Ph.D. himself), who certainly brought some dynamism to a profession that needed it (and still does today). George Duckworth never gave me a hard time about making my choice, although his generation was as different as could be: the core of the Princeton Classics faculty at the time was four senior professors — Duckworth, Frisco Godolphin, John Fine (all born in 1903), and Mike Oates (born 1904) — who were not only Princeton Ph.D.s, but had been Princeton undergraduates together.

In short, George Duckworth never tried to dominate, but encouraged me and others to find our way and *fata* and to strike out on our own. After all, he had set an example in his own scholarly work. He did not play it safe after the acclaim of *The Nature of Roman Comedy*. He experimented — this includes his attempt to find parallels between one of the great epics of India, the *Mahabharata*, and the *Aeneid* — along with pursuing more traditional lines of inquiry. A time-consuming labor that could be: he scanned all extant Latin hexameter poetry manually. Ten years later, this was fast food for the computer. But that is immaterial. What matters is that George Duckworth was a "pro-fessor" in the best tradition: he had his own bent of mind and therefore encouraged others to develop their own; he never stopped working and looking out for new horizons; and he was both authoritative and humane. It may be corny to talk about gentlemen scholars, especially in connection with Princeton, but they are a dying breed. I was truly privileged to study with one of the best, who had a full scholarly life that he generously shared with a rank beginner like myself.

READING LIST

Foreshadowing and Suspense in the Epics of Homer, Apollonius, and Vergil (Princeton: Princeton University Press, 1933)

T. Macci Plauti Epidicus (Princeton: Princeton University Press, 1940)

The Nature of Roman Comedy (Princeton: Princeton University Press, 1952)

Structural Patterns and Proportions in Vergil's Aeneid (Ann Arbor: University of Michigan Press, 1961)

Vergil and Classical Hexameter Poetry (Ann Arbor: University of Michigan Press, 1969)

Donald Drew Egbert

School of Architecture

BY ROBERT VENTURI[1]

I took Donald Drew Egbert's course on the History of Modern Architecture four times. I sat in on it as a freshman, was the slide projectionist as a sophomore, took it for credit as a junior, and taught in it as a graduate-student teaching assistant. Other architecture students at Princeton over several decades were also drawn to it, became devotees, and were influenced by it. What attracted us was not a dramatic style or arresting pronouncements — Egbert virtually read his lectures from his very complete notes while sitting down — but his lack of jargon, the clarity and elegance of his plain talk, and the balance and common sense of his approach. We were attracted also by the

[1] Copyright Robert Venturi. First published as the Foreword to Egbert's *The Beaux-Arts Tradition in French Architecture* (Princeton: Princeton University Press, 1980), pp. xiii–xiv; edited and expanded, September 1995. Also, it appears in a slightly varied form in my new book, *Iconography and Electronics upon a Generic Architecture* (Boston: MIT Press, 1996).

rich range yet meticulous order of his material, by his conviction, but also by his openness. We were thrilled by the discoveries he lead us to, not to mention the lessons we incidentally learned in architectural composition that we directly applied to our work in the drafting room.

As a historian of Modern architecture Egbert saw this subject as a part of the whole complex of nineteenth- and twentieth-century culture and his eyes were open to realities of that time that more doctrinaire historians, bent on proving points, couldn't see. For Egbert the influence of the École des Beaux-Arts, for instance, was an important part of the complicated architectural history of the nineteenth and twentieth centuries. On the other hand, for Sigfried Giedion, the famous Harvard historian of the time, Beaux-Arts architecture was a "transitory fact." Although history was not bunk for Giedion — as it was for most architectural Modernists from the 1940s through the 1960s — it was subject to simplified and personal interpretation that allowed as "constituent facts" — again Giedion's phrase — some of the historical antecedents of Modern architecture (for example, some spatial qualities of Baroque architecture and certain early industrial forms) but excluded, as transitory facts, other antecedents, the main one being the architecture of the École des Beaux-Arts. (Giedion acknowledges Henri Labrouste mostly for his cast iron.) Egbert's history of Modern architecture was inclusive — a complex evolution rather than a dramatic revolution made up of social and symbolic as well as formal and technological imperatives.

Never doctrinaire, Egbert was seldom in the mainstream; he focused in the 1940s on Beaux-Arts architecture when Giedion's spatial-technological, Bauhaus-oriented view predominated in art history. His *Social Radicalism and the Arts*, published in 1970, countered another important trend in Modern architectural history, pressed by Henry-Russell Hitchcock and Philip Johnson, whose influential introduction of the International Style had de-emphasized the radical social content of the Modern movement and set the stage for the dominance of formalism in the evolution of

Modern architecture in America. Egbert studied history to search for truth, never to prove points. How unusual this is was borne out for me when I learned from a European friend that the fame of *Social Radicalism and the Arts* among European historians is matched by their surprise that its author was not a Marxist. Some of the research for this book involved arduous travel in central European countries right after World War II by a shy person not in robust health.

Another irony of Egbert's position is that the Museum of Modern Art later acknowledged the significance of the École des Beaux-Arts in the history of Modern architecture. In the takeover, Egbert, the original protagonist, whose unpopular stand was ignored for decades by the Modern architectural establishment, was not recognized, although two of the three historians who worked on the exhibition were former students of Egbert at Princeton.

Donald Egbert did not prescribe ideology: he opened up directions — directions not dreamt of in my philosophy — where I could perceive Modern architecture not as an end, but as the current and latest part within an evolution. We students were truly students within a liberal process of education, not seminarians being given "the word." Architecture for us would evolve beyond our time and by implication through our own creativity. And there is something Donald Egbert's teaching did not imply: that architecture as an academic discipline is superior to architecture as a professional discipline, an attitude prevalent today — despite his own focus on scholarship. And this accommodation could make of us knowing workers whose talents were enriched by knowledge.

I now realize that Donald Egbert became my mentor during my postgraduate years at Princeton and the early years of my practice. I often visited him in his McCormick Hall office crammed with books, expecting understanding and support. During those visits he might ask profoundly difficult questions about architecture — some that would haunt me and to which I might find answers only years later. Thus he has influenced me actively all my life.

As a Princeton alumnus who had majored in architecture as an undergraduate, Donald Egbert wrote knowingly and lovingly of his university campus and its ethos. This perception of the significance of the familiar made us students aware that the everyday and not necessarily the ideal can be a stimulus for art.

Egbert's openness had a later, gratifying effect on me. I have learned almost always to expect, when I meet an author whose works have influenced me or a former teacher who has meant much to me, that he will be unable to accept the direction my work has taken and will not see himself in it. This was never the case with Egbert and I value very much a letter he wrote soon before he died praising a book I co-authored, *Learning from Las Vegas*; this appreciation came from an Ivy League WASP and scholar par excellence! He also wrote in that letter: "Of course the difference between a historian and an artist is that the historian has to try to be objective (though he never can succeed completely), whereas the good artist-architect has to be a man of utter conviction." Donald Drew Egbert combined both traits as a friend, a teacher, and a scholar.

READING LIST

Socialism and American Art in the Light of European Utopianism, Marxism, and Anarchism (Princeton: Princeton University Press, 1967)

On the Arts in Society: Selections from the Periodical Writings of Donald Drew Egbert (Victoria, British Columbia: University of Victoria, 1970)

Social Radicalism and the Arts — Western Europe: A Cultural History from the French Revolution to 1968 (New York: Alfred A. Knopf, 1970)

The Beaux-Arts Tradition in French Architecture (Princeton: Princeton University Press, 1980)

Eric Frederick Goldman

Department of History

BY DANIEL J. KEVLES

In the early 1940s, Eric Goldman began work on the ambitious, critical history of modern American reform that he eventually titled *Rendezvous with Destiny*, taking the phrase from the speech that he had thrilled to hear Franklin Roosevelt deliver in 1936, at Franklin Field in Philadelphia. In part, he wanted to analyze and recount the development of the grand tradition of liberalism in the United States. Yet he also hoped that the book would make a difference in the life of his country. What people believe about the past helps shape their attitudes towards the present and the future, he held. To him, history was a weapon for social change, and he passionately wanted to help change the United States.[1]

[1] Eric often explained to me his view of the social role of historical writing. I am indebted for research assistance in composing this essay to Peter Neushul

Eric was eager to change the world because he had learned early in life that much of the world was not very pleasant. Born in Washington, D.C., in 1915, he grew up in Baltimore, Maryland, in a grinding poverty that drove his mother into a mental sanitarium. Eric's earliest memories were of a dilapidated one-ton Chevrolet truck from which he helped his father, Harry Goldman, a crusty but caring man, eke out a living selling fruits and vegetables — until the Depression wiped out the business and his father turned to struggling as a taxi driver.

Eric's mother, Bessie Chapman, was descended from English Protestants; his father's family were German Jews who had come to the United States from the region of Alsace-Lorraine. Eric was confirmed as a Protestant, but his father withdrew him from the church Sunday school when one day the other students hounded him as a "dirty Jew." While in high school at Baltimore City College, he came to know young Edward L. Israel, the city's leading reform rabbi and an outspoken advocate of social justice. Israel got him bar mitzvahed, hired him to lead a Sunday discussion class for the princely sum of $10, and awakened in him an inclination to be a social crusader.

Eric's street education kindled cynicism and skepticism about self-proclaimed virtues, but the skepticism and cynicism were tempered by his encounters with decency and opportunity. The Baltimore public school system, recognizing him for the prodigy he was, kept skipping him and on graduation in 1931, as he turned sixteen, awarded him the single scholarship available at his high school to the Johns Hopkins University. He immediately declined the honor at the urging of his father — Harry Goldman could

and for suggestions and comments to Robert Dallek, Richard Challener, Charles C. Gillispie, Ashbel Green, Marius Jansen, J. Morgan Kousser, James McPherson, and Wendy Wall. I am also grateful for assistance in obtaining archival materials to Patricia Marks; Ben Primer, Princeton University Archivist, Seeley G. Mudd Manuscript Library; James Stimpert, of the Ferdinand Hamburger, Jr. Archives, The Johns Hopkins University; Kenneth Schlesinger, at the Archives of *Time* magazine, and David Wigdor, of the Manuscripts Division, Library of Congress.

not see that a college education would get you anywhere unless getting somewhere was already ensured by your family background — but the principal of the high school successfully pressed the senior Goldman to reverse his position. At Hopkins, Eric supplemented the scholarship with odd jobs, including one reporting for the *Baltimore Sun*, where H. L. Mencken took him under his wing. Mencken, a redoubtable cynic, demonstrated that cynics could be the kindest of people when Eric sent him an essay he had written. Mencken told him gruffly that the essay was no good but conveyed to him with equal gruffness that he showed some promise, and sat Eric down for hours in his living room to teach him to write a good sentence.

Eric started at Hopkins with no clear idea about what he would do in life. He relished Rabbi Israel's willingness to offend members of his congregation by leading hunger strikes and labor demonstrations and, for a time, thought seriously about becoming a rabbi. But he had doubts about a clerical future and Mencken reinforced them in a letter:

> It is very hard to advise you, but certainly it seems to me that you should not go in for theology if there are any doubts, however slight, in your mind. Once you have become a rabbi it will be extremely difficult to escape. On the whole, I think you had better wait until you are more settled in your desires.[2]

Eric's vocational desires increasingly ran to history, partly because it was one of the few academic subjects that he liked and partly because several Hopkins history professors strongly encouraged him. Entering Hopkins with standing as a sophomore, he skipped his bachelor's degree and proceeded directly into graduate work. His formal advisor was W. Stull Holt, a specialist on federal agencies and a student of historiography, whom Eric later extolled as "infinitely generous and wondrously capable of calling out the best in the worst of us."[3] Frederic C. Lane, a tall, reedy

[2] Mencken to Goldman, December 5, 193?, in my possession. Copy in the Eric F. Goldman Papers, Library of Congress, Washington, D.C.

[3] Marius Jansen and Richard Challener, "Eric Frederick Goldman," a memorial read to the Princeton University faculty meeting, May 1, 1989.

man of old New England stock who was an authority on Venetian history, became something of a second father to Eric, feeding him steak for several months at the Lane farm in New Hampshire when he came down with pernicious anemia and appointing him an instructor at Hopkins, in 1935, when he finished his master's degree. Eric dropped out of graduate school for a year, but returned, without knowing exactly why, to complete his Ph.D. in 1938, at age twenty-two, and continued at Hopkins as an instructor.

Charles Beard got to know Eric when, in the fall of 1940, he came to Hopkins for two years as a professor to organize a program in the history of American civilization.[4] Beard termed Eric "an asphalt flower," seeing in him a defiant, irrepressible urban bloom. He made Eric his assistant. Eric remembered that Beard "would talk with a fascinating ease, shifting without interruption from some esoteric matter of history, to the price cows on his farm were bringing, to the stupidities of his fellow man."[5] Eric, admiring Beard as much as he did Mencken, and knowing that they both held bourgeois civilization in contempt, got the two men to eat a lunch together with him. The occasion was a disaster, Eric in his youthful enthusiasm not having realized that Beard the liberal social reformer and Mencken the anti-democratic elitist would do little more than bristle at each other. Yet while Eric held Mencken in high regard for his iconoclasm and literary genius, he revered Beard, who had wanted to change his America and wrote *An Economic Interpretation of the Constitution* as a way of doing it. It was from Beard that he got the idea that you could write books and articles that might persuade people to think differently about the certitudes of the present and future by

[4] Beard to Alan Nevins, September 18 [1940], Alan Nevins Collection, Professional Correspondence, Columbia University, Box 18. I am indebted for this reference to Wendy Wall. Beard to Isaiah Bowman, February 12, 1941, The Ferdinand Hamburger, Jr. Archives, The Johns Hopkins University, RG 02.001, Office of the President, Series 1, File #55 (History Department) 1941.

[5] Eric F. Goldman, "Autobiography." This is a series of rough autobiographical notes that he dictated in the late 1980s, a copy of which is in the Goldman Papers, Library of Congress.

exposing the contradictions and self-interest that undergirded the related shibboleths of the past.

One day in 1941, Eric was told by the history department chairman, Kent R. Greenfield, that his appointment as an instructor would not be extended beyond the next academic year. As Eric remembered it, Greenfield, ashen-faced, said that Isaiah Bowman, president of Hopkins, had told him that the university did not want Jews on the faculty. Eric subsequently understood that Greenfield, Lane, and Holt all objected, without effect.[6] The documentary record does not provide direct support for Eric's recollection of why he was fired, but it is consistent with his account.[7] Eric's scholarship, writing, and teaching had dazzled his teachers. In a letter of recommendation, Greenfield wrote that his undergraduate lectures were "among the most brilliant" he had ever heard and that he had won "a place for himself in the work of the Department and in the respect and affection of all of its members which we should be hard put to it to fill."

In the spring of 1942, Eric was touted for a history instructorship at Princeton not only by his supporters at Hopkins but also in glowing letters from Beard, Samuel Eliot Morison, Avery Craven, and Merle Curti. Several appeared to go out of their way to commend him against the stereotypes that helped fuel the era's anti-Semitism within as well as outside of academia.[8] Professor

[6] Eric recounted his firing from Hopkins to me many times and also set it down in the "Autobiography."

[7] The decision to fire Eric was, in fact, Bowman's. Eric believed that Beard resigned in protest, but while in February 1941 Beard did tender his resignation from the university effective the end of May, his letter to Bowman was cordial and his stated reason was that the cognizant committee of the Hopkins Academic Council had declined to approve the programmatic initiative in the history of American civilization. (Greenfield to Bowman, April 3, 1941; Greenfield to Ira Hirschman, April 2, 1941; Beard to Bowman, February 12, 1941, Hamburger Archives, The Johns Hopkins University, RG 02.001, Office of the President, Series 1, File #55 [History Department] 1941.) And Eric was not alone in his perception of Bowman.

[8] Greenfield to Hirschman, April 2, 1941, ibid.; Beard to ?, March 18, 1942; Curti to ?, March 18, 1942; Morison to ?, May 16, 1942; Craven to ?, April 10, 1942, President's Records, Princeton University Archives, Seeley G. Mudd Manuscript Library.

Joseph R. Strayer, the chairman of the Princeton History Department, called him for an interview, and appointed him an instructor at the University. Eric always wondered why Princeton, which then had few, if any, Jews on its liberal arts faculty, hired him. He speculated that Strayer had heard about the nastiness at Hopkins and wanted to make a statement — a theory that Strayer later told him was simply wrong.

Whatever the reason, in 1942 Eric came to Princeton. However, never too sure that he wanted to be an academic — he always disliked being called "Doctor" Goldman — he was all the more uncertain after the Hopkins experience, and especially about such a career in the Princeton of that day, with its manifest social snobberies. He volunteered for the armed services but was rejected for medical reasons. When in April 1943, *Time* magazine offered him a job as a contributing editor at the handsome salary of $5,200 a year, he asked for a raise and a promotion to assistant professor, an indication that he might have a future at Princeton. Although only twenty-seven, he had already proved himself a remarkably productive scholar. In 1941 he had edited *Historiography and Urbanization*; early in 1943 he had published *John Bach McMaster, American Historian*, which had originated as his master's thesis. Another book was in press, *Charles J. Bonaparte, Patrician Reformer: His Earlier Career*, which had begun as his doctoral dissertation. The University nevertheless being reluctant to grant the promotion, he went to work for *Time* on a trial basis. Strayer, worried about losing him, urged the case for promotion to President Harold W. Dodds, pointing out that the senior members of the History Department "agreed that Mr. Goldman was the most promising instructor in American history whom we had had in the last fifteen years" and expressing his "hope that it will be possible to do something unusual in order to retain an unusually gifted man."[9]

The University granted the promotion, and Eric returned to Princeton in the fall, but he remained restless, keeping one foot,

[9] Strayer to Dodds, May 14, 1943, ibid.

and sometimes both, in the larger world. During the mid-1940s, he flitted between Princeton and a New York-centered life of writing. He also collaborated with Fred Lane on *The World's History*, a high school text that was published in 1947 and sold hundreds of thousands of copies.[10] That year, the University promoted Eric to associate professor with tenure and he received a Library of Congress Fellowship in American Civilization for work on *Rendezvous with Destiny*. By then, he had come to know Joanna Jackson, a gifted and adventurous young musician from Charleston, West Virginia, who had come to New York shortly after the war. By night she sang in a Greenwich Village club named Maric's Crisis and by day she worked in the New York Public Library, gathering information and ideas for the book. The couple was married in 1952, and Jo would work with Eric on all his subsequent writing projects.[11]

In October 1952, *Rendezvous with Destiny* was published — to a lengthening critical silence that left its author worried and grumpy but that Orville Prescott, the most influential book reviewer in the country, ended gloriously on December 17 in the daily *New York Times*. Prescott, apologizing for having overlooked the work when it was published two months earlier, called it "one of the most learned, one of the most enlightening, and one of the best-written historical works in a long time," adding, "Of this year's possible candidates for the Pulitzer prize in history, it seems to me the most deserving." The book was awarded the 1953 Bancroft Prize for distinguished work in American History and it established Eric Goldman as one of the nation's most prominent and provocative interpreters of modern American civilization.

By the time *Rendezvous* was published, Eric was beginning work on a new book, a study of the United States after 1945. Princeton assisted his work by appointing him a senior fellow of the Council of Humanities in 1955, the year that it also promoted him to

[10] Lane, Goldman, and E. Hunt, *The World's History* (New York: Harcourt Brace, 1947).

[11] Eric had been married twice before, each time briefly.

full professor. The Guggenheim Foundation granted him one of its coveted fellowships for 1956. The book appeared in August 1956 as *The Crucial Decade: America 1945–1955* and immediately jumped to the *New York Times* best-seller list. Although the *Chicago Sunday Tribune*, conservative and neo-isolationist, predictably disliked the book, the weight of critical opinion was with William S. White, who, writing in the *New York Times*, called it "an alert commentary upon the life of a people, full of their bad taste, their frustrations, and fears — and their gallantry as well."[12]

Eric once remarked to me that the research that goes into a book is like a woman's slip — it shouldn't show, not in the text. It didn't show in *Rendezvous*, though its prodigiousness was evident from the source notes, the historiographic elaborations, and the discussion of the methods that he used to reach his points of interpretation and analysis. All of Eric's works were grounded in deep probing of a vast array of materials that varied, depending on the book, among public and private documents, magazines, newspapers, pamphlets, and court records. Wherever possible, he supplemented these sources with interviews and correspondence with people who figured in his account and/or their relatives, friends, and associates, asking them to comment on the resulting text. "The trouble is, they do comment, and then I don't know which is worse — their memory or my research methods," he once said.[13] A stickler for accuracy, Eric checked all his material before an article or book went to press. I remember his emerging from his office during a bout of checking and telling me about a tree that figured in a scene of his narrative: "One newspaper says cherry tree. Another says apple tree. Goldman," he chuckled, "says 'tree.'"

Eric was a brilliant writer. How he became one was probably partly revealed in the simple advice he once gave me: If you want to write well, read good books, pay attention to how the authors do it, and write a lot. Eric wrote all the time, drafting, revising,

[12] *New York Times*, August 26, 1956, p. 6.
[13] *Princeton Alumni Weekly*, March 16, 1956.

polishing. From Mencken he learned to craft taut prose and sentences that sang in the American idiom. He had a knack for finding the exact word and devising the memorable image. (Robert Taft's campaign smile was "as radiant as a very small and very lopsided persimmon.") Eric made vivid vignettes of historical actors high and low one of the trademarks of his work, and he loved to incorporate in his text anecdotes or quotations that would express a trend or reveal character with humor and punch.

Few could match Eric in the writing of what he called a tone piece, an essay that captured the mood or climate of a period. A classic example of that genre was his "Good-By to the 'Fifties — and Good Riddance," which appeared in *Harper's Magazine* in January 1960, having originated as a final lecture to his undergraduate course on modern America. Here he skewered, among other things, the "false piety and religiosity which has slithered its way to astounding popularity," and the proclamation that the front-running Republican candidate for vice-president was "a wonderful new man, because he intermittently stops using slander as a political weapon and has ceased making dogs the subject of his high policy declarations." To Eric's mind, the climate of the 1950s was "the dullest and dreariest in all our history," yet the nation had never "been more ripe, more begging for mockery, for satire, for wit."[14]

Eric practiced analytic narrative history — that is, history that told a story while weaving analysis into the tale. He drew on works in social science, including studies in anthropology, psychology, political science, and economics, but he did not think of history as a social science expressing or testing laws of human behavior. To his mind, historical writing was fundamentally an art form. It was most definitely not a search for a timeless, absolute Truth. Eric held that works of history should be grounded in extensive fact and rigorous argument and that the historian should be as objective as possible in treating his subject. He also held that how-

[14] Eric F. Goldman, "Good-By to the 'Fifties — and Good Riddance," *Harper's Magazine* 220 (January 1960), 27–29.

ever energetic the attempt to avoid bias, the work would inevitably be influenced by the historian's view of the present and vision of the future. Eric brought that conviction to the extensive book reviewing he did in many publications, including the *New Republic* and the Sunday book sections of the *New York Times* and the *Herald Tribune*. He typically related history books to the present the way he framed Henry May's *End of American Innocence* in the Sunday *Times* for October 18, 1959: "The years immediately before American entrance into World War I, so engagingly colorful and so impudent, have proved a natural attraction for historians in the Nineteen Fifties, when so few things appear engagingly colorful and so many Americans seem incapable of impudence."

Eric's views on the contingency of historical truth were rooted not only in general epistemological considerations but also in the extensive explorations of historiography that were part of his early scholarship, particularly his biography of John Bach McMaster. McMaster pioneered the history of ordinary Americans — what came to be called social history — in his multi-volume *History of the People of the United States*, the first volume of which he published in 1883 while he was teaching engineering at Princeton. Eric appreciated McMaster for enlarging the scope of historical subject beyond politics, but he discerned that McMaster's "conception of the people came close to being a democratic way of avoiding completely democratic thinking." McMaster found some of the people worthy of castigation, particularly economic upstarts like anti-Hamiltonians and mid-nineteenth century immigrants, whom he regarded as un-American. The people whom McMaster glorified, Eric wrote, were actually the great middle class of white, Anglo-Saxon Protestants, and his *History* helped make "history vote for McKinley."[15]

Eric — the product of the Depression and the Baltimore streets — enlisted history on behalf of the New Deal and the welfare

[15] Goldman, *John Bach McMaster, American Historian* (Philadelphia: University of Pennsylvania Press, 1943; reprint, New York: Octagon Books, 1971), pp. 24–25, 50, 142–144.

state. While the power of economic interests shaped his understanding of modern America, he held that forces were at play in the United States that were not fundamentally economic. The forces included the kind of personal decency that Fred Lane and Charles Beard had shown him, a willingness on the part of many Americans who were old stock and well-to-do to open the doors of opportunity to those who were not. To Eric's mind, the most important of the forces was status — the drive to maintain it or achieve it or both. The patrician reformer — the theme that he explored in his book on Charles Bonaparte and developed, among many others, in *Rendezvous*, notably in his treatment of Franklin Roosevelt — was a reformer partly because he had an interest in conserving social stability but also partly because his reforms would defend his position in society against plutocrats ambitious to replace him.

Eric relished writing about the people and their diverse ways. In *The Crucial Decade*, he of course analyzed McCarthyism, the Eisenhower Republican acceptance of the welfare state, and the country's ultimate embrace of internationalism; but he also recounted the dizzying social changes that accompanied the prosperity of the post-war years, including television, suburbia, the baby boom, TV dinners, frozen foods, installment buying, Mickey Spillane, religion, popular music, organized crime, and the Kinsey Report. He gave intellectual point to such trends, relating them to elections and public policies and to the stories of socioeconomic groups who were not white Anglo-Saxon Protestants. Unlike McMaster, his people included Catholics and Jews and blacks. Status aspirations loomed larger in Eric's interpretive thinking during the Eisenhower years, when the prosperity of the period diminished the economic differences between old-stock Protestants and white ethnic and religious minority groups. His books recounted the demands of such groups not only for access to the wonder of America but also for recognition and respect in it, and analyzed how they were, in greater or lesser degree, increasingly attaining it all through a combination of public and private action. He made Jackie Robinson's flashing cleats speak for an era of remarkable social change.

Eric loved the United States for its democratic credo, yet while he celebrated the changes that the credo had brought about in the twentieth century, he was also unhappy with salient features of postwar America. He deplored the fifties' indulgent materialism, as though the point of reform had been only to put a barbecue in every backyard; its discouragement, even after McCarthyism, of adventurous, iconoclastic thinking; and its slowness to deal with the longstanding issue of race. He was a liberal who was also critical of liberalism itself. He judged that its moral authority had been undermined by a tendency to surrender to political expediency and end-justifies-the-means thinking. He was troubled by the acquiescence of many liberals in the idea that getting ahead was all that counted, no matter the cost to decency or, in the case of the advancement of group interests, even to liberalism itself.

In *Rendezvous*, Eric developed the analytic theme that liberalism had long been weakened by inner difficulties and that the pursuit of group interests was one of them. Reformers, he argued, had fought in a variety of ways to return power to "the people," but "the people" were in reality a collection of different interest groups, not all of whose demands promised a more just and equitable society. Eric's thinking on the point was very likely shaped by trends during the years when he was writing *Rendezvous* — the Truman years — when two long-standing constituencies of reform, organized labor and agriculture, often ran athwart the well-being of the urban middle-class. Yet Eric was acutely sensitive to the fact that the interest groups that had to be juggled in the New Deal-Fair Deal coalition were not only economic ones. Indeed, I suspect that his outlook on the matter was influenced by the interplay between his own experience as a half-Jew — he had experienced discrimination by Jews as well as by non-Jews — and the increasing empowerment of religious, racial, and ethnic minority groups in the United States. Eric, who naturally appreciated the real difficulties of Jews, soon understood a good deal about those that beset other minority groups, but he understood, too, how those difficulties could intensify minority-group consciousness. In *Rendezvous*, he wrote of how in the 1920s the white, Protestant majority's insulting and browbeating emphasis on Americanization "stimulated all racial, religious, and nationality prejudices, and the resulting discrimination hurried all minorities along the way to minority chauvinism." He pointed out that, at times, group interests and liberal aims might happen to coincide, but that often they did not. He understood and sympathized with the increasing postwar emphasis on minority-group interests, but he also worried that the same emphasis increasingly jeopardized the overarching public interest in, for example, civil liberties, especially freedom of expression, a democratizing education, and a temperate, united front in foreign policy.

Eric's unblinking eye contributed to the wild popularity of History 307, his Princeton course for undergraduates on the history of modern America. The course regularly enrolled some 300 to 450 students, which, at a time when the number of sophomores, juniors, and seniors totaled about 2,250, meant that 15–20 percent of eligible students were taking it. Time and again Princeton seniors voted Eric "best lecturer." Like his writing, his lectures were textured with colorful vignettes, resourceful wit, and razor-sharp deflations of pomposity and cant. But the course appealed because, in many ways, the undergraduates of the era increasingly represented the America Eric was critically analyzing — a get-ahead America where white minority groups were flooding through the open gates of opportunity, joining old-stock whites in a prosperity that was delicious but also troubled by conflicts and anxieties. The conflicts and anxieties formed inchoate questions that Eric's teaching articulated: How to maintain intellectual independence in an era of conformity? How to maintain freedom against the power of big government, big labor, and big corporations? How to hold one's identity as a Catholic or a Jew while aspiring to acceptance in a predominantly Protestant country? How to make it in America without losing one's conscience or soul? How to be a responsible citizen in a world teetering on the edge of Armageddon?

In 1957, Eric remarked to a reporter for the *Daily Princetonian*, "We're in a transitional period from the attitude of the 30's and 40's when everyone thought there were simple answers to everything." He made clear to History 307 students that, in his opinion, old certitudes would suffice for very little about the United States, now a global power in a world bristling with nuclear weapons. In the fall of 1958, bringing an ultimate certitude within their sights, he challenged a small group to revise the U.S. Constitution in lieu of a final examination, pointing out that, having been written in an agrarian society, the founding document might warrant recasting for an age of urban industrialism and intercontinental missiles. The project was derided in some of the national press — for example, the Indianapolis *Star*, which declared that when Professor Goldman's students finished disposing of the Constitution, he "might try his hand at the Bible, a document turned out by some ancient Jewish cattle men and farmers."[16] The students in the course thought better of the project than did the *Star*. The revision tended to strengthen federal power over state power, executive power over legislative power, and civil liberties and civil rights. History 307, in convention assembled, adopted the document by a vote of better than two to one.

That semester I was a student in History 307 — my friends in the liberal arts had told me that it was a must, even for a physics major like myself — and I came into direct contact with Eric through the Constitution project. The experience prompted me to consider becoming a historian. Eric put me in touch with Professor Charles C. Gillispie, who taught with eloquence and persuasiveness that science has a history that merits study. But not least — though not only — because of Eric, I wanted to work in American history. In 1961, after a year away, I returned to graduate work in history at Princeton to study under him, thinking in some vague way that I might combine my interests by studying

[16] *The Daily Princeton*, January 15, 1959.

the history of science in America. The subject was of little concern to most historians at the time, but Eric encouraged my inclination towards it. His graduate seminar, the year I took it, was devoted to the domestic history of World War I and, typically for Eric, was organized around writing a major research paper. Mine concerned the wartime use and postwar impact of intelligence testing in the American army and it eventually became my first published article.

Before long, my vague intentions were given specific direction by Eric's endless interest in what was shaping America — in this case, the rise to power of American scientists, particularly physicists. He played a key role in arranging for I. I. Rabi, a Nobel laureate in physics at Columbia University, to visit in the Princeton History Department during the 1961–1962 academic year as a Shreve Fellow. The Shreve Fellowship had been established to foster historical studies that would ascertain the reasons for the "decay, degeneracy, extinction and destruction" of nations, a purpose that Eric gleefully pointed out to me. The idea behind appointing Rabi to the post — he was the first non-historian to hold it — was that he would help the humanists at Princeton learn how better to integrate science and its culture into their courses (presumably, one might have supposed, to forestall the decay of American civilization in the late twentieth century).[17]

Eric and Rabi established a group of scientists and historians in Princeton — it included J. Robert Oppenheimer, Henry DeWolf Smyth, Donald Hamilton, Donald Hornig, John A. Wheeler, David Herbert Donald, Charles Gillispie, and George F. Kennan — that met periodically at Rabi's home during the fall of 1961 to explore the issue. Eric arranged for me to be appointed recording secretary and to be invited to write a paper for the group's consideration that would outline a modern American history course incorporating the development and role of science. The group's meetings were an eye-opening, once-in-a-lifetime encounter

[17] Press release announcing Rabi's appointment, September 19, 1961, Isidor Isaac Rabi file, Princeton University Archives.

with living history and proved to be one of the most influential elements in my graduate education. The paper I wrote, combined with my own conversations with Rabi, led to my dissertation and ultimately to my first book.

To my knowledge, very few graduate students wrote their doctoral dissertations under Eric, but his impact on twentieth-century historians of his day was extensive. It was achieved largely through his writings, but at Princeton especially it was accomplished through talk. Eric's principal pedagogical milieu was not the classroom but the living room, dining room, and restaurant. Much of my graduate education and a good deal of my general education were products of the "seminars" — he liked to call them that — that Eric conducted over lunch, dinner, or drinks. It was not in his nature to be directly or imperatively didactic. (At one point, History 307 got so crowded that the University, to save on preceptors, asked Eric to try the experiment of lecturing three times a week instead of twice. Eric so cherished one student's evaluation of the experiment that he had it framed and hung on the wall of his study: The course content is fine, it read, but "three times a week of Goldman is too much.")

Eric was a remarkable conversationalist, at his best captivating, informative, intense, funny, self-deprecating, and warm. Apart from fishing, talk was his only hobby. He loved to probe the news in the day's papers (he read several, not only the *New York Times* but the *New York Post* and a Hearst paper if he could find one, so that he could know what *all* the people were about). Like Mencken, he was fascinated by the origins of the new words and phrases that continually enrich the American language, and he liked to speculate on what the linguistic innovations revealed about changes in American culture. He relished the good story, the pungent wisecrack, and the offbeat amusement. He particularly liked to probe questions of identity and character. He would see someone in a restaurant or on the sidewalk and imagine from clothes and demeanor what the person's life situation might be. His musings on character reinforced my own instinct for keeping individual human beings in my mind's eye when considering social and political trends, historical or otherwise. Eric's observations were also lessons in discernment, suggesting, for example, that conservatives could be, and that liberals were not necessarily, decent human beings.

Following Beard's example, Eric found his main audience beyond the world of academia in the literate world at large. He was unabashedly what is nowadays called a "public intellectual." He lectured widely. In 1953 and 1954, sponsored by the State Department, he held forth in western Europe, construing his mission to be that of a one-man truth squad trying to clean up the damage done by Roy Cohn and G. David Schine, the two minions of Senator Joseph McCarthy who in the spring of 1953 had gone on an eighteen-day rampage ferreting out Communism from American information services abroad. The State Department liked Eric's performance so much that, in 1956, it sponsored him on a lecture tour of India. He reached a still broader public through essays and articles that appeared in the *Reporter*, *Atlantic Monthly*, *Saturday Review of Literature*, and the *New York Times Magazine*.

In such popular writings, Eric used history — sometimes comically, usually seriously — to make a contemporary point. He had long been interested in the history of women (he had earned Mary Beard's gratitude for inviting her to talk on women and the family in his Hopkins seminar, a subject, she noted, that was then "tabu to some dictators of historical lecturing"). In 1961, in an article in *Holiday*, he measured modern women, so many of them frenetically juggling the duties of home, family, and career, against Carrie Chapman Catt's expectations for them and declared that they had "emancipated themselves right smack into serfdom." That piece drew a flood of mail, not all of it admiring.[18]

Eric's general audience grew enormously when, on November

[18] Mary R. Beard to Eric Goldman, April 17, 1941, Goldman Papers, Library of Congress, Box 12; Eric F. Goldman, "The Oppressed Emancipated Woman," in Clifton Fadiman, ed., *Party of Twenty: Informal Essays from Holiday Magazine* (New York: Simon and Schuster, 1963), p. 146.

29, 1959, he took over as moderator of the NBC television program "The Open Mind." The program was an intellectual roundtable that was broadcast for a half hour over stations in the New York and Boston areas; on October 1, 1960, it was upgraded to an hour and sent out over the NBC network (it was also broadcast over the Voice of America). "The Open Mind," which had no sponsors, was a sustained spontaneous conversation, the kind that was perfect for Eric's gifts as an intellectual guide and provocateur. Sometimes he profiled single figures ranging in type from the writer Katherine Anne Porter to James R. Hoffa. Usually he assembled a roundtable of people balanced in points of view — one memorable program included Malcolm X and James Baldwin — to explore timely subjects such as civil rights, medical care, foreign policy, religion in America, the women's movement, or the treatment of animals. Expressing his bent for bringing history to bear on contemporary issues, his panels might include historians — for example, Gordon Craig on the strength of German democracy and John Morton Blum on Eisenhower. The "Open Mind" won Emmies in 1962 and 1966.

In the early 1960s, Eric was riding high, both in Princeton and in the larger world. In 1962, the University granted him a coveted McCosh Fellowship and appointed him the first incumbent of the Philip and Beulah Rollins Professorship of History. Eric's books were enormously popular. In 1956, Vintage Books, the Knopf paperback imprint, had brought out *Rendezvous* with an original and sprightly cover drawing by Ben Shahn, and in 1961 it published his updated *The Crucial Decade — and After: America, 1945–1960.*[19] Both books sold steadily and well (their combined sales would eventually exceed a million copies). Eric was writing a new book about an incident early in the century at Coatesville, Pennsylvania, a steel town in the southern part of the state, in which a white mob lynched a black man by burning him alive. He viewed the lynching, a harrowing account of which he published

[19] New York: Alfred A. Knopf, 1965.

in *American Heritage*, to have been in part an explosive expression of the antagonisms that had been developing in Coatesville between the Eastern European immigrants who had come to the town for the work in steel and the blacks who had been migrating there from the South for work in whatever they could find. Eric had been attracted to the subject for a characteristic combination of reasons — the dramatic features of the story and the historical window it opened on the tensions emerging as the civil rights movement of his own day marched north.

In 1961, Eric was elected and, through succeeding years, was repeatedly re-elected president of the Society of American Historians, an organization that honors distinguished writing in American history. He was one of a group of nationally known writers and intellectuals that included Richard Rovere, C. Vann Woodward, Richard Hofstadter, and Arthur Schlesinger, Jr. to whom educated Americans of the day turned for understanding and analysis of current issues. Their presence on the national scene of letters and affairs, lasting far longer than fifteen minutes, was sustained partly by the enormous postwar expansion of higher education and its products as well as by the comparative lack of pluralism in the national media and in the nation's opinion-making constituencies. Yet it also thrived on the deep and authoritative knowledge, the humor and wit, and the manifest, unembarrassed love of country and devotion to its general interests that these public intellectuals brought to the task of interpreting the United States.

In December 1963, Eric began working for the administration of Lyndon B. Johnson and in March 1964, the White House announced his appointment as Special Consultant to the President of the United States. Eric's appointment permitted him to continue teaching at Princeton and moderating "The Open Mind." Eric threw himself into the job, setting aside the Coatesville book and much else in his passionate eagerness to serve his country. He had swiped at Johnson in his article bidding farewell to the 1950s, marveling at the devotion that the then-Majority Leader of the United States Senate showed to the interests of oil and gas and at

Eric F. Goldman with President Lyndon B. Johnson.

his willingness to compromise the heart out of legislation. Now he responded to Johnson's genuine eagerness to ameliorate the bread-and-butter lives of the American people and to that Southerner's resolve, once he was in the White House, to deal at long last with the issue of race. I remember vividly, when I arrived in Washington in June 1964 for a brief stint as an assistant to Eric, the glowing excitement he felt over being in a position where he could roll up his sleeves and help make America over.

In a way, the White House job was Eric's ultimate opportunity to recruit history to the cause of changing the United States. In the speeches he drafted and the memoranda he wrote, he often drew on the past to articulate strategies and directions for the development of Johnson policies. Eric provided his own account of his White House years, which ended in the fall of 1966, in *The Tragedy of Lyndon Johnson,* a best-selling book, part memoir and part history. Suffice it to add here my impression that Eric was exhilarated and effective during the tonic months in 1964 when Johnson drove to surpass Franklin Roosevelt's record on domestic reform legislation and in early 1965 when his legislative successes achieved torrential proportions. But during the summer of that year, much of which I spent in Washington researching a book, Eric's influence seemed to have been impaired by the anti-Vietnam War turmoil that had arisen with the escalation of the conflict. He left the White House because of his own distress about the war and his inability by 1966 to do anything about it, or about much else.

In Princeton during the late 1960s and through the 1970s, Eric's courses remained popular, but he grew increasingly out of sorts with the University. He felt that many of his colleagues held his association with the Johnson White House against him, despite his own convictions against the war, which he declined to emphasize to them. He believed that if there was to be a military draft it should be genuinely democratic, without exemptions for college students, which was, he judged, unpopular in the Princeton community. He was also unhappy with the University's — and the country's — increasing emphasis on affirmative action insofar as he understood it to mean going beyond establishing equality of opportunity to achieving equality of results, and he found somewhat alien the issues of personal and social identity as they came to be expressed in the 1970s. His history department colleagues Marius Jansen and Richard Challener later wrote of him, probably with these years particularly in mind, that he was "tough, suspicious and difficult," adding, "Chairmen and deans did not rise up to call him blessed."[20]

Eric was also frustrated in his principal writing project, a book on the 1960s that he found difficult to get under control. Although NBC had canceled "The Open Mind" in 1967, he remained in public demand, writing articles and reviews and, in 1975–1976, serving as a monthly guest essayist on the CBS "Morning News." But he was soon distracted from all such activities by deep worry about his wife, Jo. In 1977, at age fifty-four, she was attacked by cancer of the palette, underwent a major operation, and began a difficult rehabilitation. It was now twenty-five years since their wedding and the publication of *Rendezvous with Destiny*. In a preface to Vintage Books' twenty-fifth anniversary edition of the work, Eric wrote of Jo: "In the middle of her silver-anniversary year, she was suddenly struck a harsh personal blow; she reacted to it with

[20] Jansen and Challener, "Goldman," May 1, 1989.

sheer guts, a constant concern with others involved, a genuine gallantry."

Eric continued to hold friends at Princeton in affectionate regard and to be helpful to a variety of people, including me, extensively. We corresponded regularly across the country — after several months in the White House, I had joined the faculty of the California Institute of Technology — and I visited him on my trips East. He was particularly encouraging in my project for a book on the history of American physics, listening to my ideas, giving critical readings to drafts of the manuscript, and bolstering me in my sometimes flagging resolve. He made clear that he continued to believe that writing a good book was worth the effort, and in numerous ways he made me think that I might be capable of doing it.

During the 1970s, Eric spoke with increasing seriousness about retiring early from Princeton, possibly to a semi-rural area where he would write and fish and contemplate the world. He and Jo were zeroing in on a place in North Carolina when, in March 1980, he suffered a serious stroke. In April, Jo, who had beaten the cancer, died suddenly, a victim of the extraordinary stress of his illness. Eric eventually managed a partial recovery from his stroke, but he had lost the ability to read easily and to use his right arm well enough to write. He might have found ways around those disabilities to continue as a writer and commentator — he certainly had plenty to say about the United States in the 1980s — but Jo's death had broken something in him. After he retired from Princeton, in 1985, he became increasingly preoccupied with establishing a memorial to her.

Eric died in February 1989, before having hit upon a memorial that he considered appropriate. However, he had willed almost his entire estate for the purpose and asked me to advise his executor on the fulfillment of his wishes. In 1992, as the principal remembrance of Jo, the estate established the Joanna Jackson Goldman Memorial Lecture in American Civilization and Government to be delivered annually at the Library of Congress and expanded into a small book. The aim of the memorial is to invite writers and analysts of distinction to probe and provoke fresh thought about issues of contemporary importance in American life. That purpose seemed to me consistent with the ferocious love of the United States, the bedrock belief in its credo — "that ordinary men and women have a right to peace, material comfort, self-respect, and a touch of joy in living," as he wrote in the preface to *The Tragedy of Lyndon Johnson* — and the enduring eagerness to harness iconoclasm and intellect to achieving those ends, all of which Eric maintained to the end of his life. He would have told the young Americans of any day what he told his History 307 students in 1959, at the end of his celebrated lecture on the need for humor in the United States:

> This rendezvous of yours is up a fantastically craggy incline. Perhaps you will permit me to suggest that you will know more where you are going, that you will get there more surely, if early in the climb you will sweep away the debris of the past, if you will brush aside with all the wondrous powers of youth's mockery the half-truths and the inanities of another generation's cosmic thinkers, newspaper pundits, and, let me say it, another generation's professors of history.[21]

READING LIST

John Bach McMaster, American Historian (Philadelphia: University of Pennsylvania Press; London: H. Melford, Oxford University Press, 1943)

Charles J. Bonaparte, Patrician Reformer: His Earlier Career (Baltimore: The Johns Hopkins University Press, 1943)

Rendezvous with Destiny: A History of Modern American Reform (New York: Alfred A. Knopf, 1952; 25th Anniversary Edition, New York: Vintage Books, 1977)

The Crucial Decade: America 1945–1955 (New York: Alfred A. Knopf 1956)

The Tragedy of Lyndon Johnson (New York: Alfred A. Knopf, 1969)

[21] *Princeton Alumni Weekly*, September 25, 1959.

Donald Ross Hamilton

Department of Physics

BY WILLIAM HAPPER

Donald Ross Hamilton — what a fine name for a professor at Princeton University, with its Scottish Presbyterian beginnings! I first got to know Don when I enrolled in the graduate course on electricity and magnetism in 1960. Don was a warm but distinguished professor in traditional college tweeds. He taught "E & M" with the self-confidence of a creator of the field, as indeed he was. His work on microwave radar during World War II had helped to save many lives. Don's beautiful papers on microwave tubes in the classic MIT radar series are still good reading.

I remember the wonderful informality of Don's course. He was not always fully prepared for his lectures, and it was reassuring to see him struggle with some obscure point. We students concluded that there might be hope for us if our professor had difficulties with physics from time to time. Don used to sit down frequently on top of the desk and chat, rather than stand at the blackboard. I found that informality very reassuring. Only slowly did it dawn on me that Don sat down because in 1960 he was already having trouble standing for long periods because of multiple sclerosis. Before the course was over, Don was walking with some difficulty and sitting down in front of a viewgraph machine where he would write on a blank transparency to illustrate his lectures.

Perhaps sensing that I had no idea what research to do, Don invited me and a few other students to join his weekly seminar on models of nuclear structure. These seminars were held on Thursday evenings at Don's home in Wyman House, the seat of the dean of the Graduate School, a position Don held with distinction from 1958 until 1965. During these seminars, a large blackboard would be rolled out into the living room, and the assembled participants, students, post-docs, and assistant professors, would harass the designated speaker with questions about the shell model, the symplectic group, or any other issue loosely related to the topic of discussion. Throughout the discussion Don would bubble with enthusiasm for the topic, infecting the whole group with his intellectual excitement. It was wonderful training for public speaking. Precisely one hour after the seminar began, Don's gracious wife Pat would always set out refreshments, typically hot cider and donuts, so the seminar ended promptly and was followed by half an hour of relaxing conversation about "cabbages and kings." Many students, myself included, were first attracted to Don's group by Pat's refreshments. Only later were we fully hooked by the physics. Don enjoyed these seminars immensely. From time to time, his little dog would run through the room, almost as excited as Don by the events of the evening. Don used to joke, "Yes, his name is spelled Robby, not Rabi."

Don's measurements of the nuclear spins and moments of radioactive nuclei were in fact a legacy of his own student days at Columbia University with I. I. Rabi, a Nobel laureate in physics. As his Ph.D. thesis work, Don perfected Bill Cohen's beautiful zero-moment method of measuring nuclear moments. Had radiofrequency spectroscopy not been invented during the period of Don's thesis work, the zero-moment technique would have been the method of choice for precision measurements. After leaving Columbia, Don was selected to be a prestigious Junior Fellow at Harvard University. In 1940, while he was still a very young man at Harvard, he wrote the very first theoretical paper on angular correlations of nuclear gamma rays, a work that was years ahead of its time. After World War II, the study of angular correlations in nuclear physics developed into an important scientific field, and the first reference was always to Don's seminal paper. Don once told me with some pride, "You know, because of that paper, people sometimes think I am a theorist!" In fact, Don was a good theorist and a good experimentalist, and he never made a very sharp distinction between them, as evidenced by his development of the hexapole focusing magnet for atomic beams machines, a device that is found today in the United States time standard, the Cs atomic beam, as well as in hydrogen masers. This wonderful ability to do either theory or experiment was another legacy of Don's training by Rabi. When I left Princeton with a fresh Ph.D., Don sent me to Columbia where I got to know Rabi very well. It was a big help at Columbia to be viewed as one of Rabi's many intellectual grandsons, thanks to my "Doctorvater" Don Hamilton.

Don's group was just right for me. As I recall, my thesis instructions were "Help us figure out how well the nuclear shell model works for the f-7/2 shell by finding some interesting spins and moments to measure." Of course, Don and his good friend Rubby Sherr, who ran the Princeton cyclotron, kept a discrete eye on the students to be sure they did not flounder too badly. In retrospect Don probably hid some of the problems we thought we had discovered in not-too-hard places — like a mother cat bringing home live prey for her kittens — but the experience of digging out the physics for ourselves was the finest training you could get. I had the pleasure of using Don's hexapole atomic beam machines to show that a crucial early measurement of the magnetic moment of Mn-52m, done with Don's method of perturbed angular correlations by a less-than-gracious competitor, was in fact wrong by nearly a factor of 100.

The cyclotron-atomic-beams group always included bright young post-docs, assistant professors, and visiting professors. I had the good fortune to have one of Don's imaginative and lively young assistant professors, John McCullen, as my mentor. Other wonderful coaches from the Hamilton-Sherr group were Oakes Ames, Aaron Bernstein, Ben Bayman, Russ Roberson, Herb Funston, Igal Talmi, and Larry Zamick.

In spite of Don's magnanimity, he could not completely suppress his competitive instincts, especially toward his intellectual siblings from Columbia. When I was a graduate student, our main rivals in the atomic beam business were the Berkeley group of Bill Nierenberg, Don's fellow Rabi student from Columbia. Don had a lot of affection for Bill, and I have grown to admire him, too. However, Don set high standards for his group and he expected us to check and cross-check any measurement before publication. On one occasion I remember the closest thing to criticism that ever escaped Don's lips in my hearing: "That Berkeley group! They measure four or five points, fit a curve to it and publish a magnetic moment." For the most part, however, Don would overlook almost any flaw in his fellow mortals, and find something supportive to say about them. As we celebrate 250 years of "Princeton in the Nation's Service," Don's legacy lives on in the many people he influenced and the ideas he created during his service to Princeton.

READING LIST

"On Directional Correlations of Successive Quanta," *Physical Review* 58 (1940): 122

With Julian K. Knipp and J. B. Horner Kuper: *Klystrons and Microwave Triodes* (Lexington, Massachusetts: Boston Technical Publishers, 1964)

Elmore Harris Harbison

Department of History

BY JERROLD E. SEIGEL[1]

I first met E. Harris Harbison, appropriately enough, through one of his books. As a college senior I was assigned *The Christian Scholar in the Age of the Reformation*, and it struck me so forcefully with its ability to find the center of arguments and debates, and to understand how intellectual and moral passions grow up in particular contexts to nurture insight and nudge people toward action, that I hoped right away I might become his student. Once I was lucky enough to have that happen I came to know things about him, both trivial and important, that don't enter into the impersonality of print: that he was called "Jinks,"

[1] In writing this memoir, I have drawn freely on the material that Theodore Rabb and I together assembled to introduce our jointly-edited volume, *Action and Conviction in Early Modern Europe: Essays in Memory of E. H. Harbison* (Princeton: Princeton University Press, 1969).

that as an undergraduate he had conducted the Triangle Club Orchestra, that he was a famous teacher in a department filled with fine teachers, that the ideal of the Christian scholar was not just a subject he wrote about but something close to the center of his life, that his manner contained an almost indescribable mix of quiet sympathy and irrepressible, sometimes caustic wit.

Jinks Harbison was born in Sewickley, Pennsylvania, in 1907, graduated from Princeton in 1928, and took his Ph.D. at Harvard under Roger B. Merriman. He returned to Princeton to join the History Department in 1933, remaining there to teach (he became Henry Charles Lea Professor in 1949) until his early death in 1964. By the time I arrived to study with him in the fall of 1958 his health had already begun to trouble him, and most of us believed that he was the model for a character in Carlos Baker's novel *A Friend in Power*, the professor whom the search committee would have chosen to be president of the university had medical worries not interfered. But we seldom saw any signs of physical weakness until close to the end.

It amused him to joke that his colleagues liked to label him as "the departmental Christian," and given what many people might take that to mean in the era of the culture wars, recalling what it meant to him brings a breath of fresh air. What ought to characterize "the Christian who is also a historian," he wrote, is not some "'philosophy of history' which is the necessary outcome of his Christian belief," nor an attention to religious subjects in his writing and teaching; instead such a person should be "known by his *attitude toward history*, the quality of his concern about it, the sense of reverence and responsibility with which he approaches his subject." That's a tall order, but one sign that Jinks Harbison actually filled it is that many of us who worked with him shared none of his religious convictions, yet we never doubted that we benefitted from something special about the way he approached his subject, and us. In the days when the rather detached mood common to American universities in the late 1950s had not yet begun to give place to the passions and commitments of the 1960s,

Jinks stood out as a person who believed that teaching and scholarship needed to be enlivened with some animating concern, and he told young historians that their students would want to know why the subjects they pursued mattered to them, as the people they were. Calmly and without insistence, he brought to those quiet years some of the spirit of conviction abroad in his own time as a student and young scholar in the 1930s; it was quite in character that he contributed an essay to *Socialism and American Life*. He was the first person I knew who called attention to the absence of women among the contributors to a grand cooperative work of history.

The subject of Jinks Harbison's first book, *Rival Ambassadors at the Court of Queen Mary*, was diplomatic history, a topic somewhat out of fashion today, but formerly more highly valued both as a key to the history of state-building and international relations, and for the chance it gave to construct careful, concrete narratives based on materials often still in archives and private papers. (Felix Gilbert, who shared interests and even students with Jinks Harbison from his nearby post at the Institute for Advanced Study, once recalled that his teacher, Friedrich Meinecke, believed that only two subjects, biography and diplomatic history, were concrete enough for fledgling historians to be trusted with.) But Jinks's history of diplomacy in the sixteenth century went beyond these features of the subject; its real concern was to understand the challenges and dilemmas posed by practicing a profession decried almost from the start for the intrigue and dishonesty it fostered (an ambassador, as the saying had it, was a person "sent to lie abroad for his country"), in an age when many people who entered public life were moved by the passions of faith. *Rival Ambassadors* already recognized implicitly a point that Harbison's friend J. H. Hexter would later formulate more explicitly: what we know as modern secularization was never merely a matter of replacing religious concerns with worldly ones, but a process in which each grew in intensity as it fed off the other.

Given such an interest, it is perhaps not surprising that much of Jinks Harbison's later work turned more directly to matters of conviction and consciousness. There he could consider not just the way that human imperfection muddied up the search for salvation with the dirty business of getting and keeping power, but also the ways that people come up against their most human limitations in the very act of trying to approach divinity and truth. A luminous example is the following comment on a great religious and secular text, Erasmus's *The Praise of Folly.*

> These are light-hearted words with serious undertones, the words of a man who takes his calling seriously and himself lightly. . . . Erasmus knew his calling as a Christian scholar to be serious and important, but he also knew the presumption in it, the presumption that taints all human aspirations and must often amuse a loving God. In a word, he believed that intellectuals are both necessary and ridiculous. This is the meaning . . . of Huizinga's remark that "only when humor illuminated Erasmus's mind did it become truly profound."

Much of this was intended to apply to himself, no doubt, as well as to the rest of us, a reminder to those who think they live the life of the mind about how quickly their doings can become empty and foolish if they take themselves too earnestly. Such skepticism about scholarship and intellect, combined with Jinks's understanding of how ideals are twisted by their insertion into systems of power relations, and his awareness and sympathy for the suffering and excluded, would, I believe, have made him at least ready to think open-mindedly about the new forms of skepticism, the new emphasis on power as a condition of intellect, and the new attention to how exclusion and oppression work, that have established so salient a presence in our universities today. But as far as the skepticism and the sense that intellect is necessarily corrupted by its involvements go, I suspect that any sympathy for these new currents would have run rather quickly up against some limits, ones that appear in the following remark from one of his essays.

> It may be suggested, without any intent to blaspheme, that the best professional historian's ideal here is theoretically the same as the Christian's: to see Luther as nearly as possible as his own Lord saw him,

> in all his weakness and strength, his compromises and triumphs, his freedom and his compulsion, so that in the resulting judgment justice is perfectly tempered with mercy. As a matter of fact, close and persistent study of Luther and his whole age by professional historians has brought us closer at least to the possibility of such a judgment than was conceivable a century ago, simply because we knew too little then. Mere knowledge is no guarantee of sound judgment of men and movements, either in historical study or in ordinary Christian living, but it is often the beginning of true understanding.

Reading this passage together with the one cited above on Erasmus gives a pretty good sense about the spirit of Jinks Harbison's scholarship and teaching.

Yet remembering him as a Christian scholar runs the danger of making him appear meeker and more compliant that he was, a kind of Chipsian figure. He wasn't like that. For one thing, his skepticism and sense that judgment was also a duty could make him strict and critical toward others. In his seminars you were listened to with attention, but if you said something unconsidered or foolish you were kindly but firmly made to know it. I remember well the pages of comments he wrote about the draft of my dissertation, some of them appreciative and admiring, but many others determined to make me think again about the places where I hadn't been at all hard enough on myself, had been too quick to take the evidence to mean what I hoped it did, hadn't subjected my own arguments to the scrutiny they required. He was devoted to undergraduates and they to him (asked the secret of the famous Harbison preceptorials, one told me "He always asks the right questions"), but his skepticism could blossom there too: about the comprehensive exams still given to history seniors in the 1960s he let fall the truth, "Only the questions change, the answers are always the same." Maybe that (or perhaps some other doubting judgment) lay behind the incident I witnessed when, as a first-year instructor, I was sitting with him when a senior colleague appeared to offer his suggested questions for those same exams: "Oh that's all right — just throw them in the wastebasket."

The department (and University) to which Jinks Harbison belonged was vastly different from the one that bears the same name today. One way to state the difference is to recall the now almost unimaginable sense of unity and common purpose that drew its members together, despite all their marked personal differences. One could go from course to course, period to period and country to country, and find a still-homogeneous body of students attending lectures and doing readings that shared a few basic themes and assumptions: the bourgeoisie was always rising, modernity was a unified and recognizable phenomenon, and the West was the place where history unfolded. "Whig history" was an object of criticism, but some of its spirit still walked abroad. There was a certain narrowness in such ways of thinking, and a certain innocence too (which is not to say that they had only innocent effects); our academies today are more broadly open and diverse, and in some ways more sophisticated and self-aware. I for one welcome these changes, and I would not want to go back to that other day; in important ways I think Jinks would have welcomed them too. But in gaining these qualities something has also been lost. Perhaps remembering Jinks Harbison may put us in mind of what that something is.

READING LIST

Rival Ambassadors at the Court of Queen Mary (Princeton: Princeton University Press, 1940)

The Age of Reformation (Ithaca, New York: Cornell University Press, 1955)

The Christian Scholar in the Age of the Reformation (New York: Charles Scribner's Sons, 1956)

Christianity and History: Essays (Princeton: Princeton University Press, 1964)

Philip Khûri Hitti

Department of Near Eastern Studies

BY OLEG GRABAR

My memories of Professor Philip Khûri Hitti, the *shaykh* as we graduate students of the early fifties used to call him with a mix of affection, humor, and reverence, are centered on a very specific event and on a set of images.

The event took place on a cold day of late January 1951. I had gone to see him in the office he occupied on the third floor of Firestone Library, right by a staircase leading up to a small cafeteria from which we, poor graduate students, were excluded in those days of strongly enacted hierarchies in universities and elsewhere. I had written to him before graduating from Harvard in June of the preceding year to say that I had specialized in medieval history, that I had taken two years of Arabic, and that I was considering doing graduate work in some form of Near Eastern Studies, uncertain, however, whether I would stick to the Middle Ages or become involved with the more glamorous and allegedly more relevant present. I had added that I had no money to invest in further studies and that I intended to earn some before applying formally to the Graduate School. Now, in January, having just arrived from Paris where my family lived, I was on my way to Detroit to a job at General Motors that was apparently waiting for me through the kindness of the father of the wife of a Harvard graduate student met on the boat from New York to Le Havre. Such were the ways of the Ivy classes in those days! The exact chronology of what happened next is not entirely clear to me now, almost forty-five years later, but the result is certain. Either on that same day or on the following one, Professor Hitti admitted me as a graduate student and provided me with a sizeable fellowship without, at least to my knowledge (and all other likely witnesses are long gone), consulting his colleagues or deans (there weren't as many then). I enrolled in the second semester of that very year, a week or two after meeting Professor Hitti. I never got to Detroit until much later when I was teaching at the University of Michigan. I occasionally feel that, had it not been for Professor Hitti, I might have become an early version of Lee Iacocca. I also wonder whether he really did not consult with at least one dean, but mostly I marvel at the open ways of the University then, at least when one was a man with the right pedigree.

The story illustrates two very remarkable features of Professor Hitti: his impulsive generosity to those he liked (and he usually decided very rapidly who these were) and a powerful sense of purpose which could not be altered once its course had been set.

The images of Professor Hitti engraved in my memory are those of a teacher in action. Two characteristics of that teaching are unusual enough to bear recalling. He used to gather graduate students in his house for "the" basic seminar in Middle Eastern history that was in fact the history of Syria, Palestine, and vaguely Egypt, with a few rare extensions beyond the core Semitic and especially Arab lands. The seminar always met in the evening for reasons that I do not recall. We would all sit uncomfortably in the Hittis' living room and comment on reading assignments, while the *shaykh* would nod occasionally and correct our bibliographical references. At the time I thought the seminar dealt too much with technical trivia and not enough with grand interpretations of history. In fact I don't remember having learned much history from it, but much later I realized that it was not history that Professor Hitti was teaching us, but how to organize our work as budding historians. He had elaborate theories on the making and use of file cards, on the ways to find books in libraries, and especially on the lives and institutional allegiances of our elders and predecessors in the field of Near Eastern Studies. In a tradition that has its sources in Muslim religious learning and in medieval practices everywhere, he wanted us to know that we were entering a world shaped by others, that we would shape it in our own ways, and that it was important to know and to honor those who preceded us. Wittingly or not, he was giving us a lesson in humility. The academic life toward which most of us were destined was presented as a succession of priestly scholars known to each other and anonymous to others, a bit like the stained glass windows in the Princeton chapel with names of mostly forgotten scholars (he made us all find and read the two names in Arabic letters he had designed for the chapel) still welcoming future generations into their company.

Another constant of Professor Hitti's teaching was the class in advanced Arabic, which always met in his office. We sat at a round table, and the student nearest to him on his right was always the first to be called for reading, translating, parsing in Arabic, and commenting on whatever passage had been assigned. The trick was to enter the room first, sit on Professor Hitti's left and have time to prepare something brilliant while the first student to the right would slowly go through the text. I am embarrassed to admit how pleased we were when time ran out before it was our turn, for the teaching of Arabic was a sacred duty of Professor

Hitti and he could be quite amusingly tough on those who made mistakes. I still wince at his hilarity when I confused a bath with a pigeon through a mistake between two different types of "h" in Arabic, or when I developed a complicated explanation for the presence of a woman's breast and a lion in the same hemistich when in fact these were names of Arab tribes. It is no doubt true that modern methods of teaching difficult languages like Arabic are far superior to the old-fashioned sitting at the table, if not at the feet, of a teacher. And Princeton, under Hitti's benevolent guidance, was, I believe, the first university to teach Arabic through people who pronounced it rightly instead of knowing only how to parse it properly. Yet no machine, no tape, no phonetic writing can give the love of the language, its playfulness, its endless varieties, with the same intensity as that short, old (he was then younger than I am now), smiling teacher sitting at the same table as his taller students and feeling, I am sure, that none of them would ever really learn Arabic to perfection, none would speak it or even read it with the pleasure he enjoyed in doing either, but all would sense the presence of something beautiful and exciting yet inaccessible to them. And the students would long cherish the memory of the one who brought it all to them.

It is more difficult to feel as enthusiastic for Professor Hitti's scholarly legacy. Except for his wonderful translations with significant commentaries of Baladhuri's *Futuh al-Buldan* (The Origins of the Islamic State), a major source for early Islamic history, and of Usamah Ibn Munqidh's *Kitab al-I'tibar* (An Arab-Syrian Gentleman and Warrior in the Period of the Crusades), a delightful memoir of a very unusual observer of his fellow men, most of Professor Hitti's learned output has not withstood the test of time. It is, of course, true, that his *History of the Arabs*[1] reads easily and pleasantly and was in some ways ahead of anything available at that time, at least in English. But its narrative presents a history that seems to have stopped being exciting some-

[1] New York: Macmillan, 1936, with many subsequent editions and corrections and with innumerable translations into many languages.

where around 900 A.D., with everything after that consisting of what Hitti called "petty dynasties" and a few successes like Ibn Khaldun, the great fourteenth-century sociologist of history, or the glittering Alhambra, in the midst of sad chaos and alien interventions. History is seen quite differently now, as is well demonstrated by a recent best-seller whose author, much younger than Philip Hitti, came from the same Lebanese Christian background and fully acknowledged his spiritual debt to Hitti: Albert Hourani, *A History of the Arab Peoples.*[2]

But the important point is not that Hitti's book belongs to another time. This is as scholarship should be, as new generations do see and understand things differently. The interesting point is rather that the book's title and much of its content and style reflect two far more original sides of Professor Hitti. One was his profound commitment to making the history and the views of Arabs, in the past or today, heard everywhere, through their accomplishments as well as through their political ambitions and emotional attitudes. For instance, he took on quite early the cause of Palestinian Arabs and testified in Congress on their behalf. He was deeply proud of his own past and would convey to us his pride in a people as well as in a language. This pride extended to his students, and retrospectively I feel a bit embarrassed that I could not respond to his request to rewrite the chapter on art in one of the later editions of his magnum opus.

The other side of his work struck me particularly as I reread the story of his life and accomplishments. In contrast to the prejudices and even snobbery of Princeton and of all comparable American institutions, Europe and European scholarship were almost totally absent from his concerns. His was a direct pipeline between the mountains and hinterland of Lebanon and an America in which he saw the tolerance of behavior and the generosity of spirit that characterized for him the first century and a half of Islamic rule over North Africa and western Asia under his beloved

[2] Cambridge, Massachusetts: Harvard University Press, 1991.

dynasty of the Umayyads. And Princeton University was to be the center for the successful operation of that pipeline.

READING LIST

Translator: Baladhuri, *The Origins of the Islamic State* (New York: Columbia University Press, 1916)

Translator: Usamah Ibn Munqidh, *An Arab-Syrian Gentleman and Warrior in the Period of the Crusades* (New York: Columbia University Press, 1929)

History of the Arabs from the Earliest Times to the Present (New York: Macmillan, 1936)

Edward Dudley Hume Johnson

Department of English

BY ROBERT L. PATTEN

"One of the most incisive minds on the Princeton faculty," the *Daily Princetonian* declared in 1955.[1] What made Dudley Johnson's English 202 course unique, according to his students, was his insistence on providing, instead of critical interpretations of selected works, magnificently organized and fact-crammed lectures on what Dudley called "the background against which the books should be read." The danger of dryness was avoided because Dudley so effectively communicated his own enthusiasm; but, he emphasized, "I don't dramatize." Instead, he stated the themes of the course in the first lecture and reiterated them throughout the semester. Those

[1] "Johnson: Organized Brilliance," *Daily Princetonian*, March 24, 1955. Subsequent quotations in this paragraph come from this source.

themes were highly personal, idiosyncratic, and independent of the narrow orthodoxies prevailing in Victorian studies when Dudley began his career. Instead of New Criticism, he supplied cultural context, attending to "the impact of ideas on the creative image of the artist."

Dudley's reconstruction of Victorian literature had led in 1952 to the publication of a landmark book, *The Alien Vision of Victorian Poetry*. Having been informed by the Department of English several years earlier that there would be no tenure track appointment in Romantic literature, as those positions were already filled, Dudley abandoned his first loves, for the artist Thomas Rowlandson, the novelist Sir Walter Scott, and the poet Lord Byron, and turned his attention to the Victorian poets Alfred Tennyson, Robert Browning, and Matthew Arnold. He detected in all three a need to conceal private visions from public scrutiny, and he translated their codes of concealment in order to overthrow the reigning orthodoxy that Victorian poets were unproblematic spokesmen for the age. That interpretation was not popular at the time of its publication; one conservative critic fulminated that we should "stop reading into Victorian poetry didacticisms and personal symbolisms that the poets never intended."[2] Over time, however, Dudley's thesis became so fundamental to Victorian studies that it seemed unremarkable, passé. But less than a year ago, three of the most distinguished senior scholars in nineteenth-century studies, on being asked who Dudley Johnson was, responded in unison by reciting the name of the book and judging it still one of the best and most influential readings of Victorian literature.

Dudley, being Dudley, could not read or teach quite like anyone else. In the sixties he shared English 202 with Robert Bernard Martin, a junior colleague who later took early retirement and wrote several prize-winning biographical studies of Victorian writ-

[2] Merle M. Bevington, Review of *The Alien Vision* in *South Atlantic Quarterly* 53, no. 1 (January 1954): 154–155.

ers. One day, when Dudley was lecturing and Bob precepting, Dudley rushed into Bob's office.

"Could I borrow your glasses? I've just discovered that I left mine at home."

"Well, certainly, Dudley, but they're a very different prescription."

"Never mind, they're glasses."

When Dudley began his lecture, he peered down at his blurry notes, then over his borrowed spectacles at the class. "This is the first time," he quipped, "that Professor Martin and I have ever seen Victorian literature in the same way."

Dudley reached Princeton students in part because he had been one himself, in an era of male privilege and obligations. Born at "Grasmere," the family home in Alton, Ohio, Dudley grew up in Columbus across the street from James Thurber. Though sick a good deal in his early years, he managed to participate in sports (crew, football) and other student activities while attending St. Paul's School in Concord, New Hampshire. In the midst of the depression, September 1930, Dudley entered Princeton, where several relatives, including Dr. C.F.W. McClure, had preceded him; since his father died before Dudley graduated, he listed his permanent address as Dr. McClure's home, 1 Battle Road. Intending to pursue a career in journalism, Dudley won the Biddle Sophomore Essay Prize and was active in the University Press Club and the *Nassau Literary Magazine.* He also had a flair for drama, writing plays and reviews and startling his neighbors when the still he operated in his rooms in Campbell to circumvent prohibition exploded, blowing the front door off its hinges. He majored in the Department of Romance Languages and graduated magna cum laude and Phi Beta Kappa. The 1934 *Nassau Herald* recorded that "Dud" was "an Episcopalian and a Democrat." A Rhodes Scholarship took him to Oriel College, Oxford, where he earned a B.A. in English literature. Then he matriculated at Yale, obtaining his Ph.D. in 1939.

Princeton hired Dr. Johnson as an instructor in English for $2,000 a year. When the United States declared war, Dudley obtained leave to join the navy. He rose from ensign to lieutenant-commander, serving on the USS Iowa and in North Africa before writing the account of enlisted personnel for the official *Administrative History* of the Navy in World War II. He also drafted a play and considered an offer from the University of North Carolina at Chapel Hill to head their creative writing program. But Professor Gordon Gerould offered a three-year appointment as assistant professor, and that Dudley accepted: "I value a chance to return to Princeton more highly than any other opportunity."[3] In 1950 he was appointed Philip Freneau Preceptor and in 1952 he was promoted to associate professor. Subsequently he served as professor (1961–1973), chair of graduate studies and later chair of the Department of English, and from 1973 until his retirement in June 1977, Holmes Professor of Belles-Lettres, the oldest humanities chair in the University.

During these years, while writing a succession of important articles, a superb though often overlooked study of Charles Dickens, and two splendid anthologies of nineteenth-century British writing, Dudley also served as an administrator. Fair, honest, dependable, and a good judge of people and policies, Dudley quickly earned the respect of senior administrators, not just at Princeton, but also at the Modern Language Association. When in 1955 he was offered the position of executive secretary of the MLA, an appointment carrying a large salary, a full professorship at New York University, and editorship of the most important journal in the field of literature, Princeton's chair of English, Carlos Baker, wrote a strong letter to Dean Douglas Brown, recommending a hefty increase in salary "to show our real confidence in Dudley" and to counteract the generous terms of the competing offer. Over the succeeding decades Dudley was appointed to the advisory board of major scholarly journals in his field; he also

[3] E.D.H. Johnson to Gordon Gerould, March 22, 1946, Faculty File, Princeton University Archives.

served twice (1969, 1972) as chair of the Committee for the George Jean Nathan Award in Dramatic Criticism.

In 1966, Dudley's four-year term as chair of graduate studies elicited this tribute: "He is a tireless, efficient, and imaginative administrator, completely selfless in his dedication to the programs and work of the Department . . . he should certainly be the first to be considered for the Chairmanship of the Department when it becomes vacant."[4] Following that advice, the University appointed Dudley chair for two terms, 1968–1974; in the opinion of Carlos Baker and A. Walton Litz, who succeeded him, Dudley may have been the best chair in decades. While administering, he "never relented in his determination to teach with his customary devotion and skill . . . invariably [he] stood near the top of the students' ratings."[5]

His administrative dedication was not an escape from pedagogy; it was an inseparable part of it. Dudley, who probably had suffered his own share of absent-minded professors as a student, never dispensed vague advice or missed deadlines for recommendations. George Rupp, Class of 1964, president of Columbia University, recalls Dudley's mentoring with particular affection:

> I had the great good fortune to have Dudley Johnson as my advisor while I studied in Germany for my junior year. He was unfailingly helpful and attentive. In the summer before I left, he worked with me as I completed my junior papers. During the year we kept in touch, and in the spring we arranged for me to take my junior exams — which included a comparative section on English and German literature — in Munich. Throughout this process of advising at a distance, Dudley Johnson was a model of what an advisor should be. I will always be deeply grateful to him.[6]

George Landow, professor of English and Art History at Brown

[4] Undated, unsigned memorandum from E.D.H. Johnson's file, Faculty Files, Princeton University Archives.

[5] Carlos Baker in consultation with A. Walton Litz, "Faculty Salary Recommendation Form," January 20, 1975, E.D.H. Johnson's file, Faculty Files, Princeton University Archives.

[6] E-mail, George Rupp to Robert L. Patten, December 13, 1995.

and expert on hypertext, took a graduate seminar on Ruskin from Dudley during his senior year. That experience reoriented George's life, deflecting him from medical school to graduate work in English. Thereafter he always did what Dudley said he should do. "My attitude toward students, teaching, and the profession," Landow believes, "have been shaped largely by him."[7] And Ulrich Knoepflmacher, Dudley's student, colleague, and successor at Princeton, summed up the experiences of many when he declared that Dudley "gave himself totally to educating his students, both undergraduate and graduate."[8]

Lecturing, administering, mentoring — Dudley did all these things with skill and professionalism. And professionalism of a particular sort was his hallmark. Born into easy circumstances, blessed with a rangy, athletic body despite his frequent chest and stomach ailments, possessed of a craggy virility (Marjorie Hope Nicolson called him a "handsome lion") and an austere yet courtly manner, and conscious of his own presence and theatricality despite his rooted dislike of histrionic lecturers, Dudley commanded his world with patrician assurance and dignified reserve.

Dudley worked hard at his undergraduate lectures. He also knew tricks for putting the material across and pointing up the highlights. In those days a teacher could smoke in class. Dudley used a cigarette as theatrically as Bogie or Bette. The *Daily Princetonian* described the forty-three-year-old lecturer's technique: "From the moment the distinguished, graying man, conservatively-dressed and composed, exhales the first puff from the cigarette placed in the holder which is his trademark, heads are bent over notebooks as the students labor feverishly to keep up with the flood of facts which Johnson pours out 26 times a year."

[7] E-mail, George Landow to Robert L. Patten, December 23, 1995 and January 3, 1996.

[8] Avani Mehta, "Victorian Age authority dies, served as department chair," *Daily Princetonian*, undated clipping, E.D.H. Johnson's file, Faculty Files, Princeton University Archives.

"Gentlemen," he would say, then suck in smoke, extract the cigarette with an audible pop, slowly exhale, and resume. He was sufficiently conscious of this way of punctuating a lecture that he passed it on to graduate students. "Just as you get to the climax of your argument," he would say, "stop and light a cigarette to build suspense."

Dudley had a distinctive, though variously interpreted, sartorial style. In the 1950s undergraduates thought him "conservatively-dressed." In the 1960s he was more venturesome: he might wear a window-pane plaid shirt, paisley tie, suede or embroidered vest, and a hound's-tooth jacket tailored from a bolt of cloth his mother wove in Nova Scotia, with a silk foulard handkerchief nattily arranged in the breast pocket. An American advisee said Dudley dressed "superbly," but his English friend and art dealer, Peyton Skipwith, thought the tweed suits "over-loud." Whatever the outfit or opinion, students remembered Dudley for a mode of dress far more personal and riveting than the conservative suits displayed in Langrock's windows.

In the 1960s Dudley hit his stride as an influential teacher of graduate students. He often said that his students were his publications. His wide reading and preference for focusing on the cultural background of literature empowered him to direct dissertations on an extraordinary range of subjects: Romantic poets, Victorian humanism, Victorian attitudes toward the Renaissance, Thomas Carlyle, Charles Dickens, George Eliot, and John Ruskin among others. His intense love of the visual arts, which led him to collect fervently and to write a magisterial book on British genre painting, also prompted him and his students to examine ways Victorian illustrators and artists fused word and image. "I . . . think of him," Professor William Burgan writes, "as above all a teacher *for* students, not just *of* students." Other faculty had their own interpretations to disseminate to acolytes; Dudley, Burgan continues, "was actually eager to efface himself, to put his students in touch with literature and with their own deepest responses to it, easing access and communicating his own passionate enthusiasm but at the same time trying to get himself out of the way."[9]

For several years Dudley served as graduate placement officer, a highly rewarding post in those days when graduates were deluged with job offers even before they had finished their dissertations. "Don't come in and just tell me that you want a position — there are too many of them," he told George Bornstein, now professor of English at the University of Michigan and a renowned Yeats scholar. "What you must do is come in and say that you want a job at a New England men's college, or in California, for example, and I'll be glad to help you."[10]

The disruptions of the Vietnam War years troubled Dudley's chairmanship and his educational principles. "I think that Princeton is surviving with reasonable credit the crisis through which we are passing," he wrote in May 1970, "thanks in no small part to an enlightened administration and a devoted faculty . . . I wonder if the world in which I have lived so much of my life has not gone for good, leaving a very different world in which I shall never really feel at home."[11] Despite his fears, students in the 1970s flocked to his lectures in record numbers; he maintained that Princeton became a much better, more civilized and intellectual place, after it admitted women. But the rapid and extreme changes to which universities were subjected in those years did wear him down. The ethos of formal civility, the standards of intellectual greatness and objectivity, and the validity of aesthetic judgments all came to be challenged, indeed overturned. In 1977 he elected early retirement. He spent the succeeding decades engaged with his family, traveling and hiking, and writing about British art.

Dudley thought that his "capacity for forming friendships" brought him most reward.[12] Like many others, my friendship with him grew out of his generous empathy and boundless fascination

[9] FAX, William Burgan to Robert L. Patten, February 13, 1996.

[10] E-mail, George Bornstein to Robert L. Patten, December 20, 1995.

[11] E.D.H. Johnson to Robert L. Patten, May 27, 1970.

[12] Peyton Skipwith, "Professor Dudley Johnson," *The Independent*, January 2, 1996.

with British culture. His cultivation and learning opened many doors; he was welcomed in stately homes, by connoisseurs of art and literature, and by devotees of the English landscape. But he never featured his own access or distinction; instead he was a tireless coach, advising, consoling, encouraging, praising, and occasionally administering a necessary corrective. None of these gifts was available, however, until one had earned Dudley's respect. He demarcated the stages of what Bill Burgan calls a "phased progression toward informality": from a frosty "thank you" interrupting an incompetent seminar report one might, if lucky, progress to "a superlative report," an "extraordinary chapter," and even to a glass of sherry at his home on Linden Lane following graduation.

What we remember are moments of contagious excitement: the way he read the denouement of "The Last Tournament" in Tennyson's *Idylls of the King*— "Mark's way," shouts King Mark gleefully as he splits Tristram's skull — or the wry comment after reading an etiolated passage of Arnoldian seduction: "Gentlemen, is *that* what you say to your wife after the third martini?" He also taught by example an attention to accuracy, economy, and elegance of expression. And he communicated an unshakable belief in the nobility of the professoriat, with its obligations to instruct dedicated students and to investigate the finest achievements of the human spirit. At the end of our frequently digressive, inconclusive seminar discussions, Dudley would half-smile and dismiss us, saying, "I always like to raise more questions than we can answer." He left us with the sense that the mysteries of literature and art would remain unsolved, however hard we tried.

READING LIST

The Alien Vision of Victorian Poetry: Sources of the Poetic Imagination in Tennyson, Browning, and Arnold (Princeton: Princeton University Press, 1952)

Editor: *The World of the Victorians: An Anthology of Poetry and Prose* (New York: Charles Scribner's Sons, 1964)

Editor: *The Poetry of Earth: A Collection of English Nature Writings, Selected, With An Introduction and Critical Prefaces by E. D. H. Johnson* (New York: Athenaeum, 1966)

Charles Dickens: An Introduction to His Novels (New York, Random House, 1969)

Paintings of the British Social Scene from Hogarth to Sickert (New York: Rizzoli, 1986)

Edward Ellsworth Jones

Department of Psychology

BY DANIEL T. GILBERT

Trends in marriage may come and go, but in academic life one does not usually take the name of one's dissertation advisor. Nonetheless, I suspect that no amount of aging or accomplishment will change the fact that I and two dozen other social psychologists will always be known to our field as "Ned Jones' students." Indeed, I think that most of us would not have it another way.

I met Ned in 1981, when I came to Princeton to pursue my Ph.D. in social psychology. New graduate students usually have to choose between two kinds of advisors — the brilliant and busy opinion-leader with whom they may or may not have a weekly audience, and the substitute parent who will shower them with kind attention because he or she has very little else to do. Neither I nor any of Ned's students ever made that choice. Our advisor was arguably the most eminent social psychologist of his day, and yet he was also the doting, avuncular professor whom students come to trust, admire, and later in life, imitate. With each of us, Ned somehow found the balance between being a supportive friend who evoked our humanity and our integrity, and a challenging mentor who pushed and prodded us to think deeply and clearly about things that really mattered. At one moment during a meeting with a poorly prepared student, Ned might put his size-13 feet up on the desk and close his eyes until the student timidly inquired, "Are you awake?" to which he would respond, "Barely. But keep talking." At another moment he might console a student whose year-long labors in the laboratory had been a wash: "Science is about trying and failing, and you should be proud of the fact that you've done both so well." He was sardonic and sweet, and the more he teased, the more you knew that you were respected and liked. He quietly dared us to be great, and he did not make gushing noises when, on occasion, we were.

Ned was such an awkward, unassuming man, that it was sometimes difficult for his students to remember that he was a giant in a field that he shaped and cherished for nearly forty years. From his early development of attribution theory, the actor-observer effect, and the correspondence bias, to his later work on self-handicapping, social stigma, and strategic self-presentation, Ned built a significant piece of the foundation on which modern social psychology rests. Although his contributions seemed remarkably varied, each was in essence a meditation on one question: How do ordinary people orchestrate and penetrate the mysteries of their own behavior?

Ned began by assuming that ordinary people consider behavior to be a joint function of a person's enduring predispositions and the situation within which the person's behavior unfolds. He argued that the ordinary observer who wants to understand others must determine whether the other person's behavior provides evidence of enduring dispositions ("He's a moron" or "She's very kind") or of external constraints ("His test was too hard" or "She's sucking up to her boss"). In 1965, Ned and his student, Keith Davis, offered social psychology its first formal model of this "attribution" process. Their landmark paper introduced correspondent inference theory, which suggested that rational observers should use a special set of inferential rules to determine whether or not an actor's behavior provides evidence of a corresponding disposition or an external constraint. His experimental work showed that people generally used those rules — with one important exception. Although the rules suggested that rational observers should not infer dispositions from actions that are performed under great duress (e.g., a political prisoner's confession does not mean that the prisoner really believes what he is saying), Ned's experiments showed that people do, in fact, infer dispositions under such circumstances. The fact that the rational canon of correspondent inference theory was violated so clearly and so often never ceased to intrigue Ned, who turned an experimental anomaly into one of social psychology's magnificent obsessions. Ned was captivated by the fact that people tend to draw inferences about others even when they are aware that the other person's behavior was situationally induced and that the other person was merely "doing what anyone would do under the circumstances." Much of his empirical work over the next twenty years explored the causes and consequences of this phenomenon.

Ned's work heralded the beginning of "the attributional approach" in social psychology, and by the early 1970s, attribution theory had replaced dissonance theory as social psychology's premiere theoretical engine — a position it retained for more than a decade. After accepting the Stuart Professorship at Princeton University in 1977, Ned extended his work to address the problem of strategic self-presentation — a topic he had set aside after a promising early interest. (His book on the topic, *Ingratiation*, won the Century Psychology Series Award in 1963.) Ned realized that if people use inferential rules to understand the actions of others, then they must surely use those same rules to their advantage when they are themselves the objects of another person's scrutiny. In a sense, Ned viewed social interaction as a sport in which people work hard to learn the truth about others who work equally hard to prevent them from learning it, and he was endlessly fascinated by the subtle tactics people use to shape others' opinions of them. His work on self-handicapping and strategic self-presentation provides an extraordinarily insightful analysis of these tactics and their implementation in daily life. Indeed, Ned was so delighted by the artful parry and skillful thrust of the simplest interpersonal event, that some suggested his attribution theory was merely a stepping-stone to the study of such tactical maneuvers. Ned explicitly denied it. "I just studied what my students told me to study," he said. Ned may have been self-effacing, but his students always knew who was really steering the boat and who was merely paddling.

Fiercely competitive at the poker table and on the tennis court, Ned was in most other settings a gentle, modest man who never quite seemed to understand why others considered his work so important. Indeed, it was this rare combination of humility and humanity that made him such a beloved colleague and mentor. He built major graduate programs at both Duke and Princeton, personally trained many of the influential social psychologists of subsequent generations, and received virtually every award his field could offer. These accomplishments and accolades made him feel both proud and uneasy, and it was the uneasiness that endeared him to just about everyone. He was a Fellow of the American Academy of Arts and Sciences (1982) and a winner of psychology's highest award — the American Psychological Association's Distinguished Scientific Contribution Award (1977). But he was proudest of the Distinguished Scientist Award (1987) given to him by the relatively small Society for Experimental Social Psychology. On the day he accepted that award, someone referred to him as "Mr. Social Psychology," and we who were gathered that evening had never seen him so moved. I believe that no title — neither President nor Lord nor King — could have honored him more. He was devoted to his discipline in a way that few ever are. Ned appreciated the vitality, accessibility, and creativity of social psychology, but perhaps more than anything, he appreciated its devotion to empirical analysis, which he saw as the surest road to knowledge. That road was rocky, treacherous, and sometimes impassable; but Ned followed it with determination, always teaching his students that it is more difficult and more pleasurable to find truth than to invent it. He felt that scientists won the right to speak on a topic by devoting a lifetime of service to it, and he had little tolerance for psychologists who chose to bypass the tedium of the laboratory and go straight into what he derisively called "the wisdom business." Indeed, it was only after four decades of service to his topic that Ned was convinced to collect his own wisdom in a single volume. That book, *Interpersonal Perception*, stands as one of the true treasures of social psychology — a profound and personal analysis of social life that remains a fitting testament to his unique mixture of conservative scientific values and liberal imagination. The book was published in 1990, when Ned was 64 years old. When asked when he intended to begin work on his next book, he replied, "In another forty years." Ned felt that he'd had his say. On July 30, 1993, after a day spent bodysurfing, playing with his grandchildren in the ocean, having his annual cigar and an occasional martini, he died unexpectedly, surrounded by the close-knit family whom he so deeply loved.

So what do we say about Ned in the final analysis? He wouldn't stand for gushing noises. That much I know. But I think he would have been pleased to hear us say this: Ned Jones was a good guy who told the truth. Yes, there it is. Ned was a very good guy. And indeed, he gave us many truths. Those truths were never shocking or outrageous or unbelievable. They were not revelations. Ned's truths were elegant, simple, astute observations that were just so right — so perfectly on the money — that the moment you heard one you realized that you could have thought of it yourself, except that . . . well . . . you hadn't. When Ned gave you a birthday present it was never a card-shuffling machine or an electric corkscrew. It was a brown tie. Similarly, he did not give psychology exotic intellectual gifts that will end up in the attic except when they are being trotted out for a history lesson. Instead, he gave us stuff we really needed. He was the master of telling us what we didn't quite know, and in a too-short life, he hit that sweet note again and again and again.

There are people who change your life, people who don't, and then there are people like Ned who change it in such a way that you can hardly imagine what it would have been without him. I hear people say about Aristotle and Einstein that their intellectual influence is so pervasive as to render them invisible. My friend and mentor, Ned Jones, is almost invisible to me now. His vision of social psychology so permeates my own that I can hardly tell that I am looking through him anymore. Maybe that's inevitable and maybe that's even good, but before he disappears altogether, I am pleased to remember him, and to share those memories with the Princeton community.

READING LIST

With Harold E. Gerard: *Foundations of Social Psychology* (New York: Wiley, 1967)

Attribution: Perceiving the Causes of Behavior (Morristown, New Jersey: General Learning Press, 1972)

Ingratiation: A Social Psychological Analysis (New York: Irvington Publishers, 1975)

Interpersonal Perception (New York: W. H. Freeman, 1990)

Louis Landa

Department of English

BY CALHOUN WINTON

Several years ago, soon after Louis Landa's death in March, 1989, I was invited by the editor of a scholarly newsletter to write a memoir of him. I begged off, on the grounds that I felt close to him and that his death was too recent. That may still be the case. One's relationship with Louis was, I think for most of the graduate students whose work he supervised, difficult to define and express.

On the one hand, he appeared as the skeptical but unyielding defender of such Enlightenment values as reason, balance, and common sense: the somewhat austere prose stylist who once returned to me a research paper in which I had used the term "infighting" when describing an eighteenth-century political controversy. Written in the margin was his advice, "Eschew the jargon of the prize ring." Landa's own work, including what is still the basic treatment of its subject matter, *Swift and the Church of Ireland*, embodied a kind of prose lucidness that escaped banality by an underlay of irony, Addisonian, perhaps, rather than Swiftian. It was an irony exercised in conversation as well: the late Bob Towers, one of his students, told me that he congratulated Louis for a narrow escape from a deadly illness, late in his life. "Well, yes," Louis said, deadpan, "If it hadn't been for the timely ministrations of my dear wife, I'd be in Heaven now."

As the remark indicates, his wife Hazel, who survives him, was always a presence in their relationship when we, his students, knew him and an important element in another and apparently contradictory aspect of his character: his warmth and generosity of spirit. Dinner at the Landas' house, entirely produced and served by Hazel — no one was allowed in her kitchen — was a festive occasion without the incessant intellectual competitiveness characteristic of too many academic meals. Drinks before a wood fire in the living room with Hazel's delicious hors d'oeuvres; no more guests than could be seated comfortably around the dining table; fine food and claret and amusing conversation: a stress-free environment, in the modern jargon which Louis would eschew.

Louis Landa came from a small town in south Texas, Hallettsville in Lavaca County, and it may be that this environment produced a certain simplicity of manners in him, and a reduced sense of expectations. To former students, now nervous assistant professors, who complained that their latest book had been inadequately reviewed, he would counsel, "A good book will make its own way." He was born in 1901: his was Texas before the oil boom, of course; an agricultural state in the midst of the long, world-wide agricultural depression. Low key. Baseball was the preferred recreation and Louis never lost his love for the game.

He graduated from the University of Texas in 1923 and received an M.A. at Columbia in 1926, serving as an instructor in the meantime at Oklahoma A. and M. He and Hazel Schaeffer, of Corpus Christi, were married in 1928 and spent their honeymoon year in a second-floor flat in Annapolis, overlooking the campus of St. John's College where he taught. A few years ago at their request I located the dwelling and reported that it was still in use and in good trim. During the Depression years Louis studied at the University of Chicago, teaching there for ten years as an instructor of English.

Ten Depression years as an instructor, but this was a university in the full tide of its greatness, with a humanities faculty of almost unparalleled vitality: Ronald Crane, Elder Olson, Richard McKeon, Norman Maclean, W. R. Keast, George Sherburn, Bernard Weinberg, to name only some of the literary scholars there at the time. Although not strictly speaking a "Chicago Aristotelian" himself, Landa was profoundly influenced by them, personally and professionally. Sherburn directed his dissertation on Swift. Ronald Crane had established the annual bibliography of eighteenth-century literature in 1926, "English Literature 1660–1800," published in the summer issue of *Philological Quarterly*, and Landa became its co-editor in 1942. This was one of the earliest annual bibliographies of literature and a distinctive feature was the evaluation of works published, succinct but decisive. If the scholarship, or the prose style, was defective the editors called attention to the defects. There is no doubt that the annual bibliography has been a strong and healthy influence in the rebirth during the last sixty years of literary scholarship on the eighteenth century; it has continued to the present as *The Eighteenth Century: A Current Bibliography*. I have often thought that there was a distinct carryover into Landa's own career of this habit of concise evaluation. Certainly he exercised it in commenting on his graduate students' work. The *Bibliography* also of course required exceptionally broad and deep reading in the field.

While the *Bibliography* reinforced Landa's scholarly specialization, Robert Hutchins' university curriculum worked in the opposite direction, emphasizing breadth of knowledge and continuing faculty-student dialogue. The combination of specialization and Great Books teaching experience must have seemed attractive to the small English Department at Princeton. Landa had been promoted to assistant professor at Chicago in 1942 and in the spring of 1946 Professor Gordon Gerould, then chairman of the Princeton department, recommended that President Harold W. Dodds offer him an appointment as associate professor. "After prolonged investigation of scholars in the field of the Eighteenth Century," Gerould wrote, "we believe that Professor Landa is the best man who could be found to carry on and stimulate the study of that period. . . . We know him to be an excellent teacher on both the undergraduate and the graduate levels, and to have wide interests that will make him useful in all our departmental work. . . . His vigorous and delightful personality will make him a welcome addition to our group."[1] Gerould's judgment proved accurate on all counts. Letters from Herbert Davis, then president of Smith and a leading Jonathan Swift scholar, and from D. Nichol Smith of Oxford, doyen of British scholars in eighteenth-century studies, recommended him enthusiastically. President Dodds offered him the appointment and Landa came to Princeton in the fall of 1946.

He was in residence here for the rest of his life, except for occasional leaves, including two appointments as a Guggenheim Fellow. His graduate course was not, as I recall, particularly distinctive: heavy reading assignments, oral reports by students, additions and corrections to the reports by Landa, who in my day, before the risks were known, often smoked a cigar. The course was, that is, conducted like most of the other demanding graduate courses in the department, though entirely unlike those of his former Chicago colleague Gerald Bentley, described in this volume by Suzanne Gossett.

Landa's greatness as a teacher and mentor was in guiding gradu-

[1] Letter of April 16, 1946, Louis Landa's faculty file, Princeton University Archives. Other factual materials are also derived from this file.

ate students to topics for their dissertation that would be both feasible and productive of publication, if the student wished to publish. If a report involved an author whose work you found interesting, you could ask Landa and he would summon two or three possible dissertation topics out of the air, as it were. Or rather out of his encyclopedic knowledge of the field, of course. Graduate students, at least in literary studies, are characteristically unfocused, and Landa's was a great gift.

As for the research and writing itself, you were essentially on your own, though Landa was always available for consultation and most conscientious about returning drafts quickly, suitably annotated. This, too, was a gift for the hard-pressed graduate student and by no means the universal practice, in my observation. He was very busy, with his teaching — always both graduate and undergraduate courses at Princeton — and with the annual *Bibliography* until 1955, and with his own work. *Swift and the Church of Ireland* appeared in 1954 and his textbook edition, *Gulliver's Travels and Other Writings*, which is still in print and widely used, in 1960. Much of his most important work appeared in essays and articles, a convenient selection of which was published by the Princeton University Press in 1980, *Essays in Eighteenth-Century English Literature.* Meanwhile his graduate students were going out to careers in academic life. John Loftis and Keith Stewart were, I believe, the first two, in 1948 and 1949: Loftis to Stanford and Stewart to Cincinnati. James King at McMaster was, I believe, the last, in 1969. There were many others and they have been as a group, I think, remarkably productive teachers, scholars, and academic administrators. A *Festschrift* of original essays, largely written by his former students and edited by three of them, was presented to him in 1970. As the years passed the students would send him copies of their books, and Louis carefully placed them in a bookshelf on the left side of the living-room fireplace. By the end of his life the collection extended from floor to ceiling.

That is the way I like to remember him, sitting there before the fire, surrounded by his books.

READING LIST

Swift and the Church of Ireland (Oxford: Clarendon Press, 1954)

Editor: Jonathan Swift, *Gulliver's Travels and Other Writings*, (Boston: Houghton Mifflin, 1960)

Essays in Eighteenth-Century English Literature (Princeton: Princeton University Press, 1980)

The Agustan Milieu: Essays Presented to Louis A. Landa, ed. Henry Knight Miller, Eric Rothstein, and G. S. Rousseau (Oxford: Clarendon Press, 1970)

Leon Lapidus

Department of Chemical Engineering

BY ERNEST F. JOHNSON[1]

Leon Lapidus first came to Princeton in 1951 as a research associate in Professor Richard H. Wilhelm's program in chemical sciences at what is now the Forrestal Campus. His previous training included two degrees from Syracuse University in the city of his birth, a doctorate from the University of Minnesota, and a post-doctoral fellowship at the Massachusetts Institute of Technology.

At Minnesota he was the first of a long line of outstanding scholars produced under the tutelage of Neal R. Amundson, a front-rank chemical engineer and mathematician, who set much

[1] This memoir is based in large measure on the Memorial Resolution for Leon Lapidus prepared on May 31, 1977, by Ernest F. Johnson, William R. Schowalter, and Richard R. Toner.

of the tone of chemical engineering research from the late 1940s and into the 1990s.

In 1953 Lapidus joined the chemical engineering faculty at Princeton as an assistant professor. He was promoted to associate professor in 1958, professor in 1962, and in 1970 he was appointed the Class of 1943 University Professor. From 1968 until his untimely death on May 5, 1977, he served as chairman of the Department of Chemical Engineering. Throughout most of his tenure as chairman he was the elected member from Division IV on the Faculty Advisory Committee on Appointments and Advancements, making his membership on that important committee one of the longest in the history of the University.

Professor Lapidus was a teacher-scholar in the best Princeton tradition; he was also a skilled administrator. Indeed, a colleague in another department commented that Leon was the ultimate exemplar of the ideal all-round faculty member because his research productivity increased even as his administrative responsibilities grew.

With a rare gift of being able to communicate often abstruse and difficult material clearly and enthusiastically, Professor Lapidus gained a wide reputation as lecturer, a reputation that was reflected in the student ratings of his courses. His contributions to teaching were not limited to classroom instruction, however, inasmuch as he was the author or co-author of four major textbooks. In collaboration with his first mentor, Neal Amundson, he edited the definitive work on chemical reactor theory, written as a memorial to Richard H. Wilhelm. In particular his books on digital computation and on optimal control theory had widespread use as teaching tools. The book on chemical reactor theory was published during the week of his death.

It is ironic that both Wilhelm and Lapidus succumbed to heart attacks during their tenures as departmental chairman. Their lives had other parallels. Both served long terms as directors of graduate studies for the department, and both served relatively long terms as chairmen. Both attracted outstanding graduate students to their tutelage, who, in turn, have made distinguished contributions to the profession in academic and industrial circles. And both won all the major awards available to them.

In 1955, just two years after joining the Princeton faculty, Professor Lapidus introduced a new course in numerical methods of computation. This course marked the beginning of his professional concentration on the application of numerical analysis and computer techniques to problems in chemical engineering. Over the years he extended the breadth and depth of this application with special attention to problems in the simulation, control and optimization of chemical process systems. More than fifty graduate students participated in this work, and many of these students have occupied important positions on major faculties throughout the world, including the chairmanships at the University of Texas, the California Institute of Technology, and Northwestern University, for example. The fruits of this work, comprising five books and some 135 articles in scientific journals, have had a major impact on the way engineers in general, and chemical engineers in particular, approach problems.

Many awards went to Professor Lapidus for his prodigious scholarship. He won the Professional Progress Award and the William H. Walker Award of the American Institute of Chemical Engineers. In 1976 he was elected to the National Academy of Engineering, the third member of the Princeton faculty so honored. He was Chemical Engineering Lecturer for the American Society for Engineering Education, Reilly Lecturer for the University of Notre Dame, Lacey Lecturer for the California Institute of Technology, Mason Lecturer for Stanford University, Distinguished Lecturer for the University of Michigan, and Organization of American States Lecturer at La Plata University in Argentina.

Widely sought as a consultant to industry, Professor Lapidus also served on the editorial advisory boards of the *Journal of the American Institute of Chemical Engineers*, the *International Journal of Systems Science*, the *Chemical Engineering Journal*, and he was editor of Control Series, Blaisdell Publishing Company. He was also a member of the Visiting Committee to the Department of Chemical Engineering at the California Institute of Technology.

Few members of the Princeton faculty were as avid boosters of Princeton athletics as was Leon Lapidus. Though he never missed a home basketball game, he was no mere spectator. He was an active player and promoter of tennis, especially among young people. At the time of his death he was president of the New Jersey Tennis Association. Furthermore, he transmitted his enthusiasm for the game to his children, Mary and Jay, both of whom he coached to tournament calibre and national ranking. Jay, who entered Princeton in the fall after his father's death, had become by his junior year the strongest tennis player in the history of the University.

A devoted husband and father, Leon Lapidus most of all appeared to enjoy those activities which included his close-knit, immediate family circle: his wife, the former Elizabeth Ralmes, whom he met and married when he was in graduate school in Minneapolis, and his children Mary Ralmes and Jon Jay.

On May 5, 1977, while interviewing a prospective coach for women's tennis at Princeton, Leon Lapidus suffered a fatal heart attack in his office. Thanks to the generosity of his many friends and associates a gracious social lounge for the Department of Chemical Engineering was dedicated in the main floor of the Engineering Quadrangle in his honor.

The outstanding productivity and achievement of Leon Lapidus were the result of an unrelenting diligence and an extraordinary efficiency. He came to his office daily before 8:00 a.m. to meet with students and faculty colleagues and to teach his courses, invariably carrying a full teaching load, despite the demands of the chairmanship and his University committee duties. Shortly after 10:00 a.m. he was on the tennis court playing with his wife and occasionally others. Afternoons and evenings were spent at home working, preparing the small pile of neatly handwritten material to be typewritten the following day.

READING LIST

With H. A. Deans: "A Computational Model for Predicting and Correlating the Behavior of Fixed-Bed Reactors," *American Institute of Chemical Engineers Journal* 6 (1960): 656

Digital Computation for Chemical Engineers (New York: McGraw-Hill Book Co., 1962)

With R. Luus: *Optimal Control of Engineering Processes* (New York: Blaisdell Publishing Co., 1967)

With J. H. Seinfeld: *Numerical Solution of Ordinary Differential Equations* (New York: Academic Press, 1971)

With N. R. Amundson, editors: *Chemical Reactor Theory: A Review Dedicated to the Memory of Richard H. Wilhelm* (Englewood Cliffs, New Jersey: Prentice-Hall, 1977)

Solomon Lefschetz

Department of Mathematics

BY FRANKLIN P. PETERSON

Solomon Lefschetz was born in Moscow on September 3, 1884. Shortly thereafter his parents moved to Paris, where he grew up and got his education. Even though very interested in mathematics, he feared that as a foreigner he could not pursue a career in mathematics in France. He took a degree in mechanical engineering instead, and after graduation in 1905, came to the United States to study and work at the Westinghouse Company in Pittsburgh. In November 1907 he was the victim of a testing accident and lost both of his hands. Soon after, he lost interest in his engineering work and decided to return to his real love, mathematics.

He entered the graduate school at Clark University in Worcester, Massachusetts, in the fall of 1910 and received his Ph.D. in June 1911. While at Clark he met another student of mathematics, Alice Berg Hayes, who would later become his wife. After his studies at Clark he spent thirteen years in the Midwest, two at Nebraska and eleven at Kansas, before coming to Princeton in 1924. He did much of his early pioneering mathematical work while in Kansas, where he thrived on the mathematical isolation prevalent in the Midwest at that time.

In 1924 he came to Princeton as a visitor, but soon he received a permanent appointment. From 1933 to 1953 he was Henry Burchard Fine Research Professor, and from 1945 until his retirement in 1953 he was chairman of the Department of Mathematics. He died in 1972.

The loss of both hands would handicap most people. But Lefschetz, with the constant help of his wife, met and overcame his loss. He not only made fundamental and important contributions to his first field, algebraic geometry, but he then made similar contributions to algebraic topology and showed that the study of topology was important to the understanding of algebraic geometry. Later, when he was over sixty, he made important contributions to a third field, differential equations, and made applications to control theory. (The "Biographical Memoir" written by P. Griffiths, D. Spencer, and G. Whitehead provides an excellent description of his mathematical ideas and his influence on his field.[1]) Solomon Lefschetz was a complete, great mathematician.

I came to graduate school at Princeton in the fall of 1952 and wrote my Ph.D. thesis under Norman Steenrod, who was one of Lefschetz's best students. What follows are various recollections of Lefschetz which I hope will give the reader some feeling for the man.

Lefschetz was not only a very original and creative mathematician, he also had a strong personality. He was, in short, a "character." Here is a ditty that was around when I was a graduate student:

[1] Phillip Griffiths, Donald Spencer, and George Whitehead, "Solomon Lefschetz, 1884–1972," *Biographical Memoirs of the National Academy of Sciences*, vol. 61, pp. 271–313.

Here's to Lefschetz, Solomon L.,
Irrepressible as Hell,
And when he's laid beneath the sod
He'll then begin to heckle God.

He liked to challenge speakers in seminars. When I was a graduate student, Lefschetz, already retired, would usually ask a question during the first five minutes of the lecture in the topology seminar. Then he would invariably fall asleep. What continued to amaze the audience was that when he was awakened by the applause at the end of the lecture, he always asked a relevant question.

Lefschetz was fluent in a number of languages, and sometimes translated lectures. Once he was asked to translate a half-hour of Russian and many formulas. He did this easily by saying, "You try to get the final formula from the first one."

I remember an incident at a very large topology conference in Mexico City. A speaker had gone way past his time with a not very interesting talk. The person in charge was W. Hurewicz, a famous algebraic topologist. When the speaker was still talking ten minutes over his allotted time, Hurewicz stood up to signal to him that his time was up — to no effect. A few minutes later, Hurewicz took a step towards the lecturer — and then two or three more. At this point, to the delight of the audience, Lefschetz got up and pushed Hurewicz towards the lecturer. This, at last, had the required effect.

Lefschetz had very high standards for himself, and he applied them to people he hired. He made the Princeton Mathematics Department the best by hiring top people. I suspect he was quite ruthless in dealing with deans, presidents, and faculty, but the reward was in the outstanding quality of the department he built. Times have changed in the last fifty years, and it would probably be difficult to build such a department now using his methods. He believed that a second-rate department which hires its own Ph.D.s soon becomes third rate. When asked why Princeton hired *its* own, he said that when you are at the top, there was nothing else you *could* do.

Lefschetz hunted for top-quality graduate students wherever he went and wherever they could be found. He visited Mexico, for example, and a sequence of fine graduate students began coming to Princeton, starting with José Adem, who later began a very successful mathematical center in Mexico City.

When Lefschetz proved his major results in algebraic geometry, the standards of rigor in that field were much lower than we expect today. It was said that he never stated an incorrect theorem and never gave a correct proof. This gives some of the flavor of the times. When two famous Princeton faculty members, Kunihiko Kodaira and Donald Clayton Spencer, told Lefschetz that they had finally given a rigorous proof of one of his major theorems, he said, "You babies! I knew that twenty years ago!"

Mathematicians will appreciate another example of his lack of rigor: When I was a first-year graduate student, Lefschetz gave a course of lectures on Riemann surfaces. "I must define a Hausdorff space," Lefschetz said in one of them. "Now, what are the axioms? Oh yes, I remember: every point has a neighborhood and every neighborhood has a point." As a careful, literal-minded, young graduate student, I was shocked. As I soon found out, however, this was a wonderful course.

Lefschetz did not hesitate to frighten as well as to confound students. In the first week I was at Princeton, he met with newly arrived graduate students. He asked each of us to look at the person to his right and then at the one to his left. He told us that only one of the three of us would become a real research mathematician. My companions and I took his remark to heart.

There was at the same time a lenient side to his character. For example, there is the story of my French exam. Like many of my fellow students, my knowledge came from reading Bourbaki with a dictionary for a few weeks and thinking I knew something. (Bourbaki's books,[2] popular then, were in very clear French and written for non-expert French speakers). The thing to do was to

[2] Including Nicolas Bourbaki, pseud., *Algèbre* (Paris: Hermann, 1947–); *Éléments d'histoire des mathématiques* (Paris: Hermann, 1960); *Théorie des*

ask Professor William Feller to administer the French exam, because he would ask you to pick out a book in French from his bookcase, and if you picked out Bourbaki, he automatically passed you. Unfortunately, he was on leave when I needed to take my exam. I asked Professor Ralph Fox. He gave me something to translate which I couldn't read. I flunked, and Fox told me to try Lefschetz instead. This worked well. I passed, and I saw the other side of Lefschetz. The French exam was the beginning of a friendship between a young graduate student and a famous 60-year-old mathematician. It lasted until his death.

Solomon Lefschetz was a great mathematician and an interesting person. He had a wonderful influence on his own students and his "grand-students." His influence on mathematics and on Princeton University was very strong and very positive. It was a great pleasure to know him.

READING LIST

Algebraic Topology (New York: American Mathematical Society, 1942)

Lectures on Differential Equations (Princeton: Princeton University Press, and London: H. Melford, Oxford University Press, 1946)

Introduction to Topology (Princeton: Princeton University Press, 1949)

Differential Equations: Geometric Theory . . . (New York: Interscience Publishers, 1957)

Luther Pfahler Eisenhart, 1876–1965: A Biographical Memoir (New York: Published for the National Academy of Sciences by Columbia University Press, 1969)

Selected Papers (New York: Chelsea Publishing Co., 1971)

ensembles (Paris: Hermann, 1939); and *Topologie générale* (Paris: Hermann, 1940–1953).

William Arthur Lewis

Department of Economics and The Woodrow Wilson School of Public and International Affairs

BY JOHN P. LEWIS

In 1961 the idea of wooing William Arthur Lewis, then vice-chancellor of the University of the West Indies in Jamaica, to join the Woodrow Wilson School and the Department of Economics began to be mooted among the elders in those jurisdictions. Gardner Patterson, Director of the Wilson School (as its leader then was called) pressed the case; Arthur and Gladys Lewis visited in March 1962, and on August 26, the Sunday papers announced that Lewis would join the Princeton faculty a year hence. Lewis was arguably the most distinguished of the five outstanding appointments to the Wilson School and adjoining disciplinary faculties that the great gift from the new "X"

Foundation (later to be revealed as the Robertson Foundation) supported that year.

Two things were notable about the reporting of the appointment. The University was not bashful about the eminence of the appointee. In the press release it used the same language employed in the document seeking his U.S. visa: "Dr. Lewis has been recognized as the world's most eminent authority in the interdisciplinary field of economic growth and political and social change in the emerging countries." At the same time the headlines in such places as Indianapolis and Seattle read, "Princeton Names Negro Professor." Arthur Lewis was the first black appointed to tenured full rank at the University.

Arthur's eminence was as a development economist, but when he became a credentialed economist (London School of Economics, undergraduate degree, one of two firsts in his class in 1937, Ph.D. as soon as 1940) there *was* no field of development economics. He helped create it. But meanwhile, along with United Kingdom government work during the war, he taught and wrote general economics at the London School of Economics. Three books — a well-regarded global, mostly macroeconomic, survey of the interwar period, a rigorous treatise on overhead costs, and *The Principles of Economic Planning* — all were published in 1949, the same year in which, at the age of 34, he moved to an endowed professorship at the University of Manchester.

As a native of a developing region (Lewis had been born in St. Lucia in the eastern Caribbean in 1915) his mind had been turning increasingly to the particular problems of poor countries trying to catch up with Western industrialization. That it had come into quick focus was revealed in 1951 when the United Nations, well ahead of academe, assembled five economists (one Chilean, one Indian, one Lebanese, one American, and Arthur Lewis) to produce a report, *Measures for the Economic Development of Under-Developed Countries*, which Arthur drafted.[1]

[1] New York: United Nations Department of Economic Affairs, 1951.

I shall return to the 1951 report because it links Arthur to another economist and the two of them all the way to 1979. But, first, this recollection of Lewis requires an initial reference to his 1954 article, "Economic Development with Unlimited Supplies of Labour" in the University of Manchester's economic journal, *The Manchester School.* This was not only Lewis' most important writing; most development economists consider it the single most influential article in the history of the field. It set forth what, ever since, has been known as the Lewis Model: In a poor country with a redundance of unskilled, presumably rural, labor (Arthur said he was thinking of India), workers could move to a modernizing, presumably industrializing and urban sector for some time without bidding up wages or reducing food supplies. Their augmentation of productivity would fuel the economy's growth engine by increasing the savings (and the investments) of "the savings classes."

The Lewis Model became so central to the conceptual architecture of development economics that, in the 1970s, when Lewis was recruited by the World Bank to give a lecture as one of the "pioneers" of development economics, he naturally harked back to the moment when he thought the great idea had first occurred to him. The story he told was about walking in Bangkok one morning in 1952. Years later, I was able to tell him that the essence of his 1954 model was already present in his 1951 United Nations "experts" report. He had simply forgotten his own intellectual evolution.

Although Lewis may have been the youngest of the five United Nations "experts," and his colleagues were distinguished (D. R. Gadgil, for example, was the leading Indian economist of the day), Arthur, quite clearly, was the leader of the group. To economists, it was amusing that his American colleague, Theodore Schultz, the outstanding agricultural specialist, got talked into joint-authoring a hypothesis that the marginal product of farmers could be zero. (That was heresy for a Chicago economist, and subsequently Schultz spent a good deal of time rebutting it.) That the two of them, Arthur Lewis and Theodore Schultz, were chosen to share the Nobel Prize in Economics in 1979 suggests, perhaps, that the Swedes have retained a lurking sense of humor despite their earnestness in administering the prizes.

Arthur was extremely productive during the 1950s, writing a seminal book, *The Theory of Economic Growth*, in 1955 and doing a great deal of real-world consulting in developing areas, particularly in the Gold Coast (now Ghana) in 1953 and 1957–1958. After coming to Princeton, he continued to devote as much time as possible to public service in the development field, but he was exceptionally conscientious about meeting classes and attending to the rest of his teaching. He was extremely good at the teaching, being widely regarded as one of the best Ph.D. thesis guides in the department.

In 1967 and 1968, Presidents Woods and McNamara of the World Bank collaborated on the appointment of a high-level commission to review the status of development and development policy. Arthur was a member of the select group that, aided by a strong staff, took on this task under the chairmanship of former Canadian prime minister Lester Pearson. The "Pearson Report" came out in the fall of 1969.[2] Early that winter, during my first year of deaning at the Wilson School, Arthur came to me and said that a new Caribbean Development Bank was being formed, that he had been asked to be its first president (nothing was more predictable), that he had laid down a set of conditions he was sure they wouldn't meet, that they had accepted all of them, and that he therefore needed to resign from Princeton. I said nonsense: we would give him a leave of absence — two years to start with — and were determined to get him back.

To our delight — Bill Bowen, the University's president-to-be at that point, had a big hand in persuading him — Arthur

[2] Lester B. Pearson et al., *Partners in Development: Report of the Commission on International Development* (New York: Praeger Paperbacks, 1969).

returned after three years of work setting the Caribbean Development Bank in motion. What he contributed to the launching of that institution was in no way merely cosmetic. He talked tough sense to his Caribbean peers about the realities, limitations, and potentialities of their economic and political predicament. He drove as well as presided over the establishment of an efficient, self-reliant, compassionate but accountable subregional development banking operation. I have just been associated with a Canada-centered review of the several regional development banks, and although the Caribbean Development Bank is much the smallest, arguably it has been the best so far. That record of achievement traces back, quite plainly, to the effects of Arthur's formative work.

Reference to the Caribbean Development Bank interlude also permits an anecdotal introduction to one of Lewis' great conceptual talents. This was a gift for coming up with big, simple, profoundly important ideas before they had occurred to many others. The Lewis Model was such an idea. In 1977 we got a clutch of others. They came in lectures that the Princeton University Press published in a short book entitled *The Evolution of the International Economic Order* in 1978. Early in the 1970s, while he was at the Caribbean Development Bank, Lewis had been invited to give the annual Wilson School lectures funded by Eliot and Elizabeth Janeway, but Arthur replied that he could not possibly do so at a time when, while preparing the lectures, he would lack access to a major research library. So he gave them in 1977 after he returned to Princeton, and after having had more than three years of renewed access to Firestone. His research work showed — although, as I say, the best product was a boldly simple set of ideas that so clarified listeners' and readers' thinking that it was almost embarrassing. But they were fresh ideas grounded in careful research.

There were three in the 1977 Janeway lectures. One was simply empirical: Whereas much development theorizing saw "ISI" (import-substitution industrialization) as the source of developing countries' foreign debt problems, actually it was the building of urban infrastructure (ports, railroads, urban transport, power, communications) that accounted for most foreign borrowing.

The other two big ideas were linked and central to his argument. What needed to be explained was the enormous gap between developed-country and developing-country (or "northern" and "southern") real incomes per capita. A proximate answer was the difference in productivities between the South and the Northwest ("North" as in North-South, "west" as in East-West). The geographic location and head start of the industrial revolution had been seen as the big difference. But, Lewis now pointed out, Great Britain's industrial revolution had been preceded by a revolutionary rise in agricultural productivity that raised the worth of farm work in Britain far above that in Bihar. The enhanced value of a man spread to the bulk of industrializing Britain. The urban-industrial breakthrough was rooted in agriculture. That was linked idea A. But why did the gap in income and output per capita between North and South persist for so long? That, said idea B, was because of segregated migration. The multitudes of Asia and Africa, except when they came as slaves, gained little access to white Northern areas of colonization, where the settlers imported British living standards or better. The "Southerners" from India, China, and elsewhere went mostly to the tropics and near-tropics, where they imported the real wages and living standards of Bihar. That, said Lewis, was the skeletal architecture of the past three centuries; it was only now beginning to break down.

Arthur was not easy to pigeonhole in disciplinary terms. He thought of himself as an economist's economist — and indeed he was, in terms of his mastery of and devotion to the historical body of economic thought. He certainly was a leader of and central to the department. And yet he was far more historical than was typical of late twentieth-century economists, including those at Princeton. And while he did meticulous and insightful work on statistical time series (a major work, *Growth and Fluctuations, 1870–1913*, appeared in 1978 and contained the research that underlay the 1977 lectures), Lewis was not a mathematical economist in the modern sense. Indeed, despite his unidisciplinary self-styling, Arthur was embraced by Princeton political scientists as one of the few students of genuine political economy. His abundance of real-world experience had left its mark.

Let me fold the rest of these comments into the proposition that Arthur was superbly qualified to be the first senior black on the Princeton faculty. In the first place, he had a comfortable, warranted self-confidence. He enjoyed and appreciated his honors — his knighthood in 1963, the Princeton honorary degree in 1988 five years after retirement, some thirty other honorary degrees, his presidency of the American Economic Association in 1983, above all, the Nobel Prize — but he did not need them for reassurance. As he would tell Princeton minority students, Arthur had grown up and worked in cultures where his was the majority race. At any rate (he would say privately) his mother had taught him that "We can do anything they can do" — and he had found this to be the case. He had excelled at every turn.

When preparing to go to India for the first time, I met Lewis at the United Nations in early 1959 while he was working as No. 2 to Paul Hoffman in what would become the UNDP (United Nations Development Program). He was scathing in his comments about Indian economists. What took the edge off that was his equally scathing remarks about American economists. What took the edge off both was his gaiety. He had an infectious giggle. Later one learned that, for all his dutifulness to issues and obligations, he had a puckish streak. At his retirement dinner in 1983 he stood up, said he had been told he must speak for ten minutes, launched almost immediately into a detailed recollection of a meeting of the Pearson Commission with the Pope in 1969, looked at his watch, announced, "The ten minutes are up," and sat down.

Arthur's self-confidence never intruded on one's affection for him. He was an exceptionally light heavyweight. But one cannot testify confidently about his inborn immunity to pomposity, because any such impulse was so deftly and decisively nipped by his wife, Gladys. Gladys Jacobs Lewis deserves an article of her own.

She enhanced Arthur's life and work in a myriad of ways, and was a valued member of the Princeton community in her own right. Together they cherished their fine daughters, Elizabeth and Barbara.

Arthur's blackness was paradoxical. He never lost sight of it himself, and never ceased to be a role model to black and other minority students. In a sense he was distant from them because of sheer elevation. But there was no stand-offishness. He worked at analyzing their separate problems, counseling them, speaking to them in small and larger groups. His last book — lectures at Harvard — was a labor of love on a racial theme.

The real irony was with Lewis' professional colleagues. Some of the press thought he had been hired so that the University could make a racial statement. His colleagues completely forgot that. He was simply the best. For most of them, long before the end of his tenure, Arthur Lewis was the leading social scientist in the University.

Lewis died in June 1991 and, after a state funeral, was buried in his native St. Lucia. His great friend and admirer, Dean Donald Stokes, spoke for the University. Among Sir Arthur Lewis' strongest perceived loyalties were those to his family, to economics, to the cause of economic development, to welfare-enhancing government interventions, to blacks, and to the Caribbean. It was clear that, long since, Princeton had been added to that list, and it is therefore appropriate that his papers are to be found among the Public Policy Papers at Princeton's Seeley G. Mudd Manuscript Library.

READING LIST

Industrial Development in the Caribbean (Trinidad: Guardian Commercial Printers, 1950)

"Economic Development with Unlimited Supplies of Labour," *The Manchester School*, May 1954

The Theory of Economic Growth (London: Allen & Unwin, 1955)

Development Planning: The Essentials of Economic Policy (New York: Harper, 1966)

Aspects of Tropical Trade. Wicksell Lectures (Stockholm: Almquist & Wiksell, 1969)

The Evolution of the International Economic Order. The Eliot Janeway Lectures on Historical Economics in Honor of Joseph Schumpeter (Princeton: Princeton University Press, 1978)

Growth and Fluctuations, 1870–1913 (London: Allen & Unwin, 1978)

William Wirt Lockwood

Department of Politics and The Woodrow Wilson School of Public and International Affairs

BY MARIUS B. JANSEN

When William Lockwood accepted a position as Assistant Director of the Woodrow Wilson School in 1946, he wrote with anticipation of two aspects that had made the position attractive to him: The University was giving its full backing to a new, experimental curriculum in public and international affairs, and "there will be opportunities to develop instruction in the Far Eastern field, where Princeton now has no one." From then until his retirement in 1971 as Professor of Politics and International Affairs, Lockwood was tireless in efforts to implement that "experimental curriculum." He instinctively saw what was needed to shape the program's most distinctive form, the policy conference, into an instrument that helped to vitalize the education of majors in public and international affairs over the decades that followed. He was also central in developing instruction in Asian studies. By the time of his retirement, Princeton's programs had produced hundreds of students whose education had prepared them for encounter with Asia at many levels. Many students in his Politics 313 could testify, as has Don Oberdorfer, principal diplomatic correspondent of the *Washington Post* for seventeen years, that "Bill Lockwood gave me a running start in Asian affairs, a fascination that provided the focus of my professional life."

Everything in Bill's earlier life came together to provide the breadth of experience and preparation that made his role successful. It began with a rock-firm strength of character and values. Lockwood was born in Shanghai in 1906, son of the general secretary of the Young Men's Christian Association there. His family still retains his copy books and essays done at the Shanghai American School. In these and in the careful records he kept on his travel "home" to Indiana, where he graduated Phi Beta Kappa from DePauw University in 1927, one senses the discipline and order that went into the mature man as person and as scholar. "He that ruleth his own spirit is greater than he that taketh a city," reads one sentence in a fifth-grader's hand, while another reminds the young scholar that "Fine manners are the mantle of fine minds." His friends and his students would long remember, in the words of one colleague, the "combination of urbanity with fineness of discrimination and principle" that distinguished Bill.

After graduating from DePauw, Lockwood went on to Harvard for work in economics. He began with plans to work on the balance of payments between the United States and China, but as the Japanese invasion distorted Chinese policies and statistics he found himself increasingly drawn into work on Japan. He drew on this for his M.A. thesis, which he offered on Japan's foreign trade since 1886. This marked the beginning of a career of specialization on the economic history of Japan, work that would see fruition a quarter-century later in his classic work, *The Economic Development of Japan.*

The intervening years, with the discipline of America's Great Depression and World War II, were a period of preparation that provided variety and breadth far beyond that available to later specialists. From 1929 to 1934 Bill taught economics at Bowdoin, and his marriage there to the vivacious and talented Virginia Chapman made for adventure and joy in each successive stage of his life. In 1934 he left Bowdoin to take up a research position with a broadly based organization that pioneered scholarship on contemporary East Asia, the American Committee of the Institute of Pacific Relations in New York. His Shanghai experience had already made Bill a charter member of a close-knit society of Old China Hands, and the new position brought him into contact with academic, government, and business advocates of better relations with Asia through many conferences and symposia. In 1940–1941 he advanced to Secretary of the IPR.

This was of short duration, for the outbreak of war in the Pacific found the government eager for Lockwood's services. He was consultant for the State Department's Studies of Relief and Postwar Rehabilitation of China before moving to the Office of Strategic Services, in a role that soon took him to China, where he served as staff officer with the rank of major for General Chennault's Fourteenth Air Force at Kweilin. In 1944–1945 he served the State Department as Assistant Chief, Division of Japanese and Korean Economic Affairs. By the time Lockwood took up his work at Princeton at the age of forty he was recognized as an important member of the small group of American Asia specialists, although he had not yet begun the book with which his name will always be associated.

Bill was a generalist. His departmental home was the Department of Politics, but he had only limited interest in the specializations that began to divide that discipline. His graduate training was in economics, but the increasingly mathematical bent of postwar economics confirmed his preference for economic history.

His area of interest was Asia and particularly East Asia, but aside from some of the language he had absorbed in childhood, he had little Chinese and less Japanese at a time when country and language specializations became increasingly demanding in major centers of learning. But he was not at all possessive about any part of his competence; he welcomed new abilities and approaches as they came along, though he also viewed them with skeptical detachment if they veered too far from the framework he had settled upon. Nor was he possessive about his field, or fired by ambitions to be an institution-builder instead of an architect. He left details of program building to others.

What Bill wanted to do was to concentrate his efforts on the preparation of a generation of students for the requirements of the postwar era, students who could combine something of his range and balance. The Woodrow Wilson School was his natural home, and there he was the first of Princeton's East Asia specialists. All of his experience came into play in his teaching. School conferences and task-force groups profited from his ability to bring in people he had encountered in the years before he came to Princeton, contacts that he maintained and widened in stays in Asia during academic leaves. In addition to Bill's School conferences and seminars, many more learned about Asia from his carefully organized lectures in Politics 313.

Lockwood followed his students' careers closely, and continued to help them long after they left Princeton. Oberdorfer recalls that Lockwood's "superb network of contacts opened doors for me everywhere and provided help when I needed it." Professor Thomas Havens of the University of California (Berkeley) remembers that "my very first Japan course was Politics 313. During that semester Bill suggested, in his low-key way, that I think about 'teaching English that summer at the Osawa Company in Tokyo', as others had done . . . Bill went so far as to suggest inexpensive ways to fly to Tokyo via Guam and Taipei." Havens went, and a career in Japanese history followed. "In many ways," he says, "I owe Bill and Yoshio Osawa '25, my father's classmate at both Lawrenceville and Princeton, my start in Japan." Charles Stevens, whose career in law would later lead to lengthy periods of work and residence in Hong Kong and Tokyo, remembered how, years before, "his introductions were wonderful, often far over the head of the lowly students (like me) who followed them up." Many others could tell similar stories showing how, as Oberdorfer puts it, "Bill's erudition, his deep knowledge and above all his love for Asian cultures and people inspired me as I began my career."

Lockwood was also an architect of East Asian studies nationally. His background, his experience, and his judgment made him someone to whom people turned for counsel. He was often a consultant for the Ford Foundation and travelled throughout Asia to watch its new programs in operation. He helped organize the "country" committees by which the Social Science Research Council structured foundation support for area studies. As director and then as president of the Association for Asian Studies he continued his oversight of what had by then become a burgeoning national effort. Professor John Fairbank of Harvard University predicted that "any future research on the history of United States East Asian Studies will find Bill part of the inner core."

Lockwood's writing, particularly his shorter pieces, are notable for the breadth and measure of his comparative evaluations. Adam Smith's *Wealth of Nations* is examined with Asian economic history in mind, and Japan is compared with India. At the time of his death he was working on a study of the relationship between education and development. There was a catholicism of interest, and before Firestone Library shifted from cards to bar codes library borrowers could encounter Bill's name on signout cards with astonishing frequency.

Lockwood could be found wherever good judgment and breadth of experience could serve the growth of interest in Asia. During his years as member of its editorial board, Princeton University Press became known for the quality and authority of its books on Asia and especially Japan. As Havens' story of his summer teaching opportunity in Japan shows, Bill also took close interest in the work of Princeton-in-Asia. That small foundation began the postwar period by sponsoring a handful of student language teachers for summers in Taiwan or Japan; today it selects and assigns close to one hundred students, about half of them from Princeton, for year-long internships throughout Asia. Bill was a valued contributor to discussion and study groups at the Council on Foreign Relations and frequently attended University Seminars at Columbia University.

As founding father of the study of Japanese economic history in the United States, Lockwood played a particularly important leadership role. Scholars who later came to hold sharply different interpretations of Japan's political economy held him in equally high esteem. Of his direction of a conference dealing with the role of the state in Japan's economic development, Professor Hugh Patrick of Columbia later wrote that "Bill's intellectual and personal style brought the field together, rather than splitting it into hostile camps. Instead of trying to score debating points, he quite simply sought truth and wisdom. Very quietly, he became a model to emulate. His wide-ranging interests, his quizzical countenance with cocked eye, his good humor, his deep concern for learning — all these were reflected in his leadership of that conference." Bill's students and colleagues will recognize in this description his quiet but masterful direction of preceptorial and seminar discussions.

Bill's major work, *The Economic History of Japan*, remains a landmark in Japanese studies. It was the first comprehensive economic history of modern Japan in a Western language. In Henry Rosovsky's words, "most students of this subject will begin with Bill's book, and if they remain with Japan they will go back to it again and again." As is often the case with influential Western books about Japan, the book has enjoyed wide readership in Japan and influenced study there as well.

A glance at what was available before shows how Bill moved the field. During the 1930s, authors had tended to see Japan through the disorder produced by Japanese militarism and aggression, and they saw its expansion dictated by an economy built for war, manned by underpaid workers who were unable to afford the products of their labors. The result was a Japan brought, by economic necessity, to inflict its products and ultimately its soldiers on its neighbors.

Lockwood saw different things. As Rosovsky put it at the time of Bill's death, "Bill, in his normal low-keyed manner, managed to dispose of most of the oversimplified theories concerning Japan's economic success . . . and drew for us a much more complex and realistic picture that was short on slogans and long on truth." The Lockwood book stressed the role of private initiative. He warned that it was easy to exaggerate the role of the state because it was so visible. "Big and dramatic innovations like railways and great banks and holding companies," he wrote, might provide the scaffolding, "but the structure itself was built, brick upon brick, by myriads of individuals and experiments and commitments."

The same balance characterizes a perceptive chapter Lockwood entitled "Japan's New Capitalism" in a conference volume he edited in 1965, *The State and Economic Enterprise in Japan.* In the three decades since it was written the growth of Japan's economy has, of course, changed the picture profoundly; the calculated hesitation about future growth that characterized Japanese writing in those years is reflected in what now seem rather somber assessments. But the merit of the chapter, and of the scholar who produced it, is its measured willingness to consider and discuss alternative, frequently wide-ranging differences. The question of state participation in Japanese economic planning and direction has now become an issue on which scholarly analysts divide sharply, but Bill's contribution remains a splendid place to begin in thinking about these issues. It serves also to remind us how important his example and person, and his quiet but incisive questions, made him to all those who have continued the work he began.

READING LIST

Trade and Trade Rivalry between the United States and Japan (New York: American Council, Institute of Pacific Relations, 1936)

The Economic Development of Japan: Growth and Structural Change, 1868–1938 (Princeton: Princeton University Press, 1954)

"Economic and Political Modernization: Japan," Robert E. Ward and Dankwart A. Rustow, eds., *Political Modernization in Japan and Turkey* (Princeton: Princeton University Press, 1964), pp. 117–145

Editor: *The State and Economic Enterprise in Japan: Essays in the Political Economy of Growth* (Princeton: Princeton University Press, 1965)

Robert Helmer MacArthur

Department of Biology

BY EDWARD C. COX

I arrived at Princeton in the summer of 1967 as a member of the Biology Department and the new Program in Biochemistry. Most of the members of the Biology Department were away for the summer. I had not yet met my chairman in Biology, John Bonner, but when he returned from Margaree Harbor for the fall term, one of the first things he did was introduce me to Robert MacArthur, the Class of 1877 Professor of Zoology. Robert had recently moved to Princeton from the University of Pennsylvania. John showed me into Robert's office, which was a very large empty space on the second floor of Guyot Hall, where the Biology library is now housed. It was clear to me that Robert did not set much store by material surroundings. He sat at a bare table somewhere near the center of this almost empty room. In one corner there was an old wooden case containing drawers of stuffed mouse skins he had collected as a boy in Ontario. He shyly told me he could never do that again. Killing and stuffing animals, he said, was too high a price to pay for the progress of his kind of science. He asked me several questions about my work on the biochemical basis of mutation, and then I set off to meet the eccentric Egbert G. Leigh, Class of 1962, housed on the next floor.

MacArthur had just published *The Theory of Island Biogeography* with E. O. Wilson, the first in the distinguished "Princeton Monographs in Population Biology" founded by MacArthur shortly after his arrival at Princeton. This book, which I picked up in the University Store, was revelatory. I was trained as a biochemist and had been strongly influenced by the founders of one branch of molecular biology and genetics whose credo was always to think of simple qualitative experiments that could give yes or no answers to important questions. I believed that most, if not all population biologists reveled in complexity and resisted reductionist thinking. Some of my friends called them stamp collectors, somehow anti-scientific in their thinking.

A quick read through *The Theory of Island Biogeography* showed me that Robert MacArthur did not at all fit this stereotype. There were several features about this new book that jumped out, but the one that most impressed me was this: MacArthur was a great and bold reductionist who had the courage to formulate the simplest possible hypothesis in mathematical terms, and then use qualitative arguments to compare his mathematical ideas to field data, whose preeminence he deeply believed in. This approach must have shocked and even threatened some of his contemporaries, for here was a man who showed how one might reduce the complexities of the natural world to simple, testable, hypotheses. The book had a profound and enlightening effect on me, because it opened up the possibility for simplifying theory in a discipline bedeviled by the great complexity of community interactions, especially competition between many species for space, mates, and food.

One of the consequences of Robert's simplifying approach was, of course, that in detail some conclusions would turn out to be wrong! Many ecologists have made much of this fact. Indeed, MacArthur was not himself unaware of this weakness — after all, if you seek simplicity in this complex natural world, you are bound to lose some of the nuances along the way. Still, he had the independence of spirit and the self-confidence to believe that his approach, with all the risks, could advance understanding in the discipline he cared most about. This may be his most lasting contribution to biology.

Although I worked on the biochemical basis of mutation when I first met Robert, and had occasionally thought about the biological "fitness" of mutation, I saw for the first time that it might be possible to test some of the current ideas which were rooted in population biology more than biochemistry. This led to a series of papers on the subject, the first two with an undergraduate, Tom Gibson, Class of 1970, whom Robert had sent to me. Our work, which discovered that high mutation rates seemed to help bacterial populations, turned out to be one of my most interesting scholarly experiences at Princeton, although at the time many of my senior colleagues must have seen it as a distraction and a want of self-discipline. For myself, however, it was marvelous, and something I would not have tried without Robert's influence.

MacArthur's general sense of what was important and how to approach it was well formed while he was still a graduate student at Yale, and may be easily seen in an early paper "On the Relative Abundance of Bird Species," published in 1957. In it, he discusses three models for species abundance based on three ways of looking at the distribution of niche size and number. This was his second paper. This work is accessible, and begins with a statement of his views, which were at the heart of all his work:

> Earlier investigations, discussed elsewhere, fit known statistical curves of uncertain biological meaning to data. A more fruitful approach seems to be to predict curves on the basis of simple biological hypotheses and to compare these with the data.

He then goes on to construct a model of how bird habitats might be constructed and sets each model up as an Hypothesis, rather like a mathematical paper beginning with a series of conjectures. The Hypotheses are simple: I — the habitats (or niches) might be non-overlapping (each species of bird feeding on food and in territories that are discrete and different from each other); II — they overlap; and III — they are "particulate," which is to say they are separate in space rather like urns in which marbles or counters can be placed. He then worked out the consequences of each model for one-dimensional niches, and compared them to bird census data, favoring Hypothesis I. Although there were problems with the agreement between the model and the data, especially for very rare or very common bird species, Hypotheses II and III were not even close to the expected distributions, and so could be dismissed. This ability to simplify and rule out alternatives in such an elegant way excited me when I first read this paper, and it excites me now on re-reading it. It is a marvelous example of the reductionist's art.

Two other features stand out. The paper has a self-confidence and forthrightness about it that is astonishing. Laconic in tone, it may even appear arrogant to some readers: "Early investigations . . . ," "A more fruitful approach. . . ." It also contains at least two errors, one mathematical and later corrected (fortunately, it worked to secure the main conclusion) and the other, the chief result, printed sideways on the page so that the two principal axes of the only data in the paper are reversed. I know nothing of the history of these errors, but in my mind's eye I can see Robert saying "Well, these things are bound to happen, and anyway, it's pretty easy for the reader to see what went wrong."

Finally, two themes central to later work are already in place: what can be learned by studying spatial variation and species diversity; and the distinction between what to expect in populations whose structure does not change with time, modeled by equilibrium theory, and those that do. The former can be rather more easily modeled, and that was one reason why he chose bird species in the abundance paper. The latter is much more difficult, but would become a major theme later on.

Many of MacArthur's ideas are in all basic texts. One, developed at length in *The Theory of Island Biogeography*, is that organisms will develop different food-gathering and reproductive strategies depending on the kinds of selective pressures they face. The two kinds of strategies are referred to as *r* and *K* strategies because as long as populations are growing without bound, their rate of increase may be characterized by a constant *r*. On the other hand, when resources run out, and populations are limited by food and space, they reach the carrying capacity of the environment, which can be characterized by a constant *K*. The idea that selection on *K* could be substituted for organismal fitness in the classical population genetic work of Haldane and Fisher led Robert to write an influential paper while a graduate student, "Some Generalized Theorems of Natural Selection," a title that also gives the reader a hint of his self-confident approach to difficult problems. The paper was nothing less than the reformulation of a famous theorem in population genetics to include the idea of the carrying capacity *K* of the environment.

Brine shrimp and oyster larvae are often said to be "*r* selected," for example, whilst most mammals are *K* selected: the former are produced in great numbers, multiply rapidly, and are left to fend for themselves upon hatching, while mammals typically grow slowly, family size is small, and there is a large parental investment spanning many years, traits all thought to be characteristic of species that have reached the carrying capacity of their environment. These ideas had truly great heuristic value, and for a period of roughly ten years the experimental literature was discussed and often reinterpreted through the *r* and *K* lens. It led, obviously, to some rethinking about life history strategies; but it also influenced how one thinks in general about evolutionary strategies. What, for example, should the adaptive strategy be for an organism that finds itself in an unpredictable environment, where the future is uncertain? Where it is certain? Collaborators and students of MacArthur asked all of these questions and many more. In my own research, I asked whether or not we can deduce anything about selective forces simply by looking at mutation rates, which themselves evolve.

The Theory of Island Biogeography, whose title seems to admit of only one, discusses *r* and *K* selection and the idea that species abundance on islands can be understood as equilibria between migration and extinction rates. It focuses on how we account for the number of different species on islands that have apparently been colonized by immigrants from the mainland and from islands nearby. This is an old question, and it arises from observations on both the diversity and relative abundance of island species. MacArthur and Wilson thought about the problem in particularly clear terms. They assumed that the number of bird species on a model island was a consequence of two factors: the chances that immigrants would find the island in the first place, and the chances that, having found it, they would persist.

With this simple clarifying idea MacArthur and Wilson could then show, among many other things, that the size of the island and its distance from the mainland were very important determinants for easily understood reasons: small islands are small targets for immigrants, however they may arrive; for islands of equal area, the one farthest from the mainland represent the smallest target, and hence the number of different species should be lower; island size is usually related to diversity of habitat, so that the chances of an effective colonization increases with island size; islands act as stepping stones to other islands, and this leads to complications. And so on. I continue to find this style of thinking very impressive. We start with a simple idea and pursue its clarifying ramifications for a remarkable length, not only formulating testable hypotheses as we go, but calling into question current dogma.

Lest I leave the reader with the impression that Robert

MacArthur was primarily a modeler or applied mathematician, let me briefly outline a description of a classic field study that made up the body of his Ph.D. thesis. His field studies were based on careful observation of warblers in conifer forests of the Northeast, and were published a year or so after his paper on niche overlap, described above. The problem was that several different species of warblers appeared to occupy the same niche. That is, they could all be observed feeding on the same tree, which poses a theoretical problem, for the following reason: The evolution of a new species occurs when an animal or plant evolves to occupy a niche that is unoccupied. When the process is over, there are often two species, one in the old niche and one in the new. Each is highly tuned to exploit the niche in which it finds itself, and in general therefore we expect "one niche one species." The various finch species observed by Darwin in the Galapagos is the textbook example. By careful quantitative field work, Robert MacArthur demonstrated that conifers were in reality not a single niche, as one might conclude, but many, and that the various warbler species on a single tree co-existed because they occupied different characteristic spaces. This work is a classic example of how careful field work can resolve an important issue, and is also widely used in current texts.

The Princeton Biology Department was transformed by MacArthur's appointment in 1965. The department was tiny by 1960s standards, and, like many Princeton departments, could only afford to cover a few areas in each major discipline. There were no population biologists at Princeton, nor had there been any, and thus MacArthur's recruitment could be seen as an effort by the University to expand into new fields. This may indeed be true, but Princeton has another tradition, and it is as likely that the chairman and his colleagues simply could not resist the opportunity created by the University of Pennsylvania's unhappy luck, and so recruited Robert because of his great originality and incisive ways. In the event, the department could not have done better.

READING LIST

"On the Relative Abundance of Bird Species," *Proceedings of the National Academy of Science USA.* 43 (1957): 293–295 (Three models for species abundance based on three ways of looking at the distribution of niche size and number.)

"Population Ecology of Some Warblers of Northeastern Coniferous Forests," *Ecology* 39 (1958): 599–619 (A field study showing that different species of Warblers divide up a conifer into different niches.)

"Some Generalized Theories of Natural Selection," *Proceedings of the National Academy of Science USA* 48 (1962): 1893–1897 (A reformulation of a famous theorem in population genetics to include the idea of the carrying capacity *K* of the environment.)

With E. O. Wilson: *The Theory of Island Biogeography* (Princeton: Princeton University Press, 1967) (Discusses *r* and *K* selection and the idea that species abundance on islands can be understood as equilibria between migration and extinction rates. First in an influential series of population biology monographs founded and edited by MacArthur.)

With R. May: "Niche Overlap as a Function of Environmental Variability," *Proceedings of the National Academy of Science USA* 69 (1972): 1109–1113. (MacArthur had earlier asked why there seems to be a limit to the number of species feeding on a resource or occupying similar space. This paper supplies an elegant answer. His co-author May was appointed to MacArthur's Chair upon Robert's untimely death in 1972.)

Fritz Machlup

Department of Economics

BY BURTON G. MALKIEL

On January 30, 1983, shortly after his eightieth birthday, Professor Fritz Machlup died of a heart attack. With his death, Princeton University and the economics profession lost one of their most prominent, most productive, and most versatile scholars. For the present writer and for many, many others, Fritz Machlup was an important teacher and mentor and a close, affectionate, and trusted friend whose memory will always be treasured.

In this essay I would like to develop three of the many admirable attributes of Fritz Machlup. First, Fritz was a scholar of incredible breadth, vision, and distinction, who displayed an uncompromising integrity. His writings, lectures, and conference leadership were at once extraordinarily influential and characterized by an élan, elegance, grace, and style not usually associated with the economics profession. Second, he was a man with an almost superhuman capacity for work who, in the brief periods he allowed himself for relaxation, played as hard as he worked. And yet, third, Fritz was a man of uncommon warmth who, despite being perpetually over-committed, was unstinting in the time he gave to causes in which he believed, such as academic freedom, and in the help that he offered students, colleagues, friends, and those oppressed by tyranny.

Machlup was born in Wiener-Neustadt, Austria, near Vienna, on December 15, 1902, and matriculated at the University of Vienna in 1920. He received his doctorate in 1923 upon completing his dissertation, "Die Goldkernwahrung" (Gold Bullion Standard), written under the direction of Ludwig von Mises. Publication of this work in 1925 marked the beginning of a great scientific and academic career.

During this time in Vienna, Machlup was also a businessman. While still a student, he became an active partner in his family's cardboard-producing concern. The company owned two factories, one in Austria and one in Hungary. In 1927, he became a member of the board of directors of a cartel of Austrian cardboard manufacturers. He often talked about his business career during classes, insisting that his business experience was very helpful in his scientific work on monopolies, competition, and other topics.

Early in 1933, Machlup came to the United States on a Rockefeller scholarship and visited Columbia, Harvard, and the University of Chicago where he met many of the world's leading economists. In May 1935, he received his first appointment as professor, from the University of Buffalo. While on leave during the first semester, Machlup liquidated his business interests in Austria. He spent several months at the London School of Economics and in Cambridge, England, before beginning his lectures in February 1936. In 1947, after having served in the United States government for three-and-a-half years during World War II, Machlup accepted a position at the Johns Hopkins University. In 1960, Machlup was called to Princeton University to succeed Jacob

Viner as the Walker Professor of Economics and director of Princeton's International Finance Section. In 1971, the year before his retirement from Princeton, Machlup began to teach regular courses at New York University. He received a professorship in economics from New York University in 1972 and continued teaching there until his death.

One of the most prolific writers in the economics profession, Fritz Machlup wrote thirty-four books and more than two hundred articles on subjects ranging from international trade to domestic patent laws, from microeconomic theory to macroeconomic policy, from the history of economic thought to the criteria and tests of valid knowledge. One could easily imagine an economics student assigned to read a Machlup article in every course he or she was taking. Many of his works have been translated into foreign languages, including French, German, Italian, Japanese, Russian, Spanish, Swedish, and Serbo-Croatian.

Machlup's articles remain today as the classic and still most lucid and punctilious statements of and solutions to some of the most central problems in economics. His work on equilibrium in the foreign-exchange markets and balance-of-payments adjustment is the basis for every modern text in international finance. His book on the foreign-trade multiplier, showing how shocks in one country are transmitted to the entire world economy, is as valid and relevant today as when it was written in 1943.[1] His defense of marginalism and the principle of maximization still stands as one of the foundation stones of microeconomic theory. During his lifetime, his academic achievements were recognized by his election to the presidencies of the American Economic Association, the International Economic Association, the American Association of University Professors, and by many honorary degrees and gold medals. With respect to political economy, Machlup was a firm liberal in the old, classical sense and was a co-founder of the

[1] *International Trade and the National Income Multiplier* (Philadelphia: The Blakeston Co., 1943).

Mont Pelerin Society dedicated to preserving nineteenth-century liberal ideals.

Fritz Machlup was not satisfied to concentrate his efforts on the development of economic theory. He was also keenly interested in policy-making and in shortening the cultural lag between academic discovery and practical implementation. There is no better illustration of Machlup's consummate skill in this area than his efforts, which began in 1964 at Bellagio, to organize conferences of academic economists and official government ministers and central bankers to discuss reform of the international monetary system. No one played a more central or constructive role in the fascinating interaction between academic economics and diplomatic negotiation. Challenged by the then-Secretary of the Treasury, Douglas Dillon, who planned a thorough study of the international monetary system *without* the help of academic economists because he believed academics were incapable of agreeing on anything, Machlup initiated and led this unique enterprise with inimitable skill and unquestioned authority. The very fact that such meetings continued to be held for many years, usually several times a year, by overburdened official participants is the best demonstration of how useful they were considered to be.

At the first meeting at Bellagio, the conference, under Fritz Machlup's leadership, isolated the differences in factual assumptions and normative judgments that underlay the difference in policy prescriptions by the participants and provided a taxonomy of the problems of the international monetary system that rapidly became the standard statement of the issues. At these meetings, the participating government officials were shocked to hear many of the academics argue that the sacred Bretton Woods system was doomed to self-destruct and to hear them recommend what the officials considered the impractical system of freely-flexible exchange rates. Yet within a decade, the major currencies of the world were left to float freely in the market. While the force of events was undoubtedly as important as Machlup's missionary work in producing that outcome, there is no question that these influential conferences prepared official government ministers to acquiesce in the acceptance of floating exchange rates and had a major influence on the development of the international monetary system.

The second set of attributes of Fritz Machlup that I would like to recall includes his integrity, courage, and his enormous capacity for work. The standard eight-hour work day was very much a vacation schedule for Fritz, whose normal work day consisted of two or three shifts and who did not follow the biblical admonition to rest on the Sabbath. "Sleeping is for sissies," he would often say.

One of the first economists to examine knowledge as an economic resource, he began during his seventies (when most people would be enjoying a comfortable life of retirement) an incredibly ambitious ten-volume study entitled *Knowledge: Its Creation, Distribution and Economic Significance.*[2] Three of those volumes were completed before his death.

In the brief period Fritz Machlup allowed himself for play, he was an avid sportsman. An excellent skier and fencer, he would only ski down the most challenging alpine slopes. In his seventy-ninth year, he won two bronze meals in skiing competitions with much younger men. This he accomplished despite his misfortune a few years earlier to have broken his hip while fencing with an especially agile teenager. A lover of classical music, he particularly enjoyed Wagner's operas and Mahler's symphonies, which he would listen to with scores in hand.

Kenneth Boulding composed the following verse, which describes the tempo of Machlup's activities:

> Oh, happy is the man who sits
> beside or at the feet of Fritz
> Whose thoughts, as charming as profound,
> Travel beyond the speed of sound,

[2] Princeton: Princeton University Press, 1980.

All passing as he speeds them up,
Mach 1, Mach 2, Mach 3, Machlup.
With what astonishment one sees
A supersonic Viennese
Whose wit and vigor, it appears,
Are undiminished by the years.

Fritz Machlup also displayed enormous courage and effort in fighting for the causes in which he believed deeply. He was a lifelong defender of academic freedom. During the Vietnam War, when the Princeton faculty was busily passing manifestos of condemnation, he was often a lone force reminding us with grace that in an academic institution each of us may express his or her own views, but that neither the university administration nor the faculty can express a view for us. It took enormous courage and integrity in that emotionally-charged atmosphere to speak out on the floor of the faculty as Machlup did, arguing that "this institution or its faculty as a body has no brain and no heart and should have no mouth either."

But to me the most endearing attribute of this important man was that someone with such a strong sense of dedication to work was also such a warm and compassionate friend who always had time for students, colleagues, and friends. In the 1930s, soon after he was established at Buffalo, Machlup helped many economists leave Nazi Germany before it was too late. One of those who was aided wrote me shortly after Machlup's death about the efforts Fritz had made on his behalf. Fritz managed to engineer a scholarly invitation that enabled this professor to leave Germany. Fritz then invited him to stay with the Machlup family while beginning a series of negotiations to find him an academic job in the United States. Let me quote from the letter I received:

> I got to love them all and wrote to my wife on the second day: "The Machlups are such charming people that I cannot find words to describe them." Though I had met them five years earlier in Vienna, I had then not had a chance to learn how really wonderful they were.

There followed in the letter a description of how Fritz secured him a job, helped his wife to immigrate via Canada, and later spent many days helping him polish his first book written in English. The letter concluded:

> You know, I am sure, what such sacrifice of time meant for Fritz. I can only repeat what I said in the Preface to my book: "He has given so generously of his time and editorial skill that I cannot find words to express my gratitude."

Fritz Machlup was an extraordinarily passionate, inspiring, and dedicated teacher who always gave freely of his time to students. He imparted certain indispensable techniques of analysis and of model-building, invaluable habits of clarity and consistency in the use of concepts and language, and most fundamentally, a love of truth and discovery that had a major influence on graduate students. A universal sentiment among all of Machlup's advisees was appreciation of the extraordinary amount of time he devoted to them. Quick reactions to drafts and consistent encouragement would be given to those whose theses were well in hand, a flood of ideas to those unable to find a suitable topic, and gentle prodding to the dilatory. Machlup was a meticulous record keeper. If a student had not delivered a promised draft of a chapter by the first of the month, a gentle reminder would be forthcoming on the second day of the month. He was never too busy to see students and would regularly go out of his way to accommodate their needs. At Princeton, the Machlup home was always open, and students often enjoyed an evening of intellectual stimulation and uncommon hospitality. The warmth and charm of Mitzi Machlup always made such occasions especially memorable.

My own relationship with Fritz Machlup went through many stages, that of his student, his colleague and, most important, his close and admiring friend. At Princeton, during the summers, we would regularly have a brown-bag lunch together on the roof outside his tower office in Firestone Library. Our conversations would range over such topics as international economics, nineteenth-century liberal values, academic freedom, skiing, and speculative common stocks likely to double over the next year. I shall always treasure the memory of the considerable time we spent together. Much of what I have learned about economics, teaching, and clarity of exposition, I have learned from Fritz. My wish for his legacy to Princeton and to his profession is that his love of truth for its own sake, his precision and grace in the use of language, his vitality, enthusiasm, and love of teaching, and most important, his kindness and generosity will serve as a model for future economists. Fritz was once described as a man with an anti-Midas touch: if *he* touched gold, he would turn it to life. I know of no better paradigm of what a dedicated teacher-scholar and lover of truth and humanity can be.

READING LIST

The Economics of Sellers' Competition: Model Analysis of Sellers' Conduct (Baltimore: Johns Hopkins University Press, 1952)

The Political Economy of Monopoly: Business, Labor, and Government Policies (Baltimore: Johns Hopkins Press, 1952)

Knowledge: Its Creation, Distribution, and Economic Significance (Princeton: Princeton University Press, 1970)

Essays in Economic Semantics (New York: New York University Press, 1975)

International Monetary Systems (Morristown, New Jersey: General Learning Press, 1975)

A History of Thought on Economic Integration (New York: Columbia University Press, 1977)

Methodology of Economics and Other Social Sciences (New York: Academic Press, 1978)

Alpheus Thomas Mason

Department of Politics

BY WALTER F. MURPHY

"Tell me what I ought to know." That was Alph's typical greeting, one he borrowed from Brandeis. He would say it in a jocular tone, but he meant it seriously. He was always eager to learn and eager to pass on to others what he had learned. The corpus of his writings is enormous: more than a hundred articles and twenty-two books, ranging from slim scholarly monographs to hefty judicial biographies to texts and readers. One of his texts reached its ninth edition, another its fourth; one of his scholarly books sold so well that it went through three editions, with several printings for each; and his biography of Justice Louis Brandeis was a Book-of-the-Month Club Selection and stayed on the best-seller list for five months.

But the quantity and popularity of his work were distant seconds to its quality. If Alpheus Thomas Mason did not invent the field of judicial biography, he perfected it. The awards he won — among others the American Library Association and the Francis Parkman prizes — so testify. In 1956, the Pulitzer Committee voted his monumental *Harlan Fiske Stone* the prize for biography, but Joseph Kennedy intervened and used his influence to have the decision reversed and the award assigned to the book published under his son's name, *Profiles in Courage.*

Alph once remarked that everything anyone wrote was in some significant sense autobiographical. His memorial to his dear friend and former student, Julian Boyd, demonstrated his contention:

> He pioneered in a vast, unexplored field, setting standards of meticulous research, painstaking accuracy, and informed judgment which will shine as a beacon in the years ahead. Originality . . . and craftsmanship mark his legacy. . . . His very presence, speech, and literary style, even the timbre and cadence of his voice, spelled *elegance.* Some are dazzled by his English prose, not realizing that he was its master not its slave. Happiness was special, too. He enjoyed in the ancient Greek sense: "the exercise of vital powers along lines of excellence in a life affording them scope."

Everyone who knew Julian Boyd, the first editor of *The Papers of Thomas Jefferson*, recognized that Alph had captured the essence of the man; all of us who knew Alph recognized that he had also captured his own essence, including the happiness he found in fifty-five years of marriage with Christine. I used to tease him that she, who had published a novel and short stories, was really the author of many of his books. In all seriousness, he would reply that she was his constant co-author. No one person, he argued, is good enough to write a book alone. Her literary skills augmented his own. Even more important, her dedication to him — and his to her — made his life full and fully human. "Marrying Christine was the best decision I ever made," he would say. No one ever doubted it. She never recovered from his death, though she continued to live until 1995.

Coming to Princeton to be the colleague of one of the premier constitutional scholars of the age was daunting. But I took comfort in the sure thought that anyone who wrote so well and so prolifically would not have time to be a good teacher. I could not have been more wrong about Alph's history, his temperament, and even his genes. A few paragraphs from his unfinished autobiography illustrate the point and reveal his literary style:

> It would be extreme to say that my origins are 18th century. My birth in 1899 on Maryland's Eastern Shore, in a rural community 23 miles from the Atlantic, at least a generation behind the rest of the country in technological progress, makes this statement less extreme than it would seem at first thought. Dubbed the "Eastern Sho'," the DelMarVa Peninsula is flat country, suited for truck farming and fishing, especially crabs and oysters. It was then a land of broad vistas, open fields, and isolated white clapboard farmhouses, occasionally broken by patches of woodland where small boys could roam about, freely trapping rabbits and collecting pigeons. Overhead, turkey buzzards circled in graceful spirals, ever in search of prey. People travelled by horse and buggy over dirt roads full of jagged holes and deep ruts. Water was drawn by pumps from wells. Nonexistent modern plumbing necessitated the use of privies. . . . Cooking was done on wood burning stoves or "ranges." . . . Houses were lighted by candles or kerosene lamps, requiring weekly cleaning and trimming of the wicks.
>
> My birthplace was a handsome brick farmhouse . . . two miles south of Snow Hill. Congressman George W. Covington owned it. My father tilled the land and shared the crops.
>
> Pop's formal education ended in third grade, but his self-education in religion and politics continued throughout life. He was an avid reader of the Bible, which inspired him to name me Alpheus. . . . The Bible served as a source book for ideas and lively discussion with men whose formal education greatly exceeded his. A Sunday school teacher, he carried on animated conversations with the local Baptist preacher. Transcending theological issues, they got down to fundamentals. Though largely illiterate, Pop had remarkable ability to articulate ideas . . . invariably spiked with wit. I have never met his equal as a mimic and story teller. From age ten to sixteen he was my teacher and ghost writer.

> Interest in oratory and public debate moved Pop to collect speeches of outstanding contemporary orators, including William Jennings Bryan, Teddy Roosevelt, and Woodrow Wilson. At a time when money was scarce and technical equipment hard to come by, he bought a gramophone and acquired records so that I might profit by hearing speeches at their best. On at least two occasions my public speaking teacher and mentor was put to a test. Congressman Covington, ardent prohibitionist, offered a prize for students in the 4-room Girdletree School on the topic, "The Best Way to Get Rid of the Liquor Traffic." . . . My (really Pop's) speech won the prize. [Later] at a school program I memorized and delivered a highly dramatic speech from our anthology of literature, entitled "The Death Bed Scene of Benedict Arnold." I can still see my father's proud expression . . . as I received a gold medal, dated 1915.

Coming to Princeton had also been daunting to Alph. He had graduated from Dickinson College but still thought of himself as just a poor country boy. He was, he later said, naive and unpolished, "a hick" was his term, awed by the gothic grandeur of the Graduate Tower and the sophistication of his fellow students. He was also, as the son of a sharecropper, penniless. All he had was drive, determination, and talent. Fortunately, he caught the eye of "the General" — Edward S. Corwin, one of Woodrow Wilson's original "preceptor guys," the then McCormick Professor of Jurisprudence, and *doyen* of American constitutional scholars.

Corwin became Alph's mentor and also his benefactor and friend. The relationship was in many ways close, but it was always strained, for Corwin had difficulty showing warmth or affection. Still, the General, Alph said, made sure he had enough to eat when he was in graduate school and even gave him $5 when he had had to stuff cardboard inside his only pair of shoes. As autocrat — not merely chairman — of the Politics Department, Corwin also invited Alph to come back to Princeton from his first teaching job at Trinity College (later Duke University) and continued during later years to help Mason along professionally.

Yet, as much as Corwin admired his protégé's intellectual

power, he would not allow Alph to teach *the* course, Constitutional Interpretation. During Alph's first twenty-one years on the faculty, he was allowed to offer "Con Interp" only once, the year Corwin spent in China. During each week of the other years, the General summoned his preceptors, including Alph, to his study and made them recite for him, "brief" the cases that the students would read.

In some ways, Corwin's jealous protection of his turf benefitted Alph, for it meant he had to establish his own teaching niche at Princeton. And he found it in the field of American political thought, which became as central to his intellectual persona — and perhaps dearer to his heart — as constitutional interpretation. Indeed, he came to see the Supreme Court's majority and dissenting opinions on constitutional issues not as legal answers to legal problems but as clashes of political theory. His collection of essays and documents on the development of American political thought, *Free Government in the Making* (its fourth edition co-edited by his old friend and former student, Gordon Baker), remains the classic work in the field almost a half-century after it first appeared.

Alph recognized and accommodated himself to the ambivalence of his relation with Corwin. He was painfully aware of the General's faults but also appreciated the older man's magnificent learning. Even when Alph was sixty-five and had himself held the McCormick chair for twenty years, he still addressed Corwin not as "Ned," as many mutual friends did, but as "Professor Corwin." And, when Corwin died, Alph, with his own former student and now colleague, Gerald Garvey, was bringing together a series of the General's articles under the title *American Constitutional History*.

Although Alph's graduate students would fondly dub him "the fastest pen in the east," teaching, as one would expect from his background, came first in his professional life. Indeed, he would subtitle his autobiography "A Teacher's Story." He had only disdain for scholars, even great scholars, who did not love teaching.

"He's nothing but an ornament," he said contemptuously about a noted political scientist whom the department was considering. "An ornament. He doesn't care about students."

To watch him lead a graduate seminar was to watch Toscanini conduct a symphony orchestra. Each week each student had to write a paper on one of the "queries" Alph had chosen. But the students could never read their papers in the seminar. Alph would do that before the meeting, remember what each had written, and begin by asking a leading question to one of the participants. He'd listen to the response for a few minutes, then turn to another student and say, "He's claiming your paper is all wrong. Are you going to let him get away with that?" Battle would be joined; from time to time Alph would shift the topic and incite fresh antagonists, but for three hours arguments would not let up.

It was a talent he never lost. Shortly before his long, final illness, I took him and two of my preceptors to lunch at Prospect. As we put our trays down, I heard him say to one: "What do *you* think about. . . ." I missed the next part of the sentence because I had to go back through the line for tea. A few minutes later, I returned to the sound of loud voices; my two preceptors were shouting at each other, one wildly punctuating the air with waving hands. All I said was "Alphhhh." He grinned impishly and shrugged his shoulders as if to reply: "Just wanted to make sure I still have the touch." He did.

His undergraduate lectures — written out in longhand — were always polished and sparkling, evidence of his talent and practice, his father's training, Christine's literary flair, and his abiding respect for the intelligence and commitment of his students. "I've never given a lecture I didn't later publish," Alph once said. How could it have been otherwise?

He was a carrier of ideas, and no vaccine could immunize against his virus. No one who heard him could escape realizing how deeply he cared about solving intellectual problems. Nor could anyone escape the contagion of his enthusiasm for ideas and for clear thinking about them. Students, colleagues, friends, and foes were all infected.

He was not without tricks. He knew how to measure an audience and how to count a house. One day when the two of us were walking across the campus, with Alph attacking Felix Frankfurter's jurisprudence with the sort of zeal academics later reserved for Ronald Reagan and Pat Buchanan, he suddenly interrupted himself to speak to an undergraduate: "Mr. Henry, I'm so glad you're better." "Better?" the puzzled young man replied. "Better? I haven't been sick." "Oh," Alph said in a tone both puzzled and hurt, "you weren't at lecture this morning; I thought you must be ill." I needn't add that the young man never missed another lecture.

Alph could also be maddening. Whenever we disagreed on personnel matters, I, being young and foolish, would try to convince him. He'd listen politely but seldom changed his mind. "In my judgment," he'd begin. "But," I would regularly interrupt, "good judgment has to be based on evidence." Just as regularly he would spring the trap: "But *I* must have good judgment. Didn't I pick you to come here?" There was no answer, at least none that would strengthen my case.

In Sonnet Number 12, Shakespeare wrote that " 'gainst Time's scythe" no man can make defense except in his offspring. Here Alph blunted Time's blade. His daughter, son-in-law, three granddaughters, and four great grandchildren live on. But so do generations of Princeton undergraduates and graduate students, as do students from the fifteen universities at which he taught after his so-called retirement. Many of these people are now journalists, judges, lawyers, physicians, stockbrokers, and even professors. They are fulfilling Alph's usual parting command: "Carry on." If they are not doing so in the Brandeis way, certainly they are in the Mason way. And the world is much the better for it.

Unlike Thomas Wolfe, the students and colleagues of Alpheus Thomas Mason do not have to spend time "remembering speechlessly" or seeking that "lost, and by the wind grieved, ghost"; we need not cry out "come back again." For whenever constitutional scholarship is done, Alph's ghost — Alph's spirit — will be there, rustling judicial papers, recalling the wisdom of Jefferson, Madison, and Marshall, tweaking Felix Frankfurter, and reminding Americans of the joys as well as the responsibilities of "free government" and free men's — and free women's — lives.

READING LIST

Brandeis: A Free Man's Life (New York: Viking Press, 1946)

Editor: *Free Government in the Making: Readings in American Political Thought* (New York: Oxford University Press, 1949)

Security Through Freedom: American Political Thought and Practice (Ithaca, New York: Cornell University Press, 1955)

Harlan Fiske Stone, Pillar of the Law (New York: Viking Press, 1956)

The Supreme Court from Taft to Burger (Baton Rouge: Louisiana State University Press, 1979)

Editor, with Gerald Garvey: *American Constitutional History: Essays by Edward S. Corwin* (New York: Harper & Row, 1964)

The States Rights Debate: Antifederalism and the Constitution, with Selected Documents (Englewood Cliffs, New Jersey: Prentice-Hall, 1964)

William Howard Taft, Chief Justice (New York: Simon & Schuster, 1965)

Oskar Morgenstern

Department of Economics

BY MARTIN SHUBIK

Harlow Shapley, the great astronomer and father of my longtime collaborator Lloyd Shapley, once noted that the way to discuss the deceased appropriately could be summarized as "De mortuis nihil nisi Bunkum." I do not wish to talk bunkum about Oskar Morgenstern, the pioneering advocate of the application of game theory to economics, nor do I wish to present a hagiography or a discussion of his adequate supply of faults. I leave it to others to offer their versions of the "downside analysis." Instead I intend to place my view of Oskar in the context of Princeton in the early 1950s; I want to talk about Oskar and Princeton with some fondness, and with sensitivity to human processes.[1]

[1] In several other publications I have presented the complete bibliography of Oskar Morgenstern as well as many observations and recollections.

Oskar Morgenstern was controversial, but he was one of the truly great entrepreneurs and visionaries of economics. He was the first to see how useful game theory could be in providing a basic structure for the study of strategic decision-making in economics. Much of microeconomics consists of developing a virtual parody of the human being as a "rational decision-maker," whereas anyone with an ounce of either common sense or uncommon sense knows that the human being is far more a rationalizing animal than a rational animal. After the fact, we spend a great deal of time explaining why what happened in this best of all possible worlds *should* have happened. Scenarios can then be developed justifying almost anything *ex post facto.* Oskar the skeptic was a nuisance to an establishment that thought along these lines; his was a much more daring approach, and therefore he was never fully accepted by his colleagues in the Economics Department of the 1940s and 1950s. They neither understood nor appreciated him. A financial analogy is possibly apposite: Senior bondholders do not welcome interlopers who tell them that the firm is essentially bankrupt and that, unless they change their ways, they should be grateful for 10 cents on the dollar. Like the bondholders, Princeton's Economics Department was certainly competent, and somewhat stodgy. It had a few distinguished members. It was basically middle class and conservative. Oskar was upper class and radical. The mix was oil and water.

Few institutions know how to treat the entrepreneur or his new ideas, and with 20-20 hindsight it is easy to inveigh against the short-sightedness of the Economics Department at the time. But game theory — which Oskar used to great advantage in his theoretical work — was heady new stuff. The success of game theory as a tool for economic analysis took about forty years to come into its own. In 1950, an economist already trained in the prevailing fashion would have had to be naive and unworldly, or, like Oskar, possessed of considerable imagination and fortitude, to risk staking a career on something so new and different as n-person game theory. Since then, however, the work of current scholars of economic thought such as Carver, Leonard, and Weinberg have told much of the history of game theory from an objective, or at least dispassionate point of view.

Oskar's interests were not in game theory as such, however, but in basic economic theory. He was a great skeptic, unwilling to accept some of the basic tenets of his discipline. He felt that the concept of "perfect foresight" was ill-defined, for example, and that much of the work on economic statistics was sloppy in the extreme. He was an admirer and friend of mathematician Kurt Gödel, and he appreciated careful logical argument. He insisted that a high level of accuracy was required in gathering and interpreting economic data and in modeling. But he was painfully aware of his own mathematical limitations, and he had the sense to cultivate those who could supply both the mathematics and the logic that were beyond his competence — and he was able to do this with dignity and enthusiasm. I can think of no other economist who could have brought off the collaboration with John von Neumann; together, they wrote the seminal *Theory of Games and Economic Behavior.*[2]

The contrast between Oskar and his fellow Austrian economist Joseph A. Schumpeter was considerable. Schumpeter's works were peppered with phrases such as "thus I have proved" — this following a set of casual commentaries with no proof whatsoever. In contrast, Morgenstern was always aware of what he and others did not know. But, possibly because of his admiration for mathematicians and physicists, he expected too much help from these sources in the development of an economic science. Game theory, after all, had been invented by mathematicians, not by economists. In the 1940s and 1950s, game theory was one of many new gimmicks coming in to challenge conventional economic theory. Most of the more senior practitioners of the "dismal science" then (or at any time) did not need too much that was radically new in order to make a contribution to their disciplines. Once tenure

[2] Third edition, Princeton: Princeton University Press, 1953.

had been achieved, a good, comfortable, constructive academic life did not require living on a frontier. Then as now, understanding which of many new competing ideas is seminal, and not merely a fad, is not an easy task, and most of us do not do it well. As it turned out, game theory was an extremely productive model; some might even argue that it is now too well accepted. If that is so, then it is time for a few new intellectual entrepreneurs to make sure that it does not become too entrenched and ossified.

In the musical comedy *Guys and Dolls*, one song has as its chorus "Sit, down, sit down, you are rocking the boat." This line helps us to understand Morgenstern's relationship to Princeton's Economics Department. He rocked the boat — and those who preferred less exciting times were far happier with plain quiet sailing, steering clear of new techniques and new ideas. Nevertheless, a conservative American college with a competent but conservative economics department, through some miraculous circumstance, supported a distinguished scholar who, although not Jewish, was nevertheless "politically unbearable" in Nazi Vienna, where Oskar Morgenstern had been born in 1902 and spent his early years. This individual was by nature an intellectual entrepreneur and a visionary. He rocked the boat, and he rocked it heavily. The people whom he made uncomfortable did not greet this activity with joy, and thus Oskar did not become the icon of the department, as might be expected, given his innovative thinking. This honor was reserved for his more conventional and conformist contemporaries.

In spite of being an outsider, however, Oskar did have a considerable sense of context. On one occasion, when I was complaining about the opposition to game theoretic thought in economics, he observed that one had to hope to outlast the opponents. The passage of time would achieve more than rational argument could hope to accomplish.

Oskar cared about both ideas and people. In many ways he was very Viennese. He was somewhat formal in his demeanor, projecting the image of the Viennese "Herr Professor" to the random student, but he was enormously supportive of and concerned for his graduate students. He cared, and those who were his students found a warm and helpful mentor, far different from the person exhibited by his more formal façade. Yet when it came to new ideas and vision, he was as enthusiastic and dedicated as any seeker of the Holy Grail. I can think of very few economists who would encourage independence of thought in their graduate students to the degree that he did, even if he did not agree with them or even fully understand what they were doing. Enormously high IQs combined with an ability to dazzle with the accepted forms of mental gymnastics are grist for the academic mill, but Oskar was not that kind of economist. A truly dedicated innovator who does not seek to dazzle his audience is a far rarer and often more valuable asset. Oskar was such an individual.

The producers of the seminal ideas, even if some of them are wrong, are among the more fortunate human beings. They have a vision which lasts them until the end of their lives, and that vision provides them with an elixir of youth. Oskar Morgenstern was one of those fortunate beings. I saw him for the last time a few days before his death. He said to me that he regretted that he was not going to live long enough to see the pictures developed from the Saturn space probe. Even racked with pain and fully aware that his life was almost over, his concern was with being, at least, an appreciative spectator of the newest game in town.

Princeton was in many ways the right place for him to be. Placed in the context of the time, the reigning economic theory, the character of people in the department, and the general conservative attitude, Oskar was reasonably well treated. And in spite of the inability of many in the Economics Department to understand his worth, Princeton served him well. With the benefit of fifty years of hindsight we know that the seed planted by Oskar has grown and flourished, there and elsewhere. The new generation at Princeton appreciates the heritage he left.

His was a life that was highly fulfilled. His circle of friends at the Institute for Advanced Study and in town, and the support from his wife, Dorothy, provided him with a rich social and intellectual life. He was blessed with faith in his own work and the ability to make a contribution to his profession and university that is still growing. In his day, the Economics Department viewed Oskar Morgenstern and his ideas warily; now that he is safely out of the way, his views and methodology vindicated, he can and should be an icon of it.

READING LIST

With John von Neumann: *Theory of Games and Economic Behavior*, 3d. ed. (Princeton: Princeton University Press, 1953)

Economic Activity Analysis (New York: Wiley, 1954)

Limits to the Uses of Mathematics in Economics (Princeton: Princeton University Econometric Research Program, Research Memorandum 49, 1963)

The Element of Time in Value Theory: Perfect Foresight and Economic Equilibrium (Princeton: Princeton University Econometric Research Program, Research Memorandum 55, 1963)

On the Accuracy of Economic Observations, 2d. ed. (Princeton: Princeton University Press, 1963)

With Gerald L. Thompson: *Mathematical Theory of Expanding and Contracting Economies* (Lexington, Massachusetts: Lexington Books, 1976)

Selected Economic Writings of Oskar Morgenstern, ed. Andrew Schotter (New York: New York University Press, 1976)

Essays in Mathematical Economics in Honor of Oskar Morgenstern, ed. Martin Shubik (Princeton: Princeton University Press, 1967)

Dana Gardner Munro

Department of History

BY STANLEY J. STEIN

When Dana G. Munro arrived in 1930 as Princeton's first specialist in Latin American history, he had already had a meteoric career in the Foreign Service of the State Department. Graduating from the University of Wisconsin (1912) after three years at Brown, Munro went first to Europe (Munich) and then, financed by a grant from the Carnegie Peace Endowment, to Central America where he conducted a field study of political and economic conditions there. (At 91, he published privately a memoir of his field experience, *A Student in Central America, 1914–1916*, based upon his letters written home.) This research formed the basis of a doctoral dissertation for the University of Pennsylvania (1917) and his first publication, *The Five Republics of Central America. Their Political and Economic Development and Their Relations with the*

United States,[1] now a classic reference work on that area at the beginning of the twentieth century. By then he had entered the Foreign Trade Section of the State Department as an economist. During the war he trained as a pilot in the Air Force, but did not serve overseas; after the war, he returned to the State Department, and also lectured on Latin America at Georgetown University. In 1920 he married Margaret B. Wiley, a perceptive, witty, and delightful lifelong companion.

Following a brief appointment as economic consul at the Valparaiso (Chile) consulate in 1920–1921, he returned to Washington to enter the Department's Latin American Division, rising to assistant chief of division while still in his mid-thirties. He advanced rapidly in the State Department in the 1920s, at a time when there was sharp criticism at home and in Latin America of the United States government's decades-old policy of direct intervention in the internal affairs of the republics of the Caribbean (Cuba, Santo Domingo, Haiti) and Central America (Nicaragua, Panama) in support of U.S. banking, mining, plantation, and strategic interests. The Caribbean cockpit attracted some of the most talented career officers in the State Department. Dana Munro was posted to the U.S. Legation in Panama (1925–1927), then to Nicaragua, where he was responsible for oversight of its electoral process according to procedures designed by Harold W. Dodds of Princeton's Politics Department, later president of the University. In recognition of Munro's diplomatic skills he was then made chief of the Division of Latin American Affairs before leaving Washington for Princeton University. Later, from 1932 to 1934, the State Department recalled him to serve as minister to Haiti to negotiate the withdrawal of a Marine contingent that had been in place since 1915.

At Princeton from 1930 until his retirement in 1961, Dana Munro pursued three careers: teacher, university administrator, and scholar of modern Latin America. As professor of Latin

[1] New York: Oxford University Press, 1918.

American History and Affairs he initiated two undergraduate courses on Latin America covering the colonial and modern periods. These courses led to one of the early, widely used textbooks, *The Latin American Republics, A History*, which appeared in three editions between 1942 and 1960.[2] In 1936 he became chairman of the History Department, where he remained until appointment as the second director of the Woodrow Wilson School of Public and International Affairs (1939) and Tod Professor of Public Affairs. President Dodds chose Munro to provide clear direction to the School, integrate it with the University's departmental structures, and define its overall goals. During his nineteen-year tenure, the School expanded its undergraduate program, innovated the now standard junior conference courses,[3] and established a graduate professional program.

While at Princeton, Dana Munro continued to serve on an interim basis as consultant to the State Department, as member (and for a time, president) of the Foreign Bondholders Protective Council (a U.S. government-sponsored group to defend the interests of U.S. holders of foreign bonds in default since the Great Depression), and as a trustee of the Doherty Charitable Foundation. It was his recognition of the importance of his own initial field experience in Central America that led him to seek funding from the Doherty Foundation to send pre-doctoral candidates to Latin America for field research in history and the social sciences. In its thirty-seven years of operation (1948–1985), the Doherty Program for Advanced Study in Latin America funded more than 300 grantees, many of whom became outstanding figures in Latin American studies. Munro was also largely responsible for a capital grant of one million dollars (1967) from the Doherty Charitable Foundation for the University's Program in Latin American Studies.

[2] New York: Appleton, 1960.

[3] An undergraduate policy conference has about fifteen juniors leavened with three to five seniors, is built around analysis of public policy issues, involves visiting lecturers, and requires an essay by each participant. At the end of each conference, the students produce a joint body of policy recommendations.

The abiding focus of Dana Munro's scholarship remained relations between an expanding U.S. empire and the republics of the Caribbean during the first third of the twentieth century. His basic purpose, he once advised his readers, was to "describe and explain what happened rather than to defend what the State Department did."[4] In a book written shortly after he returned from Haiti, *The United States and the Caribbean Area*, Munro surveyed conditions in the Caribbean and Central America and explored the factors that led from fiscal errors and political instability to the U.S. policy of overt intervention after 1903.[5] Intervention, Munro argued, had been inspired by the necessity of "permanently stable governments" which — with U.S. oversight, if necessary — might guarantee foreign investments and avert potential gunboat diplomacy by aggrieved non-American (and unfriendly) governments. United States surveillance was not motivated, he felt, by the pursuit of commercial ends by U.S. investors.

This book was followed by two analyses published after Munro's retirement, *Intervention and Dollar Diplomacy in the Caribbean, 1900–1921* and its chronological sequel, *The United States and the Caribbean Republics, 1921–1933*. What had been a short sub-section on "Dollar Diplomacy" in *The United States and the Caribbean Area*, Munro now expanded in *Intervention and Dollar Diplomacy* into full-scale, country-by-country case studies of why and how successive U.S. administrations since the presidency of Theodore Roosevelt justified and then applied the "Roosevelt Corollary" to the Monroe Doctrine, which invariably led to intervention in Nicaragua, the Dominican Republic, Haiti, and Cuba. The driving force: "Disorder and economic backwardness" invited "imperialistic ventures by non-American powers"

[4] *The United States and the Caribbean Republics* (Princeton: Princeton University Press, 1974), p. ix.

[5] The sources of this study were mainly the annual *Foreign Relations of the United States*, State Department press releases, Congressional Hearings and a few English-language publications.

endangering the "security of the United States."[6] Three decades after leaving the Foreign Service, relying less on personal experience than the "tedious detail" in State Department materials, Munro found a leitmotif in U.S. Caribbean policy: explicit, persistent bipartisan support for maintaining U.S. "security" there. (It was probably pure coincidence that *Intervention and Dollar Diplomacy* appeared at a critical juncture in U.S. relations with Cuba's revolutionary government). Dana Munro's last study revisited what had been presumed to be the sequel to the era of intervention, the withdrawal of occupation forces from Santo Domingo and Haiti, "non-intervention" in Cuba (1925–1933) and the extension, in his view, of the Hoover administration's noninterventionism into Franklin Roosevelt's Good Neighbor Policy.

Dana Munro's studies of U.S. government policy in the Caribbean and Central America in the early decades of this century offer a conspectus of intervention via diplomacy, Marine contingents, and micro-management of the political and fiscal processes of the states intervened from the vantage point of State Department personnel in the field and in Washington. They do not pretend to provide a balanced view, rather their underlying theme is the responsibility of the U.S. government under its unilaterally mandated Monroe Doctrine to prevent non-American intervention in the Caribbean. In a dual role as participant in policy execution and, decades later, historian of that policy, Dana Munro represents a unique case of a high office holder who had experienced the frustrations of the hands-on diplomat in the field, of the policy executor in Washington confronting the Congress and the public and — years later — of the 20-20 hindsight of the historian. It was, he once confessed after examining in State Department files his own dispatches from Caribbean posts, a humbling experience for the diplomat turned historian. Through these prisms one must evaluate his historical studies.

[6] *Intervention and Dollar Diplomacy in the Caribbean, 1900–1921* (Princeton: Princeton University Press, 1964), p. vii.

He died at 97. His life was coterminous with the trajectory of the United States from relatively insignificant world power to uncontested superpower.

READING LIST

The United States and the Caribbean Area (Boston: World Peace Foundation, 1934)

Intervention and Dollar Diplomacy in the Caribbean, 1900–1921 (Princeton: Princeton University Press, 1964)

The United States and the Caribbean Republics, 1921–1933 (Princeton: Princeton University Press, 1974)

Whitney Jennings Oates

Department of Classics

BY ROBERT F. GOHEEN

Whitney Jennings Oates, known to friends and associates as "Mike," was a caring and compelling teacher, a well grounded and productive classical scholar whose concerns were broadly and passionately humanistic, and a man possessed of an unusually creative gift for organization. Beyond that was his wholeness and sensitivity as a human being — his warm, responsive readiness to bring his heart as well as his mind to every encounter and every concern. It left a legacy of respect and affection in all who had him as a teacher or friend, or who worked alongside him.

Mike Oates came to Princeton from Evanston, Illinois, with the Class of 1925. Because of illness in his junior year he did not graduate until 1926, but did so then with highest honors. In 1931 he gained his Ph.D. degree in Classics at Princeton and that fall joined the Princeton faculty on which he was to serve for the next forty-three years. He rose steadily in rank from instructor to full professor, holding in the later years, first, the Andrew Fleming West Chair in Classics and, subsequently, the Avalon Professorship in the Humanities.

As early as 1939, the then chairman of the Classics Department, Duane Reed Stuart, in recommending him for promotion to associate professor, wrote, "Mr. Oates is one of the key men in the plans contemplated for the department. He is regarded as one of the most promising and talented younger Classical scholars of the country, and in this institution has taken the lead in popularizing in the best sense the study of the literary masterpieces of antiquity. Endowed with rare traits, both intellectual and personal, he is an inspiring teacher of undergraduates and an excellent lecturer. Furthermore, he has shown convincing ability in the direction of graduate studies and in the supervision of dissertations in his favorite field, Greek philosophy."

Mike Oates' Princeton career went on to include service as Classics Department chairman, 1946–1961; chairman of the Special Program in the Humanities, 1945–1959; and chairman of the Council of the Humanities, 1953–1970. In the establishment and direction of the last he was the driving force. Meantime, he published many articles on Classical topics and edited with both scholarly care and critical acumen an important series of translations into English of major Classical authors. It included *The Complete Greek Drama* with Eugene O'Neill, Jr. (1938); *Stoic and Epicurean Philosophers* (1940, 1957); *Basic Writings of St. Augustine* (1948). In 1963 the Princeton University Press published his *Aristotle and the Problem of Virtue*, a major study and the culmination of a life work begun under Paul Elmer More. It was followed in 1972 by *Plato's View of Art*, his final publication.

As a young faculty member he was among those who gathered around Paul Elmer More, former editor of *The Nation*, nationally prominent literary critic, and scholarly interpreter of Classical and oriental thought. They regularly met in the afternoons at the

Baltimore Daily Lunch (just across Nassau Street, where Hinksons is now located) for coffee and discussion. The habit continued after Mr. More's death in 1937 and gave rise to the following verse in the undergraduates' faculty song:

> Here's to Princeton's esthete band
> Making culture's final stand.
> In the Balt they all convene,
> Hinds, Godolphin, Oates, and Greene.

And it was, in fact, in these afternoon coffee sessions, with Mike Oates as a regular participant, that many of the ideas and observations in T. M. Greene's massive, influential *The Arts and the Art of Criticism* were thrashed out. In any case, the influence of Paul Elmer More's "neo-humanism" and eventual Christian Platonism remained strong for all four of the relatively young professors named in that verse of the faculty song.

A moral drive was to mark Mike Oates' teaching, scholarship, and public activities for the remainder of his life. Indeed, in his person and in his work he stood in a long, strong line of Christian humanists who helped give the University spiritual as well as intellectual quality throughout many years. Lively and probing in mind, with a disposition for the rational pursuit of truth; imbued, in Charles Osgood's phrase, with an "affectionate concern, incorrigible and dominant, for his fellow men"; humble yet firm in the belief that the will of God imposes moral responsibility on us even when we cannot fully comprehend it — these were characteristics of the Whitney J. Oates who powerfully influenced many of us who studied under him.

Equally important and influential were his convictions about the life of the mind and the role of the faculty member. He saw the purview of the humanities to be all that has concerned, and concerns, humankind, and he upheld the interrelatedness of all fields of learning — provided that philosophy, especially the study of values, was regarded as the supreme study of them all. Another dominant idea that he impressed on his advisees was the equal and indissoluble partnership between scholarship and teaching that ought to prevail in the life of a university faculty member, each of these vital functions nourishing the other.

But to say all this falls short of conveying his particular charisma — his warmth, his empathy, his telling idiosyncracies. None who studied under him or worked alongside him are likely to have forgotten his smile as he looked up from the paperwork on his desk to greet a visitor — or his pacing of the lecture platform, coat off, hands gesticulating as he sought to make some complex idea clear — or his habitual dubbing of close associates and friends with affectionate nicknames — and his merry hosting of gatherings of young and old, often enlivened with piano and singing, at his home on Edgehill Street. And there were other occasions there where as graduate students and junior faculty members we were given opportunities to meet personally eminent visitors such as T. S. Eliot and Arnold Toynbee. Mike Oates' interest and concern embraced us all, brought us together, and stimulated many a lively discussion.

Lest the writer be mistakenly thought to be a dispassionate witness, let me acknowledge that I came under Mike Oates' influence when I entered Princeton as a freshman in the fall of 1936 and had the good luck to have him as freshman advisor. It was an influence that, in subsequent years, did much to shape my professional life. For example, taking "Classics 118, Greek Literature in English Translation," in which Professor Oates was the principal lecturer, led to my beginning the study of Greek as a sophomore and deciding to major in Classics (for which fortunately I already had a good grounding in Latin). Also in sophomore year, I was one of those taken into the then new Special Program in the Humanities — in effect, a transdepartmental super-honors program that required a senior thesis spanning at least two academic disciplines and that afforded its few students ready access to the interest and advice of the six faculty members of the interdisciplinary committee which oversaw the program. Mike

Oates was a founding member of that committee which comprised in addition E. Baldwin Smith (Art History), Asher Hinds (English), Gray Boyce (History), Ira Wade (Modern Languages), and T. M. Greene (Philosophy). Mike in particular helped guide me through my sophomore and junior years and became principal advisor on my senior thesis in which I sought to make certain comparisons between Shakespearean and fifth-century B.C. Attic tragic drama.

An affable and supportive mentor, he also could be demanding. Thus in the second term of my junior year when I normally should have continued the study of classical Greek at an intermediate level, Mike Oates pushed me into an upperclass reading course in Greek tragedy under a distinguished visiting professor from Oxford, Denys Page — what a struggle! — during which Mike would listen to my anguished sense of inadequacy but never let me withdraw. The result, as I expect he foresaw, was that I learned much more about the language and literature of fifth-century B.C. Athens in that term than I otherwise would have.

All this, however, was but a preliminary to what, in retrospect, was a long and rewarding disciple-to-guru relationship. For, it was Mike Oates who persuaded me at the end of World War II not to try to enter the Foreign Service but instead to resume graduate work at Princeton. The latter was made possible by my receiving one of the first Woodrow Wilson Fellowships in a program that he had conceived to lure qualified returning veterans toward academic careers. He himself had volunteered for military service in 1943 and served for two years as an intelligence officer in the Marine Corps in the Pacific theater. On the island of Peleliu in the spring of 1945, when an end to the war was beginning to seem foreseeable, he had become impressed by young Marines saying that they wanted to go to college if circumstances allowed, and he had become concerned that many talented college graduates in the military services might be diverted from academic careers because of the interruption and dislocation caused by military service, as had happened following World War I. So, on returning to Princeton in the summer of 1945, Mike Oates already had in mind the development of a national fellowship program to recruit into graduate study as many qualified and highly promising young veterans as could be reached by means of focused encouragement and the offer of a year of substantial financial assistance. The G.I. Bill meant initially that even relatively small supplements from private sources could go a long way. Within a very few years, Mike Oates' combination of deep personal commitment, worldwise savvy, and persuasive ability was instrumental in carrying the Woodrow Wilson National Fellowship Program from a tiny beginning at Princeton in 1945, to a nationwide competition attracting 1,500 and more nominated candidates and making 150–160 awards each year in the mid-1950s (with Carnegie Corporation and General Education Board support), to finally as many as 1,000 Fellowship awards a year through the 1960s (under Ford Foundation sponsorship). It has been called "the largest, most successful recruiting campaign in the history of American higher education."

To come back, however, for a moment to our personal involvements, when classes in Princeton's Graduate School reopened in the late fall of 1945, I enrolled in Mike Oates' seminar on Plato's Theory of Forms (Ideas). Several of us in the seminar had found that the war years had badly eroded our ability to read Greek. Not unlike my experience as a college junior, Mike's remedy for our rustiness was to have us read a dialogue a week and large chunks of the *Republic* as well. By much long and late-night effort, toward the end of the term our Greek was pretty much up to speed again. While demanding as a teacher in this way and others, Mike could also be understanding of efforts to break outside the mold of traditional Classical philology. For example, when in writing my dissertation I chose to be so heterodoxical as to want to try to apply techniques of the "New Criticism" to the interpretation of Sophocles' *Antigone*, he gave me strong encouragement

Whitney J. Oates with newly-inaugurated President Robert F. Goheen, in Nassau Hall.

and support. The book that emerged gave him undisguised pleasure.

A decade and more later, our positions were nominally reversed, but as president of the University, I continued to learn from Mike in the course of frequent discussions. These lessons stemmed from his leadership of the Council of the Humanities and its oversight or planning for such new programs for Princeton as American Civilization, Comparative Literature, the History and Philosophy of Science, Linguistics, Political Philosophy, and the Creative Arts. In this period he also brought to the campus as fellows of the Council scores of distinguished scholars and artists from many parts of the world. Many of us profited from association with them.

On the Princeton campus, Mike Oates was a perennial "favorite lecturer and preceptor" in senior class polls. An invigorating teacher of the literature and thought of the Greco-Roman period, he took an active interest in his students, both graduate and undergraduate. His friendships within the faculty likewise extended widely because of his openness, good humor, and ability to listen with genuine interest — plus, no doubt, his service on many faculty committees. At the Oates' home, one was almost as likely to encounter aeronautical engineers and physicists as fellow classicists or other humanists.

Moreover, as suggested earlier, alongside his gifts as a teacher and scholar, Mike Oates possessed a quite remarkable talent for translating constructive ideas into institutional and operational forms. His success along these lines reached often beyond Princeton, and at times it entailed considerable artistry in finding and obtaining the necessary funding. The National Woodrow Wilson Fellowship Program and the University's Council of the Humanities are but two examples — as much earlier, though in lesser degree, was his part in the establishment of Princeton's Special Program in the Humanities.

In 1955–1956, as vice-chairman of the Commission on the Humanities of the American Council of Learned Societies, he was largely instrumental in obtaining funds that rescued the ACLS from serious financial straits. He served as its treasurer from 1959 to 1970 and was a director from 1955 to 1970. Meanwhile, he was also a senator of the United Chapters of Phi Beta Kappa and its president in 1964, working to strengthen the institution's finances. In the same period, as a founding member of the National Committee on the Humanities established jointly by the ACLS, the Council of Graduate Schools, and Phi Beta Kappa, he was a principal draftsman of its 1963 report that was instrumental in the creation by the federal government of the National Endowment for the Humanities.

In all these endeavors, Whitney J. (Mike) Oates was sustained by unfailing devotion to the literature and thought of Greece and Rome. His passionate commitment to Classical ideals carried him beyond antiquarianism and the confines of philology into the continuing exploration of humanistic values — of what it is that constitutes human virtue, excellence, justice, freedom, and moral well-being.

READING LIST

The Complete Greek Drama, edited with an introduction by Whitney J. Oates and Eugene O'Neill, Jr., 2 vols. (New York: Random House, 1938)

From Sophocles to Picasso: The Present-Day Vitality of the Classical Tradition (Bloomington: Indiana University Press, 1962)

Aristotle and the Problem of Value (Princeton: Princeton University Press, 1963)

Plato's View of Art (New York: Charles Scribner's Sons, 1972)

Robert Paul Ramsey

Department of Religion

BY GILBERT MEILAENDER

I have not forgotten my first conversation — if it can exactly be described as a "conversation" — with Paul Ramsey. Having come to Princeton as a graduate student in the autumn of 1972, I wandered over to 1879 Hall on a Saturday afternoon in late summer, telling my wife I would be back soon. In my naiveté I had applied to graduate school without bothering to come for a personal interview; hence, I had never actually met the man with whom I wanted to study. The building was empty, the halls dark, as I perused a bulletin board near the department office. Down the hall came Paul Ramsey, although I, of course, did not know who he was. But he immediately introduced himself, discovered my identity, and marched me off to his office for that "conversation."

More than two hours later I finally headed home, carrying with me copies of several of his books. In the course of the conversation he had managed to discover just about everything that I had read — and, more important, had not read. I went home a chastened man.

I do not think my experience was uncommon. A fellow student of mine once called Ramsey an "intellectual whip." Whatever the topic, he probed and pushed at the argument, examining it from every angle, making of his interlocutor's argument far more than it deserved — and, in the process, inevitably dominating the conversation in his loud and boisterous manner. Not everyone liked the manner; some found it pompous. In fact, however, it was simply the manifestation of his enormous delight in the intricacy of argument. It should be no surprise that his most lasting intellectual passion was for the writings of Jonathan Edwards. He edited two volumes in the standard edition of Edwards' *Works* — *Freedom of the Will*, published in 1957, relatively early in Ramsey's career, and *Ethical Writings*, worked on during Ramsey's last years and published posthumously in 1989. (For the last lecture he gave before his retirement from Princeton, he chose to read to his class long excerpts from Edwards' "Charity Sermons.")

Robert Paul Ramsey — born a Mississippian in 1913; educated at Millsaps College (B.A. 1935), Yale Divinity School (B.D. 1940), and Yale University (Ph.D. 1943) — joined the Princeton faculty in 1944 and was named Harrington Spear Paine Professor of Religion in 1957. He taught at Princeton for thirty-eight years until his retirement in 1982. Shortly after Ramsey had begun teaching at Princeton, his father, a Methodist minister in Mississippi, wrote to warn him of the dangers of his calling: "You will be invited to all sorts of entertainments such as cocktail parties and beer suppers. . . . Read the chapter in . . . Proverbs on strong drink and when liquors of any sort is [*sic*] being passed don't forget to turn your glass upside down." His father also reminded him "not to use tobacco in any form." Students who remember Ramsey's omnipresent pipe will know that he cannot be said to have followed this paternal advice on every occasion.

Ramsey's first book, *Basic Christian Ethics*, marked the one time in his career when he set forth in systematic fashion the fundamental shape of his own approach to Christian ethics. He honored the great thinkers of the tradition — Augustine, Aquinas, Luther, Kierkegaard — by reading them not simply as historical artifacts but as his colleagues in an ongoing conversation. Often encouraged to write another "Basic Christian Ethics" much later in his career, he always declined. In effect, though, the 120-page (a distillation of an even longer draft) introduction to Edwards' *Ethical Writings* constituted Ramsey's return to those fundamental themes. His reputation was made, however, largely through his writings on the ethics of warfare and on medical ethics.

Ramsey dedicated roughly a decade of his life to just-war theory, publishing *War and the Christian Conscience* in 1961, and *The Just War*, a 550-page collection of essays, in 1968. The writings on warfare demonstrate the genuinely ecumenical character of his approach to Christian ethics. Grounded in the understanding of love he had drawn from Luther and Kierkegaard, these writings incorporate into an ethic of love distinctions and refinements that Ramsey had learned from Roman Catholic moralists. His writings on the morality of warfare did not always make him popular, especially during the Vietnam War years. Perceived as a hawk during the war, he was more precisely one who took seriously and valued "statecraft" — understanding the use of force as essential to God's "alien work" in government. Always ready to defend the use of force on behalf of those in need, he was equally ready to argue that this same concern for the innocent and needy placed moral limits on the use of force. But he did for a time become something of an outsider among his own colleagues. Gregarious as he was, it must have hurt him. Argumentative as he was, it must sometimes have been a tense atmosphere. But he seldom looked back. (Perhaps, too, he remembered the young Paul

Ramsey who, while still a student, had published his first article on "Christianity and War" in *The Christian Advocate* in 1935 — arguing the Christian case for pacifism to which he was at that point committed!)

When in the late 1960s his attention was drawn to emerging problems in the ethics of medicine, he applied himself with characteristic thoroughness. Ramsey never wrote about subjects such as medicine and war without learning as much as he could from specialists in those fields. In 1968 and 1969 he held a research appointment at Georgetown Medical School, beginning to study moral issues in modern medicine. That research became the background for the Lyman Beecher Lectures on Medical Ethics that he delivered at Yale University in 1969 — which, in turn, became *The Patient as Person*, one of the classic works in the early development of bioethics. Several of its chapters — in particular the chapter titled, in typical Ramseyan fashion, "On (Only) Caring for the Dying" — display Ramsey at his very best and remain classic discussions of important issues. A later work, *Ethics at the Edges of Life*, pursued in still greater detail questions that concern the beginning and the end of life. As always, Ramsey understood Christian love to call for and ground commitment to the weak, the dying, the incompetent, the disabled, and the unborn — those who were, to use his term, "voiceless."

Certainly to his students — and also, I think, to many of his professional colleagues — Paul Ramsey was a man somewhat "larger than life." To engage him in conversation was to be forced into constant refinement of one's view. He would probe, push, and hypothesize in a conversational style uniquely his own. As he put forward each possibility, punctuated by "hrumphs," wheezes, and puffs on his pipe, every sentence ended with a "Heh?" or a "You know?" and perhaps a boisterous laugh at a particularly pleasing point. He did not really need a response, however, as he pressed forward — every "You know?" drawing the interlocutor more deeply into the issue at hand. Moreover, if and when one managed to get in a few words and put forward an argument, Ramsey would go to work on it in this style — demonstrating its shortcomings but, at the same time, turning it into a stronger and better argument than it had been. Even when he disagreed, he invariably drew out of an argument whatever was best about it. He did that not only with students but time after time with colleagues at professional meetings.

Beyond doubt, this style could sometimes overpower students, however intriguing it might be from a distance. (Indeed, I know one of Ramsey's students who told me that he had once vowed to read none of Paul's writings for a least a year — the better to assure himself that he had some shred of intellectual independence remaining.) One spring semester I was auditing the lectures in one of Ramsey's classes because I was precepting for him. Near the end of the semester, Ramsey had to be absent for a day. At that time, an undergraduate named Bill Werpehowski (who himself subsequently earned a Ph.D. in religious ethics) was writing a senior thesis under Ramsey's direction. Ramsey decided that in his absence Werpehowski should lecture to the class on the subject matter of his thesis — which Werpehowski did. He began, however, with a few introductory remarks about how "Paul" had asked him to do this and "Paul" had suggested that — "Paul" this . . . "Paul" that. A freshman in the class, a member of one of my discussion sections, was sitting next to me. He leaned over, as Werpehowski continued, and whispered to me: "Does he call God by his first name too?" Nevertheless, overbearing as the Ramsey style might at first seem, few teachers extended themselves more on behalf of their students. Indeed, there are many academicians today who, although they were not even Ramsey's students, would have to admit that they are where they are in part, at least, because of a letter written by Paul Ramsey.

Although he liked to refer to his writing as his "poetry" and was sometimes given to rhetorical flights appropriate to the son of a Methodist preacher, his writing style was in some respects similar to his conversational style. That is, it involved chiefly a relentless probing of arguments. He would take the work of another author and scrutinize it from every possible angle. The result was a very penetrating body of writing — but, also, a very difficult one. A reader must be willing to follow the twists and turns of the argument, to watch Ramsey dissect the writing of other authors who may not be familiar. A certain patience is required, but the patient reader will almost always be rewarded. More than once I have worked my way through an issue only, at the end, to discover that Ramsey had gotten there first. He did not, however, suppose that any formulation of his would be perfect. He wrote not to settle the matter but to "continue the conversation." His students spent their years at Princeton trying to trip him up. I remember well an occasion on which I was certain that I had him. I had found an inconsistency in the argument of *Christian Ethics and the Sit-In* (1961). There we sat in his office as I laid out the problem. To my amazement he seemed unfazed. A few puffs on the pipe, a "hrumph" or two, and he responded: "Well, I never could get everything said exactly the way I wanted." For all that, he was perhaps the last tie to the era of Reinhold and Richard Niebuhr — an era in which theology still had some general purchase on public life in this country. And his writings, difficult as they are, were widely read by many concerned with the problems of warfare and medicine.

Over time, however, one tended to notice the idiosyncrasies less as the deeper and more compelling aspects of Ramsey's character came to light. He was a man moved by a deep sense of vocation. I can recall him once offering me some counsel when I was considering several job possibilities. I suggested that the more attractive position of the two might simply appeal to one's sinful ambition. To which he responded: "I'm surprised to hear you say that. There is, after all, such a thing as a sense of vocation — of applying the whole of one's powers to a calling." Spoken like a good Methodist. And I cannot recall ever hearing him say anything more characteristic of the man or of the impression he made upon me: the sense that he applied the whole of his powers to his calling.

His first book, *Basic Christian Ethics*, was dedicated — in his own "poetic" way — to the memory of his mother and father. I reproduce it here:

THIS BOOK IS GRATEFULLY DEDICATED

to my

MOTHER AND FATHER

Mamie McCay Ramsey
(June 20, 1872 – Oct. 26, 1948)
Who spent herself with serene, lavish and noble
affection and who died at last of release from
duty faithfully performed,

and

Rev. John William Ramsey
(Feb. 17, 1869 – Oct. 26, 1948)
For nearly sixty years an ordained minister of the
Methodist Church who sought by use of heart
and mind to bring people to an "experimental"
knowledge of God in Christ.

As his student I had puzzled over this dedication, but lacked the nerve to inquire about it. How had it happened, I wondered, that his parents had died on the same day? An accident perhaps? Finally, when I returned to Princeton for the occasion of his retirement, I spent an evening with him and found him, understandably, in a reflective and nostalgic mood. Working up my courage, I asked. The story was better than I could have imagined. Ramsey's father had been ill for the last years of his life, and his mother had faithfully nursed her husband. On the evening of October 26, 1948, she went into the bedroom to give him his last medication for the evening — and found him dead in bed. Relatives were notified and a doctor called. While the doctor went to examine the corpse in the bedroom and pronounce death, Ramsey's mother sat down in a chair in another room. When the doctor and the others came out of the bedroom, they found her dead in her chair. Having "spent herself with . . . affection," and having now been released "from duty faithfully performed," she had died.

Ramsey himself had been telephoned at word of his father's death, had thrown some things into his car, and begun to drive south. Only upon his arrival did he learn that he had come for the burial not only of his father but also of his mother. Reflecting that evening of his retirement, he noted that many — himself included — had said how unfortunate it was that his mother should have died then. Just when she was released from the need to care for her husband, she might have traveled a little, visited her children, and so forth. But, said Paul, after a few weeks he realized how foolish that was. She had died at precisely the right moment, faithful to the end — and "she wouldn't have wanted it any other way."

Paul Ramsey likewise was moved by a deep and abiding sense of vocation. His calling in life had many aspects, of course, some of them private and familial. He was deeply devoted to his wife Effie and his daughters Marcia, Jennifer, and Janet. But he was moved also by commitment to the discipline of Christian ethics, which he sought "by use of heart and mind" to further. In both his writing and his teaching the whole man was committed.

Paul liked to end his large lecture course with a passage from St. Augustine's *City of God.* I myself heard him do it during my first year at Princeton, when I sat in the lectures of his undergraduate course on moral problems. In typical Ramsey fashion it was a good show from beginning to end, but he saved the best for last. Anticipating the ritual of student applause at the completion of the final lecture, he wound down his stirring peroration — hrumphing and wheezing and "you knowing" all the way. Then, gathering up his papers so as to be ready to stride from the room with applause still ringing in his ears, he quoted for the students the words with which St. Augustine closes that mammoth work written over so many years: "I think I have now, by God's help, discharged my obligation in writing this large work. Let those who think I have said too little, or those who think I have said too much, forgive me; and let those who think I have said just enough join with me in praising God." That is vintage Paul Ramsey as he is best remembered — bridging the gap between Augustine's world and his own, filled with humor and delight, combining self-deprecation with a sense of self, but, above all, manifesting a sense of his calling that went, finally and ultimately, beyond loyalty to Princeton University alone.

READING LIST

Basic Christian Ethics (New York: Charles Scribner's Sons, 1950, recently reprinted in the "Library of Theological Ethics" by Westminster/John Knox Press)

War and the Christian Conscience: How Shall Modern War be Conducted Justly? (Durham, North Carolina: Duke University Press, 1961)

Nine Modern Moralists (Englewood Cliffs, New Jersey: Prentice-Hall, 1962)

The Just War: Force and Political Responsibility (New York: Charles Scribner's Sons, 1968)

The Patient as Person (New Haven and London: Yale University Press, 1970)

Fabricated Man: The Ethics of Genetic Control (New Haven: Yale University Press, 1970)

Ethics at the Edges of Life: Medical and Legal Intersections (New Haven: Yale University Press, 1978)

The Essential Paul Ramsey, ed. William Werpehowski and Stephen D. Crocco (New Haven and London: Yale University Press, 1994)

Durant Waite Robertson, Jr.

Department of English

BY LYNN STALEY

D. W. Robertson, Jr., or Robbie as he was fondly and familiarly known, was by 1969, when I arrived at Princeton, one of the pre-eminent medievalists of his generation. Together with B. F. Huppé, with whom he had published two books, *Piers Plowman and Scriptural Tradition* and *Fruyt and Chaf: Studies in Chaucer's Allegories,*[1] and R. E. Kaske, he helped to define what is known as Exegetics, or the exegetical approach to medieval literature. Robbie himself came to define an approach ("Robertsonianism") that assimilated literary texts to the vast medieval system(s) of scriptural interpretation, particularly with the publication of his major study, *A Preface*

[1] *Piers Plowman and Scriptural Tradition* (Princeton: Princeton University Press, 1951); *Fruyt and Chaf: Studies in Chaucer's Allegories* (Princeton: Princeton University Press, 1963).

to Chaucer, which posed a carefully articulated and aggressively formulated challenge to a discipline whose tenets were increasingly New Critical.[2] *A Preface to Chaucer* not only insisted on the priority of primary texts as interpretive guides to the *mentalité* of the entire sweep of the Middle Ages, but upon the high Latin and Augustinian culture of a Middle Ages conceived of in iconographic and hierarchical terms.

It is a tribute to Robbie's erudition and intellectual curiosity that he did not rest on his laurels, but continued to engage new fields. *Chaucer's London* moves away from the focus upon iconography and exegetical interpretation of scripture that underlies his earlier work and explores the topography and the political and historical underpinnings of late fourteenth-century London. *Abelard and Heloise* is likewise an excursion into the history of a period as it is revealed through and helps to make sense of the experiences of two of medieval culture's most famous lovers. The shape of Robbie's scholarly life can be seen in miniature in the last volume he published, *Essays in Medieval Culture*, which collects a wide variety of essays that adumbrate the progress of his mind. However, even then the story of Robbie's work is not complete without reference to his final consuming interest in the shape of fourteenth-century life (both lived and imaginary) as we can detect it in the manorial, legal, and ecclesiastical records that have survived. Thus, during the last period of his life, when he had retired from Princeton to live in Chapel Hill, he began yet another line of research, equally rooted in primary materials, that might, if pursued to its end, pose a subtle challenge to the methodology by which he was already known. The articles he published in retirement to a great degree anticipate the present interest among medievalists in social history.[3] Though most of Robbie's

[2] The best account of the trends in Medieval Studies and Robertson's relationship to those trends is perhaps that of Lee Patterson, "Historical Criticism and the Development of Chaucer Studies," in *Negotiating the Past* (Madison: University of Wisconsin Press, 1987), pp. 1–40.

[3] See, for example, his "Who Were 'The People'?" in *The Popular Literature of Medieval England*, ed. Thomas J. Hefferman (Knoxville: University of

last work is unpublished, existing only in the form of notes and charts, those of us who corresponded with him during those years, know how much excitement he felt at this new direction. What stopped him finally was the arthritis in his hands that made it painful for him to write or even use a computer for long stretches.

So brief an account of his writings cannot do justice either to Robbie's achievement or to the amount of controversy generated by that achievement. Students like to describe the academy as an "ivory tower," but they have not been privy to the take-no-prisoners mood of many academic conferences or to the vigor of academic exchanges whose arena is the written page. Robbie entered into the lists of Medieval Studies with the force of his vigorous mind and pen and voice; he did not shun controversy but courted it. He set himself against an academy that he saw as dominated by a liberal humanist point of view, insisting that we need not agree with or like what we find in the documents we study, that we must however look at an age, seeking to discover its peculiar terms of discourse. If those terms were manifestations of a set of beliefs that are foreign to us, if they countermand what we know of the heart, we must nonetheless honor them and recognize their use in literary texts we too often see as reflections of ourselves. Here, he anticipated the thrust of much of the "New Historical" work now being done, and many in today's academy who might shun the title can be described as "Robertsonian" in spirit, if not in letter. Throughout his scholarly life he engaged with scholars of equal weight, notably with E. Talbot Donaldson of Yale and Morton W. Bloomfield of Harvard. I think it is fair to say that there was little love lost between Princeton and these schools during Robbie's tenure. Robbie's eloquence, his massive intelligence, his dislike

---

Tennessee Press, 1985); "Chaucer and the 'Commune Profit': The Manor," in *Mediaevalia: A Journal of Mediaeval Studies* 6 (1980): 239–259; "Simple Signs from Everyday Life in Chaucer," in *Signs and Symbols in Chaucer's Poetry*, ed. John P. Hermann and John J. Burke, Jr. (University, Alabama: University of Alabama Press, 1981); "'And For My Land Thus Hastow Mordred Me?' Land Tenure, the Cloth Industry, and the Wife of Bath," in *The Chaucer Review: A Journal of Medieval Studies and Literary Criticism* 14 (1980): 403–420.

for unsupported interpretation, and his courage may have won him enemies, but they also engendered admiration and respect. Those of us who were his students, for better or for worse, saw ourselves as a special cadre, trained for warfare but expecting to be as sheep among wolves. I am being only partially fanciful here, for Robbie saw the academy as poised for a slide into the mediocrity of subjectivism.

That he found himself the spokesman for hierarchical ordering at a time when American universities were the stages for an emerging women's movement and a vociferous anti-war movement may or may not be a coincidence. Certainly he had little affinity for either of these movements, and his unhappiness with Princeton students (graduate students included) for their stand on the United States' invasion of Cambodia in the spring of 1970 was palpable. However, what remains important about Robbie in the context of the University atmosphere of the late 1960s and early 1970s is his refusal to judge students in terms of their political beliefs. He judged what he was given to read; he judged what he heard said in class, and he left his personal beliefs out of the equation. This is nowhere so evident as in his support of the few women students who came his way.

This was of course a time when women were first moving in significant numbers into graduate schools; and, though Princeton had had women before in its graduate classes, my class was the first important block of women to colonize the Graduate College. Robbie, with his faintly obscene humor, his refusal to be earnest, and his very conservative political stance, could hardly be expected to welcome the sight of groups of women around his seminar table. How then could he joke about lusty wenches or soft bosoms or beds suddenly catching on fire? How could he tell Ovid's already obscene tale of Priapus as a tale of a supposedly innocent picnic gone awry? How would he handle the Wife of Bath's rhetorical thrust and parry with his usual barrage of Classical humor and patristic citation when her sisters sat taking notes? Such an approach would not go down in today's classrooms; I doubt even Robbie could get away with it. However, what tipped the scales in Robbie's favor was his absolute integrity, his intellectual honesty, his interest in an age whose anti-feminism he never attempted to deny. That he did not deplore it is a tribute to his own historicism, for he refused to superimpose modernity upon the past. Furthermore, he may have been a "traditional man," but his traditionalism did not affect my professional career, nor that of any woman I know. On the contrary, Robbie looked at the work, cheered on the person who did the work, teased with his sweet southern manners, but always encouraged. If he called you "honey child" or grinned down the table when he hit a bawdy pun, that was part of a public performance whose own point was bound up with his sense of the Middle Ages as at once intensely serious but never overtly solemn.

His gifts to his students were many; characteristically he did not let us know how rare they were. How shall he be remembered? He could be easy and outrageously funny in class. No one could read Chaucer as he did or could seem to have walked with him through the streets of a vanished London Robbie knew intimately, sometimes eerily. His graduate seminars could be marvelous windows into the dramatic capacities, the rhetorical nuances, the flexibilities of Middle English, including its willingness to spawn salacious puns. Robbie, with his deadpan manner, mobile eyebrows, and delayed laugh would read and we would begin to understand something about the sheer size of the language Chaucer employed. Certainly I learned to read Chaucer out loud from listening to and watching Robbie, and my guess is there are many like myself who try each year to read the *Miller's Tale* with as much belly humor as Robbie could bring to class. His gift for impersonation gave life to the dead: he could stage a conversation between John of Gaunt and John Wyclif as though he had been a fly on the wall, or recount Ovid's tales in a southern accent and with down-home details that made them as meaningful as they are slyly ironic. In fact, he insisted on the ways in which humor was fundamental to meaning. "You don't have to be solemn to be serious" echoed around his table, and he was more than capable of turning this dictum upon students overly eager to impose solemnity upon Chaucerian moments. He shared his ongoing work with us, his moments of revelation, his tremendous interest in literature and cultural history. He insisted that we go the extra mile and find proof for what we said in class or dared to write in papers. He was kind. He made it possible for me to learn in ways many professors might not have by giving me the freedom to chase my ideas through Firestone Library, and I think I am not alone in saying I have rarely felt as zestful as I did in that great collection of books. He read the work we turned in quickly and willingly; he praised and criticized. The key, I think, to his approach was patience: he would not hound a student to finish chapters or to meet deadlines; working with him was self-selective in the sense that you must be able to direct yourself. Robbie then met you more than halfway, quick to promote work that he saw as significant.

He was a generous and a shy man. Many of us have spent some tense times getting to know him. He could be what I call a "tough date," answering questions meant to be open-ended with a "yes" or a "no," leaving the other party to dream up another conversational gambit. This could go on for a while until he became comfortable, when his own fund of stories would begin to emerge — childhood, gardening, travel, impersonations of important people . . . and that all-encompassing laugh. He sported a Robertson clan tie, white bucks in summer. His life was a testimony to his extraordinary discipline, physical as well as mental. He exercised consistently in the pool he had built, paid careful attention to his lifestyle. You could not know Robbie without knowing and loving Betty, whose sweetness and common sense and good humor smoothed out Robbie's rougher demeanor.

I share with so many — John V. Fleming, Thomas P. Roche, Jr., Chauncey Wood, Paul Olson, Darryl Gless, Margreta De Grazia, Gail McMurray Gibson — clear memories of Robbie's quirks, of his frustratingly stubborn approach to life, and of his absolutely fundamental courtesy. It was a moment of great loss to Princeton when in 1980 he chose to take early retirement and to leave New Jersey for North Carolina. Despite his geographic distance he continued to engage with those of us who count ourselves among his academic get. Like many, I have old letters from Robbie that are as warm, as intelligent, and as human as any I have received. His death occurred just a few days before the 1992 meeting of the New Chaucer Society in Seattle, which offered its own moment of official recognition. I think, however, Robbie would have most liked the stories Chauncey Wood and I told *sotto voce*, old Robbie stories, not at all solemn.

READING LIST

A Preface to Chaucer: Studies in Medieval Perspectives (Princeton: Princeton University Press, 1962)

Chaucer's London (New York: Wiley, 1968)

The Literature of Medieval England (New York: McGraw-Hill, 1970)

Abelard and Heloise (New York: Dial Press, 1972)

Essays in Medieval Culture (Princeton: Princeton University Press, 1972)

Henry Norris Russell

Department of Astrophysical Sciences

BY LYMAN SPITZER, JR.

The career of Henry Norris Russell was as brilliant as the stars he loved to analyze, and led him to a top position among astronomers. His close connections with Princeton, first with the town, then with the College of New Jersey, and finally with the University, make him an appropriate figure to commemorate at Princeton University's 250th Anniversary.

His family had made substantial connections with Princeton several years before Henry was born. His father, Alexander G. Russell, came from Nova Scotia in 1872 to enter the Princeton Theological Seminary, and in 1876 became pastor of a church in Oyster Bay, Long Island. Henry's maternal grandfather, Henry L. Norris, Jr., a retired businessman, came to Princeton with his family in 1874 and bought a large Victorian house at 79 Alexander Street (then Canal Street). Two years later, one of Henry Norris's two daughters, Eliza H. Norris, married Alexander Russell and moved to Oyster Bay. There in the following year their first son was born, on October 25, 1877, and named after his grandfather Norris.

Young Henry must have made frequent visits to his grandfather's house, a spacious high-ceilinged, wide-porched mansion which gradually became the focus of Henry's personal and family life. In a talk he gave almost eighty years later at the Princeton University Observatory, he mentioned that he was only a few months old when he first visited his grandfather's Alexander Street home. "I naturally don't remember much about it," he remarked, "but I have known Princeton more or less ever since."

Henry Russell was brilliant even as a child, and his parents wanted to be sure he had the best schooling. So they enrolled him in the Princeton Preparatory School; the principal (and founder) of the school was John B. Fine, a brother of Professor Henry B. Fine, a mathematician at the College of New Jersey and subsequently dean at the University; their sister, May M. Fine, had a corresponding post in the newly organized Miss Fine's School. Both his grandfather and grandmother Norris had died, but his aunt, Ada Norris (Henry Norris's other daughter), was still at 79 Alexander Street. Henry lived with her while he was at Princeton during his school and college years, and she looked after him with devotion and love as a surrogate mother.

In 1893 Henry Russell completed his studies at the Preparatory School, and entered the College of New Jersey, which during his senior year, just three days before his nineteenth birthday, became Princeton University. His entrance exams had been primarily in Latin (Vergil, Cicero, Sallust) and Greek (Xenophon, Homer). In contrast, his college work placed greater emphasis on mathematics and science; it was here that he discovered his natural interest and aptitude. Mathematical ability ran in his family.

His grandmother Norris had won a gold medal for her unequalled performance in a mathematical competition at her New York school. Similarly, some thirty years later Henry's mother won first prize in a mathematical examination at the University of Edinburgh.

Henry's fantastically wide and precise memory (virtually total recall) served him well in his college courses, and he received his B.A. with the remarkable rank of 1.02. His degree was awarded *Insigni cum Laude*, an honor given rarely if ever in earlier years at Princeton and never since. Then on to graduate school at Princeton University, with a Ph.D. degree in astronomy awarded in 1900.

While Russell had extraordinary abilities, he had not yet learned to set practical limits on his efforts, and in 1900 he had a nervous breakdown. His Aunt Ada again took care of him at 79 Alexander for much of a year, and during the following year he travelled some in Europe. By 1902, when he began three years of postdoctoral research in Cambridge, England, he had recovered his health. In 1905 he returned to Princeton with the faculty rank of instructor. Rising rapidly, he became a professor in 1910 and director of the Observatory in 1911, posts which he occupied for more than thirty-five years.

Successfully launched at Princeton University, Russell felt that he could now support a family and in 1908 he married Lucy May Cole, whom he had courted for more than a decade. She was a daughter of John H. Cole (Harvard 1870), a lawyer in New York. At Aunt Ada's heartfelt invitation, the newlyweds moved into the ancestral home at 79 Alexander Street.

No article about Henry Norris Russell can be regarded as complete unless it describes at least the salient features of his scientific research. With his strong background and interest in both astronomy and physics, Russell's scientific work throughout his active life made use of established physical laws to interpret astronomical observations, and thus to reveal the nature of the universe around us. This search into the unknown took him into many different branches of astronomy. His extensive list of publications, some two hundred in number, covers the entire horizon of astronomical research.

One area which he explored on many different occasions was the distance from the Sun to various stars. This fundamental property of our stellar system had been determined with simple trigonometry for a few stars, just as distances on the Earth's surface are often determined by surveyors. The astronomical base line needed must be a long one — the distance of the Earth from the Sun. Russell was involved in this trigonometric program during his three years in England.

Use of the Earth-Sun distance as a base line is accurate only for the closer stars. For more distant objects a longer base line is required. The distance between two stars, orbiting around each other in a visual binary system, can provide such a greater base line, whose length can be determined from Newton's laws of motion. Russell devised an approximate method for computing the distances to these binary systems and published, jointly with his associate Charlotte Moore, a table giving distances (called "dynamical distances") for some 1,700 such double stars.

An additional basic property of a star is its total mass. If the two stars in a binary system eclipse each other alternately during every period, the orbit can be determined precisely and the sum of the masses of the two stars can be accurately found. The calculations needed to compute this mass would have been straightforward with modern digital computers, but in Russell's day were regarded as forbiddingly complex. Russell, who delighted in simple, convenient solutions of apparently complex mathematical problems, devised a combination of tables and graphs which permitted a ready determination of the mass. The results obtained with his method have significantly increased our knowledge of stellar masses.

Another major characteristic of a star is its composition — what chemical elements are present and in what proportions. To explore this topic one must use a spectrograph, which splits light into its component colors or wavelengths. Since individual atoms show strong absorption and emission only at certain characteristic wavelengths, different for each element, measurement of the spectrum can reveal what elements are present in the visible surface layers of the stars. However, to understand what the spectrum is telling us, we must be able to identify for each element what its characteristic wavelengths are. In the first half of the twentieth century physicists had not fully analyzed the spectra of all the chemical elements.

To help fill this gap, Russell waded energetically into a torrent of spectroscopic research, analyzing spectra of such astronomically interesting elements as oxygen, neon, calcium, and titanium — for each element, usually the singly ionized species (missing one electron). His was a well known name among those physicists specializing in atomic spectra.

A major climax of his astronomical and physical research on spectra was his great 1929 paper, "On the Composition of the Sun's Atmosphere." This work drew the startling conclusion that hydrogen atoms were the predominant constituent, some thousand times more abundant than the familiar heavy atoms (such as carbon, oxygen, magnesium, silicon, iron) that make up the earth. Others had suggested this result a few years earlier, but Russell's more detailed and complete analysis was conclusive. The predominance of hydrogen is now believed applicable to most of the visible material in the universe.

These research programs will give at least an impression of the ways in which Russell used physical theory to interpret astronomical observations and to reveal the properties of our universe. His ideas on how this might best be done had an influence far beyond his own published papers. His informal discussions with other astronomers scintillated with suggestions for research plans, described with his usual enthusiasm, and supported by relevant facts stored in his fabulous memory. During much of his career he

Henry Norris Russell (left) with Lyman Spitzer, ca. 1950. The photograph was taken in Professor Spitzer's office in the Old Observatory, now demolished.

spent a few months each year in California, visiting the Mt. Wilson Observatory, where the world's two most powerful telescopes at that time (mirror diameters of 60 and 100 inches) were located. The observing programs carried out there, and at other observatories also, were substantially influenced by his comments and suggestions. Graduate students trained by him rose to active research posts not only at Mt. Wilson but also at Harvard and Princeton.

He remained scientifically active until his death. His bibliography includes seventeen papers published in the decade 1947–1957, mostly dealing with eclipsing binary stars and the analysis of spectra. Truly a remarkable career!

The outstanding quality of his scientific work was honored in almost every way known to the astronomical community, with medals and honorary degrees bestowed on him in this country and abroad. He was a member of the United States National Academy of Sciences and other honorary societies in this country as well as a foreign associate of a half dozen such science academies in other countries. He served as president of several societies, including the American Philosophical Society and the American Association for the Advancement of Science.

As a person, Russell's most evident characteristics were a tremendous enthusiasm combined with his tremendous memory. During my two years as a graduate student I delighted to hear him talk about any of the numerous scientific topics that interested him. I listened to him with fascination both in course lectures and in small discussion groups. He must have noticed how much I enjoyed hearing him, for he seemed frequently to talk directly toward me.

His tendency to go to sleep during colloquia was also evident. Particularly striking was his ability to wake up at the end, rise to his feet and make penetrating comments about the talk which the rest of us had just heard! Very occasionally, when seated at a table, giving a lecture in some course, he would slow down, put his arms and head on the table and doze for a few moments, while we looked at each other and wondered whether it would be better to wait quietly or to tiptoe out!

After my return to Princeton as Russell's successor, my wife and I came to know both the Russells very well. We and our four children enjoyed being with them, and they became Uncle and Aunt to our family. Our children were often engrossed watching his dexterous fingers fold paper into boats, balls, and animals for them. Occasionally during springtime we all went for picnics together, sometimes among the boulders high up on the ridge, sometimes beside Beden's Brook to see the mertensia in bloom. Especially we recall the celebrations around Christmas, singing carols together; Uncle Henry always knew the verses and sang them heartily. Then there was the tall Christmas tree in their formal parlor, with lighted candles on every branch (and a bucket of water on one side, just in case).

Uncle Henry was always friendly and encouraging to me. Both

as a person and a scientist he was an inspiration to all of us. Knowing him and Aunt May was a joy for us and remains so in our memory.

READING LIST

"On the Composition of the Sun's Atmosphere," *Astrophysical Journal* 70 (1929): 11

Modifying Our Ideas of Nature: The Einstein Theory of Relativity (Princeton: Princeton University Press, 1920)

The Composition of the Stars, being the Halley Lecture delivered on 1 June 1933 (Oxford: The Clarendon Press, 1933)

The Solar System and Its Origin (New York: Macmillan, 1935)

With Charlotte E. Moore: *The Masses of the Stars, with a General Catalogue of Dynamical Parallaxes* (Chicago: University of Chicago Press, 1940)

Harlow Shapley, *Henry Norris Russell, 1877–1957: A Biographical Memoir* (New York: National Academy of Sciences, 1958)

William Feay Shellman, Jr.

School of Architecture

BY NICHOLAS MOFFETT PYLE

William Shellman seemed to me, a midwesterner who had been an undergraduate in New England, to be compelling evidence that Princeton was indeed the northernmost Southern university. When I entered the Graduate School of Architecture in 1968, Billy (as he was universally known) was an elegant gentleman of fifty-two, with thick, curly grey hair neatly trimmed and brushed into submission and a wardrobe that ranged from somber three-piece suits to blazers with brilliantly colored trousers, all perfectly cut and immaculately pressed. No donnish disarray or comfy rumple was to be observed on his person. He was a native of Savannah, with architecture degrees from the University of Virginia and Princeton, and spoke in well-formed sentences spiced with Southern hyperbole. His voice was soft, with a Gielgudesque silkiness to it and an accent that could be taken for Mid-Atlantic or Deep Southern, depending on the subject. So gentle was his speech, in fact, that he had to emphasize his stronger sentiments with deeply furrowed frowns and belligerent juttings of the lower lip.

At that time his furrows and juttings were many. Although he was to be promoted to full professor three years later, at the time I studied with him Billy was already seen by many as outmoded, a relic of Princeton's gentlemanly past. He was to them that wonderfully archaic fellow who had designed the president's robe and the banner that hung on Nassau Hall at the commencement ceremonies, and had executed the quaint drawings of Princeton's old buildings that adorned the official University plates.[1] He was not, however, considered to be a part of any current academic or professional movement.

Billy, in turn, felt that the School of Architecture was going to Hell in a handbasket.

During my years at Princeton there was in the School of Architecture a sort of house style, based on the 1929 Le Corbusier modernist vocabulary and characterized by a rigorous refinement of formal syntax. Students helped each other master the intricacies of this system, and their work, as a result, all tended to look alike. There was considerable appeal to this process, since the style had a simple, consistent logic and a limited palette of forms that a relative novice could learn to manipulate in such a way as to seem to be producing genuine architecture. Furthermore, it had the stamp of approval from the school's preeminent design masters, who were enjoying considerable attention in the architectural press.

To Billy this was the depth of triviality. While teachers and students were busying themselves with superficial exercises, he thought, the sacred duty of architectural education was being ignored. Unless he could rescue them, Princeton architectural graduates would be sent into the world unequipped with the vital skills

[1] He even designed the splendid banner that hung over the hockey team's bench at Hobey Baker Memorial Rink, although in his lifetime it flew from a staff in his garden at sufficiently important gatherings.

needed for their profession, not even aware that they were lacking them. They could be expected only to worsen the already deplorable state of architecture.

If I make Billy sound like a fanatic or a curmudgeon, let me assure you that he was not. Looking back after twenty-five years of practicing architecture, with some eight of teaching thrown in, I think that he was justified in his concern about the siren-like perils that lured students away from their most important lessons, and correct about what those most important lessons were.

Billy taught introductory courses in architecture and the visual arts as cultural expression, and courses intended to strengthen the architectural student's visual sensitivity. He also taught a graduate course on the principles of landscape architecture. Part of what he taught us was how important architecture, of both buildings and landscapes, is to society, not just in its utilitarian or programmatic functions nor in its symbolic value, but in its ability to satisfy deeper needs of people to express and embody their values.[2]

But more often he tried to show us how buildings and streets, gardens and parks went about the jobs they were meant to do, showing us along the way how many-layered were those jobs. Lecturing to us about light he would show us how the golden recurved domes of Russian and Baltic churches catch the low near-arctic sun and reflect it gloriously when all below is descending into darkness; and how the gilt rococo carving sprawling all over the walls of the Amalienburg pavilion conspired with mirrors and candlelight to give a room for dancing the illusion of having no material boundaries. His aim was not to show us how to make a church or a ballroom, or indeed to suggest that we ought to do so, but to make us begin to understand the complexity of the tasks

[2] One example of his, which I had never heard in my several previous encounters with the subject, was to make the connection with the English Romantic landscape garden and the Enclosure Act: how the garden expressed a hatred for the patchwork division of the countryside and nostalgically recreated the previous world without enclosures.

we had before us and what preparation would be needed in order to fulfill them.

That preparation is not, of course, something that can be obtained in its entirety in a university course. There is no end to the process of learning how to make good architecture. Billy's role in the process was to open our eyes and sharpen our ability to see what is around us; to teach us to question and discern what makes an example of architecture work better or less well; to help us to appreciate the vast range of tools architects have available to adjust their works to the boundless demands made upon them; and to exercise and develop our inventive potential.[3]

Billy often used historical examples like the Amalienburg for his teaching, calling our attention to instructive points that we would not otherwise have noticed, preoccupied as we were with the latest wrinkles in design. We tended to see pre-modern buildings and landscapes either as freeze-frames in the grand stylistic procession of art history or else as illustrations of architectural theory. For instance, he loved to show the plan of his alma mater in Charlottesville, where Thomas Jefferson's original campus of the University of Virginia provides one of history's great models of architecture as the expression of ideas. When I was a graduate student at Princeton, the Jefferson buildings were generally discussed by faculty and students for their symbolic and formal qualities and for their relationship to European architectural and social thought. Only Professor Shellman discussed the ways in which the campus illustrates Jefferson's convictions about how a democratic society should teach its youth.

The greatest resource for Billy's instruction was the Princeton campus itself, a splendidly varied and eminently available trove of historical and historical-seeming architecture, landscape, and plan-

[3] This last clause is a paraphrase from a lecture he gave to students at the Royal Institute of Technology in Stockholm in 1966, where he was a visiting lecturer and critic. The lecture was later reprinted in an issue of *Arkitekten*, the journal of the Swedish architectural society, a copy of which he gave me. It was, typically of Billy as opposed to most academics, concerned with the most general of topics: "Architectural Invention."

ning. Billy was one of those sons of Princeton who had stayed on; save for periods in Savannah at the service of the war effort and his filial duty, he dwelt, studied, and taught in Princeton from his entrance to the Graduate School in 1939 to his death in 1987. He seemed to know every stone of the place and could draw readily upon its inexhaustible supply of lessons. Realizing that what we needed to learn required our directly experiencing the buildings, courts, paths, and vistas in space, time, and light with our own eyes and bodies, he led us to them and made us see and feel them.

Most of Princeton's campus was designed in imitation of a style that Billy, trained in the modernist tradition and devoted to the pursuit of truth in architecture, thought inappropriate to the twentieth century — though, of course, he loved it all and thought it quite well executed, particularly in comparison to the half-baked material currently claiming the title of architecture.[4] Princeton's academic revival architecture dated from a period when the symbolism of style itself was given great importance.[5] He used to point out with scornful glee the pronouncement carved into the stone of the archway between McCosh and Dickinson Halls:

> Here we were taught by men and Gothic towers democracy and faith and love of unseen things that do not die. — H. D. Milroy '14

"You cannot learn democracy from a building," he would crow, much less from a tower meant to simulate the ecclesiastical architecture of feudal Europe. Under Billy Shellman's guidance, however, these buildings, like the plaster casts of great sculptures used in nineteenth-century art instruction, taught the lessons of their

[4] In 1948, Billy wrote an eloquent letter to the *Princeton Alumni Weekly* railing against the construction of a "false Gothic building" for Princeton's gymnasium. The letter was in response to a pro-eclectic diatribe by a recent alumnus in the same pages, which ridiculed such notions as "a giant plastic pleasure dome." The Jadwin Gym certainly gave Billy the last chortle.

[5] The limited competition for Columbia's Morningside Heights campus yielded a classical Greek proposal, in order to achieve a modern version of Periclean Athens; a Gothic entry, which was meant to cloister innocent youth from the vicious world around it; and the winning Italian Renaissance design, which would recreate the brilliant intellectual achievements of Medici Florence.

original models. True to his modernist education, Billy admired Gothic architecture because its perceptual and spiritual attainments were inseparable from its structural aspirations. Unfortunately, this could not be said of its 1920s revival. But even the imitations could give glimpses of how architecture whose makers desired to express incorporeal concepts in light and space did so with solid earthen material, never missing a chance to create an effect but never shirking their duties of shelter and durability. We learned from Billy and these Gothic towers how mundane functional concerns of design could contribute to the aesthetic and emotional uplift of the building. Billy pointed out things that we had seen hundreds of times but that had never had any meaning for us. It would never occur to us to ask ourselves, for instance, what function a white sundial might have in a pseudo-Gothic Princeton courtyard beyond the nostalgic and the chronographic. (Notice it on your next stroll across campus towards the courtyard adjacent to the University Chapel. It was one of Billy's pet examples.)

The most basic lesson Billy taught was to learn how to look, which to Billy began with learning how to draw. Michael Wurmfeld, one of his students and an extremely able architect, said of Billy after his death in 1987, "Shellman developed the visual sensibilities of generations of Princeton architects. Drawing was always essential to his analytic method — an act of the mind followed by the movement of the hand." Another former student, Robert Venturi, one of the most influential architectural designers and thinkers of his generation, said that "Many of us at Princeton learned from him about how to look at beautiful buildings with our eyes, hearts, and minds, and free of dogma." At the faculty memorial service for Billy, his friend Professor Edward Cone of the Music Department said of him, "It was his talent for communicating what he saw, together with his insatiable desire for doing so, that made him a great teacher, not just of architecture, but of the esthetics of visual design. And not only in the classroom; to take a walk with him was to have one's own eyes opened, whether to the unappreciated worth of the frequently decried Alexander Hall, to the formal or functional defects of some new construction, or to the erosion of the careful planting on the walk to the Graduate College. To see correctly, he felt, was to see critically."

When I was at Princeton I took Billy's graduate class in the principles of landscape architecture and assisted him in his undergraduate course. In this course we had laboratory sessions that were really remedial drawing lessons, teaching students how to sketch simple objects. One might assume that university-level architecture students would already know how to do that. One might even share the widely held opinion that sketching is a skill superfluous to the practice of the architectural profession. Billy knew better. He knew that most students sketch badly, not just because of a lack of practice or talent, but because of a lack of skill in looking. They draw what they think is there, not what they really see. He knew that being able to see acutely, to understand what we are seeing, and to file that information away with all its possible connections are keys to creativity.

Some of Billy's students had the rare opportunity to continue our education by travelling with him. Billy seemed to know Rome, Venice, Florence, and Paris almost as well as he knew Princeton, and he had observed them with the same keenness. A few years after I received my degree I joined Billy on a British Victorian Society tour of later nineteenth-century Vernacular Revival houses and gardens (a historical category of extraordinary variety and inventiveness, which had been the source of much of our American suburban fantasies). The Society's distinguished guides were full of interesting historical commentary. But Billy's observations of houses by masterful architects such as Edwin Lutyens, Richard Norman Shaw, and Philip Webb, and gardens by the peerless Gertrude Jekyll, were of vastly greater value to an embryonic architect. After the tour Billy and I continued driving about, visiting cathedrals and spas, Oxford and Cambridge, villages and London. He was like a proud host showing me his finest treasures:

Look back at the tower from here! See what happens when you go down that curved street!

Most of Billy's off-campus instruction occurred not so far afield, but at his home on McCosh Circle. Billy, who was unmarried and live alone, invited students to meals quite often — lunches, usually, and dinners on such free evenings as were begrudged him by voracious Princeton society. He flattered students by entertaining us with the same attention and wit as must have held the local grandees in thrall. But it was all marvelously educational. Even hearing his David Willcocks-King's College Choir recording of the Allegri *Miserere*, which he played quite often and was the most wonderful thing I had ever heard, helped to prepare me for the moment I walked into King's College Chapel with Billy years later.

The house itself was designed by Billy for himself, one of his numerous works in the Princeton area. (His practice did extend as far as Spain, but that commission was for a Princeton family, too.)[6] Unpretentious and casual as it was, his house provided all sorts of striking illustrations of Billy's particular concerns. He would note, for instance, how the house's unusual siting (it was an L-shape pushed against one front corner of the lot) was the result of some regrettable underground utility that diagonally traversed the property. But as we sat under the eaves and looked out over the spacious rectangular back lawn walled with privets and edged with graveled paths, a broad herbaceous border extending alongside it that continued the width of the rear wing of the house, we found it hard to imagine why anyone would want it otherwise. A water main chopping across the middle of your property might be considered unfortunate, but as Billy quoted Louis Pasteur in his lecture to the Swedish architectural students, "Fortune favors

[6] William Shellman's architectural practice consisted mostly of residential work in and around Princeton, though he had done a couple of early works in Georgia and South Carolina and, during my stay at Princeton, a garden in the south of Spain for a Princeton couple. It was fascinating to observe the process of this garden's design, in which he practiced what he preached.

the prepared mind." Sipping our drinks and listening blissfully to the water dripping from a long scupper off the roof into a Japanese stone basin, rather than tunneling through a leader into the usual concrete trough, we wondered if we could ever achieve minds as awesomely prepared as Billy's.

Every room in Billy's house was a delight to be in and perfectly suited to the way Billy lived, including the rooms outside the house. Invited to rest in the little courtyard outside the dining room while Billy put the finishing touches on some pre-organized meal, we luxuriated in the intimacy and soft light of the lushly planted little space. It seemed to be transplanted, like Billy, from Savannah. Even the paving was verdant, with fat little succulents threatening to consume the bricks. In my native northern Illinois the place that outdoor room occupied would have been just a side yard, a non-place traversed without sensation on the way between the front yard and the back. At Billy's house it was to me a window into the magic we students might one day perform. I still think of it as a paradigm of what can be conjured from practically nothing by the practiced eye, the disciplined memory, and the prepared-mind memory of the inventive architect, to give beauty and pleasure to life.[7]

Billy tried to explain this process in his Swedish lecture:

> An architectural problem almost always has its origins . . . in the form of a list of accommodations, a schedule of spatial needs. . . . Such a list

[7] Another of Billy's works in Princeton, the barn he transformed into a residence for the Patrick Kellehers, illustrated even more strikingly his ability to see existing circumstances as opportunities to create new solutions to carefully formulated problems. The clients being people of formidable taste and sophistication, he was inspired and encouraged to make a place rich with surprises (the garden that caused guests to gasp when they reached the master bedroom at the top of the loft had been the hay ramp, the huge window through which they saw it, the door for bringing the hay inside); luxurious with unusual space (the intermediate levels for pitching the ever-descending supply of hay became gallery-rooms fully open to the loft); and almost dreamlike in its quiet splendor (the barnyard within the building's U-shape had become a garden laid out with gravel paths and geometric plantings, shaded with orderly fruit trees and trod by peacocks, where one could sit and look through the iron fence at the meadows beyond and think that one was, well, not in New Jersey).

> or schedule alerts and quickens your architectural imagination. . . . It acts as a trigger, which when tripped releases a flood of images, possibly at first rather general, then more detailed and broken down into smaller and smaller units of similar functions, remembered from past experience. Suppose it is a small lecture room of the size and purpose of that in which this paper was first read which you are called upon to design. If I had never been in such a room and had only scant knowledge of its use, the chances of success would be very limited. If I could remember many such rooms, not merely their names or locations but their several qualities down to . . . the most simple sort, I would have a vast reservoir from which to choose or reject. If I could unravel specific characteristics of sensory experience at the most basic level and discriminate between them, the chances for invention would be good. These remembered qualities, to list a few, would include those of sound and the ease of seeing and hearing; of illumination, texture, color and reflections; ease or fatigue in my body, seat, legs, arms, and back; the nearness or disturbing presence of other people; glare from windows or blackboards; qualities of heat and air currents; noise underfoot, noise of people outside the doors, noise from doors and hardwood made by those who are late. A man who can recover these and thousands of other images of previous sensory experience can select the tiny items that satisfy programmatic needs. The sum or addition of these choices can add up to a new set of relationships, a new order.

It is understandable, reading these words, how Billy would be impatient with students' spending so much of their precious time playing with lines and shapes on pieces of paper. That was fun, as I well remember, and to a certain extent useful and necessary. But it missed the most important point. I am forever grateful for Billy's tireless efforts to make us see that point.

Allen Goodrich Shenstone

Department of Physics

BY VAL L. FITCH[1]

In 1951, a year after Allen Shenstone had become chairman of the Physics Department, a man appeared in the chairman's office and said, "My name is Whiton. Is there a professor named Shenstone around here?" When told that Professor Shenstone was out for the day, he said, "He did me a great favor when I was an undergraduate in 1926."

When Shenstone returned the next day, he was told of the visit. As recounted in his autobiography, "I racked my brains to remember what the 'favor' could have been." He remembered

[1] In preparing this brief profile of Allen Shenstone, I have made use of an excellent biography by W.R.S. (Reggie) Garton, F.R.S., which was published in the *Biographical Memoirs of Fellows of the Royal Society* 27 (1981): 505–523. In addition, I made use of a highly interesting unpublished autobiography in Shenstone's faculty file, Princeton University Archives, Seeley G. Mudd Manuscript Library.

Whiton well, however. After graduation Herman F. Whiton had become a leading sailor of 6-meter boats and had been the winner in two Olympic games, achievements which Shenstone had followed with great interest because of his own keen pleasure in sailing. But what was the "favor?" Allen checked his academic record book and then remembered: He had flunked Whiton at midyear in the senior course in electricity. He had given Whiton a stern lecture about wasting his own time and brains as well as those of others. The "favor" was that straight talk which had made him get down to work. Whiton did very well in the course during the second term. Subsequently, "Swede" Whiton, a wealthy man, became an important benefactor to the department.

Allen Shenstone succeeded Henry DeWolf Smyth as chairman in 1949 when Smyth went off to Washington as a member of the United States Atomic Energy Commission. Shenstone served until 1960, the year before he retired from teaching. Those were years of substantial change in the department. They were years of expansion, with a shift in the emphasis in research programs. The teaching faculty more than doubled in size from twenty-three in 1949 to fifty-one when Allen stepped down. Furthermore, as a result of the McCarthy witch-hunts, they were years of turmoil in university faculties across the nation, and Princeton physics was not immune. They were years in which a hurricane blew a section of the roof from Palmer Laboratory, and a fire destroyed the cyclotron in the basement of Palmer.

Who was this man given to straight talk who so successfully steered the Physics Department through these eventful times? Allen Shenstone came to Princeton as a member of the Class of 1914 from Toronto, Ontario, Canada. His family circumstances were comfortable. His father was president and chairman of the board of the Massey-Harris farm equipment maker. It was a family of highly ordered minds, and the children were expected to perform accordingly. Even the rebellious ones succeeded. An aunt of Allen's found life at home too strict, ran away and married an itinerant printer. They ended up in Chicago, where her husband founded the R. R. Donnelley Publishing Company.

From Toronto there are, on the horizon, many possibilities for college. Why did Allen choose Princeton? Probably the most compelling reason was that three of his older cousins had attended and were enthusiastic alumni. Allen travelled alone on the train from Toronto in the autumn of 1910, the only Canadian student to enter that year. He had just turned seventeen and was to spend a large part of the rest of his long life in Princeton.

Allen graduated in the honors course in mathematics and physics — *magna cum laude* and with highest honors. From his autobiographical account of his undergraduate life it is clear that he probably enjoyed courses in literature as much as those in physics and mathematics, an interest he maintained throughout his life. After graduation, to see the West, he joined a survey crew for the summer and worked along the Fraser River in British Columbia. Subsequently, he applied to Cambridge University for graduate work and was accepted by J. J. Thomson, the discoverer of the electron, as a research student, and by Emmanuel College. He sailed for England in November 1914 on the *Lusitania.* In North America there was not yet an awareness of the enormity of the developing war in Europe, but it was immediately apparent in England. After only a brief time as a student, Allen obtained a commission in the British Army, in the Royal Engineers, in March of 1915. Early in the war, British officers were, by regulation, forbidden to shave the upper lip. Some officers opted to satisfy the requirement with only a thin line of hair, but this led to a regulation that officers had to shave the whole upper lip or none of it. Allen chose not to shave, and that accounts for the guardsman mustache that he maintained for the rest of his life.

To have spent three and a half years on the battlefields of France and survived is remarkable in itself. In his autobiography he describes many experiences where his survival was simply a matter of luck — a few feet here rather than there. In the characteristic understatement of the British, he was "mentioned in dispatches" at the time of the first battle of the Somme. Later, while on leave in England, he received the British Military Cross for bravery from the Queen herself. Reggie Garton, in his splendid biographical tribute to Allen for the Royal Society had this to say about those years as a British officer:

> Shenstone's own notes, which contain great detail of his experiences as a soldier, confirm what any friend of later years would know. Here was a man, not by nature disposed to strife or even argument or polemics, who had built into him, perhaps in part by origins — certainly by upbringing and precept — great courage, loyalty to good ends as he saw them, and complete steadfastness.

After the Armistice in November 1918, Allen was assigned to the army of occupation and was the commanding officer of the 56th Field Company of the Royal Engineers at Cologne. Demobilized in the summer of 1919, he found passage back to Canada and the family summer cottage in Smith's Cove, Nova Scotia, on the Annapolis Basin. After almost five years in the army, a good part of it spent in the dehumanizing circumstances of trench warfare in France, a summer month sailing in his beloved boat was just the right tonic, and the restorative period could begin. It was from here that he inquired of Princeton whether there were any fellowships available in either mathematics or physics. He was awarded one in physics, and in the autumn of that year he became one of two graduate students in Palmer Laboratory. His fellow student was Henry DeWolf Smyth, Class of 1918.

Shenstone still aspired to return to Cambridge and continue his work on his B.A. in research. The opportunity presented itself in 1920, when he was awarded the Charlotte Elizabeth Proctor Fellowship. Although the fellow was required to live at the Graduate College, he was allowed to spend two terms at Cambridge. But the situation there had changed. J. J. Thomson had retired, and had been replaced by Ernest Rutherford. The B.A. in research had been supplanted by the Ph.D. degree. However, in view of

Shenstone's war record, exceptions were made and he was able to obtain the degree he wanted, probably the last B.A. in research ever awarded at Cambridge.

For his thesis, at the suggestion of Rutherford, Shenstone did an experiment at the Cavendish Laboratory designed to search for short-lived radioactivity induced by alpha particle bombardment. The experiment involved detecting particles by viewing, through a microscope, the scintillations they produced when they struck a zinc sulphide screen. Different materials deposited on the rim of a rapidly rotating disk were exposed to a beam of alpha particles and particle emission was searched for just downstream of the point of bombardment. In order for the experiment to be sensitive to very short-lived radioactivities, it was necessary for the disk to be rotated at the maximum possible angular speed, producing a great amount of noise and, with the ever-present danger of the rapidly rotating disk tearing itself apart, measuring the rate at which scintillations appeared. It is easy to imagine the self-discipline required to view the roaring disk at close range through a microscope and accurately tabulate the faint flashes of light for long periods. It was a heroic one-man experiment, but it yielded a null result. The discovery of artificial radioactivity eleven years later by Curie and Joliet (for which they received the Nobel Prize) had to await the development of Geiger counters, which were much more sensitive than the older scintillation techniques used by Shenstone.

The experiment at the Cavendish was to be Shenstone's only foray into nuclear physics. He returned to Princeton to finish his Ph.D., with a thesis supervised by E. P. Adams dealing with a possible relationship between photoemission and the Hall effect. After obtaining his degree, he was appointed a demonstrator at the University of Toronto. It was there that his research interests turned to optical spectroscopy. In 1925 Princeton wooed him back with an appointment as assistant professor and with funds to construct and equip a spectroscopy laboratory. Working largely alone, he quickly established for himself an international reputation in the field. His most productive period in research was from 1925 to the onset of World War II in 1939. Perhaps his most important discovery was a phenomenon called autoionization. Independently, the same idea without the name was suggested by the Italian theorist E. Majorana. With Henry Norris Russell he proposed a spectroscopic notation which remains the standard to this day. Among his other collaborators was W. F. Meggers of the National Bureau of Standards and the great Spanish spectroscopist M. A. Catalan.

At the beginning of World War II, Shenstone volunteered his services to the War Office in London as a former officer. In 1940 he was appointed Special Assistant to the President, Canadian National Research Council. He almost immediately departed for Ottawa, where he served as a liaison officer between Canada and the United States on a wide range of technical problems. In 1942 he was transferred to London, where he continued to serve as Canada's liaison officer with Britain on wartime science. In this capacity he made many new friends, including the physicist C. G. Darwin (grandson of Charles Darwin) and physicist-turned-novelist C. P. Snow. I mention these two in particular because later they were to participate in Physics Department affairs when they came to visit Allen in Princeton. After the war he again took up his duties in Princeton and reestablished his research in Palmer Laboratory.

I first met Shenstone when I came to Princeton as an instructor in 1954. By then he was almost midway through his tenure as chairman. My initial impression was of a somewhat aloof person, very English in appearance and manner; his clothes were tailored in London and he drove English cars, Hillman and Rover, but he spoke with a Canadian rather than an English accent. The apparent aloofness was exaggerated by his having a highly protective and efficient secretary, Myrtle Farley. He also had a series of extraordinarily able administrative assistants. One of them was Leslie

("Bud") Vivian who, when he left the department, went on up the University administrative ladder. A junior faculty member like myself got his teaching assignments from Myrtle Farley; laboratory-research arrangements were made through the departmental administrative assistant. In my own case, I was totally engrossed in my research, largely carried out at the Brookhaven Laboratory on Long Island, seventy miles east of New York City. I returned to Princeton to teach classes and to see my family. The net result was that I came to know Shenstone only slightly while he was chairman. It was only twenty years later, after I married his stepdaughter, that I came to know him well.

Allen Shenstone was a remarkably direct person in his speech and in his relations with other people. He was not given to euphemisms. To Allen people did not "pass away," they died. People did not go to the "bathroom" except to take a bath. However, as we all learned, behind the somewhat forbidding exterior was a man of considerable warmth, a caring person. Allen Shenstone married twice. His first wife, Mildred (Molly) Chadwick, was an Englishwoman he had met in England during World War I. After her death in 1967 he married Tiffen Harper, a neighbor in Princeton, the widow of Raymond Harper, Class of 1918.

Shenstone's teaching was largely to undergraduates, and his research rarely included graduate students. One of them, William Martin, now of the National Institute of Standards and Technology, NIST, has recalled:

> Coming to Princeton as a graduate student in 1951, I was assigned to be A.G.S.'s research assistant. His duties as Chairman of the Physics Department took a good deal of his time, but he moved easily from meetings, etc., back to his research. The way I now think of Allen makes it difficult for me to remember why it was that, until I got to know him, he seemed somewhat unapproachable — it probably had more to do with his eyebrows than his actual character and nature. . . .
>
> Allen enjoyed teaching and showing how a thing was done, and he was a good research mentor. He knew how much to show you and how

much you should find out for yourself. In the early 1950s, one still used a mechanical calculator to reduce plate measurements [to wavelengths], search for energy levels, etc. I had never used one, and after showing me the most basic features, he said "There are tricks you will find out for yourself." I did, and had the pleasure of discovery. He also told me I should add two multi-digit numbers from left to right, so the sum would be in mind correctly. I still do that.

During the time I knew him, Allen attended fewer conferences away from Princeton than the average physicist, but he always made a strong impression when he spoke at a meeting or met younger physicists for the first time. At a conference on interferometry in Teddington in 1959, an early enthusiast for the Fourier-Transform spectroscopy described an erroneous FTS procedure by saying that the poor results made even a diffraction grating appear to be a good spectroscopic component. After this talk Allen stood up and said that practically all the existing data on optical spectra of atoms and molecules were due to diffraction gratings, the designers of new spectrometers should wait until they had done something with them before disparaging gratings, etc. He clearly spoke for many of the attendees and his comment met with general approval — the word had been given.

Wavelength calibration of high-resolution spectrometers for the IUE satellite (launched in 1978, still active!) and for the Hubble Space Telescope (HST) is accomplished by use of on-board platinum hollow-cathode lamps as sources of accurately known wavelengths. Bill Fastie of Johns Hopkins, who was chiefly responsible for the choice of the platinum lamp for standards for the IUE and the HST told me that they tried a lot of elements, and platinum looked to be the best because the spectrum had a large number of sharp UV lines. The consideration that finally convinced him, however, was that when he looked up the Pt II measurements and analysis, he found that Shenstone had done the work (1938) — he knew these data would be reliable and accurate. Since Allen's vacuum spectrograph had a resolution of perhaps 30,000 whereas the HST high-resolution instrument has a resolution of 90,000, Joe Reader and others in my group here have remeasured the Pt spectrum

> to obtain higher accuracy for the HST calibrations; nevertheless, whenever I hear about striking new observations for HST that are dependent on high spectral resolution I always remember that it all goes back to Allen's work.

Shenstone's high professional reputation was confirmed in 1950 when he was elected a Fellow of the Royal Society.

When I came to know Allen well I heard many stories from the days when he was chairman — the stories associated with the trying times that occurred during his chairmanship in the 1950s. The House Un-American Activities Committee had targeted a number of people in the department. In one case, it was a person who had received his Ph.D. and was kept on in a research position. In the eyes of the Committee, he was suspect for having attended Brooklyn College, which had a reputation as a hotbed of leftists in the 1930s, and for having parents who were still alive in the Soviet Union. A grant from the Office of Naval Research supported his research project. One day, the department got a call from an admiral in Washington, who said that the young researcher must be terminated because he appeared to be "a security risk." The department saw the gross injustice of this action, and persuaded the president of the University to call the admiral and tell him that if this was the price of the grant to Princeton, then no thank you. The Navy backed down.

Another case involved David Bohm, a young theoretical physicist of extraordinary promise who had been recruited by John Wheeler from the University of California in Berkeley, another center for leftist causes. During these turbulent years, the University fully supported faculty members who were called before the Committee — provided that they cooperated fully with the Committee. Bohm was called before the Committee in 1949 in connection with totally unsubstantiated charges that he and former colleagues at Berkeley were communist sympathizers. On principle, he decided not to testify, believing that it was not for him to betray or to tell stories on his friends. The Committee cited

Bohm for contempt of Congress, whereupon he was suspended by the president of the University and told not to set foot on campus, certainly not to use the library. Forty of the forty-one graduate students in physics signed a petition objecting to this action. The physics faculty also strenuously objected and sent a delegation to the president about the matter. The president was unrelenting. Later in the year the department voted to give Bohm, who was becoming one of the great expositors of quantum mechanics, another three-year term as an assistant professor, but this was vetoed by the Committee on Advancements and Appointments. Through all of this, Chairman Shenstone, despite the strongest feelings that an injustice had been done, felt that he could take no direct action because he was not an American citizen (he maintained his Canadian citizenship throughout his life). He did, however, introduce at a University faculty meeting a motion to the effect that, before any faculty member could be suspended or dismissed, the matter must first be brought before a faculty committee. The resolution was passed, and it remains in the Rules and Procedures of the faculty to this day.[2]

Shenstone's research was not in an area that was considered mainstream at the time, though subsequently it was to become so. He worked largely alone, at most with one or two others. He had few graduate students. Still, his influence in the physics department was profound and long lasting. He lived and worked by his own high principles and provided a pervading sense of stability and guidance in a period when research in physics was going through major changes. He always emphasized the importance of writing and speaking clearly and correctly, and the rewards that come from doing something well. He imbued those around him with these beliefs. But he was always modest about his own accomplishments and those of his family. When he was congratu-

[2] For an account of the Bohm affair forty-four years later, see David Z. Albert, "Bohm's Alternative to Quantum Mechanics," *Scientific American*, May 1994, pp. 58–67.

lated for the role his son Michael played in spiriting American hostages out of Iran, his response to congratulations was "Of course, he would see to that!" Michael, a career diplomat in the Canadian foreign service, was then responsible for Mideast and African Affairs in the Department of External Affairs in Ottawa.

Allen Shenstone died in Princeton on February 16, 1980, from a heart attack while recovering from an operation to repair an aneurism.

READING LIST

"Ultra-ionization Potentials in Mercury Vapor," *Physics Review* 38 (1931): 873–875

With Henry Norris Russell: "Perturbed Series in Line Spectra," *Physics Review* 39 (1932): 415–434

"First Spark Spectrum of Copper," *Philosophical Transactions of the Royal Society of London* A235 (1936): 195–243

"The First Spectrum of Copper (Cu I)," *Philosophical Transactions of the Royal Society of London* A241 (1948): 297–322

"Forbidden Transitions in the Palladium I Spectrum," *Proceedings of the Royal Society of London* A219 (1953): 419–425

Earl Baldwin Smith

Department of Art and Archaeology

BY DAVID R. COFFIN

Early on a Monday morning at the beginning of Freshman Orientation Week at Princeton in September 1936, a somewhat bewildered freshman was sent from the Registrar's Office in Nassau Hall to the office of Professor E. Baldwin Smith of the Department of Art and Archaeology on the third floor of the north stairway of old McCormick Hall. This was to be my first meeting with the man who would remain my mentor until his death in 1956. After knocking on his open door, I was greeted with the view of Smith perched on a tall stool poring over a drafting table. This was a position characteristic of him; it immediately put me at ease, since I had often seen my father, an architect, in the same pose. Rugged looks and a direct gaze conveyed the idea of a man who brooked no nonsense, while the receding hairline and domed forehead topping these features seemed appropriate to his nickname "Baldy," which actually referred to his name. I had been sent to Smith in his capacity as departmental representative of Art and Archaeology responsible for the academic programs of undergraduates electing the department, and as departmental representative and chairman of the recently established Divisional Program in the Humanities (later called the Special Program in the Humanities) in which I wished eventually to be enrolled. He quickly reviewed my course elections, making only one suggestion: during my first year I should be enrolled in the freshman course in architectural drawing. As his pose indicated, drafting was one of his main interests. To the dismay of most students, he believed that anyone could draw. It was simply "a matter of applying common sense to paper."

The evening before our conference I had been invited to dine with a young Cuban instructor in the School of Architecture, Eugenio Battista, who, learning that I was to enroll in Professor Smith's course in the history of ancient architecture, noted that he was one of the most popular teachers on the campus. Each year at graduation the seniors elected him their favorite lecturer. Battista did warn me that I might at first be baffled by Smith's "Down East" accent. As one familiar with New Englanders, I was more at home with the accent than was a Cuban, but my notes of the first few lectures transcribed unfamiliar architectural terms properly ending in vowels, such as "basilica," with a final "r," reflecting his New England pronunciation.

Earl Baldwin Smith was born at Topsham, Maine, in 1888. As a youth, he studied drafting and illustration at Pratt Institute for a year, where he developed his belief in the importance of drawing. He spent endless hours at the drafting table preparing the illustrations for his books, which lent a certain uniform elegance to all his publications. After Pratt he entered Bowdoin College where he graduated Phi Beta Kappa with an A.B. in 1911. Twenty years later Bowdoin honored him with an honorary Doctorate in Humane Letters. In the spring of 1911, in anticipation of his graduation, Smith wrote a letter to Dean Andrew Fleming West requesting admission to the Princeton Graduate School in the Department of Art and Archaeology, which after a check of his qualifications, was granted. During his first year he held a scholarship from Bowdoin, then in successive years he was awarded a Princeton Fellowship, followed by a Procter Fellowship, and finally the Jacobus Fellowship, the University's most distinguished graduate fellowship. Having completed his doctorate in 1915, Smith was appointed instructor in the department.

In March 1917 Smith enlisted as a corporal in the New Jersey National Guard. After officers' training at Plattsburg, he was commissioned a captain in the regular army and commanded Company H of the 312th Infantry of the 78th Division. He was wounded during the St. Michel offensive in September 1918 and, a month later, he was severely gassed at Grand Prés during the battle of the Argonne. Throughout the remainder of his life he suffered bouts of acute pain, but never revealed it to his students or colleagues. During World War II he taught aerial map reading and photographic interpretation at the Naval Air Combat Intelligence Officer School at Quonset, Rhode Island.

Professor Smith's war service may have contributed to his character, for he became a dominant member of the Princeton faculty. Everyone who met him was immediately struck by his strong personality. Often an undergraduate would use the image of an army first sergeant to describe him. During my first year as chairman of the department, Dean Brown took care to put me at my ease by recounting how nervous he had been as a novice dean of the faculty when he held his first meeting with "Baldy," then chairman of the Art Department. Smith's experience as a commanding officer served him well during his later years, too, when he officiated as Chief Marshal at University convocations, ordering and leading the academic processions under the authority of his baton.

To be a member and chairman of the Divisional Program in the Humanities was very appropriate for Smith, given the extraordinary breadth of his research. He read widely in anthropology, psychology, philosophy, and religion and instilled the same curiosity in his students. So, when as a senior I was writing a thesis on the Greek attitude toward nature in art and literature, he sent me to audit the course in cultural anthropology and to a fascinating public lecture on non-Euclidean geometry given by his friend, the eminent mathematician Howard Robertson; to William James's *Principles of Psychology*, and to articles by the philosopher Francis Cornford.

Smith's career in research and teaching demonstrated this interdisciplinary drive. His doctoral dissertation on the iconography of early Christian art was written under the guidance of Princeton's Charles Rufus Morey, who would soon be recognized as the most eminent medievalist in the country, wooed unsuccessfully by Harvard. This study was published in 1917, while Smith was in the army. Soon, however, Smith turned to the history of architecture, completing and publishing a manuscript on early churches in Syria left incomplete by another of his teachers, Howard Crosby Butler. (Smith later became the Howard Crosby Butler Memorial Professor of the History of Architecture.) While the Syrian book was basically archaeological and descriptive, Smith in his own research began to be more concerned with the meaning of architecture. His next book, on ancient Egyptian architecture, was not the traditional archaeological study, but bore the title *Egyptian Architecture as Cultural Expression.* Its last chapter was a superb consideration of habits of imagery and aesthetic attitude in ancient Egypt. After World War II, Smith's last two books considered the meaning of domical architecture in antiquity and the Early Christian era and the significance of the two-towered façade in ancient gateways and medieval churches. These books were the result of several graduate seminars. The seminars were often arduous, as the participants were obliged to view a stream of coin images, but the students learned to be thorough, and to recognize that "truth was in the details." They came to understand that moral virtue informed research. These values guided the wide ranging research of Smith's students, whether that of Alex Soper on Japanese Buddhist architecture, Alan Gowans on nineteenth-century American and Canadian architecture, or mine on Italian Renaissance architecture and gardens.

Smith's scholarly research always reinforced an intense and constant interest in teaching. In preparation for the 1912 International Conference on the History of Art, the president and eminent Italian art historian Adolfo Venturi wrote to Professor Marquand, founder and first chairman of the Princeton department, to inquire about the state of the discipline of art history in America. Marquand immediately asked Baldwin Smith, his first-year graduate student, to research the question. Smith queried some four hundred institutions of higher education regarding their courses, their instructors, and their libraries and photographic facilities in the history of art. Of ninety-five respondents, Smith determined that only sixty-eight offered adequate programs. He undoubtedly took pride in the fact that Princeton's rivals, Harvard and Yale, offered only eighteen and seven courses respectively, while Princeton had thirty-four, of which Smith himself would participate in twenty. In 1912, *The Study of the History of Art in the Colleges and Universities of the United States*, Smith's report, was published by the Princeton University Press, ensuring him a role as an authority on this aspect of American education.

Throughout his career at Princeton, Smith was involved in almost every educational innovation the University undertook. After World War I Smith and Sherley Morgan, an instructor in the School of Architecture and later its director, guided the School for at least the next thirty years "and succeeded in making Princeton's School of Architecture one of the foremost in the country."[1]

In 1925 Smith was a member of the faculty committee that devised the so-called Four Course Plan of Study in which every undergraduate would undertake junior independent work and

[1] Alexander Leitch, *A Princeton Companion* (Princeton: Princeton University Press, 1978), p. 25.

write a senior thesis, thus being actively involved in research rather than passively absorbing knowledge from lectures. Soon afterwards, Smith was chosen to be chairman of the Faculty Committee on the Library. Already Charles Rufus Morey, who succeeded Marquand as chairman, had outlined the idea for a new library to be labelled a "Humanistic Laboratory," differing in its arrangement from the traditional library building. His idea had met opposition from the administration and from the architect, who favored the customary huge warehouse to store books and a single large reading room to accommodate all users. Morey suggested that each of eight reading departments in the humanities and social sciences should have a separate section within the structure, each with its own conference room, undergraduate and graduate reading rooms with individual desks, and some offices adjacent to the books of their discipline — in short, eight departmental libraries like the physically independent Marquand Library of Art and Archaeology. Under Smith's leadership the faculty committee and then the faculty endorsed the concept.[2]

In 1935 the University issued a booklet entitled *The New Princeton Library* with brief essays by President Harold W. Dodds and the chairman of the Trustees' Library Committee, and a long one by Professor Smith accompanied by illustrative drawings by the architect Charles Klauder. Lack of money, aggravated by World War II, delayed the project. Smith spent most of 1944 touring the country, speaking to alumni on the need for the library and the concept for its arrangement. From 1945 on there is extensive correspondence between Smith and the new architect, Robert O'Connor, on almost every detail of the library, including the location and wording of memorial plaques, lighting, and the crenellations along the roof line. During the Bicentennial of the University in 1946, the cornerstone of the new Firestone Library was laid.

Smith was no stranger to controversy. In 1930 he had persuaded

[2] See Smith, "The Idea of the New Princeton Library and Its Plan," in *The New Princeton Library* (Princeton, 1935).

the University to invite architect Frank Lloyd Wright to offer the six Kahn lectures on architecture. Wright's career was at its nadir. Architects favoring traditional styles of architecture controlled the media of architectural criticism, condemning most of Wright's ideas. At the same time Wright's domestic life was featured in all the newspapers, occasioned by quarrels in court with his wife, the birth of a child by his mistress Olgivanna, later to be his third wife, and by his brief imprisonment under the Mann Act. Smith much later recalled with amusement the scandalized reaction of some Princetonians on seeing Wright and Olgivanna, then his wife, drive down Nassau Street in his open sedan.

Wright's Kahn lectures were published in 1931 as *Modern Architecture*, with a preface by Smith. Identifying Wright as a "prophet without honor in his own country," Smith indicated that the lectures were primarily to inspire young architectural students. Admitting that Wright was belligerent in his attitude, Smith noted that the lectures "are not didactic rules — rather are they sermons of an engaging, self-confident and enthusiastic artist fired with a faith, not in the machine itself, but in the power of man to master his creation, the machine, and to make it fashion new manifestations of beauty." Accompanying Wright's lectures at Princeton was the first showing of a large exhibition of photographs, drawings, and models of Wright's architecture. The exhibition then toured many institutions, although Wright later claimed that it was rejected by Cornell, Harvard, MIT, and Yale. The Kahn lectures and exhibition, combined with the appearance of Wright's autobiography in 1932, began his rehabilitation as the greatest architect produced in America.

From 1936 to 1941, Professor Smith was the Art Department's representative to the Divisional Program in the Humanities, and its first chairman. A student in the program would satisfy departmental requirements a year earlier than usual, so that his senior year could be devoted to a larger, broadly oriented senior thesis synthesizing work in several of the humanities. In the mid-1950s, with increasing student interest in specialization, Smith would often come back from meetings of the committee disgusted that some of the theses were merely departmental theses, with no attempt at bridging the humanities. The Program soon died a natural death from lack of student interest.

In 1945, when Charles Rufus Morey retired, Smith was appointed chairman of the Art Department. Despite his new responsibilities, he continued to teach at least seven or eight hours each week, including lectures in the spring on modern painting, which was one of the most popular courses on campus. It was during his chairmanship that the Creative Arts Program began to teach painting, and with his support the department accepted Bill Seitz's doctoral dissertation on Abstract Expressionism, recognized as the first dissertation on contemporary art accepted by an American university. Although the faculty taught undergraduate courses in the entire history of art, their research was limited to ancient, medieval, and Chinese art. The new appointments under Smith were of faculty interested in scholarship in the additional fields of Northern Renaissance and Baroque art, Renaissance architecture, and modern painting.

Like many New Englanders who experienced the Depression, Baldwin Smith was rather frugal in terms of money and time. His younger colleague Donald Drew Egbert once complained that Smith would buy the least expensive chairs on the market, which would collapse the first time one sat in them, while their colleague Albert M. Friend would insist on antique Louis XV chairs that no one *dared* sit in. Egbert lamented that he just wanted simple, solid chairs.

To the dismay of some of the students, Smith always scheduled his preceptorials at 8:30 a.m., so that some of the morning and many afternoons were free for administration and research. He expected the same intensive teaching schedule from his faculty as he himself pursued. During my first year on the faculty, I taught twelve preceptorial hours in two courses each term.

With all his academic activities, Professor Smith had a strong domestic life. His first wife died prematurely, leaving him with two young children. His second wife, who bore him two more children, had as dominant a personality as he did. An influential citizen of the town, she was a leader in the planning and building of a new public library.

Smith devoted his entire adult life to furthering the study of architectural history, to teaching the profession of architecture at Princeton, and to developing and refining educational methods and facilities at the University. Hospitalized during his last term of teaching, he died in March 1956, just a few months short of his scheduled retirement in June, 1956.

READING LIST

With Howard Crosby Butler: *Early Churches in Syria* (Princeton: Published for the Department of Art and Archaeology of Princeton University, 1929)

Egyptian Architecture as Cultural Expression (New York: Appleton, 1938)

The Dome: A Study in the History of Ideas (Princeton: Princeton University Press, 1950)

Architectural Symbolism of Imperial Rome and the Middle Ages (Princeton: Princeton University Press, 1956)

Henry DeWolf Smyth

Department of Physics

BY GEORGE T. REYNOLDS

On June 29, 1921, Dean of the Graduate School Andrew Fleming West wrote a memorandum to support the application of the young Henry DeWolf Smyth for continuing graduate work at the world famous Cavendish Laboratory, Cambridge University. In it, he said:

> Mr. Henry DeWolf Smyth graduated in Princeton University with the degree of Bachelor of Arts in June 1918, received the degree of Master of Arts in June 1920 and the degree of Doctor of Philosophy in June 1921. During the three academic years 1918–1921 he pursued advanced studies in Physics under Dean Magie and Professors Adams and Compton and also studied the mathematical theory of relativity with Professors Eisenhart and Veblen. In June 1921 he won by competition one of the National Research Fellowships in Physics recently established by the United States Government.

> Throughout his entire undergraduate and graduate course here, extending through seven years, he has proved himself one of the most brilliant young scholars in Physics we have ever known here. His modesty, refinement and general personal attractiveness have endeared him to us all and we believe that he will amply justify our expectations in the advanced work he desires to undertake at the University of Cambridge, to which we commend him without reserve.[1]

Enthusiastic though this recommendation was, it fell far short of predicting the outstanding accomplishments of Harry's career as a scientist, teacher, administrator, educator, and statesman.

Henry DeWolf Smyth was born in Clinton, New York, on May 1, 1898, the son of Ruth Phelps Smyth and Charles Henry Smyth, Jr. His family moved to Princeton in 1905, when his father was appointed professor of geology. My first contact with him came in the form of a telegram informing me of my acceptance to the Princeton University Graduate School for study in physics, with an assistantship stipend of $600. With characteristic graciousness, Professor Smyth concluded his telegram with the sentence: "Acceptance will not commit you if you get a better offer elsewhere." I accepted with pleasure, and have never regretted the decision, not least because it resulted in the opportunity to associate with a man of outstanding character and wisdom. He was, in the full sense of the word, "mentor" in several critical phases of my career.

As one of four graduate students entering the department in September 1940, I was assigned as a research assistant, expected to spend thirty hours per week in that capacity. In addition, Professor Smyth decided to try a program in which each new graduate student would take four courses per term. Incidentally, one of my courses, "Analytical Mechanics," was taught by Prof. E. P. Adams,

[1] Letter by Andrew Fleming West, June 29, 1921, in Henry DeWolf Smyth, Faculty File, Princeton University Archives. Although he had already been awarded a Ph.D. in physics by Princeton University, Smyth determined to continue his career with a further Ph.D. from Cambridge, which he achieved in 1923.

a fine old gentleman who, with K. T. Compton, had been the supervisor and final examiner on Smyth's Ph.D. thesis in 1921. Smyth, though busy with the administration of the department and already beginning to be involved with some research concerns related to national defense, nevertheless took a direct interest in the welfare of the graduate students and decided that the work load was indeed heavy, and modified the requirements.

Although sympathetic, he could also be direct. On the occasion when I confessed to him that I was surprised to feel overwhelmed by my courses because I had been Phi Beta Kappa in my junior year as an undergraduate, he replied, "There isn't a graduate student in the department who wasn't Phi Beta Kappa including the two who have just failed the general examination." It was not until forty years later that I learned (but not from Harry) that he had been top boy at Lawrenceville in 1914, Phi Beta Kappa and number one in his graduating class at Princeton.

By the end of the academic year 1940–1941, Smyth was heavily involved as a consultant on research projects for the National Research Council and the Office of Scientific Research and Development. At one point he was in charge of two projects at Princeton, one having to do with the separation of isotopes and the other with chain reaction. Wartime security dictated that those working on one project were not allowed to talk to those working on the other. As director of both, and in spite of his heavy work load, Smyth was able to maintain his sense of humor, pointing out that he could no longer talk to himself.

Smyth took his Princeton responsibilities very seriously. His reorganization of the freshman physics course led to a text, *Matter, Motion and Electricity*, that served nationwide for many years as a standard for introductory physics.[2] Coupled with imaginative lecture demonstrations and equipment of his design it made Princeton's freshman physics outstanding. In late 1943, teaching loads had to be increased because of the new courses designed for

[2] Smyth and Charles Wilbur Ufford, *Matter, Motion and Electricity: A Modern Approach to General Physics* (New York: McGraw Hill, 1939).

service personnel, a situation exacerbated by the number of regular faculty diverted to war research. When President Harold W. Dodds wrote to say that Smyth was urgently needed to teach extra courses, Smyth resigned his associate directorship of the Chicago Metallurgical Laboratory, maintaining a less demanding role as consultant. It is interesting to read the correspondence with Dodds on this matter,[3] in which Smyth goes to some pains to point out that "the University will just about break even" if he returns his $25 per day consulting fee to Princeton and accepts his full salary, resulting in net compensation consistent with Princeton salary guidelines (at this time about $6,500 per year).

In his role as chairman of the Physics Department, Smyth prepared an annual "Report to the President." Excerpts from them demonstrate his determination to maintain the style and quality of the department in spite of the demands of the war effort, and show that he maintained his sense of humor in the face of somewhat daunting changes:

> Compared with the year 1943-44, the past year has been relatively quiet. . . . To be sure, heavy teaching loads in elementary physics continued through most of the year and none of the regular staff was available, but . . .[4]

> Although the war ended in August, the period of reconversion in the Department hardly began until December. . . . We can hardly hope to have achieved equilibrium before the end of another year, and I do not know whether we will ever return to those happy times when writing a report for the President was the chairman's only obligation during the summer.[5]

In this report also he struck a theme that he adhered to throughout his tenure:

[3] Smyth to President Dodds, March 11, 1944, Faculty Files, Princeton University Archives.

[4] Smyth, "Report to the President" (Harold W. Dodds), 1944–1945, Princeton University Archives.

[5] Smyth, "Report to the President" (Harold W. Dodds), 1945–1946, Princeton University Archives.

> We see two great dangers in government sponsored research, first the danger of vanishing financial support, second the danger of loss of individual originality and initiative. In many ways modern experimental research has become so complicated as to require group effort, but there is always the probability that the great new ideas or discoveries will come from a single individual working with a powerful mind but simple apparatus.

Finally, in the report for 1946–1947:

> It is hardly possible to call the past year a normal one considering the Bicentennial Celebrations and the overcrowded condition of the University. Yet compared to the previous five years, life in the Physics Department has been relatively calm. We have sometimes known how many students would be in a course several weeks before it began instead of several weeks afterward and none of our staff has suddenly vanished on a secret mission of unknown duration.[6]

As a new assistant professor joining the Department in March 1946, I was privileged to experience Smyth's remarkable qualities as an administrator. He had given me responsibility for chairing the steering committee for the (ONR supported) program in cosmic ray research, as well as for overseeing the curriculum of a two-year course, the Army Atomic Energy Training Program, for selected U.S. Army officers. In meeting these responsibilities, I benefitted immeasurably from his guidance and example. He was more than a superb administrator; he brought wisdom, dignity, good manners, and a sense of humor to the tasks at hand. One piece of advice I particularly benefitted from: "When a complaint comes up for the first time, ignore it; if it is important it will come up again." I also appreciated his candor: Due to certain regulations of the U.S. Navy at the end of World War II, I was not able to take up my first teaching appointment as assistant professor until almost a year had passed. At the end of my abbreviated teaching, Professor Smyth called me into his office and said: "You are

[6] Smyth, "Report to the President, 1946–1947," Princeton University Archives.

up for re-appointment. You will also be considered for tenure. You won't get it, but you will be considered."

A symposium and dinner held on April 29, 1983, to celebrate Smyth's eighty-fifth birthday provided a perspective from which to review his truly remarkable career as scientist, educator, administrator and statesman. Although perhaps best known for his remarkable book, *Atomic Energy for Military Purposes*,[7] he was the author of a number of seminal physics papers. His Princeton Ph.D. thesis, "The Radiating Potentials of Nitrogen," was published in the *Physical Review* in 1919. From 1919 to 1934 he was author or co-author of some thirty technical scientific papers in such journals as *Proceedings of the Royal Society of London*, *Proceedings of the National Academy of Science*, *Nature*, and *Reviews of Modern Physics*. He was recognized internationally as a first-rate atomic scientist. He later described the pleasure he experienced in his research career:

> I rejoiced in all this. I liked the discipline of publication which meant that any experiment I did in Princeton must be so clearly described in print that it could be repeated in Moscow or Berlin thereby testing the accuracy of the results. I liked the excitement of comparing experiment with theory. I liked the elegance of some of these comparisons. I was indifferent to practical application believing that greater knowledge of nature enriched the mind of men and that the work was thereby justified. I liked the impersonal nature of the work and its international character. Of course there was competition but we all know that competition must be transcended by cooperation including international cooperation.[8]

Although in 1934 Smyth had "inadvertently" given up his promising research career to devote his energies to reorganizing the big freshman physics course, and then in 1935 to become chairman of

[7] Henry DeWolf Smyth, *Atomic Energy for Military Purposes: The Official Report on the Development of the Atomic Bomb under the Auspices of the United States Government, 1940–1945* (Princeton: Princeton University Press, 1945).

[8] Quoted by Val L. Fitch at the memorial service for Smyth, Princeton University Chapel, February 20, 1987.

Allen Shenstone (left) with Henry DeWolf Smyth in 1978.

the Physics Department, he published in later years several remarkable papers reviewing the field. These include "From X-rays to Nuclear Fission" in *The American Scientist* (1947). In the introduction to this succinct history of atomic physics, he warns against arrogance and conceit. "The degree of Ph.D. in physics or chemistry or some other science," he wrote, "does not automatically stamp a man as great or wise or even very bright." In the conclusion, written two years after the end of World War II, he expresses some thoughts remarkably relevant to his later national and international responsibilities:

> The thoughtful scientist reviewing his present situation is deeply concerned. . . . The achievements of the past fifty years . . . show what human beings can do when they work with disciplined minds and objective methods in a spirit of cooperation and freedom. Yet mankind has failed to understand the lesson of method. Apparently the method is inadequate for social and political problems or its use conflicts too violently with long cherished prejudices and shortsighted ideas of self interest. . . . Some scientists themselves, suddenly awakened to the world in which they live, make political pronouncements in a spirit of emotionalism and panic that would never be tolerated in their own field. . . .

The scientist "must be humble, recognizing the limits of his own knowledge. . . . He must be restrained and infinitely patient . . . think imaginatively but not emotionally . . . He must remember that he has no monopoly on brains but is merely the custodian of a method well designed to meet the kinds of problems that have heretofore confronted him."[9]

All of this original research and dedicated teaching was interrupted in 1940 by an escalating involvement in national affairs. As the result of Smyth's association with the Manhattan Project, in the spring of 1944 General Groves asked him to prepare a general report on the atomic bomb project, although it was not clear whether the report would ever be used. An outline of the whole report and a rough draft of the first half were sent to Groves in August 1944. In May 1945 Groves decided the report would be used, and asked for it to be completed by the end of June. (Smyth was also the chairman of the Princeton Physics Department during this period.) After submitting a draft of the final report to various key group leaders, Smyth completed a final revision by July 30. It was this final effort that prevented him from viewing the Trinity test on July 16, 1945. On August 2, Groves declared the report ready for submission to the printer — the facility for reproducing secret documents in the Adjutant General's Office in the Pentagon, where it was labeled Top Secret. On August 11, two days after the bomb was dropped on Nagasaki, President Truman ordered that the "Smyth Report," *Atomic Energy for Military Purposes*, be made public, and it was released to the press on August 12, 1945.[10] Professor Smyth wrote these remarkable words to accompany the publication, words that also provide insight into his motives for preparing it:

[9] Smyth, "From X-rays to Nuclear Fission," *The American Scientist* 35 (1947): 485–501.

[10] The heroic efforts of the Princeton University Press and its director, by means of which 60,000 copies of the report were on hand for delivery to book sellers by September 7, are described by Datus C. Smith, Jr., Class of 1929, in his "The Publishing History of the 'Smyth Report,'" *Princeton University Library Chronicle* 37, no. 3 (Spring 1976): 191–203.

> In a free country like ours, such questions should be debated by the people through their representatives. This is one reason for the release of this report. It is a semi-technical report which it is hoped men of science in this country can use to help their fellow citizens in reaching wise decisions. The people of this country must be informed if they are to discharge their responsibilities wisely.[11]

With this background, President Truman appointed Smyth to the Atomic Energy Commission, where he served from May 1949 until he resigned in September 1954. During this period his responsibilities on the Commission were to promote U.S. research in nuclear power. However, it is the first six months of 1954 that are most remembered by Harry's friends. Allegations questioning the loyalty of J. Robert Oppenheimer were made known by the FBI to Lewis Strauss, chairman of the AEC, and by him to the other four commissioners. A panel of three was set up to evaluate the allegations and the vote was to remove Oppenheimer's security clearance. The case then went to the Commission. As his friends knew and remembered, this case put Harry under a great strain. Although he had many misgivings about Oppenheimer's judgment in certain scientific and personal matters, he studied the evidence thoroughly and objectively and came to the conclusion that Oppenheimer's clearance should be restored. His was the sole favorable vote. The strain had contributed to his catching flu, and he was given only overnight to prepare his dissenting opinion. He stated at the time that "a professional review of the case has been supplemented by powerful personal enemies. . . . The conclusion of the Commission cannot be supported by a fair evaluation of the facts." Professor I. I. Rabi, on the occasion of

[11] *Atomic Energy for Military Purposes*, p. 226. For Smyth's own account of the circumstances leading to the conception and completion of the book, see "The 'Smyth Report,'" *Princeton University Library Chronicle* 37, no. 3 (Spring 1976): 173–189. My own involvement in the Manhattan Project at Los Alamos and Tinian was as a member of the Ordinance Division. In the 264-page report, our work received the following attention: "For the same reasons (i.e. security) none of the work of the Ordinance, Explosives and Bomb Physics Divisions can be discussed at all."

the memorial service for Professor Smyth on February 20, 1987, eloquently stated the opinion of Harry's many friends: "So one thinks of a supreme moment in a person's life when he stood out against great odds and did the right thing. That was Harry Smyth's fortune and Harry Smyth's greatness."

Upon his return to Princeton in September 1954, Smyth was appointed by President Dodds as chairman of the University Board of Scientific and Engineering Research, which led in May 1959 to his appointment by President Robert F. Goheen as the first chairman of the Princeton University Research Board, a post he held until June 1966. During this period he provided wise guidance in developing policies and practices related to government support of research, the construction of the 3 Bev Princeton-Pennsylvania Accelerator, and the expansion of research on thermal fusion. For the *Princeton Alumni Weekly*, he wrote detailed and informative overviews of "The Significance of Research in Science and Engineering at Princeton" (May 15, 1959) and "Sponsored Research" (May 22, 1959).

Those of us actively engaged in federally-sponsored research in these years came to regard him as a wise and helpful mentor. He was always available and generous with his time. This characteristic is all the more remarkable in view of the other heavy responsibilities he was carrying. From the start of the postwar period, Harry had discussed with us his concerns about the international aspects of nuclear power. He summarized these in an article, "Nuclear Power and Foreign Policy," published in *Foreign Affairs* in October 1956.

On June 1, 1961, he was appointed by President Kennedy as United States Representative to the International Atomic Energy Agency, with rank of ambassador, a post he held under Presidents Johnson and Nixon until August 31, 1970. It was during this assignment that Harry achieved international stature as a statesman. He found that matters had deteriorated in the Agency, which was torn by bitter political controversy. He initiated a program of personal diplomacy, in the firm belief that the Soviets had the same incentives to build a successful Agency as did the United States. He developed personal relationships with the Soviets and succeeded in getting results by his example of integrity, sincerity, good humor and, not least, good manners.

Dr. Glenn Seaborg, chairman of the U.S. Atomic Energy Commission throughout Smyth's tenure as ambassador to the IAEA, has made the following comment:

> Through his superior statesmanship and personal relationships with the Soviet representatives, Harry brought a calming influence which achieved an unprecedented atmosphere of rapport in the Agency. In particular, Harry Smyth played a key role in the realization of the Non-Proliferation Treaty, one of the two most important arms control agreements ever achieved. Harry's personal diplomacy, sincerity and commitment were paramount in this accomplishment.

Late in his life, Harry frequently said that the success of the Non-Proliferation Treaty gave him the most satisfaction of all of his accomplishments. In his letter of resignation to President Nixon (April 23, 1970) his first sentence read: "Preventing the spread of nuclear weapons and promoting the peaceful uses of nuclear energy have been my primary concern for the last twenty-five years." And he ended with the statement: "I intend to continue to devote my energy and attention to the non-proliferation of nuclear weapons and the promotion of peaceful uses of nuclear energy." In 1968, he was given the Atoms for Peace Award, and in 1974 he was the first recipient of the "Henry DeWolf Smyth Award for Nuclear Statesmanship," established jointly by the Atomic Industrial Forum and the American Nuclear Society.

Harry Smyth formally "retired" from Princeton University on June 30, 1966, but continued to visit his office in the Physics Department regularly. He remained active as a consultant in academic and governmental matters and chairman of the board of trustees of the Universities Research Association, 1965–1968. Most importantly, he was available to his colleagues and former students until his death on September 11, 1986.

In his autobiography, *The Education of Henry Adams,* Adams

says "a friend in power is a friend lost." This was never so in the case of Harry Smyth. There in his office we were accepted as friends, and there we could hear his anecdotes, benefit from his experience and sage advice. He enjoyed these interactions, and once told an interviewer that he left his office door open so that he could overhear the younger men describe their work: "I don't know what they are talking about, but I hear the interest and the enthusiasm, and that makes me feel good."

His awards and tributes[12] are laced with phrases containing the words "dignity," "good manners," and "integrity," but from my personal experience I would choose "wise". Harry Smyth was the wisest man I have been privileged to know.

READING LIST

Atomic Energy for Military Purposes: The Official Report on the Development of the Atomic Bomb under the Auspices of the United States Government, 1940–1945 (Princeton: Princeton University Press, 1945)

"From X-rays to Nuclear Fission," *The American Scientist* 35 (1947): 485–501

"The 'Smyth Report,'" *Princeton University Library Chronicle* 37, no. 3 (Spring 1976): 173–189

[12] I would be remiss if I did not list a few more of the national and international awards testifying to Harry Smyth's accomplishments, but even these cannot do adequate credit to the man known and respected by his colleagues and students: Woodrow Wilson Award from Princeton University, 1964; Atomic Energy Commission Citation, 1967; Distinguished Honor Award, U.S. Department of State, 1970; Distinguished Service Award from the International Atomic Energy Agency, 1977; and, also in 1977, an Honorary Doctorate from Princeton University.

Harold and Margaret Sprout

Department of Politics

BY VINCENT DAVIS, MAURICE A. EAST, AND JAMES N. ROSENAU

The academic study of international relations during the 1920s and 1930s in the United States had its roots in diplomatic history and international law. The subject matter and the perspectives brought to it were largely dominated by the legacy of Woodrow Wilson, the Paris Peace Conference, and the establishment of the League of Nations. With remarkably few exceptions, American teachers and writers on international subjects anticipated a new era of international cooperation, the abolition of secret diplomacy, and a stable peace into the indefinite future. There were, however, a few scholars who did not accept this optimistic scenario and began to revolutionize the field of international studies.

Among them must be listed Harold Sprout, born in 1901, and

Margaret Tuttle Sprout, born in 1903. A young couple who met as undergraduates at Oberlin College, the Sprouts did not enter the international field immediately. They married after Harold's graduation from Oberlin in 1924 and then went to the University of Wisconsin, where he studied law and Margaret completed her A.B. After one year in Madison they transferred to the Law School of Western Reserve University, expecting to practice law in Painsville, Ohio, in partnership with Margaret's father. One more year of legal study, however, led to the conclusion that the practice of law was not for them, and they returned to Madison in the fall of 1927. In 1929 the University of Wisconsin awarded Harold a doctorate in political science and law and Margaret a master of arts in political science and geography. They spent the 1926–1927 academic year at Miami University of Ohio, where Harold obtained a fill-in faculty appointment, and 1929–1931 at Stanford University, where he had a similar position.

In 1931, when the Great Depression virtually wiped out the academic job market, Harold had the good fortune to receive an instructorship at Princeton University, which was to remain their base for the rest of their professional careers, stretching out for approximately half a century. Although Margaret's affiliation with Princeton was much less formal, her participation in Harold's research and writing was so thoroughgoing that it is not possible to record an evaluation of the latter's work as if it were the output of a single scholar. For Margaret did far more than copy-edit Harold's manuscripts; indeed, she was so completely a partner in their intellectual enterprises that it was never clear who originated which of the many rich formulations and insights that pervade their work. Hence, not only did the title pages of Harold's major contributions list Margaret as a co-author, but those who study and teach in the field of international relations (IR) make no distinction between them. Rather, it has become quite habitual to refer to "the Sprouts." Both as students of the Sprouts and as practitioners in the IR field, we have been neither able nor willing to break this habit, and thus what follows is cast as much in a plural as in a singular form.

Throughout the desperate early and middle 1930s, Harold clung precariously to the lower rungs on the faculty ladder in Princeton's Department of Politics. He eventually reached the rank of full professor, served as department chairman (1949–1952), and was then appointed to the endowed Bryant chair in geography and international relations in the Department of Politics. In 1969 he became professor emeritus upon reaching sixty-eight, the mandatory retirement age at that time. He died in 1980.

Along the way, Harold held visiting appointments at the University of Pennsylvania (1938), Columbia University (1948–1950), the University of Denver (1950), Nuffield College, Oxford (1955), and Rutgers University (1970). In the mid-1940s he was briefly a member of the Institute for Advanced Study in Princeton. He conducted most of the negotiations that successfully resulted in the movement of a number of professional scholars from Yale University in the context of the establishment of the Center of International Studies at Princeton University. His own membership in the Center was continued by appointment to a research position coincident with his retirement from the teaching faculty.

Not least among the important innovative departures which the Sprouts brought to the study of international relations in the 1930s was an emphasis upon the interconnections between national and international politics — "linkage politics," as it later came to be called. This intimate relationship between a nation's internal politics and its foreign policies had been commented upon by Plato in his writings around 400 B.C. and Clausewitz in his writings in the early nineteenth century, among others. But IR scholars during the first four decades of the twentieth century often ignored relationships between parts and wholes, until the Sprouts and a few others began to underscore these ties in the late 1930s.

The Sprouts initially pursued this linkage perspective in the publication of their first major book in 1939, *The Rise of American Naval Power: 1776–1918*. This monograph also contained several other major themes which were to pervade much of their remaining work. In many cases, these themes foreshadowed important developments in the professional literature of the field as a whole. For example, their conceptualization of the "styles of statecraft" of national actors in the international arena was an operationally researchable and behaviorally tenable version of the older and somewhat discredited notion of "national character" and its effects on foreign policy. From another perspective, the attempt by the Sprouts to differentiate among states on the basis of foreign policy behavior antedates what subsequently came to be known as the study of "comparative foreign policy."

Their work on the Navy introduced them to Alfred Thayer Mahan's earlier writings, and Mahan's work in turn whetted their lifelong interest in the interplay between geographic factors and new developments in science and technology. In a very real sense, *The Rise of American Naval Power* can be said to represent one of the early attempts to assess the impact of science and technology on international politics. Mahan's work also served to stimulate the Sprouts' interest in the British Navy and, subsequently in the British social, political, and economic system more generally. Finally, and related to all of their other emerging interests, the Sprouts' first book on the Navy generated their continuing focus on the relationships between man and his geophysical environment.

These various concerns were brought more sharply into focus in the context of an examination of a specific major instance of international negotiations, in the Sprouts' second book — a sequel to the first — which dealt primarily with the Washington Conference on the Limitation of Naval Armaments of 1921–1922. Although essentially a case study, *Toward a New Order of Sea Power: American Naval Policy and the World Scene, 1918–1922* merged the focus on national actors into the context of the international system. And it also contained early hints of a recognition of systemic actors in addition to nation-states — actors in categories that later came to be called IGOs (intergovernmental organizations) and NGOs (nongovernmental organizations). In this sense, too, the Sprouts' early work foreshadowed major themes that emerged much later in the IR literature.

The next major milestone in the Sprouts' scholarship was the publication in 1945 of their basic textbook, *Foundations of National Power: Readings on World Politics and American Security*.[1] It was compiled during World War II at the request of Secretary of the Navy James V. Forrestal, who felt that American naval officers were inadequately educated in a fundamental subject indicated by the book's title and subtitle. Used for many years in the training of naval officer candidates in many different Navy schools and programs, the book was put into commercial circulation by D. Van Nostrand in 1946 and a revised edition was published in 1951. Notwithstanding its origins as part of the Navy's ROTC curriculum, the book was a remarkable intellectual achievement in that it avoided being a reflection of the tumultuous but essentially transient political passions of the wartime period. Thus, rather than reflecting a narrowly parochial American perspective, it was a major effort to devise analytical categories and concepts for studying the behavior of any nation-state within the context of a complex global system composed not only of national actors, but of other kinds of actors as well, all operating within a conditioning environment made up of human as well as nonhuman elements. It examined the newly fashionable concept of power not in hortatory, normative, or mystical terms, but in terms of capabilities measured against possible goals within analyzable restraints and constraints. The book included readings not only from political science, but from geography, psychology, sociology, and even from the physical and natural sciences. In this sense it clearly anticipated the growing conviction among specialists in international

[1] Princeton: Princeton University Press, 1945.

studies after World War II that their field required significant and substantial contributions from many disciplines and areas of knowledge.

The early 1950s involved the Sprouts in fertile and fruitful interactions with a number of their colleagues at Princeton University. Although their early work on the Navy had utilized a focus on nation-states as the primary actors in international politics, it was also clear that they viewed the "nation-state" as a collective noun referring to politically organized groups of human beings in social systems. Always carefully avoiding anthropomorphic and teleological fallacies, they insisted from the outset of their scholarly careers that nations were composed of individuals, that the decisions of nations are at root the decisions of officials who represent or speak for other people, and that one critically important way to study the behavior of nations is to study the perceptions and actions of national decision makers. It is hard to escape the conclusion that the landmark monographic essay by Richard C. Snyder, Henry W. Bruck, and Burton Sapin, *Decision-making as an Approach to the Study of International Politics*,[2] was at least in part a product of the interaction between the Sprouts and these authors who were younger colleagues in the Department of Politics. The Snyder monograph sharply focused and systematized insights and perspectives clearly evident in the earlier work of the Sprouts.

In the middle 1950s the Sprouts returned to one of the basic themes first evident in their work on the Navy. This theme could have been summarized under the rubric of "geographic factors," but the Sprouts were unhappy with the way in which other analysts tended to treat such factors. In the first place, they were dissatisfied with a tendency to view geographic factors as permanent and immutable. They saw the significance of geography to

[2] Originally published in June 1954 as monograph #3 of the Foreign Policy Analysis Series, Organizational Behavior Section, Princeton University, the monograph was subsequently reproduced in Richard C. Snyder, H. W. Bruck, and Burton Sapin, eds., *Foreign Policy Decision-Making: An Approach to the Study of International Politics* (New York: The Free Press of Glencoe, 1962).

be a function of social choices concerning the allocation of resources as well as a function of the level of technology at any given time. In the second place, they were displeased with the deterministic rhetoric which so often pervaded the geographic literature. Social choices appeared to be foreclosed in such literature, and this in turn obviated the need for conceptualizing any operational linkages between human behavior and the geographic factors. The Sprouts refused to accept this kind of reasoning because they refused to abandon the conviction that human beings are the fundamental actors in all social systems — actors with thought processes and decisional options.

Put differently, they persistently avoided a common tendency to endow social systems with anthropomorphic and teleological qualities, and the reverse tendency to endow neither humans nor their social systems with discretionary options in an ironclad natural order. At the same time, the Sprouts were not prepared to argue that geographic factors were inconsequential in human and social affairs. Accordingly, they framed a conceptualization of human beings and their social systems as units within a comprehensive surrounding element embracing "the total aggregate of factors in space and time, to which an individual's behavior may be oriented or otherwise related (excepting only the environed individual's own hereditary structures and characteristics)." The Sprouts did not like the terms "geographic" or "environmental" to refer to this total aggregate of factors, because these older terms had too many restrictive and narrow denotations and connotations in earlier literature. They thus borrowed the French word *milieu*, and they spelled out their conceptualization of the environed unit in its possible relationships to its environment in their path-breaking monograph, *Man-Milieu Relationship Hypotheses in the Context of International Politics.*[3] A year later they elaborated other aspects of the argument in a paper entitled "Environmental Factors in International Politics," read by Harold

[3] Published in 1956 by the Center of International Studies at Princeton University.

at the annual meeting of the American Political Science Association in September 1957. Eventually, they refined and sharpened their thinking on this subject in a book-length statement, *The Ecological Perspective on Human Affairs: With Special Reference to International Politics.*[4]

Subsequently, in *An Ecological Paradigm for the Study of International Politics,*[5] the Sprouts elaborated on the implications of an ecological approach to the study of world politics. The more important ramifications of this elaboration included (a) a greater emphasis on lower levels of abstractions, with the human actor as central to international political analysis; (b) an increasing awareness of the interdependence of human efforts to control the environment; and (c) an appreciation that coping "with the diverse, cumulatively enormous, and still proliferating human capabilities to alter the condition of existence, even survival, upon this planet constitutes the ultimate problem of international politics." The concern with this "ultimate problem" served as the basic organizing idea of their subsequent book, *Toward a Politics of the Planet Earth.*

Many of these conceptualizations and perspectives were also summarized in the Sprouts' textbook, *Foundations of International Politics,*[6] but this work was much more than a restatement of the man-milieu and ecological framework. Its first 69 pages continues to be one of the most succinct and readable expressions of the basic logical and intellectual processes applicable to international studies. Indeed, it was such a valuable statement of these processes that a number of scholars argued in favor of publishing those 69 pages as a separate handbook for the benefit of students. The next three chapters, something over 100 pages, constituted an equally valuable delineation of the elements of the international system, encompassing not only newer insights and perspec-

[4] Princeton: Princeton University Press, 1965.

[5] Published in 1968 as Research Monograph #30 by the Center of International Studies at Princeton University.

[6] Princeton: D. Van Nostrand, 1962.

tives emerging in the IR literature of the 1950s and 1960s but also incorporating up-to-date and operationally tenable versions of older concepts such as "power," "political potential," and "capabilities." The remainder of the book was in some respects an updating of the material in *Foundations of National Power*, but the very change in the title suggested the extent to which older substances and terminology had been reconceptualized into a broader, more global perspective. It was no mere exercise in pouring old wine into new bottles; on the contrary, it was the culmination of a career's work in carefully defining and refining basic human and physical factors into a paradigmatic synthesis of greater analytic utility in research on international politics.

In 1978 the Sprouts published *The Context of Environmental Politics*, a book they regarded as perhaps their culminating masterwork, embracing and synthesizing as it did the dominant and involving themes in their research and writings for more than two decades since the middle 1950s. Some of those themes can be briefly summarized in the following statements from their works: (1) political scientists should not stand idly by while the political aspects of environmental deterioration are dealt with by nuclear physicists, aerospace engineers, and technocrats; (2) any program for spending large sums of public money for environmental improvements is likely to run into political trouble if they are put ahead of comparable outlays for eradicating poverty; (3) business executives who are necessarily driven by profit motives will tend to exploit the natural environment and to put domestic social circumstances into a low-priority category, such that only governments can assert a broader public need and demand for environmental maintenance and restoration; and (4) governments, particularly the government of the United States, will find it exceedingly difficult if not impossible to offset the pressures for environmental exploitation from the business community, because interest groups and the public at large believe in a hedonistic utopia. If these themes now sound commonplace, given the growing numbers of scientists and scholars and other publicans who subsequently stressed similar messages, it remains the case that the Sprouts were virtually alone for several earlier decades in reaching these conclusions from their interdisciplinary social science research.

Most scholars are fortunate if they experience one brief burst of impressive creativity in their lives, surrounded by less creative periods that are dominated by elaborations of earlier ideas, occasional book reviews, perhaps edited books of readings, and other useful but routine chores. The work of the Sprouts, however, represented an extraordinary accomplishment from the outset, opening up many fruitful avenues of inquiry. Never experiencing the intellectual arrest that is the fate of most of us, they continued to traverse and enlarge the avenues that they pioneered. Always in the forefront and sometimes well in advance of the frontiers of research in a number of important directions, it is notable that the foregoing themes evident in their work still appear fresh and vital some forty years following the Sprouts' first explorations of a wide-ranging intellectual territory. They always worked at their own pace and followed their own star, never seeking to accommodate transient intellectual fads merely for the sake of being fashionable, but also never missing an opportunity to build on the best work of contemporaries, young and old, in their work.

The measure of a person, even in academic life, is by no means to be assessed solely in terms of the impact and enduring value of his or her published scholarship. It is a rare person who combines distinguished thought and research with the human qualities of the superior teacher. Yet the Sprouts fall into this category, and their students as much as their publications constitute their monument. They belonged to that earlier generation which believed that the best place for academicians to do their work was at home within the academy. Following World War II they did stay home to work while younger generations experimented with newer career-building modes characterized by frequent travel on the conference and convention circuit as well as by a variety of consulting assignments for governmental agencies. The Sprouts never confused motion with progress nor publicity with stature, and they achieved both progress and stature in remarkable degree by sticking to what they did best: thinking, researching, and teaching.

Their distinguished students included not only a number of scholars who wrote their doctoral dissertations under the supervision of the Sprouts, but also many who merely took an occasional seminar under their direction, only to discover later that even a single seminar was sufficient to have produced a lasting influence. Their "students" also included younger departmental colleagues and associates at Princeton and other colleges and universities who gained from counsel and correspondence with them. This is not to suggest that their impact was limited to those who later attained distinguished records of their own in academic life, because their students also included many who achieved positions of prominence and responsibility in public affairs.

Aside from their creativity as scholars and teachers, the Sprouts exhibited other qualities which endeared them to all who came in contact with them. Their warmth and openness and readiness to help was immediately evident to incoming students and colleagues alike. Margaret's involvement in affairs of the Princeton community made her an excellent source of information and guidance for the newcomer. Harold's years spent in the University gave him the wisdom to be able to get things done. During his tenure as graduate student advisor for the Department of Politics, his true concern for helping others was quite evident; many students were grateful to Harold for favors granted, doors opened, or crises eased. It was in his role as graduate student advisor that Harold initiated and strongly supported the admission of women into the graduate program of the Department of Politics.

This openness and enthusiasm displayed by the Sprouts was contagious in many respects. Harold's respect for the work of others was a source of inspiration and encouragement. Whether it was the work of one of his colleagues at Princeton, or a book or an article written by a scholar at some other institution, or the research project or dissertation of a graduate student, Harold's enthusiasm and interest would often become quite intense. Perhaps it was this same personality trait — this ability to become involved and enthusiastic — which kept them so up-to-date in the field of international studies. Their course syllabi and writings always reflected the most current standards of scholarship, and references were frequently made to works by others on the frontiers of the field.

In summary, it can be said without qualification that the Sprouts had a profound impact upon several generations of IR scholars and, indeed, upon the history of the discipline itself. In some cases, the impact involved the relationship of teacher to student; in others it stemmed from the influence of one scholar's ideas upon another; and in yet others it was rooted in the relationship between scholars sharing a common concern for the problems of world politics. The example Harold and Margaret Sprout set through their writings, their teaching, and their human kindness will serve as lasting mementos for all those who know of them and their work.

READING LIST

The Rise of American Naval Power, 1776–1918 (Princeton: Princeton University Press, 1939)

Toward a New Order of Sea Power: American Naval Policy and the World Scene, 1918–1922 (Princeton: Princeton University Press, 1940)

Toward a Politics of the Planet Earth (New York: Van Nostrand Reinhold, 1971)

The Context of Environmental Politics: Unfinished Business for America's Third Century (Lexington: University Press of Kentucky, 1978)

Joseph Reese Strayer

Department of History

BY WILLIAM CHESTER JORDAN AND TEOFILO F. RUIZ

His office was immensely long — at least it seemed so to naive young graduate students who entered it for the first time. On either wall were shelves so heavy with books — including many very old and rare books — that they sagged under the weight. At the far end of the room, at a cluttered desk, was the "Great Man." His gravelly voice did not disappoint. There was authority in it and wisdom and a touch of humor (though it took time to recognize this) and, most important perhaps, patience.

Seminars with Joseph Strayer, held in his office and under the spell of his voice, were unlike any instruction that either of the authors of this memoir had experienced before. They usually consisted of long disquisitions on the week's problem in medieval history, three-hour monologues without interruption. Or, rather, occasionally they were interrupted with a pointed technical, even obscure, question from the *magister*. Every head in the office went down when a pause, a half-grin, or an arched eyebrow gave warning of one of these questions coming. There was hope of being passed over in obscurity. And the questions, at first, seemed pointless. It took time, again, to discern their purpose: we were not only to read everything assigned and read it with care, but with such care that each detail became intimately a part of ourselves, as if it were a fact of our own emotional and material lives.

On rarc occasions the monologues yielded to assigned reports from the students. But then the voice of authority would intervene and become the voice of the critic and skeptic. Challenges came to details and to overall interpretation and sometimes led to long commentaries so full of erudition and insight that the student who had given the report began to feel embarrassed at the thinness of his own effort and ashamed that he had once thought it worthy.

Nearly everything in graduate school in those days — certainly the courses — seemed designed to bring self-important, confident graduate students down to earth roughly and to remind them emphatically of their ignorance. Change was in the air. Vietnam would shatter the old ways. Professors would become more approachable. (It would take time to realize that the new familiarity was as much of a mask in its own way as the Olympian remoteness of the older generation.) But Strayer was emphatically of the older generation. Colleagueship had to be earned through the crucible of overwhelming self-doubt. The danger was that the unrelenting coldness of the experience would so damage egos that there was nothing left to salvage. The word used by Strayer and his colleagues to describe graduate students who did not make it through the program from the 1930s deep into the 1960s was "terminated." It was a brutal word and accurate. Yet, it was also well known that almost no one who had come to work with Strayer was ever terminated.

Here is where the virtue which the man enjoyed in abundance — patience — paid such dividends. No one in our experience received a paper back from Strayer which did not have something positive written at the head or in the margins. The worst comment, we came to learn, was, "This needs a little more work"; the best, "This could be publishable." But there would also be an enormous number of question marks in the margins, suggesting that the master was puzzled or doubtful about this or that fact or interpretation we had come up with.

To go back now and read those papers, see those question marks and compare his comments is to discover the embarrassing truth. "This needs a little work" meant "I have queried a number of places, and it is clear that your Latin is bad. You can barely read French, let alone old French. You don't get your facts right. But we let you into the program and come hell or high water you're going to be a medievalist by the time you leave." "This could be publishable" meant "If you work your butt off, check your facts, improve your dreadful prose, and verify every single one of those pretty awful translations you made, there might one day be a publishable article that comes out of this."

Among ourselves the laconic written comments which we refused to go behind at the time were a prize to be venerated. They meant or were interpreted to mean that our naive hopes were legitimate. Just a little more work, just a little more effort and we might enter the ranks of real scholars. There is no doubt that without the generosity of his remarks and the unmitigated patience of the man in the face of students, like us, who had so much to learn, we would not have had the wherewithal to endure the rigors — the perpetual winter — of graduate education in history at Princeton.

In many other ways, beyond his enduring patience with our shortcomings, Joseph Strayer turned the winter of our graduate work into a promising spring. His engagement with and support of his students extended far beyond our graduate years. It lasted until the end of his life. Whether in the form of letters of recommendation, timely advice on professional matters, suggestions for fellowships, he was always willing to help. It seemed to us that whenever we gave him a paper, an early draft of an article or a longer manuscript, he would put aside whatever he was doing and turn all of his attention to our work. In a few days a much revised and annotated new version would be in our hands. His comments, which addressed matters of style and choice of word or phrase as well as content, revealed Strayer's commitment to his students.

Joseph Strayer loved to teach and once remarked to one of us that he found it difficult to be away from the classroom for too long. In 1971, when he had to go abroad for a few months on a research trip, he had Gaines Post, the distinguished historian of medieval law and a graduate-student classmate of his at Harvard, come out of retirement to teach the students he left behind. He did so not only to see his students protected and cared for but also to bring his good friend back into teaching.

Not surprisingly, for reasons of this kind and many others, Joseph Strayer commanded a wide and loving loyalty from most of his graduate and undergraduate students. At the gathering honoring him on his retirement, friends and former students poured into Princeton from all over the country. Out of his earshot, for there was still that sense of awe we all felt, they regaled us with cherished anecdotes of his earlier years, his teaching, his cigars, his imposing presence, his legendary efforts on their behalf. There was love and care in the telling, a sense of extended kinship among all of us who had shared the benefit of the same master.

Strayer also taught us the pleasure of research in medieval history. In our first years at Princeton a life of scholarship seemed to us a half-understood, only a half-possible thing at best. He led us to the sources, showed us how to handle and work with manuscripts, encouraged us to go abroad to do archival research. He uncovered to us the excitement of attempting to reconstruct the past from sources hitherto unused and see them from completely new perspectives. To us his insights and commitment to archival research and a life of scholarship came as a revelation and as a most worthy example to follow.

Why was Joseph Strayer so sympathetic to his students? His own upbringing in a family of educators may have given him insight. His father, George Drayton Strayer, was a specialist in the new field of educational theory at the turn of the century; his brother Paul taught at Princeton, and they shared experiences; and his wife, Lois Curry Strayer, had herself been a student of the great developmental psychologist, Jean Piaget. From all these quarters he might have gained useful knowledge, and he certainly wrote extensively and with a professional air on the teaching of history, publishing eleven articles on the subject from 1930 to 1970.[1]

More important, we think, to his philosophy and practice of education was Strayer's own experience as a student. Years after his retirement, one of the authors of this memoir convinced him to allow some conversations on his life to be recorded.[2] Unfortunately they were too brief to give a full picture of the man and his career, but they do reveal that he relished the memory of his teachers, especially those from his undergraduate days at Princeton. He was, however, remarkably reticent about his graduate education — on or off tape — and what little he vouchsafed in casual conversations late in life was more negative than positive. He had an abiding conviction that his most famous teacher, the greatest name in academic medieval studies in America in this century, Charles Homer Haskins, did not give him the encouragement and praise he deserved. He respected and admired Haskins. He wrote a superb memoir of his life for the *Dictionary of American Biography*.[3] And he never ceased to commend the quality of his scholarship or the fundamental importance of his role in making

[1] A complete bibliography of Strayer's writings appeared in a volume of his collected essays, *Medieval Statecraft and the Perspectives of History* (Princeton: Princeton University Press, 1971).

[2] A copy of the tape, which is in the possession of Teofilo Ruiz, has been given to the Princeton University Archives.

[3] "Charles Homer Haskins," *Dictionary of American Biography*, 22, Supplement 2 (New York, 1958), pp. 289–291.

American scholarship on the Middle Ages respectable to European historians. But he missed having had, it was clear to us, the kind of praise that he himself would later shower on far lesser lights.

The remarkable scholarship which Joseph Strayer himself produced is, on assessment, extremely fine. It has "stood up well," to borrow the phrase that was the highest praise he could give to the scholarship of those among his predecessors, Haskins chief among them, whom he admired most. His work is lucid and economical in style. He loathed to waste words.

Although the end of his career saw a veritable explosion of publications from Strayer, one of his most distinguished colleagues, Jerome Blum, for whose appointment Strayer was responsible, lamented once in conversation that what should have been the period of his friend's greatest productivity coincided with World War II and the first decade or so of the Cold War, when service to his country drew Strayer away from the study of the Middle Ages. Blum was quick to add that Strayer never, to his knowledge, displayed any regret over his choice. And his service to government informed the scholarship of his later years. There is an authority about his writing on the state that still dazzles undergraduates, graduate students, and mature scholars alike.

All of his varied experiences — doing research in Europe in the 1920s when the great civilization was still far removed from its attempt at suicide in the Great War, his consultancies to the Air Force and the Central Intelligence Agency, his service on the Princeton Borough Council, let alone his numerous positions within the Department of History, including his long chairmanship (1942–1962) — gave substance to his historical analysis of state formation and institutions. He was particularly interested in the interplay of bureaucracy and political leadership in the two countries, France and England, that, for good or ill, became the models for so much of the rest of the world. One of his two famous undergraduate courses was called "Europe in the High

Middle Ages"; it was largely about France with a deep bow to England as well. The other was "English Constitutional History," a title which speaks for itself.

But if his own interests seem, at first glance, so focused and perhaps now somewhat old fashioned, it is wise to recall that he always saw the problems of French and English political development in global terms. (His graduate course in the Woodrow Wilson School covered the emerging states of post-colonial Africa and Asia as much as medieval and early modern Europe.) Moreover, his intellectual curiosity knew almost no bounds. High problems in theology appear to have held little interest for him; and except for Castro's Cuba and its role in Cold War diplomacy, Latin America occupied little of his time (it was the only field he never precepted in his fifty-odd years on the faculty). Otherwise he was interested in everything, a fact which translated into an openness in graduate teaching that persuaded him to encourage students to do dissertations on Castilian and Catalonian history, on German and Imperial history, on Sicily, and in various areas of intellectual history.[4] At the other end of the pedagogical scale, his last great scholarly achievement was bringing the thirteen-volume *Dictionary of the Middle Ages*[5] to fruition. Designed for high school and college students (but as useful for mature scholars), the *Dictionary*, of which he was planner and editor-in-chief, is a fitting monument to a man whose whole life was dedicated to the teaching of young people and the perpetuation of a scholarly tradition of the study of the Middle Ages, as rich as it is admirable.

[4] Here is a random selection: Robert Lerner, "The Heresy of the Free Spirit in the Thirteenth Century" (1964); William Percy, "The Revenues of the Kingdom of Sicily under Charles I of Anjou, 1266–1285, and Their Relationship to the Vespers" (1964); John B. Freed, "The Mendicant Orders in German Society, 1219–1273" (1969); Rhiman Rotz, "Urban Uprisings in Fourteenth-Century Germany: A Comparative Study of Brunswick (1374–1380) and Hamburg (1376)" (1970); Elaine Robison, "Humberti Cardinalis libri tres adversus simoniacos: A Critical Edition with an Introductory Essay and Notes" (1972).

[5] *Dictionary of the Middle Ages*, 13 vols. (New York, 1982–1989).

READING LIST

The Administration of Normandy under Saint Louis (Cambridge, Massachusetts: The Medieval Academy of America, 1932)

With Charles H. Taylor: *Studies in Early French Taxation* (Cambridge, Massachusetts: Harvard University Press, 1939)

Feudalism (Princeton: Van Nostrand, 1965)

On the Medieval Origins of the Modern State (Princeton: Princeton University Press, 1970)

The Albigensian Crusades (New York: Dial Press, 1971)

The Reign of Philip the Fair (Princeton: Princeton University Press, 1980)

William C. Jordan, Bruce McNabb, and Teofilo Ruiz, eds., *Order and Innovation in the Middle Ages: Essays in Honor of Joseph R. Strayer* (Princeton: Princeton University Press, 1976)

Oliver Strunk

Department of Music

BY KENNETH LEVY

Oliver Strunk was one of the founders of American musicology, and during the middle decades of this century its most influential and versatile practitioner. His scholarly background was auspicious. His father, William Strunk, was Cornell's celebrated professor of Old English. The elder Strunk's "little book," *The Elements of Style*, retouched by his disciple E. B. White, continues to introduce thousands of Americans each year to the proper use of their language. Oliver's career had a bumpy start. As a precocious sixteen-year-old, he was enrolled at Cornell, but he gave that up for independent study of musical performance and composition. For a while he supported himself in theaters, playing the piano or organ background for silent pictures. There are stories of T. E. Lawrencesque motorcyclings, and of an impetuous early marriage that was soon annulled.

At twenty-four he was back at Cornell for a first exposure to the young discipline of musicology, under the German-educated Otto Kinkeldey. Then he spent the next year (1926–1927) in Berlin, where the German musicological scene was flowering, with such authorities as Abert, Wolf, Sachs, Schering, and Blume. That was the last formal education Strunk would have, and when he returned home, it was to uncertain prospects. He never earned an undergraduate or graduate degree, so an academic career seemed closed. And musicology itself was practically unknown in American universities. In his later twenties, Strunk found employment at the Music Division of the Library of Congress; while based in Washington he married Mildred Altemose, and in 1931 he published a first scholarly article, on "Vergil and Music." When the post of chief of the division fell vacant in 1934, Strunk's extraordinary talents were recognized and he was chosen over more mature candidates. In 1936, the University of Rochester tendered an honorary doctorate of letters; that was his first and — through his active career — his only academic credential. The role of librarian offered professional fulfillment, and he might have spent his career at it. Then Princeton intervened.

During the early 1930s, music was rarely taught at the University. What meager attention the subject received went largely to providing for Chapel services and the concert series in Alexander Hall. There was no academic department. A turning point came in 1935, when President Harold W. Dodds persuaded Roy Dickenson Welch to leave Smith College in order to build a formal program in music at the University. This began as a wing of the Department of Art and Archaeology, and it would not attain full status as an independent department until a decade later. Roy Welch was a splendid choice. He was a person of great personal charm and well-honed political instincts, and also a brilliant undergraduate lecturer. Neither a composer nor a musicologist — he had trained as a pianist in Germany — he had no particular ambition to be a postgraduate instructor. But he had the wisdom to attract to Princeton the outstanding person in each of those fields. In composition, that was Roger Sessions, who with Aaron Copland was the most accomplished composer of the American generation. In musicology, it meant Oliver Strunk, who stood practically alone in the field. In 1937 he was enticed to the University by an assistant professorship. Over the next three decades, his reputation for intellectual and human qualities would attract to the Graduate School the majority of the nation's musicological talents. In this past generation, the programs at Chicago, Cornell, Berkeley, Illinois, New York University, the City University of New York, Rome, Harvard, and Oxford, among others, have been headed by Princetonians he trained.

Oliver Strunk was a reserved person, slow to speak, with little in the way of small talk or hail-fellow manner. He loved telling a good anecdote and the laughter that went with it, yet in social situations he often stood shyly on the margin, and conversations with him could be punctuated by painful silences where neither party seemed to know what to say next. He lacked the flair for lecturing to undergraduates, and his rare offerings for the general student tended to produce respect mingled with yawns. He was gently chided for that by Princeton administrators, and was not advanced to full professorial rank until he was over fifty. With graduate students, it was another matter. In his chosen field, he was again quiet and slow, but the force of intellect and imagination cast a spell around the music seminar room. The graduate students adored him. Lewis Lockwood, the present-day Strunkian at Harvard, in a recent publication recalled "Strunk's ability — matchless in my experience — to handle large-scale problems in music history in quiet lectures and with magisterial economy of expression. . . ." He never took on the airs and graces of the great professor. Instead, he dealt with the graduate students as equals — as a humble fellow-seeker of enlightenment. To be on that basis with the most formidable of musicological minds was a transforming experience for all who experienced it.

Strunk's intellectual horizons were wide. It often seemed to his students that there was no area of the field where he had not achieved absolute control of what everyone else knew, and then, without ever belittling, that he had a better notion of how that knowledge might be interpreted. His wider reputation was based on a brilliantly executed historical anthology of other peoples' writings about music. But he published only a small fraction of the scientific work he did. He never produced an independent book of his own. In fact, all his published writings, apart from one field of particular specialization, are collected in a volume of precisely 200 pages. Yet the great storehouse of his wisdom and information was available to all students and colleagues, and through his initiative and example he spawned the work in many of today's fields — fields as diverse as medieval plainchant, thirteenth-century polyphony, the fourteenth-century "newer" and "subtler" polyphonic arts, fifteenth-century Flemish-Burgundian mass styles, Venetian seventeenth-century opera, Haydn, Beethoven, Wagner, and Verdi. On each, just a seminal article or two, but enough to get others on track. And the historical shapes as Strunk envisioned them have generally withstood the test of time.

Perhaps the most extraordinary feature of Strunk's career was that the sole field where he made a major contribution was the obscure one of Eastern Orthodox (Byzantine) Church plainchant. It was a forbidding area, where few could follow him, but the bulk of the life's work was there, sustained throughout his last four decades. It began almost by chance, though with a link to Princeton that was influential in his decision to leave Washington and come to the University. During the mid-1930s, professors Albert M. Friend and Kurt Weitzmann of the Department of Art and Archaeology projected a facsimile edition of a thirteenth-century Byzantine hymn book, preserved in the library of Koutloumousi monastery on Mount Athos. Its appeal for them was its cycle of pictorial illuminations. But that book was also filled with musical notations, and the scrupulous art historians cast about for enlightenment on those as well. The search led to Strunk, who, as it turned out, claimed no competence in such matters; at the time he did not know a word of Greek. But where there was a problem, Strunk was interested, and he thought he might take a look. As the nature and scope of the problem became clear, the initial look turned into a passion that remained for the rest of his life. The year 1942 saw a first paper on Byzantine music, and he went on to a flow of related contributions, often in little-known journals, that gave future direction to the field. He was responsible for establishing a sound theoretical basis for the transcription of the Byzantine notations of the twelfth and thirteenth centuries into Western notation; for developing methods of transcribing the previously impenetrable paleo-Byzantine and paleo-Slavonic notations; and for opening up major musical repertories that were previously ignored or poorly understood. The full collection of Byzantine papers, reprinted in 1977, came to 350 pages.

Strunk was a tall, gaunt man, at times scarecrow thin, and with a Sherlock Holmes quality to his person and his mind. Students remember him, poised at the blackboard, mute for a full minute or two while he formulated what he wanted to say; at times there was an unlit cigarette in one hand and a long chalk in the other, and there was speculation as to whether his concentration would lead to lighting up the wrong white stick. When the formulation came, it was worth the wait. He combined intellectual skepticism with a knowledge of cultural context and an ingenuity in evolving and exploiting various methods of inquiry. Reluctant to create broad theories or deal with generalities, he liked to take apparently small-scale, self-contained problems and develop far-reaching conclusions based on irrefutable facts. His teaching, like his writing, was influential far beyond its immediate scope, and it was marked by an exceptional generosity with ideas and information.

Strunk was a founding member of the American Musicological Society, the first editor of its *Journal* (1948), and its president

(1959–1960). He served on the editorial board of the *Monumenta Musicae Byzantinae*, and was its director from 1961 to 1971. His honorary awards included membership of the Royal Musical Association, the Danish Academy and the British Academy, as well as an honorary doctorate from the University of Chicago (1970). In 1961 he received the American Council of Learned Societies' prize for distinguished scholarship in the humanities.

The Strunks had no children; there was only the scholarly output, and the cadre of younger scholars to whose intellectual and personal outlooks his example gave focus. In his later years, the flow of royalties from his father's book allowed him to retire early, and just before his sixty-fifth birthday he and Mildred took up residence in a villa at Grottaferrata in the Alban Hills, south of Rome. One attraction was the thousand-year-old Basilian monastery of Saint Nilus, in a walled enclosure above the lovely town, where Byzantine-style chants are regularly sung; its first-class theological and liturgical library also supplied his professional needs. For some years, life was agreeable, but the final years were difficult. Mildred passed away in 1973. As Oliver's own afflictions increased, the gentle-hearted monks did what they could to lighten burdens for "il professore." He passed away just short of his seventy-ninth birthday. With Mildred, he is buried in the Cimitero Protestante in the southern part of Rome, near the grave of Keats.

READING LIST

Specimina notationum antiquiorum, Monumenta musicae byzantinae, Série principale, Vol. 7 (Copenhagen, 1966)

Essays on Music in the Western World (New York: W. W. Norton, 1974)

Essays on Music in the Byzantine World (New York: W. W. Norton, 1977)

H. S. Powers, ed., *Studies in Music History: Essays for Oliver Strunk* (Princeton: Princeton University Press, 1968)

Hugh Stott Taylor

Department of Chemistry

BY WALTER J. KAUZMANN

Hugh Taylor, the fourth dean of the Graduate School (1945–1958), was born, raised, and educated in Lancashire, England. His father was a glass technologist, with a laboratory in his home. Hugh was thus exposed to scientific experimentation from his earliest years and went on to study chemistry at the University of Liverpool, from which he obtained his D.Sc. in 1914. During the years 1912–1914 he had done research in Stockholm and Hanover under two of the most prominent physical chemists of the time. There and at Liverpool he was exposed to some of the most important frontier problems of the day in the relatively young science of physical chemistry.

In 1914 he came to the United States, expecting to stay for a year or so. He accepted an instructorship at Princeton, where he remained for the rest of his life. Bright, hard working, well-organized and personable, he settled into the life of the Chemistry Department, the University, and the community. But World War I was raging, and from 1917 to 1919 he chose to live in England, where he undertook important war-related research. Returning to Princeton in 1919, he rapidly climbed the academic ladder, becoming chairman of the Chemistry Department in 1926, a position he retained for twenty-five years. During this period he built the department into one of the best in the country through his own scientific research, through appointments of able men to the faculty, and through the construction of the Frick Chemical Laboratory.

During World War II he was again heavily involved in war research, this time in Princeton (a large group at the University was responsible for developing an important component of the immense plant required for separating uranium isotopes at the Oak Ridge project of the Manhattan District). At the end of the war he became dean of the Graduate School, where he presided over a thirteen-year period of expansion and important change. He retired from the faculty in 1958, having reached the mandatory retirement age of sixty-seven, but continued a busy and productive life for many years.

I came to Princeton as a graduate student in the fall of 1937, intending to become an organic chemist. I was appointed as research assistant to Professor Eugene Pacsu, who, however, was away on leave during the first term. He had an ingenious idea for the chemical synthesis of sucrose (common cane sugar) which had not yet been achieved in the laboratory (and indeed has not yet, I believe, been accomplished without the use of biological catalysts). During the fall term I worked hard at making a large quantity of the raw materials required for the synthesis; Pacsu's post-doctoral associate supervised me in this work. When Pacsu returned from his leave and I proudly showed him what I had made, he snorted "Is *that* all you've done?" Some time thereafter I was told to see Professor Taylor, who said to me "Professor Pacsu does not think you are cut out to be an organic chemist." I was utterly crushed, but Taylor immediately went on to say that my record showed that I had a good background in physics and mathematics. Perhaps I should consider talking with Professor Henry Eyring about working with him. This is one of the most important pieces of advice that I have ever had and I shall be eternally grateful for it — and not only for the advice itself, but also for the manner in which it was offered. I did go on to do my thesis with Eyring. After World War II Eyring left Princeton and I was appointed to fill his position on the faculty.

Despite the impression Taylor often created by the rapidity with which he dealt with the personal problems that came to his attention, he was a warm, caring person at heart. This was demonstrated in my case by the care that he, as chairman of the department, took in passing on to me Professor Pacsu's evaluation of my prospects as an organic chemist. Ordinarily one would have expected this to be dealt with by the chairman of the Graduate School Committee, but when he learned of my situation, Taylor must have felt that he should take care of the problem himself. I know of a number of other painful personal situations in which Taylor quietly took matters into his own hands to see that they were handled quickly, properly, and discreetly.

Hugh Taylor was a sensible and flexible dean of the Graduate School. Several changes in policy illustrate the point. At the time I came to Princeton all graduate students were required to sign a pledge that they would not marry while they were graduate students. Taylor later explained to me the rationale for this rule: Princeton University felt that it had a moral responsibility to its students to see that they were able to keep body and soul together. If the student married, this responsibility would be extended to his spouse and possibly to his children. The University felt that it had the right to require of the student that this responsibility be restricted. I was far from ready for marriage at the time and had no hesitation in signing the pledge, but a number of my graduate-student friends did violate the pledge, and they were penalized and severely criticized. Their faculty advisors found

Jeremiah Finch, Hugh Stott Taylor, and J. Douglas Brown at Commencement 1958, when Dr. Taylor received a citation on the occasion of his retirement as dean of the Graduate School.

means of supporting them, however, and they were able to complete their degrees. One of those who violated the rule, incidentally, was the physicist Richard Feynman. Behind this was a touching and tragic story that is now well known. Dick was deeply in love with a girl who was dying of tuberculosis, and he felt justified in violating the rule.

When Taylor became dean of the Graduate School in 1945 World War II had just ended and graduate schools were flooded with married veterans. Thus it was at the beginning of his tenure as dean that the Princeton marriage pledge fell by the wayside, and he accepted the change. But another archaic requirement remained: the Princeton Graduate School did not accept women. This rule was removed under Taylor's successor and during Robert F. Goheen's presidency — the first step in Princeton's rapid transition to becoming co-educational. Although I never discussed this matter with him, I am sure that Taylor would have approved of the change; but the University was not yet ready to accept it while he was dean.

An amusing situation arose in connection with one of the rules for student conduct established at the founding of the Graduate

College: gowns were to be worn at meals served in Procter Hall. This rule was still in force when Taylor became dean just after World War II. As can be imagined, a number of students were not favorably impressed by this tradition held over from what they considered a bygone era. A petition was drawn up, signed by a large number of students, and presented to the dean. He rejected it, saying that there were some things that were not decided by majority vote. But students who wished to dine without gowns were then accommodated in another dining room where gowns were not required.

Taylor's teaching was highly effective. His interests were very broad, and he included in his graduate course in physical chemistry many topics that were extremely useful to me in my own later research. His outside contacts included outstanding scientists in the most active research areas. I recall vividly that during my stay as a graduate student there were symposia on several of these areas in which leaders in the fields spoke in the Frick Chemical Laboratory. What a boon this was to us as graduate students!

Taylor retained his British citizenship, and in 1953 he was knighted by the Queen. Thereafter we often addressed him as "Sir Hugh." He was also a devout Catholic and involved in church activities, among them the establishment of a Catholic chaplaincy at Princeton in 1928. In the 1950s he became involved in several church activities at the highest levels; he was honored by the Pope in recognition of these services.

A painful incident occurred in 1957 when the Catholic chaplain began publicly attacking various members of the faculty, alleging incompetence, atheism, or dangerous political opinions (this was at the height of the McCarthy era). I understand that Sir Hugh made efforts within the church to have the chaplain silenced, but without success. This situation was eventually resolved by President Goheen, who was then just assuming office. In one of his first actions as president he rescinded the University's recognition of the chaplain and withdrew the use of University facilities. Soon thereafter the chaplain was transferred elsewhere.

Sir Hugh's scientific activities centered on the study of the mechanisms and rates of chemical reactions. Although the idea originated with others, he was among the first to recognize the role of free atoms and "radicals" in chemical reactions; many important experimental studies were made in his laboratories in this area. His studies in Britain during World War I involved the use of solid catalysts in the production of ammonia from nitrogen and hydrogen (the so-called Haber Process, which made it possible for the Germans to manufacture high explosives although cut off from South American sources of nitrates). This led Taylor to the highly interesting study of the scientific basis of catalysis of chemical reactions at solid surfaces — an area of tremendous industrial importance as well and one which is still only incompletely understood. Thanks to Taylor's activities and many publications, Princeton became a major center of this study. There is general agreement today that academic science should take cognizance of the needs of industry — but Taylor was actively doing this well over half a century ago!

Taylor, however, might well have considered his most important scientific discovery to be in quite a different direction: it was the discovery of Henry Eyring, a remarkable young, daring, and creative scientist who was bringing the powerful tools provided by quantum mechanics to the study and understanding of chemical reaction rates and mechanisms. Eyring had spent several years in Germany learning quantum mechanics in the early 1930s, shortly after it had been developed. He had returned to the United States and joined the faculty at the University of Wisconsin as an instructor, but the faculty there were not sufficiently impressed and they let him go. Hugh Taylor heard him speak at a meeting, immediately recognized the immense significance of the ideas Eyring was trying to promote, and invited him to Princeton and fostered his career on the faculty. Eyring's presence on the Princeton chemistry faculty brought many outstanding students and postdoctoral associates to Princeton.

Another of Taylor's accomplishments at Princeton was his involvement in the construction of the Frick Chemical Laboratory. The story here could go back to Taylor's first years at Princeton. He once told me of the following incident, which deserves to be more widely known. Henry Clay Frick, the wealthy industrialist and associate of Andrew Carnegie in the Pittsburgh steel industry, somehow became interested in Princeton and was induced to serve on the board of trustees. After some University function, Frick was walking down Washington Road with Hugh Taylor, at the time a mere instructor as I understand it, yet already with a presence that made it possible for him to walk down the street with one of the wealthiest men in America. At the present intersection of Washington Road and William Street, Frick pointed with his cane to a plot of vacant land and declared that someday a new chemistry laboratory would be located there. At that time the department was housed in an inadequate building. World War I intervened; at the end of the war Frick was approached to make good on his promise. He thought it over, then said that the price of steel was too high, but would surely come down and he would respond at that time. Unfortunately Frick died soon thereafter, and it was necessary to seek the promised money from his daughter; eventually she gave a handsome sum to the University. At about this time the chemistry building burned down and the need for a new building became urgent. Taylor, who was soon to become chairman, took an active part in planning the new laboratory. The building was dedicated in 1929 and even today seems a masterpiece — lovely on the outside (especially when the wisteria is in bloom) and fresh and attractive within. I have been told that its principal shortcoming is that its interior walls are so well built and so clean that it is a problem to rearrange laboratories and offices to meet new needs. And the building stands, of course, on the land to which Frick pointed while walking with Taylor, when Taylor was beginning his Princeton career.

Sir Hugh was also instrumental in bringing the Textile Research Institute to Princeton and arranging the close relations between the Institute and the University whereby graduate students can conduct their thesis research in the Institute's laboratories under the guidance of Princeton faculty affiliated with the Institute. This is another example, nearly fifty years old, of a trend that is now being encouraged by government agencies such as the National Science Foundation as well as by a number of influential members of Congress. Taylor was clearly in tune with some of today's notions of the relationships between universities and the society in which they are embedded.

Another development of importance to the University in which Taylor was deeply involved was the purchase of the land and buildings of the Princeton campus of Rockefeller Institute. After World War II the trustees of the Rockefeller Institute decided to move the facilities and personnel from the Princeton campus back to the parent Institute in New York. This facility had been on the market at a high price, but was not moving. The University was able to purchase it at a reasonable price, and it became the James Forrestal Research Center.

Lady Taylor played an important role in Taylor's career at Princeton. He had married Elizabeth Sawyer in Princeton in 1919, after his return from England. She, like Hugh, was a Lancastrian, and a graduate of Liverpool University. Warm-hearted and well-liked by all, she provided ideal support for Hugh in his many activities. Her death in 1958, at the time of Hugh's retirement, was a severe blow. In her memory, and in recognition of her concern for the welfare of graduate students, the Lady Taylor Fund (now the Sir Hugh and Lady Taylor Fund) was established to assist graduate students who face family medical emergencies.

Clearly, Hugh Taylor's presence on the Princeton faculty over a period of nearly fifty years had an enormous effect on the state of the University — an effect that remains very much in evidence today.

Willard Thorp

Department of English

BY THOMAS P. ROCHE, JR.

Willard Thorp was one of the last teachers to carry on the old Princeton tradition of teaching seminars in his home. In the spacious library of the house at 428 Nassau Street we would find Willard seated in the window seat looking out on the garden, with the inevitable cigarette dangling from his lip. The smart ones headed right for the blue couch in the dark corner near the fireplace to avoid Willard's inquisitive eye, and then the reports would begin and were somehow finished, and Willard would take over, running the rest of the three hours like a preceptorial: discussion was the mode, and it was pretty wide-ranging, which gave Willard the opportunity to get up at least once during every seminar to pluck down his autographed copy of the book under discussion. He had an instinct for assigning reports; as a recent arrival from New

Haven I was assigned the "Connecticut Wits" and was informed that New Critical methodology would not be really helpful with Timothy Dwight, a conclusion that I had reached immediately after the assignment had been given a week earlier.

Three hours later, we all adjourned to the sitting room where Margaret presided over a proper tea table, with the inevitable Thorp dachshund (Redburn in 1954)[1] and a very large plate of cookies done for the occasion by Winnie, the large and silent cook. The first tea was something of a trauma for most of us, who were unused to balancing teacups and cookies without mishap and who most certainly were not accustomed to find our hostess on hands and knees stuffing dog biscuits in our cuffs. The second week most of us wore cuffless trousers. At Christmas, in addition to the tea Willard sat down at the baby grand and played carols; we sang and Redburn howled, which Margaret assured us was the dog's custom when Willard played. The elaborate, old-fashioned scenario was something of a joke to all of us then, but we enjoyed it, and it is a tribute to the Thorp's ingenuity in restaging these ancient ceremonies that they come so easily to mind now forty years after they occurred.

Willard was always in danger of becoming a parody of himself, but underneath the well-dressed, smooth flamboyance and bonhomie we came to know the tough mind and kind heart that characterized the real Willard. Above all he was loyal, to his students, his friends, his alma mater Hamilton College, and most especially to Princeton and his work here.

After graduation from Hamilton in 1920 and one year as a graduate student at Harvard where he earned a Master's degree, Willard accepted a bid to teach at Smith where he was an instructor (1921–1922) and assistant professor of English (1922–1924). It

[1] The Thorp dachshunds (a single potentate at a time) had two dynasties, the first Wagnerian with "Fafnir," etc. and the second Melvillian, the last of which, "Toby," Willard dispatched to another home on the day that Margaret died.

was an important time in his life because it was there that he met his future wife, Margaret Farrand, and Roy Welch, who later came to Princeton as the first chair of the newly formed Department of Music. Willard came to Princeton in 1924 as a Procter Fellow where his main field of scholarly interest was Elizabethan drama (fostered no doubt by the presence of Thomas Marc Parrott), which eventuated in his doctoral dissertation on the rise of realism in the drama. It is the least significant of Willard's books, which may well explain his hasty progress to Dryden and the songs of the Restoration stage and soon thereafter to the Victorians and to *Poets in Transition*, on which he worked with his mentor Parrott. We tend to forget these earlier works because of Willard's allegiance to the field of American literature and his participation in its creation. His early edition of Melville was an important landmark in the rehabilitation of Melville as a serious American writer. He was one of the four major editors of the still pertinent *Literary History of the United States*. His bibliography, in addition to the books and anthologies, consists of over sixty articles and more than 160 reviews of books.[2] For his contributions to the humanities he was awarded an honorary degree of Doctor of Letters by Princeton in 1978.

Willard Thorp was important, not only because of his critical works but also because of his networking with most of the New Critical generation of critics and poets. He was a close friend of Allen Tate and his wife Caroline Gordon, who were married for the second time in the Thorp library. It was through his friendship with Tate that he became an honorary member of the Southern Agrarians, out of which association grew Willard's influential *The Southern Reader*. I believe it was through Tate's intervention that Willard and Margaret became friends of T. S. Eliot and his

[2] For a complete list of books, contributions to books, articles, and reviews, see "The Published Writings of Willard Thorp: A Checklist," compiled by Steven V. Justice, *Princeton University Library Chronicle* 54, nos. 2–3 (Winter–Spring 1993): 259–287.

wife Vivien during the sabbatical year the Thorps spent in Lincoln's Inn,[3] and later in the year that Eliot spent at the Institute for Advanced Study where he wrote *The Confidential Clerk.* It was Margaret Thorp who persuaded her old Smith friend, Emily Hale, to deposit her long correspondence with Eliot in the Princeton Library; Ms Hale sealed it from the public until 2016.

I brought Lyndall Gordon, who was completing her biography of Eliot, to see Willard late in his life. She was very much interested in the Hale-Eliot correspondence, to which she could have no access. Willard almost became the Chesire cat when he assured her that nothing could be done about the prohibition, but he added, "You might look at my correspondence with Sam Monk, in which I told him all about the letters, and my library file is open." In the last year of Willard's life Lyndall brought one of the first copies of her book, *Eliot's New Life*, to Willard, in which he is copiously thanked for solving her dilemma about the Hale correspondence.

Within the University Willard was influential in bringing Roy Welch to Princeton as the first chair of the Department of Music. He was also one of the originators of the Friends of the Princeton University Library and thus is responsible for the enormous growth of the rare book collection. I have no doubt that it was Willard who persuaded Julian Boyd, librarian of the University, to accept the donation of the F. Scott Fitzgerald collection for the library, to which Boyd was opposed on the grounds that it was too modern. Willard was everywhere for every liberal cause, and most of his enthusiasms have proved benefits for the University. He was a founding member and director of the Program in American Studies, to which he left his considerable fortune when he died. Most of Willard's teaching energies were directed to undergraduate teaching, but it was he and Lawrance Thompson who were the first to give graduate seminars in American literature. Nor should we ignore the long line of dissertations done under Willard's

[3] Margaret Thorp's Diary of that year, now in the Rare Book Room of the Firestone Library, tells an amusing story of their first luncheon with the Eliots.

supervision: Thomas Henney (1939), Howard Horsford (1951), Edgar Smith Rose (1955), Severn Duvall (1955), Jesse Bier (1956), Carl Hovde (1956), James Meriwether (1958), Andrew Hook (1960), Charles Fish (1964), John Clum (1967).

Two more long-term relationships should be mentioned. The first was Willard's influence on Harvard Professor Robert Chapman and the poet Louis Coxe, who produced a still-notable dramatic version of Melville's *Billy Budd.* The relation with the Coxe family continued in that Willard and Margaret summered in the Coxe home in Brunswick, Maine, while the Coxe family migrated north to Nova Scotia, which left the Nassau Street house available for three summers while I was a graduate student, enjoying the luxury of a large kitchen and an even larger library. This relationship has continued through Louis's son Robert, my junior supervisee, and his son, Charles Olav, who is now a member of the Class of 1997. All of them came to see Willard in his final years.

The second is Dr. Thomas Maren, Class of 1939, who left the graduate school to pursue a medical career in pharmacology, most recently at the University of Florida. His annual visits were a source of inspiration to Willard, who got free medical advice in return for the latest "happenings" in literary studies. Now that he is retired (but still working) Maren is giving courses in American literature to medical students at Florida and has established a fund in honor of Willard to support summer dissertation work of graduate students in English.

Willard had always earned the admiration and respect of all his students, many of whom continued to visit him at home long after he retired. But there was a problem in that Willard's arthritis was beginning to cause real pain, which made the stairs to the second floor bedroom a further problem. We toured all the nursing homes in the area, in each of which Willard would ask a magisterial question, "Can this room hold a baby grand?," for example, to which the reply was always negative. We settled on a live-in cook and housekeeper, Mrs. Pipe, a delightful widow who moved in and took charge. Within a couple of weeks Willard was complaining of putting on weight because of her German cooking, which he loved, and she was complaining that he was dictatorial and did not let her do her work without supervising. The real problem was that Willard did not want someone in the house all day, wanted his freedom to be alone. Mrs. Pipe departed soon thereafter, amicably and amply rewarded.

The solution we fixed on was to have a graduate student use the guest room, have cooking privileges, shop for Willard and drive him to the few outside appointments he still had. Food would be supplied by Meals on Wheels, one of the most inventive responses to aging that Princeton has found. Willard was delighted and immediately found the title for the graduate student; each was to be known as "the incumbent." At this point neither Willard nor I realized how many incumbents there would be, but as I recollect there were Robert Black, now a lawyer, followed by Mary Harrison, who was Grace Lambert's mistress of the stable and needed a room, and then Verlyn Klinkenborg, now at Harvard, Bruce Redford, at Chicago, Steven Justice, at Berkeley, and Scott Wayland, still in Princeton and married to Beth Harrison, the office manager of the Department of English. This long succession of mainly graduate students gave Willard a new grip on life. He badgered them, advised them on their dissertations, and generally regarded the incumbents as wayward but beloved offspring.

During this period his arthritis kept him from his piano and his typewriter, and he all but gave up the notion of finishing his history of the Graduate School, until Aaron Lemonick, then dean of the Graduate School, persuaded him to call in an assistant. It was Minor Myers, Jr., Princeton doctorate in politics and president of Illinois Wesleyan University, who courageously took charge, and the manuscript ballooned into completion — so much so that the exquisite editorial skills of Jeremiah Stanton Finch, emeritus professor of English and secretary of the University, were called on to trim the manuscript to the sleek and final form that appeared in 1978. Histories of parochial educational institutions are not high in the scale of genre studies, but the troika that created *The Princeton Graduate School: A History* have every reason to feel proud of their contribution. Willard was delighted that the work had been finished.

More public but not so well remembered today was Willard's part in the Library of Congress' award of the Bollingen Prize in Poetry to Ezra Pound in 1949, which generated much controversy and resulted in the prize's being moved from the jurisdiction of the Library of Congress to Yale University.[4] A little background is necessary to understand Willard's importance in the literary community of the forties. In 1943 Archibald MacLeish, then Librarian of Congress, appointed Allen Tate as Consultant in Poetry to the library. Tate suggested to MacLeish that Congress establish a body of Fellows in American Letters to advise the consultant and the librarian about developing the collection and selecting annually the incumbent of the Chair of Poetry in English. The first fellows were appointed in May 1944. Tate, who automatically became a Fellow after his year as Consultant, also suggested to MacLeish the establishment of an annual prize in American poetry and persuaded Huntington Cairns, the head of the Bollingen Foundation, to underwrite the award. The Prize was announced in 1948, and the jury was to be the Fellows in American Letters, who in that year included Tate, Robert Penn Warren, Louise Bogan, Karl Shapiro, Robert Lowell (all of whom had succeeded Tate as Consultant in Poetry) and Conrad Aiken, W. H. Auden, Katherine Garrison Chapin (Mrs. Francis Biddle), T. S. Eliot, Paul Green, Katherine Anne Porter, Theodore Spencer, and Willard Thorp (Spencer and Thorp the only academics, strictly speaking). The final vote went overwhelmingly to Ezra Pound's *Pisan Cantos*, which had been published in 1948 by New Directions, Shapiro casting the only negative vote and Green abstaining.

[4] I am indebted to the account given in William McGuire, *Bollingen: An Adventure in Collecting the Past* (Princeton: Princeton University Press, Bollingen Series, 1982), pp. 208–216.

Pound at the time of the award was in St. Elizabeth's Hospital in Washington where he had been committed as legally insane to avoid the more serious charge of treason for his broadcasts from Italy during World War II in support of the Fascist cause. He had been arrested by the U. S. Army in 1945 for treason and had been kept in a detention cage near Pisa for six months, during which time he wrote the first draft of the *Pisan Cantos.* The outcry against the award was summed up by a headline in the *New York Times*: "Pound, in Mental Clinic, Wins Prize for Poetry Penned in Treason Cell." The controversy quickly escalated into a battle about anti-Semitism and Fascism, the "new" poetry represented by Pound and Eliot, and other political allegations from the press that augured the emergence of the McCarthy era, led most vociferously by the poet Robert Hillier. The Fellows held firm to their decision and issued a point-by-point refutation of Hillier's charges, which, issued as a press release by the Library of Congress, was neglected or reported only in small bites by the press. It was written by a sub-committee of the Fellows: Leonie Adams, Louise Bogan, Karl Shapiro, and Willard, who was especially proud of his part in this controversy. I know of this only because I stopped by to have a drink with Willard on the day after Robert Penn Warren died, 16 September 1989. Willard rather sadly said, "So now I am the last." I, not understanding the relation of Warren's death to Willard's seniority, asked and was told, with mounting liberal indignation at every savored sip of bourbon, the whole story of the Pound controversy and finally understood that Willard was in many senses the last of the brave but conflicted defenders of the rights of poetry against the claims of a politically correct world. The battle, nonetheless, had been lost in 1949 when Congress passed a resolution that the Library of Congress should abstain from awarding prizes.

Willard's and Margaret's influence continues in the support their estate gives to the Program in American Studies. In the week that I am writing this tribute, the Program has just presented a two-day conference on the Centenary of Edmund Wilson, which was an intellectual triumph that would have delighted Willard and Margaret.[5] They both were devoted to the cause of liberal education at Princeton. We can only hope that we live up to their expectations of us.

READING LIST

The Lost Tradition of American Letters (Philadelphia: Philobiblon Club, 1945, reprinted *Princeton University Library Chronicle* 54, nos. 2–3 [Winter–Spring 1993]: 188–206)

The Lives of Eighteen from Princeton (Princeton: Princeton University Press, 1946)

A Southern Reader (New York: Alfred A. Knopf, 1955)

Moby-Dick; or, The Whale, by Herman Melville. With an introduction and notes by Willard Thorp (New York: Oxford University Press, 1947)

With Minor Myers, Jr., and Jeremiah Finch, *The Princeton Graduate School: A History* (Princeton: Princeton University Press, 1978)

[5] The *Princeton University Library Chronicle*, volume 54, nos. 2–3 (Winter–Spring 1993) devoted the whole issue to honoring Willard's career and contains one of the lectures given by Alfred Kazin as the first of the Willard and Margaret Thorp Lectures, pp. 240ff.

Melvin Marvin Tumin

Department of Sociology

BY BERNARD BECK

Princeton does not have a law school, but during the years when I was a graduate student in sociology there, it offered a unique curriculum in advocacy through the work and character of Melvin M. Tumin. The Department of Sociology was still two years in the future when I took the Suburban Transit bus from New York City's Port Authority Terminal in the late Spring of 1958 to have my first look at Princeton. At that time, sociology was a stepchild discipline in the Department of Economics and Sociology, a strange, amusing, rough-hewn, impaired sort of pursuit amid the ancient noble academic lineages that flew Princeton's colors and maintained her greatness. Although it was a recent arrival on campus and had not yet won full legitimacy, sociology at Princeton had an impressive faculty who had made distinguished contributions in theory, demography, survey research, organizations and industrial relations.

The graduate program was committed to excellence as well. The eight of us who entered our first year in the autumn of 1958 were told often that we had been hand-picked. Few in number, we were nevertheless the largest entering group up to that time. Typical of sociologists, then and now, we were a motley, diverse aggregation. We found a faculty who were themselves excellent, diverse, and ill-assorted. Sociology was, fortunately, a raffish gypsy lot in the traditional surroundings of Old Nassau. We were an early foretaste of the bohemian turn the American academy was about to take in the 1960s.

No one was more homespun, more dashing, more gaudy, more irrepressible, more passionate, more oppositional, more rebellious, more intellectual nor more aristocratic, more courtly, more devoted to *noblesse oblige* than Mel Tumin. He reminded me of an improbable combination of Zorro and Joe Hill, Zero Mostel and Clarence Darrow. Most unlikely of all, he was an archetype of the social researcher at mid-century, devoted to the ideal of a rigorous, objective social science, but one of the few who put that science in service to the needs of people in need.

At that moment in the 1950s, post-war quietism and red-baiting had produced a safe, conventional, academic social science. Mel, on the other hand, made noise and generated embarrassment by insisting on the intellectual respectability of egalitarianism as a theory and the moral necessity of activism in practice. The theoretical foundation for his position was expressed in a series of articles and commentaries in dialogue with the leading mainstream sociological theory about inequality, propounded by Kingsley Davis and Wilbert E. Moore. Moore was Tumin's senior colleague in the Princeton department, so their monumental debate was conducted in person within Princeton's ivied walls.[1] Before

[1] Their dialogue was also carried on in print. See Kingsley Davis and Wilbert E. Moore, "Some Principles of Stratification," *American Sociological Review*

the word "relevance" became the name of virtue for a generation, Mel insisted on making his sociological work relevant to social and political movements for class, racial, and ethnic equality. He paid a price for it in his career at Princeton, but he never missed a payment.

I was certainly not the first child of poor immigrants to work his way up through city schools, trying to become "somebody." By the late 1950s, that story had almost become commonplace. But not quite. The final stage of my climb to the heights, graduate study at Princeton, was for me a solo journey up an unmarked path. A month or so short of my graduation from Brooklyn College in 1958, I was waylaid in a corridor by one of my sociology professors, Leo P. Chall, founder of *Sociological Abstracts* (whose death, ironically for me, came in the same year as Mel Tumin's, almost four decades later). In his typically conspiratorial manner, he took me aside and posed to me a fateful question: "How would you like to go to Princeton?"

Leo thought that the graduate program in sociology at Princeton might have some openings, that it was not yet as well known a graduate department as some others, and that I might look good to them. I was excited by the prospect, and he went into action on my behalf. Leo was as good as his word. In a very short time, very late in the academic year, I had an appointment to see Marion Levy in Princeton. Almost as an afterthought, Leo mentioned that I might also see Mel Tumin, who supervised graduate study there. I might find him somewhat gruff and formidable, but I was not to worry. Down deep, he had a heart of gold.

I went off to the appointment in a newly bought but ill-fitting suit, hopeful and fearful. After all, this was Princeton. I found Marion Levy to be a handful, sharp, challenging, rigorous in the interview, as he was for the five years I studied with him and learned how to think. This was what I expected Princeton to be

10, no. 2 (1945): 242–249, and Melvin M. Tumin, "Some Principles of Stratification: A Critical Analysis," *American Sociological Review* 18, no. 4 (1953): 387–394.

like, the Big Leagues, not for sissies. It was stimulating, but not relaxing. Then it was time for my meeting with Mel Tumin. Now, I thought, I have to see the gruff one?

He happened to be out of his office when I got there; his secretary, Freda Milner, who later became a good friend of mine, called him at home to tell him I had come. Soon he arrived, changing the atmosphere completely in a way that was a personal signature, with broad, flourishing strokes. He burst in with greetings and apologies, energetic, risible, expressive, spontaneous and warm. He welcomed me, looked after my comfort, made me feel at home in what were for me very unfamiliar surroundings. When I rode the bus back to New York at the end of that day, I felt at last that I might have some business at Princeton, after all. And I wondered how anyone could have thought that I needed to be warned about Mel.

It was a perfectly reasonable idea. As I got to know Mel, I found that he was indeed a scrapper. He was assertive, obstinate, demanding, combative and uncompromising. As I would describe him at a memorial session of a national sociological association in 1994,[2] he could be a loudmouth, a crank, a troublemaker — but only toward those who were powerful and oppressive, only on behalf of the abused and the victimized.

I remember Mel with love and admiration not only for the special care he took of me on that first day, throughout my graduate student years at Princeton, and during the many years after I left. Caring and supportive mentors are many in the academy, but my personal gratitude is only the beginning. Mel did a great deal for many other students, especially those from modest or obscure backgrounds who came to Princeton as to a foreign land. Mel helped in a thousand practical ways. More importantly, he showed those diamonds-in-the-rough that they were indeed in the right place at Princeton, that they belonged, that they had

[2] Bernard Beck, "Caring about Social Problems: Loudmouths, Cranks, and Troublemakers," presented at the Annual Meetings of the Society for the Study of Social Problems, Los Angeles, August 5, 1994.

proper business there, and that they need not abandon their identification with the places they had come from in order to accommodate to Princeton. Mel showed us all that a Princeton sociologist could go home again.

From among the countless incidents and episodes that reveal Mel at his finest and that showed us how sociology could be properly done, three stand out for me. The first involved his challenge to traditional practices of racism and inequality in the eating clubs of Princeton itself. As a teacher of undergraduates, Mel ventured beyond the conventional presentation of the sociological literature. Mobilizing students into a social research team to investigate life on campus, he unearthed findings that showed disturbing forms of bigotry in the conduct of the "bicker" system by which students were selected to be members of the clubs. He brought these findings to the attention of the administration, calling for prompt action to ameliorate the situation. When things did not change, he went further. In the finest tradition of social research, he made his findings public, creating a scandal which generated sufficient pressure to compel the University to reform bicker, guaranteeing universal access and making the system accountable for its role on campus. Princeton was transformed for the better, and everyone who knew about the process was given a splendid and powerful lesson about the proper role of the social scientist in society: scientific rigor, important substantive questions, responsible action to correct injustice. Mel had made trouble for the University, but in the process he had done it the greatest service by calling it to live up to its highest ideals.[3] He was never forgiven for it.

The second episode grew from Mel's involvement as a sociological expert-witness in a school desegregation suit during the early 1960s. By that time, the Department of Sociology had become an independent unit, with Charles Page, the long-time editor

[3] He presented the intellectual rationale for this approach in his presidential address to the Society for the Study of Social Problems: Melvin M. Tumin, "In Dispraise of Loyalty," *Social Problems* 15, no. 3 (1968): 267–279.

of the *American Sociological Review*, called in to serve as its first chairman. Shortly before a day when Mel was scheduled to testify in a school desegregation suit in Federal District Court in Wilmington, Delaware, he invited a number of the graduate students to accompany him on the drive down, to observe sociology at work in the world of social action. Such applications of sociology were not rewarded in the academy, and they were time-consuming and exhausting. But Mel undertook a heavy schedule of testifying, consulting, and applied research in service to his cherished values of racial, religious, and social justice.[4] There were other prominent sociologists at Princeton who also had consulting schedules that produced healthy fees for modest impositions on their time and energy. One of the most eminent consulted with a major American corporation; one day, he explained to us with becoming irony that he was not troubled by the ethical issues of the arrangement because, in his judgment, he never told them anything that could be of the slightest use to them. Mel never made it easy on himself that way. In his public activities, he carried out an ideal of university service, an academic patriotism as exemplified by Woodrow Wilson himself. In the process, he showed his students that sociology could operate in a wider arena than the campus quadrangle or the learned society, even if it earned him no merit badges.

The third incident was Mel's brief but shining career as the coroner of Mercer County. Mel discovered in the early 1960s that although Mercer County, Princeton's home county in New Jersey, had changed from a coroner system to an appointed professional medical examiner, the office of coroner had never been taken off the books. He waged a brief, intense campaign as a write-in candidate for the office. In the absence of any opposition (since no one else was aware that the office existed), Mel was elected. Although there was no provision for him to carry out any duties of office, in fact no physical office space assigned, no state auto

[4] A good example of this kind of work is his book *Desegregation: Resistance and Readiness* (Princeton: Princeton University Press, 1958).

Melvin Marvin Tumin (left) and Bernard Beck, in ceremonial robes and displaying important documents, in Tumin's office at Princeton, Commencement Day, June 1964.

license plate, no stationery, no perquisites other than a certificate that he occupied the post, Mel was delighted with his political debut. It pleased the performer in him, the prankster, the fancy-dresser, and the play-actor. It also made a more serious point: that democracy and political participation must be cherished, that they must never be allowed to drift into routine business-as-usual, reserved for experts. And it said that no matter how respectable the working-class boy from Newark had become at Princeton, he would always find ways to debunk hierarchies and conventional pieties. That is still a necessary workout for sociologists, who need to remain skeptical and unseduced to do their jobs.

This playful streak showed us all that sociology was a matter of the utmost seriousness, but never grim, and that a good joke was always the most elegant theory. It showed itself to me again on the June day in 1964 when I attended Commencement at Princeton. I had completed my degree requirements a year earlier, but had rushed off to begin a post-doctoral fellowship in Copenhagen. I returned to Princeton on that day, with my mother, to don doctoral robes and march in the academic procession for her sake. Afterward, we went to visit Mel in his office. Seeing me in my robes with my diploma case, he hastened to put on a silk bathrobe that was there for some reason and to brandish a copy of *Mad Magazine*, so that we could take pictures together. It was a symbol of our mutual affection, of his satisfaction in my achievement and of his irreverent amusement at the pompous solemnity of it all. Congratulations, he seemed to be saying, but don't take it too seriously.

Mel Tumin taught me a lot of sociology and he took great, loving care of me. He welcomed me into the sanctum of his family so that I could know and cherish his wife, Sylvia, and his sons, Jonathan and Zachary. He was a hell of a sociologist, and he was a *mensch*. I will miss him forever, and so will Princeton.

READING LIST

Caste in a Peasant Society: A Case Study in the Dynamics of Caste (Princeton: Princeton University Press, 1952)

"Some Principles of Stratification: A Critical Analysis," *American Sociological Review* 18, no. 4 (1953): 387–394

With Arnold S. Feldman: *Social Class and Social Change in Puerto Rico*, (Princeton: Princeton University Press, 1961)

"On Inequality," *American Sociological Review* 28, no. 1 (1963): 19–28

"Business as a Social System," *Behavioral Science* 9, no. 3 (1964): 120–130

"The Functionalist Approach to Social Problems," *Social Problems* 12, no. 4 (1965): 379–388

Social Stratification: The Forms and Functions of Inequality (Englewood Cliffs, New Jersey: Prentice-Hall, 1967)

Jacob Viner

Department of Economics

BY WILLIAM J. BAUMOL

Scholarship was, clearly, Jacob Viner's passion. His meticulous pursuit of scholarly research extended well beyond the boundary of conventional economics and gave him the status of a legend among the members of the English and History Departments. In the Princeton library there was no work too obscure nor any too peripheral to his areas of interest to escape his attention. There was no scarcity of volumes whose borrowing cards reported that he was the only one in many decades to have taken them out. Each elicited a profusion of careful notes written by hand on a number of file cards and carefully indexed. The result was an incredible erudition that was provided unstintingly to anyone who came to him for information. For example, when Bill Bowen and I were conducting our study on the economics of the performing arts we came across data on the finances of an American theater during the late colonial period. Since the data were expressed in contemporary currency (pounds, as I recall) I came to Jack for information on its purchasing power. There followed a delightful two-hour lecture on differences in the currencies of the various American colonies, their comparative rates of inflation during the decades preceding the Revolution, and what little was known of their purchasing power. The next day I received the precious file cards indicating the sources of the information and offering further details.

I will tell only one other (verified) tale of the many I can recount to illustrate his fantastic stock of knowledge. During a trip to a nearby university a young member of the faculty came to him and indicated that he had come across an undiscovered American mathematical economist of the nineteenth century. "You mean Charles Ellet," was Jack's immediate comment. The astonished young man asked how he knew this, to which Viner answered, "That's simple — Ellet is the only American economist of the nineteenth century who is undiscovered."

But an equal passion of Viner's was the desire to transmit to others his love for scholarship and the importance of meticulous standards in its pursuit. That, above everything else, was what his students obtained from him. He summed up his thoughts on the subject in a memorable (and amusing) essay, "A Modest Proposal for Some Stress on Scholarship in Graduate Training," whose title spells out its thesis.

Viner's own scholarly work focused on what many would consider obscure and esoteric subjects. His last years were devoted to research on the economic aspects of Christian theology, centered upon the sixteenth and seventeenth centuries and the writings of the Scholastics, the Jesuits, and the early Calvinists, among others.

Yet Viner was hardly a full-time resident of the ivory tower. He held a number of important government positions, starting with a post at the United States Tariff Commission from 1917 to 1919. He was special assistant to the secretary of the treasury from

1934 to 1939 and again in 1942, where he played an important role in the formation of U.S. monetary policy. Later, he acted as special consultant to the Department of State and the Federal Reserve Board. Much of this occurred during the administration of Franklin D. Roosevelt, but this is not to be taken to imply that he was an avid partisan of the New Deal. Rather, he maintained an impartial position very much in the middle ground, opposed to government intervention on a large scale, but holding that government has an important, if limited, role to play in the economy, as elsewhere.

Viner was born in Montreal in 1892. His parents were immigrants. His undergraduate studies were at McGill University, where his teacher was Stephen Leacock, noted more as a humorist than as an economist. His graduate studies were carried out at Harvard, where his qualities were recognized early, and where he formed a close friendship with F. W. Taussig, the most noted economist then on the Harvard faculty.

Jacob Viner came to Princeton in 1946 after a very distinguished career at the University of Chicago that spanned twenty-seven years, beginning in 1919. He had been promoted to full professorship in 1925 at the early age of thirty-three — something virtually unheard of at that time. During his period on the Chicago faculty he produced pathbreaking writings on the theory of international trade and on the analysis of behavior of firms and industries. For many years he served as editor of the *Journal of Political Economy*, transforming it into one of the leading journals in economics. Many of his students afterward achieved fame, among them Paul Samuelson, Milton Friedman, and a number of other future winners of the Nobel Prize in economics. Attending his classes is reported to have been a terrifying but memorable experience, and many of his students bravely chose to return for another dose of his instruction. A number of them have commented that this was the finest learning experience they had ever undergone. It is also worth noting that his classroom manner belied his true kindliness and wonderful sense of humor that charmed everyone who knew him well.

During his twenty-four years at Princeton the flow of Viner's distinguished contributions to the economic literature continued undiminished. The focus of his writing shifted somewhat. He devoted less of his attention to trade theory and policy and more to the history of ideas. New articles and new books continued to flow from his pen, many of them written in straightforward and nontechnical prose that is a model of command of the English language and the ways it can be used most effectively. Several of his books and papers make excellent reading for those who have no training in economics or related fields.

When Viner came to Princeton in 1946 anticipations were high, and they were never disappointed. He was an exceedingly helpful colleague, indeed, his mind was an indispensable resource for many of us, as has already been illustrated. Colleagues from other departments (and throughout the world) regularly turned to him for help on research problems. The cliché, "He was unstinting with his time," understates the generosity with which he responded to such requests.

But none of this is sufficient to capture his impressive and magnetic personality and that of his delightful and profoundly intelligent wife, Frances. It seems to me that they contributed to the community most manifestly by virtue of that personality, which meant, for example, that the atmosphere at any gathering they were scheduled to attend would brighten noticeably upon their arrival. When Viner spoke up at a seminar there was no one whose attention went elsewhere. In short, he and his wife were a phenomenon that was unforgettable. Though they were modest, kindly and affectionate, that did not diminish the magnitude of the effect of their presence. From the moment of their arrival they occupied an important and noted place in the community, adding to the depth of thinking and to the vitality of its intellectual life.

READING LIST

Studies in the Theory of International Trade (New York and London: Harper & Brothers, 1937)

A Modest Proposal for Some Stress on Scholarship in Graduate Training. Address before the Graduate Convocation, Brown University, June 3, 1950. (Providence, Rhode Island, 1950)

International Economics (Glencoe, Illinois: Free Press, 1951)

The Long View and the Short: Studies in Economic Theory and Policy (Glencoe, Illinois: Free Press, 1958)

The Intellectual History of Laissez-faire (Chicago: University of Chicago Law School, 1961)

The Role of Providence in the Social Order: An Essay in Intellectual History (Philadelphia: American Philosophical Society, 1972)

Religious Thought and Economic Society: Four Chapters of an Unfinished Work, ed. Jacques Mealitz and Donald Winch (Durham, North Carolina: Duke University Press, 1978)

Essays on the Intellectual History of Economics, ed. Douglas A. Irwin (Princeton: Princeton University Press, 1991)

Gregory Vlastos

Department of Philosophy

BY ALEXANDER NEHAMAS

With one exception, I remember the teachers who have been most important to me over the years with a sense that, at least while they and I were talking, I was close to the center of their world, that they and I were somehow the only people who mattered, that perhaps a small part of their life was actually lived for my own sake. The exception is Gregory Vlastos.

And yet Vlastos is the person from whom I learned the most in graduate school, and for many years thereafter. He paid the closest attention to his students and his effect on them has been deep and long-lasting: many of us openly admit that we still judge what we write, on whatever subject, by standards we imagine we have taken over from him. My own sense of his presence is so strong that I am acutely concerned with his reaction had he been alive to read the short memoir I am now composing, and I am being careful not to write anything he would have had reason to reject. On the other hand, I am less concerned with whether what I say here would have pleased him. And though such an attitude may appear ungrateful, it is essential for all those affected by Vlastos to face and acknowledge it if we are to understand Vlastos' intense but distant relationship to his students and collaborators and the manner in which he exercised his remarkable influence on the University and on his discipline in general.

Gregory Vlastos, who was (an unusual combination) both Greek and Presbyterian, was born in Istanbul and emigrated to the United States in order to study divinity and to join the church. He was ordained a minister but eventually decided to take a graduate degree in philosophy and to pursue an academic career. He received his doctorate at Harvard and taught for a number of years at Queen's University in Ontario. While at Queen's he published works of Christian Marxism and a series of brilliant essays on early Greek, or "Presocratic," philosophy. He also developed a lifelong fascination with Socrates, though he did not feel comfortable enough to publish his main ideas about him until the last decade or so of his life.

Vlastos moved to Cornell in the late 1940s and began writing almost exclusively on Plato. His work was heavily influenced by the analytical approach to philosophy which had by then become dominant at Cornell and other major American philosophy departments. Vlastos gave clear, sometimes formal reconstructions of Plato's arguments and read Plato as a thinker who addressed issues of immediate concern to contemporary philosophers. His approach attracted very wide attention. Along with G.E.L. Owen, who was formulating a similar approach at about the same time in England, Vlastos established the study of Greek philosophy as a central branch of academic philosophy in America.

He came to Princeton in 1955. His influence on the Philosophy Department, which he chaired twice, was immense. Vlastos was a very acute judge of intellectual ability. Through the philosophers he helped attract here and the standards he applied to the administration and governance of the department, he was instrumental in turning Princeton into one of the world's leading centers of analytical philosophy. He also became a central figure in the intellectual life of the campus, and was, for many years, an influential presence on the "Committee of Three." His standards were, as always, extraordinarily strict and his voice carried great weight: the Princeton faculty still owes much of its character to him. On an even broader scale, he was instrumental in the creation of a number of institutions crucial to philosophy and to the humanities in general, including the Council for Philosophic Studies and the National Humanities Center in Research Triangle Park, North Carolina. He was also involved in the negotiations that resulted in the creation of the National Endowment for the Humanities.

Vlastos' life at Princeton was highly regimented; its timetable was widely known, and awe-inspiring. When he had no other obligations, he would wake up at 5:00 A.M. and work in his study until noon. He would then come to the University for lunch, classes and appointments. He would return home for an early dinner, and work again until about 10:00 P.M. when he would go to bed, ready for another cycle. During brunch at his house one Sunday, he told us that he had awakened at 4:00 A.M. that morning in order to make up some of the time he was losing because of the invitation he had extended to us. I remember finding that slightly amusing and seriously confusing.

Vlastos had the reputation of being an extraordinary lecturer, though he generally did not let his graduate students attend his undergraduate classes, which he claimed were too elementary and therefore unsuitable for us. According to one undergraduate student, who went on to write a dissertation under his direction, Vlastos began each lecture by presenting one very complex question which, by the end of each period, he had succeeded in making comprehensible and engaging to everyone in the group. He was very generous with his students and encouraged their efforts unstintingly.

His graduate seminars were astonishing. They were huge, attracting most of the graduate students in Philosophy, many from Classics, and a sizable number from various other departments. Vlastos would arrive for the first session with a syllabus of often more than twenty single-spaced pages. It contained a general introduction to the topic of the seminar and a description of the overall approach Vlastos would take; it also offered a breakdown of the subjects to be discussed each week, a sketch of the position Vlastos would defend, a list of topics which he would assign to a student for a class presentation, and a detailed, annotated bibliography. He expected the text of the student presentation three days before it was to be delivered. He read the paper overnight, made extensive comments on it and discussed it in detail with its author, making sure it was clear and comprehensible. The seminar was divided into two parts: during the first, Vlastos read from a set of prepared typewritten notes, which he always distributed in advance; the second part consisted of the student presentation.

Discussion in the seminar was extraordinarily intense. Vlastos' graduate teaching was inseparable from his research and, in his utterly disciplined manner, he expected to produce at least one, perhaps two scholarly papers out of each of his gradate seminars. We considered it our task to argue every single issue in the greatest detail with him in order to help him polish the arguments that everyone in the field would be reading in a few months. It was, of course, Vlastos himself who had made that our task. His ability to provoke productive disagreement was unparalleled. In a manner quite mysterious to us at the time, he had convinced us that it was our moral responsibility to understand various philosophical issues and to defend our position against his.

In the seminar, he exhibited the most peculiar and frustrating combination of features. On the one hand, he displayed a deep humility in regard to his ability to understand and master the problems he discussed, and a genuine need for our cooperation and assistance. On the other, he made it obvious that it would be anything but easy to make him change his mind on any issue. I remember tens of occasions when an exhausted student would slump down, speechless after a long dialectical bout, while Vlastos cheerfully proceeded to the next topic on the day's agenda with the remark (tinged with an irony to which I shall return) that he hoped he would prove less intransigent and more amenable to enlightenment this time around: "A brilliant effort, Mr. . . . (we were almost all men then), but I remain unconvinced. Perhaps Mr. . . ., from whom we will hear now, will have better luck."

Luck, of course (as Vlastos well knew), had nothing to do with it. And on occasion, a solid knowledge of Plato's texts and their interpretation, combined with philosophical ingenuity and relentless persistence, did have the effect he invited from us, and Vlastos would publicly acknowledge that a particular student had enabled him to see a matter correctly for the first time. Though such occasions were rare, they were also precious: not just because they were accompanied by a sense of personal triumph but even more because they demonstrated that effort, persistence, and the ability to marshal the various tools we were gradually acquiring through our education could establish a contact of minds, and perhaps bring us closer to the truth. The difficulty of winning an argument against Vlastos, the rigor with which we had to present our case if we were to move him from his position, and his genuine gratitude when he felt he had been set right only added to the sense of well-being that we felt at the time. I can recall nothing to match the heady enthusiasm that accompanied such moments.

I believe that all of Vlastos' students learned what counts as a telling argument, when to be and when (as happens much more often) not to be satisfied with our intellectual efforts, through such interactions with him. His exacting standards, as I have already said, have become ours, and he is, to that extent, a part of what we all are. And yet there is something deeply impersonal in the gratitude with which I remember him.

Such a reaction is disturbing. It suggests that in thinking about him I am distinguishing between his being an admirable teacher on the one hand and a warm, approachable person on the other. This does not mean that Vlastos was not a nice man or that he was nasty to his students, but it does imply that his intellectual interactions did not involve the affective side of his personality directly. Vlastos must have had a deep personal stake in the philosophical questions that occupied him. Yet he never revealed what it was, and he kept the private aspects of his personality separate from his teaching. Some teachers are successful because they elicit their students' love and in return promise, and sometimes offer, their own. Vlastos' gift was his uncanny ability to provoke his students into the fiercest intellectual struggles simply through the intensity of his own interest in his field. He engaged in such struggles with the utmost seriousness, but he was also in a curious way partly absent from them. Though he was not at all detached from the issues he discussed, the rift between his personal and his intellectual motives appeared to detach him from the people with whom he discussed them. Given our current ideology regarding the relationships we expect professors to have with their students, many may not be comfortable with the thought that one might be an admirable teacher without also necessarily being an affectionate person. One can; and it is important, if we are to appreciate correctly the varieties of good teaching, to be aware of this fact.

The reason, then, for my impersonal reaction to Vlastos — a reason that explains why I care whether what I say about him is true but less whether it would have pleased him — is that the primary goal of his own teaching was itself impersonal. He was deeply committed to making the study of Greek philosophy central to his discipline, and he was exercised by a series of philosophical questions raised by the Presocratic philosophers and Plato. He wanted answers to these questions, and he took his students as collaborators in his own projects of search and research. He was of course concerned with our improvement and he paid close attention to us and our work; no one ever wrote more detailed or more helpful comments on my term papers or on the essays I continued to send him years after we had both left Princeton. He had a serious stake in us, but that stake was purely intellectual. In order to answer his questions, he needed the best collaborators he could find, and he was for that reason willing, even eager, to help us become as good philosophers as we could be: the better his students, the more likely he was to get help from them with his work and the more likely it was that Greek philosophy would continue to flourish. But that was just what made his attitude toward us so impersonal.

Vlastos' attitude was the effect of his leading a life in which the central role had long ago been assumed by the play of ideas and in which many personal relationships had been subordinated to such play. On one occasion, he invited me to a picnic at the beach. I remember how excited I was at the prospect of an encounter which, I thought, would for once be purely personal. And I also remember my astonishment when it turned out that the picnic was an occasion for another student to read, in the middle of Long Beach Island, a set of comments criticizing a paper on "The Individual as an Object of Love in Plato" which Vlastos had recently completed.

Vlastos, in short, treated his students and collaborators (and sometimes his colleagues as well) as apprentices. His attitude could on occasion appear harsh, especially to young people, but it had the supreme virtue of being totally unsentimental. In today's climate, when successful teaching is confused with enabling students to feel proud of themselves whatever their concrete accomplishments, Vlastos' invitation to join him in his pursuit, to suffer through it primarily for his sake and, in the process, to learn how to engage in it for ourselves can almost provoke a nostalgic reaction. Vlastos cared about ideas. He trained us, and trained us well, because he believed that it was a good thing for his field to thrive and for his questions to be answered. But he did not, nor did he ever suggest that he did, do so for our sake. His primary responsibility was always to himself. So we are grateful for his actions, though not necessarily for his motives. And our gratitude is for that reason impersonal, though not for that reason diminished.

No discussion of Vlastos can be complete without touching on his irony. It was an irony that sometimes undercut his humble claims that philosophical problems were just too hard for him and that he had to rely on his students' superior — younger and more agile — intellects. It also undercut his confessions that he was slow and stubborn and that he found it almost impossible to understand other people's views and to benefit from their talents. It was an irony that made him seem less humble, but also a more capable dialectician and better at listening to others than he claimed to be.

His ironic temper pervaded his personality and reached every one of its aspects, except one: I don't think anyone has ever doubted that Vlastos' desire to answer the philosophical questions he cared about was as deep and genuine as it could possibly be. And through this combination of irony of manner and seriousness of purpose, Vlastos came personally very close to the single philosophical personality that occupied him intellectually for most of his life — the Platonic Socrates.

The Socrates Vlastos came close to is not the character he described in the book he finally wrote a few years before his death. That benevolent oldster wends his way around Classical Athens in an effort to help his fellow citizens confront their ignorance and thereby save their souls, and uses irony only as a pedagogical tool in order to incite them (and us) to pursue that for which he cares above anything else: "If you are to come to the truth, it must be by yourself for yourself."[1] *That* Socrates is a man who is primarily concerned with the welfare of others.

The Socrates Vlastos resembles was, instead, a man who was primarily concerned with his own improvement. Convinced that knowledge of the nature of goodness was indispensable for living

[1] Gregory Vlastos, *Socrates: Ironist and Moral Philosopher* (Cambridge: Cambridge University Press, 1991), p. 44.

a good life, and acknowledging that that was a knowledge he lacked, he marched through Athens looking for anyone who might impart it to him, all the while intimating that he did not really believe his audience would know what he was after: he asked for help but expected little of it. He was eager to explain to others what he wanted from them, willing to learn from them whenever they were able to teach him, and happy if, in the process, they improved themselves as well. But that last was not his purpose: what he primarily cared for was himself. And it was by caring for himself that he sometimes was of benefit to others.

Just as this last is not a criticism of Socrates, the fact that Vlastos elicits the impersonal gratitude I have described is also not a criticism of him, unless we think that teachers can be good only if they make their students' welfare their primary concern. That is not true. Teaching comes in many varieties. Though good teaching does sometimes spring from genuine concern for students, it is not always the case that genuine concern produces good teaching: one must have something to tell one's students, a valuable idea to communicate to them. And one of the best ways to communicate a valuable idea is to take one's students as collaborators in the effort to discover that idea for oneself. Students are essential in such an effort and they profit immensely from it, but they are not the reason for which the effort is undertaken.

That is what Gregory Vlastos did during the many years he taught at Princeton, and for many years afterward. He showed us what a life is like in which devotion to ideas is often more important than affection for people. Not everyone will approve of such a life or want to pursue it. But universities are meant to create a space for it, to make it possible for some people to live it and to enable others to learn about and from it. Vlastos provided an almost perfect example of such a life. He thus also provided a perfect example of what a certain kind of teacher could be. Since he placed much greater significance on being right than on pleasing people, I believe that this short memoir exhibits just those features and incorporates just those standards which he valued and encouraged his students to develop for themselves. In that way, it is, I hope, not simply a description but also a manifestation of his continuing influence and importance.

READING LIST

Christian Faith and Democracy (New York: Distributed by Association Press, 1940)

Platonic Studies (Princeton: Princeton University Press, 1973, 1981)

Plato's Universe (Seattle: University of Washington Press, 1975)

Studies in Greek Philosophy, 2 vols. (Princeton: Princeton University Press, 1995)

Socrates: Ironist and Moral Philosopher (Cambridge: Cambridge University Press, 1991)

Socratic Studies (Cambridge: Cambridge University Press, 1994)

E. N. Lee, A.P.D. Mourelatos, and R. M. Rorty, eds., *Exegesis and Argument: Studies in Greek Philosophy Presented to Gregory Vlastos* (New York: Humanities Press, 1973)

Ira Owen Wade

Department of Modern Languages and Literatures

BY RONALD C. ROSBOTTOM

We all thought that he not only looked, but acted like Voltaire, the inimitable *philosophe* whom he spent his career studying and interpreting. The photograph on the book jacket for his *Intellectual Development of Voltaire* (1969) bears uncanny resemblance to the patriarch of Ferney, but the shot used most often in official publications reminds me of Woodrow Wilson, another self-conscious Princeton intellectual. Like his subject, Ira Wade had a decided tendency toward irony, never saying directly what he meant, for he knew that if his interlocutor had to figure it out, his point would be made even more pertinently. He was also unafraid of engaging the big picture, even when he was criticized, or worse, patronized, for trying to discover the "form and structure of the

Enlightenment." Hadn't Voltaire himself invented the "discipline" of world history?

My favorite Wade anecdote goes something like this: Crossing campus burdened with two full briefcases, he was stopped by a student who said: "Those look heavy, Mr. Wade." Hefting his bags, he answers: "It's the French Enlightenment." "The Enlightenment?" "Yep, where it came from, what it was, and where it's going." That was his plan, and it was carried out before he died. Mr. Wade certainly was bold in his aims: "The task of the historian of ideas is to make some coherent sense of the activity of people thinking, saying, doing, becoming. . . . His ultimate goal is the apprehension of [a civilizations's] inner reality, what is often called the spirit of the age."[1] There were — and are — those who said that he never successfully completed his task, that his work remained inconclusive, a combination of the history of ideas and a fuzzy, idiosyncratic methodology that would enable the discovery of the "organic unity" of a civilization. But, then, this is what Voltaire was about as well: trying to understand what the cultural mind-set of his time was, so as better to live and work, and, in Ira Wade's case, to teach.

It always seemed to me, who had come up from Louisiana just to study with him, that Ira Wade's persona was a combination of fragility and toughness. He was physically small, and, by the time I had a class with him, nearly frail. This was in the autumn of 1964, his last year of full-time teaching at Princeton. One of his colleagues assured me then that Wade in his prime at Princeton had been a red-haired firebrand: intense, highly strung, arrogant. But, by the time I arrived, he had become a more reflective man, working alone, with diligence, to sum up his career.

He had published a great deal since the 1930s,[2] and could have

[1] *The Intellectual Origins of the French Enlightenment* (Princeton: Princeton University Press, 1971), p. xvii.

[2] See Ronald C. Rosbottom, "An Annotated Bibliography of the Writings of Ira O. Wade," in Jean Macary, ed., *Essays on the Age of Enlightenment in Honor of Ira O. Wade* (Geneva: Droz, 1977), pp. 376–385.

rested on the many laurels his work had brought him. But he had a point to make, and make it he would. Was it a promise to his beloved Mabel, who had died after a cruel illness in 1965, or was it just part of the toughness that seemed to inhere in him? All that matters is if you want to know Voltaire, start with Wade. His oeuvre remains one of the richest sources for information on that writer, his thought, and his time.

Wade's first book was *The Clandestine Organization and Diffusion of Philosophic Ideas in France from 1700 to 1750*, a work that showed the way, well before it was fashionable, to the study of the relationship between ideas and their diffusion. (It is good that Robert Darnton, presently a member of the University's Department of History, continues the tradition with his masterful corpus on publishing and the diffusion of ideas in pre-Revolutionary France.) From the publication of his work on clandestine ideas to the end of his career, Wade would ask himself and his students how "real" these ideas were that we think defined the Enlightenment. Who knew about them? How did they get into the culture and thus into the minds of the writers that we would come to identify with the *esprit philosophique*, especially Voltaire? Building on the work of the great literary historians of late nineteenth- and early twentieth-century France, Wade transformed the results of archival research into an analytical critique of that most ineffable of human creations: civilization.

He also produced — in the 1940s and 1950s — three exceptional studies of Voltaire: on Voltaire's didactic and affective relationship with Mme. du Châtelet, his one great love (1941); a critical edition of one of his best and most important *contes*, *Micromégas* (1950); and, in recognition of the bicentennial of the publication of the Enlightenment's most beloved legacy, *Voltaire and "Candide"* (1959), derived from his own discovery of the only prepublication manuscript of Voltaire's tale. Wade considered *Candide* the bravest work that Voltaire wrote, not because it could have caused him even more trouble with the authorities, but because it was a self-critique of all that the writer had done before he wrote the tale at the age of sixty-three. It was an example of personal and intellectual courage by a man past middle age still unafraid of changing his mind. Wade saw himself, I sensed, reflected in this image of Voltaire, for he wanted to leave a similar magnum opus, and would do so with the publication of a massive three-volume work on the Enlightenment, *The Intellectual Origins of the French Enlightenment*, and *The Structure and Form of the French Enlightenment*: "where it came from, what it was, where it's going."

Wade was fascinated with the possibility that a civilization, like any human text, could be comprehended. If we could but decode and then teach the structural components of any one civilization, we could understand them all. As far back as the late 1940s, he had argued at Princeton for the establishment of an interdisciplinary undergraduate program in European civilization (whose spirit, I trust, still informs the University's present Program in European Cultural Studies), one that would encourage students to use the methodologies and content of the liberal arts — social sciences, languages, history — to study European cultures. In a fictional dialogue — another of the Enlightenment's favorite genres — in the *Daily Princetonian* (May 1955), Wade put in a student's mouth the following description of what would become SPEC (Special Program in European Civilization): "We go at it a little differently. First we learn the language, then we study the country's arts and letters, then we analyze its institutions, then we look at its manners and customs. We try to understand its role in history, we absorb some of its ideals, we enjoy its beautiful productions, we try to understand its 'queer' actions. In time, we conceive of this foreign people as thinking, feeling, living, and from this picture, admittedly incomplete, of others, we gain some perspective on our own thinking, feeling, living." After having informed the curriculum of the Department of Modern Languages and Literatures, SPEC was added to the University's curriculum in 1960.

There had been little doubt about which period I would concentrate on after my Ph.D. qualifying examinations, but when it came time to choose my dissertation topic, I decided *not* to follow in Ira Wade's footsteps, that is, not to work in the "history of ideas." Rather, I wanted to analyze the French Enlightenment from another perspective — through the study of narrative fiction. I chose to write on the novels of Marivaux, known until then primarily as a playwright. When I finally informed Mr. Wade — and I do remember putting this meeting off several times — I noticed an impatiently disguised distaste. Marivaux had, after all, been the object of much cruel criticism from Voltaire: I am sure Mr. Wade saw him as a lightweight and a *littérateur* to boot, certainly not a man of intellectual substance, not a *philosophe.* I never quite recovered from that look of dismay; thirty years later, as I remember this moment in my young career, I still cringe. I had let the old guy down: I was his last chance to influence a new generation, and I had chosen to be a literary critic.

But Mr. Wade was always the gentleman, and we stayed in touch — and friends, I know — until his death. That's what one remembers the most about him, not his obsession with discovering what gave the Enlightenment form, but his courtliness, and his self-deprecating humor. He loved telling stories about and laughing at himself, especially at his obsession with the Internal Revenue Service. (The IRS was for him the symbol of all of the arbitrary authority that his man Voltaire had railed and written against two hundred years before.) He told me once how he had spent a bootless three hours in a Parisian bookstore waiting to catch a glimpse of Anatole France, whom he had heard frequented that establishment. He worked hard at being an unpretentious man, and this little story of his seduction by fame was neutralized by his amusement at having wasted time to no fruitful end. He would often catch himself in mid-pretension, and prick the hot air balloon he felt growing. To a student reporter: "Being a teacher, I have tried to collect not facts but wisdom. But when I couldn't get the wisdom, I sure enough went back to the facts."

Ira Wade taught at Princeton for more than forty years, and

when he gave his last lecture in 1965, the *Daily Princetonian* wrote an editorial on his demeanor, and on the self-effacing way he ended his career. Though he consistently mocked his ineffectualness as a lecturer, he was cited more than once as one of the best lecturers at the University. He was John N. Woodhull Professor of Modern Languages, had been awarded the Légion d'Honneur from the French Government and the Madison Medal from Princeton itself. He did all the things one had to do as a teacher and administrator in a major university, but it was by his teaching that generations of students knew him, a teacher too modest to a fault about his skill, yet passionate about *why* he had given his life to present the Enlightenment. Great teachers are often men and women of understated confidence in their abilities, people who are so sure in their intellectual faith that they have no need to perform. That was Ira Wade. He knew that he was asking very big questions, and that he was leaving many of them unanswered. But he had confidence in the value of what he was doing, and knew that asking questions is one of the defining characteristics of an *enlightened* person. Mr. Wade taught me that the life of the mind is not for the timorous, that patience in a scholar is indeed a virtue, and that teaching is most successful when it forces the student to ask questions the teacher has no shame in admitting that he cannot answer.

READING LIST

The Clandestine Organization and Diffusion of Philosophic Ideas in France from 1700 to 1750 (Princeton: Princeton University Press, 1938; reprinted 1968)

Voltaire and "Candide": A Study in the Fusion of History, Art, and Philosophy, with the Text of the La Vallière Manuscript of "Candide" (Princeton: Princeton University Press, 1959; reprinted 1972)

Voltaire's "Micromégas": A Study in the Fusion of Science, Myth, and Art (Princeton: Princeton University Press, 1950)

Voltaire and Madame du Châtelet: An Essay on the Intellectual Activity at Cirey (Princeton: Princeton University Press, 1941; reprinted 1967)

The Intellectual Development of Voltaire (Princeton: Princeton University Press, 1969)

The Intellectual Origins of the French Enlightenment (Princeton: Princeton University Press, 1971)

The Structure and Form of the French Enlightenment, 2 vols. (Princeton: Princeton University Press, 1977)

Ronald C. Rosbottom, "Ira Wade's Enlightenment," *Studies in Burke and His Time* 14 (1972–1973): 133–154

Jean Macary, ed., *Essays on the Age of Enlightenment in Honor of Ira O. Wade* (Geneva: Droz, 1977)

Kurt Weitzmann

Department of Art and Archaeology

BY GEORGE GALAVARIS

As a young student of art and archaeology in Greece, where I come from, I had heard Kurt Weitzmann's name. Later, a book of his, *Illustrations in Roll and Codex*, came into my hands accidentally. It was a formidable book, difficult to read and understand; however, at the time, I had a feeling that the book was most important. This impression was proven correct when I studied the book properly, and I was able to realize how fundamental it was for the study of the origins of book illustration. It brought to the fore the classical roots of medieval book illumination and developed a method for its study, a kind of "picture criticism" relevant but not identical to the textual criticism used by philologists in preparing editions of ancient texts.

When I first encountered the book, what impressed me most was the author's vast knowledge. The book was published in

Princeton for the Department of Art and Archaeology as part of a series, *Studies in Manuscript Illumination*, edited originally by Albert M. Friend and after his death by Kurt Weitzmann. I knew nothing about the series, but came to realize how essential the books were for medieval scholarship. Through the announcement of the series in the printed book, Professor Friend became another name for me. These names and their books led me to the discovery that the Department of Art and Archaeology at Princeton was one of the most important centers for the study of Early Christian, Byzantine, and Western medieval art, with emphasis on the first two periods. There were other illustrious members of the Art Department, scholars working in these fields who had produced famous books, among them Ernest T. De Wald and E. Baldwin Smith.

In the late 1950s, a scholarship brought me to Princeton, to the renowned Art Department, for graduate work. Kurt Weitzmann was away, at Saint Catherine's Monastery on Mount Sinai, taking part in an expedition organized by Princeton and the Universities of Alexandria and Michigan. There were five expeditions to Saint Catherine's between 1956 and 1965, all of them intended to photograph and eventually publish the artistic treasures of the God-Trodden Mountain. Weitzmann's interests were centered on manuscripts and icons. Indeed, the study of icons was to form the crown of his illustrious career, for the monumental publications that followed his expeditions to Saint Catherine's brought to light a wealth of works of paramount importance for students of Christian art, and enhanced the leading role played by the Princeton Art Department in the study of Byzantine art. By then, Weitzmann, who in essence had brought Byzantium to America, was considered by many to be the foremost Byzantinist of our time.

That first year in Princeton I worked with Professor Friend, a great personality, a great teacher, and Weitzmann's close friend and collaborator. In his home on Mercer Street, Friend held a seminar on early Christian churches in Jerusalem. At the time I found the project to reconstruct the churches on paper strange, for most of them were gone. But it was exciting, for it had the fascination of a fairy tale. My assigned task was to research the relevant texts, with which I had considerable facility. At the beginning of the seminars, Professor Friend would play Bach on an old gramophone before we adjourned to fifth-century Jerusalem. While we read the texts and saw pictures and visited Jerusalem, we spoke about Byzantine emperors and learned empresses. We gossiped about them; we followed them as they ran with curious monks eager to build churches "for the love of God, the salvation of the soul, and the defence of the correct doctrine." But we also saw these "real" figures sitting with their "entourage" in their palatial halls, knitting and reciting Homer, a Homer, however, whose text, in the process of the recitation, had become a biography of Christ. In all this Kurt Weitzmann was always mentioned: "He would have approved of this. He would have added to the argument by producing some unknown photographs."

Weitzmann's task was (and I heard this for the first time in Professor Friend's seminar) to reconstruct lost manuscripts and to fill the gaps in those extant in the libraries of various Eastern monasteries. In reconstructing the churches and the manuscripts, Friend and Weitzmann aimed at the reconstruction of an entire period, its artistic tastes, its ideology. In doing this, they stressed the continuity of tradition and its importance for a civilization. A new world, almost of mythical dimensions, was opened to me.

Weitzmann was present not only in Friend's seminar. He was physically in Sinai, yet he was everywhere. In the corridors of the old McCormick Hall, the older students would come and ask "Have you taken Weitzmann's course? You must," they would say, "especially if you are interested in Byzantine art, for Weitzmann *is* Byzantine art." The irony of the matter was that Weitzmann never taught an undergraduate course on Byzantine art. He offered a half-course on medieval art, of which Byzantine art constituted only a fraction. Byzantine art was reserved for graduate students, and it focused on Byzantine manuscripts and ivories.

In due time, Weitzmann returned from Sinai, and I was notified that he expected to see me. His small office in the old McCormick Hall was a famous place for those who pursued medieval art seriously. I approached him feeling uneasy. Here was a young student trying to converse with the great professor venerated by everyone. This is how I have described this meeting in my introduction to Weitzmann's memoirs, *Sailing with Byzantium, from Europe to America*, a book that constitutes an essential document for the history of Byzantine scholarship in Europe and America — and for the history of Princeton.

> He was sitting against a small window so that at first I saw an outline which was gradually filled with an image. A man in a light brown suit, spectacles, light eyes, fair hair and a face that spoke of energy and kindness. He could laugh. My initial fear was instantly dissolved. My intuition was, or rather I felt sure, that this was the beginning of a most fruitful relationship between the young man who desired to learn and the teacher who was eager to give.[1]

I should add that the ice was completely broken when Weitzmann surprised me by addressing me in my native Greek, in which he was fluent, and did not miss the opportunity to reveal his love and admiration for Greece. Later, much later, when the Program in Hellenic Studies was established in Princeton (by then Weitzmann had retired), he told me how happy he was for such developments, especially because he was a firm believer in the continuity of Greek civilization.

Kurt Weitzmann became my mentor. In another meeting in the same small office, which had access to a mezzanine from which he could survey his domain — the famous manuscript room, the desks, covered with photographs, on the lower floor — he gave me a set of photographs made in Sinai during the latest expedition. They were photographs of an unpublished manuscript containing the sermons of the great church father, Gregory Nazianzenus, Patriarch of Constantinople in the fourth century.

[1] *Sailing with Byzantium, from Europe to America. The Memoirs of an Art Historian* (Munich, 1994), p. 9.

I was to write a paper on it. Eventually, I studied all extant illustrated manuscripts of the sermons, wrote my dissertation on them — all this under Weitzmann's guidance — and I had the honor to see a book published in the series *Studies in Manuscript Illumination*, which I had long admired.

As he gave me the photographs, Weitzmann discussed each one of them, describing the beauty of the manuscript (which I was to hold in my hands much later) with such enthusiasm and excitement that it became not merely a volume of painted pages but a great work of art representing an exciting period in the cultural life of Byzantium. It represented a lost but resurrected world. I learned that illuminated manuscripts were not objects; they were transformed into real people who could guide the student through the paths of a civilization. And while Weitzmann was talking to me about the photographs, there were stories about Sinai, the artistic oasis in the desolation of the desert. I was to experience this desert repeatedly when I became Weitzmann's collaborator in the Sinai project, and I continue to do so now. With the stories of Sinai came stories of Athos and other monasteries in the Christian East. Some of these stories can be read in his memoirs. Every specific object, whether manuscript or icon, had a story behind it, and behind these objects were, once again, real persons.

Kurt Weitzmann in his formidable graduate seminar (I have given some glimpses of it in my introduction to his memoirs) was interested not only in the changes in iconography, in the way compositions were preserved or transformed by the hands of artists or copyists, in their sources in the ancient past, but also in the manner in which they were visually presented, that is, in their style. Above all, there was always a discussion of the meaning of these images. Weitzmann was in control. He could move from ancient Greece and Rome through late medieval art. The precision of his language, the richness of the content of his discourse, and the intonation of his voice with its strong German accent left a lasting impression on anyone who was fortunate enough to be present in his seminar. Often the audience included established scholars as well as graduate students. He insisted on teaching us that "the existence of a work of art in the world of art had to be proven and to be integrated in the spirit of the imaginable of the Middle Ages." I should mention that the discussions that followed the presentation of each paper were continued by the students in the rooms of the Graduate College, often until the early morning hours. We all went on arguing about our "wonder." I believe it was this "wonder" that educated us.

Kurt Weitzmann would read everything I wrote and in countless meetings would criticize every line, correct and improve. He would produce photographs unknown to me to make a point and to complete his argument. He was indeed formidable. And yet he never made me feel crushed before "Christ-Pantocrator." He was hard on himself and hard on me. He demanded hard work and devotion to my own task. He had his own way to show his satisfaction with my accomplishments and at the same time to urge me to do more. In correcting or improving my work, he would open windows for future projects, future development.

Apart from regular meetings in his office, there were walks, especially on Sunday mornings, in the Princeton woods and along the lake. He would give me then the chance to discuss the project I was working on, and give me also the benefit of his reaction. There was always a dialogue, in which the difference in our ages did not exist. Weitzmann treated me as a colleague, and would converse with me not only on art history but also on poetry, contemporary literature, and even on the events of the day. He was an avid reader. He read everything that had to do with the world of ideas. And he would always relate his readings to his own personal experiences. A reading of a Stefan George poem would bring to mind a salon in Berlin or a letter by Ernst Kantorowicz who was a friend of the poet. Listening to a new recording of an opera would take him back to a performance of the Meistersinger of Nürnberg in which Beckmesser overshadowed poor Walter von Stolzing. Weitzmann was not a Wagnerian, and we argued constantly about this; nevertheless, he enjoyed visits to the Wagner

Kurt Weitzmann (right) with George Galavaris in Luzern, Switzerland, July 1977.

house at Tribschen, near Luzern, and showed special interest in the copies of musical manuscripts displayed there. Through such meetings and conversations my own knowledge was enriched, and I developed links with the past that no book could give me. There was a human relationship growing, too, one that gradually took the form of a great friendship.

Most of Weitzmann's summers in Luzern were devoted to reading and catching up with news from "the world." Our conversations continued long after my departure from Princeton, and so did the human stories. He was eager to hear news from Mount Athos, Patmos, and above all from Sinai. He would ask for details about monks and places. For him the monks and nuns were "*his* monks and *his* nuns." He regretted that he could not return to Saint Catherine's, but he knew that he was never forgotten by the monks and was happy for this. He was also happy to realize that his scholarship and learning had radiated east and west, through his students.

For most of the year, Weitzmann worked like a Benedictine monk. The monks of Mount Athos had given him the name of an eastern holy man, Saint Kodratos, and I do not know which

Eugene Paul Wigner

Department of Physics

BY ARTHUR S. WIGHTMAN

Eugene Paul Wigner, who won the Nobel Prize in Physics in 1963, was surely one of the most distinguished scientists ever to serve on the Princeton faculty. The breadth of his interests and the depth of his original contributions were remarkable, as the eight volumes of his *Collected Works* will attest.[1] In the present article I make no attempt to outline what is in those eight volumes. Instead I assemble a collection of anecdotes concerning Wigner's activities as a teacher.

Wigner was first appointed to the Princeton faculty in 1930. He served continuously until his retirement in 1971, with the exception of the year 1937–1938 when he resigned his Princeton position to accept a professorship at the University of Wisconsin.

[1] *The Collected Works of Eugene Paul Wigner*, ed. J. Mehra and A. S. Wightman (Heidelberg: Springer Verlag, 1992–1997).

He had an extended leave during the Second World War (1942–1944) which he spent working on the plutonium-producing nuclear reactors that provided the explosive for the Nagasaki bomb. He also spent a year's leave (1946–1947) as director of research at what later became Oak Ridge National Laboratory. He continued to teach sporadically even in retirement.

An account of Wigner's style as a teacher in 1929, as seen by European graduate students in the Leiden seminar of P. Ehrenfest, occurs in reminiscences of H.B.G. Casimir:

> Ehrenfest understood at once that group theory provided the clue to understanding the semi-quantitative rules of the vector model on the basis of quantum mechanics. He invited Wigner to Leiden. That was not entirely successful. The trouble was that Wigner was too polite to be clear. It is obvious that if someone lecturing to theoretical physicists would spend considerable time explaining how to solve a simple quadratic equation then the audience would be insulted. To Wigner many things appeared to be just as simple, so he carefully avoided explaining them. (After all, according to a slightly apocryphal legend, he himself had learnt group theory from Johnny von Neumann on one rainy Sunday afternoon.)[2]

When Wigner and his fellow Hungarian, John von Neumann, showed up in Princeton in the Spring of 1930, recommended for their visiting positions by the same P. Ehrenfest,[3] Wigner took the measure of his colleagues and the students, and changed his tactics. In his reminiscences he says:

> The Princeton Physics Department was hardly interested in quantum mechanics. Howard Percy Robertson followed it but his interest was largely a formal one. The manipulation of the symbols of quantum mechanics was a game at which he was quite skilled. But he much preferred relativity theory.

[2] H.C.B. Casimir, "My Life as a Physicist," in *Pointlike Structures Inside and Outside Hadrons*, ed. A. Zichichi (New York: Plenum Press, 1982), pp. 97–712, especially p. 699.

[3] See *The Recollections of Eugene P. Wigner As Told to Andrew Szanton* (New York: Plenum Press, 1992), p. 129.

> The most important theoretical physicist at Princeton then was E. P. Adams, and his interest in physics was entirely macroscopic, classical mechanics, a bit of electrodynamics. There were a few others at Princeton who knew quantum mechanics, but most of them were mathematicians. And they knew it as an abstraction, not as a precious link to personal experience.[4]

Wigner's memory fails him here: prominent among Princeton theoretical physicists was E. U. Condon. He certainly knew and used quantum mechanics effectively. He, together with P. M. Morse, had published in 1929 a widely used textbook on quantum mechanics.[5] But, in any case, in his first teaching assignments in Princeton, Wigner did not assume that the students knew much quantum mechanics. There is material evidence for the elementary character of his Princeton courses in the 1930s in four sets of lecture notes which have survived in Fine Hall Library:

1930(?)	Quantum Mechanics (Notes by ?)
1931	Electron Theory of Metals, Notes by George H. Shortley
1932–1933	Lectures on the Theory of the Solid State, Notes by Fred Sutz
1936	Fall Nuclear Physics Notes by L. Eisenbud

It is a notable feature of all these notes that they deal with the fundamental physical phenomena using a minimum of mathematical formalism. The students who took those courses got a sound and thorough introduction firmly based in experiments. It is also worth noting that, during this same period, Wigner was publishing research papers that were virtuoso displays of group theoretical techniques.[6]

One can speculate on the influence of Wigner's Princeton experience on the book that he published in the year following his first appearance in Princeton, *Gruppentheorie und Ihre Anwendung*

[4] *Recollections of Eugene P. Wigner*, pp. 133–134.

[5] E. U. Condon and P. M. Morse, *Quantum Mechanics* (New York: McGraw-Hill, 1929).

[6] See *Collected Works, Volume II: Nuclear Physics.*

auf die Theorie der Atomspektren.[7] He had started it in Germany with the encouragement of M. von Laue. What I can say about it from personal experience is that for graduate students after the second World War there were three books to choose from: Wigner's classic book, Hermann Weyl's classic book *Gruppentheorie und Quantenmechanik*,[8] and B. L. van der Waerden's classic book, *Die Gruppentheoretische Methode in der Quantenmechanik.*[9] Which was the best to learn from was very much a matter of taste. Spectroscopists much preferred Wigner; high-flying theoretical physicists, Weyl; and pragmatic mathematicians, van der Waerden (it was shorter).

It is worth noting in passing that von Neumann, who shared an office with Wigner in old Palmer Laboratory, also taught a physics course of which the notes have survived in Fine Hall Library: 1932 — Lectures on Quantumelectrodynamics, Notes by A. H. Taub. Von Neumann also approached his subject in an elementary way. Most of the notes are devoted to elementary quantum mechanics and classical electrodynamics. A somewhat fancier version of this course appeared as part of von Neumann's classic book, *Mathematische Grundlagen der Quantenmechanik.*[10]

In his research in the 1930s Wigner was running a three-ring circus. He continued his pioneering work on the theory of chemical reactions; he was also a pioneer in the rapidly developing area of nuclear physics; and for a brief period he made fundamental contributions to solid state physics. It was in this last area that he had his first three graduate students, Frederick Seitz, John Bardeen, and Conyers Herring. Every theoretical physicist should have such

[7] Braunschweig: Vieweg, 1931; English translation by J. J. Griffin (New York: Academic Press, 1959).

[8] Leipzig: S. Hirzel, 1928; 2nd ed., 1931; English translation by H. P. Robertson, *The Theory of Groups and Quantum Mechanics* (London: Methuen & Co. Ltd., 1931).

[9] Berlin: Julius Springer, 1932.

[10] Berlin: Julius Springer, 1932; English translation by James J. Griffith, Princeton: Princeton University Press, 1955.

students; they sprang full-formed from the brow of Zeus. Needless to say, all three became pillars of solid state physics. It is interesting to note that Seitz was actually recruited as an undergraduate at Stanford by E. U. Condon. When Seitz got to Princeton, Condon was too busy to take him on as a thesis student, so he referred him to Wigner. (Condon was busy writing a famous book, *The Theory of Atomic Spectra*, with G. H. Shortley.)

In the spring of 1930, at the end of their first term in Princeton, the Physics and Mathematics Departments offered Wigner and von Neumann five-year appointments with a special arrangement: half a year in Princeton and half a year wherever they liked (Berlin). The German end of this evaporated when Hitler came to power in 1933. That year von Neumann was appointed to the new Institute for Advanced Study, which at that time resided in the old Fine Hall, now Jones Hall. Wigner's position was transformed to a year-round appointment.

When Wigner's term as a visiting professor of mathematical physics ended in 1935, he was offered and he accepted a three-year reappointment, but he was bitterly disappointed because he expected be offered a permanent position in an endowed chair, the Thomas D. Jones Professorship of Mathematical Physics. So, in 1937, he resigned to accept a professorship at the University of Wisconsin. He returned in 1938, when the University changed its mind and offered him the chair. This was the position he occupied until his retirement in 1971.

Shortly after Wigner returned to Princeton, the news of the discovery of nuclear fission reached North America and Wigner was swept up in a completely new venture, the research and development leading to nuclear weapons and power. Since the story of his adventures has been so eloquently told in his *Memoir of the Uranium Project* and in Alvin Weinberg's annotation[11] of his papers on nuclear energy, I will not sketch it here. Suffice it to say that his activities as a group leader working on the design of

[11] See *Collected Works, Volume V: Nuclear Energy.*

plutonium-producing reactors also involved a kind of teaching, a kind that he had never done before. He turned out to be very good at it.

My first encounter with Wigner was in print. As an undergraduate in New Haven, I happened on an article reviewing the book *Symmetry Properties of Nuclear Levels*, written by Eugene P. Wigner and Eugene Feenberg. I felt as though I had stumbled out of the jungle to find an ancient Mayan city replete with pyramids and calendar stones. Even if you didn't know any Mayan history, it was obvious that something interesting had been going on there! I had not the faintest idea how to derive all those beautiful Wigner and Feenberg formulae for supermultiplets, but I made a resolution to find out as soon as the war was over.

The first time I actually saw Wigner in action was in the spring of 1946. When I got out of the Navy, I passed through Princeton on my way home and attended my first Princeton seminar. The speaker was Fritz London, his topic, the London theory of superconductivity. In the question period, Wigner posed a very polite but non-trivial question and was very persistent in trying to get an answer satisfactory to him: Was the theory gauge invariant and, if not, what were the physical consequences? This was my first but not last experience with one of the ways Wigner taught.

My Princeton thesis adviser was John Wheeler, so I saw him regularly. During the autumn of 1947, when Wigner had returned from his year at Oak Ridge, I scheduled a weekly appointment with him, too. Wigner accepted this gracefully if perhaps not gratefully. (I was determined that the U.S. taxpayers should get their money's worth from my G.I. Bill support.) We talked about a variety of topics and I was impressed by his penetration to the heart of the matter, once we had succeeded in locating the physical question at issue. At one stage, before my thesis topic had been finally settled, I tried to convince Wigner to let me work with him on the mathematical foundations of quantum field theory. On that he was very firm: no, expressed in a polite, oblique Hungarian style.

Eugene P. Wigner (center) with John A. Wheeler (right) and a student.

Other graduate students of the era were luckier. For Ted Newton, he had a beautiful problem: the group theoretical characterization of the position operator for relativistic particles; for Ed Jaynes, a theory of ferroelectricity; for George Snow, the extension of R-matrix theory to three-body final states; for Ted Teichmann, general properties of nuclear reaction cross-sections and level widths; for Tom Phillips, the theory of wave equations on de Sitter space; for Marcos Moshinsky, relativistic equations for interacting particles; for Bill Sharp, Racah algebra and the contraction of groups; for Joe Ehrman, irreducible unitary representations of the infinite de Sitter group. We all felt lucky to have known the great man.

By the terms of his professorship, Wigner was not required to teach, but he was obliged to lecture on his own work. He always felt a moral obligation to teach, however, and he did so regularly. His particular favorite was the introductory graduate course in thermodynamics and statistical mechanics.

Over the years quite a number of postdoctoral visitors came to work with Wigner, including Erdal Inonu from Turkey, Igal Talmi from Israel, and H. Salecker from Germany. I always felt that these visitors greatly increased Wigner's effectiveness as a teacher of graduate students by providing an impedance match. If you didn't understand something in nuclear physics you could talk to Talmi. If he felt he could answer completely he would do so, but if not he would take it up with Wigner.

After his retirement Wigner was persuaded by the Physics Department to come back and give one last course. The notes were originally taken by Stuart Freedman and revised by Wigner for publication as "Interpretation of Quantum Mechanics." It is a brilliant exposition of the von Neumann-Wigner point of view. He saved some of the best for last.

READING LIST

The Theory of Groups and Quantum Mechanics (London: Methuen & Co. Ltd., 1931)

"Foreword," *Physical Science and Human Values: A Symposium* (Princeton: Princeton University Press, 1947)

With Leonard Eisenbud: *Nuclear Structure* (Princeton: Princeton University Press, 1958)

Group Theory and Its Application to the Quantum Mechanics of Atomic Spectra, translated from the German by J. J. Griffin (New York: Academic Press, 1959)

Two Kinds of Reality (Chicago: Open Court Publishing Co. for Edward C. Hegeler Foundation, 1964)

"Events, Laws of Nature, and Invariance Principles," in *Les Prix Nobel in 1963* (Stockholm: Norstedt, 1964), pp. 120–132

Symmetries and Reflections: Scientific Essays of Eugene P. Wigner (Bloomington: Indiana University Press, 1967)

"Interpretation of Quantum Mechanics," in *Quantum Theory of Measurement*, ed. J. A. Wheeler and W. H. Zurek (Princeton: Princeton University Press, 1983), pp. 260-314

The Recollections of Eugene P. Wigner As Told to Andrew Szanton (New York: Plenum Press, 1992)

Richard Herman Wilhelm

Department of Chemical Engineering

BY JAMES WEI

Richard Herman Wilhelm was a principal founder of the scientific approach to the design and operation of chemical reactors, where things are made through chemistry for the benefit of mankind. He organized and led the chemical engineering graduate program at Princeton for many years and made the department a major source of professors for the best universities in the country and a source of leaders for important industries in the United States. He became chairman of the department and served in that capacity for fourteen years. He influenced the careers of two generations of students and colleagues, and he was responsible for converting me from an industrial researcher into an academic.

Dick was born in New York City in 1909 and went to public

schools there. He obtained his B.S. in 1931 and his Ph.D. in 1934 from Columbia University, where Arthur Hixson was chairman of the Chemical Engineering Department. Dick married Hixson's daughter, Rachel, and they had three children: Karen, Joan, and David. The young couple moved to Princeton in 1934, where Dick was an instructor in chemical engineering at the invitation of Joseph Clifton Elgin. The chemical engineering program at Princeton was founded in 1929 by Sir Hugh Taylor, who hired Elgin as the program's first faculty member and sent him to the Massachusetts Institute of Technology (MIT) for eight months of post-doctoral studies. John Whitwell arrived in 1932, and the three of them taught all the courses and advised all the students. After three years as an instructor, Dick became an assistant professor and was the principal driving force in developing an outstanding graduate program. It became clear that to make a quantum leap in the stature of the department, a doctoral program would be needed, and Dick was instrumental in persuading the Visiting Committee and the University administration to start the first engineering doctoral program in 1942. The first Ph.D. was awarded to Raymond Wynkoop in 1948.

I first met Dick Wilhelm in 1958 when I was working in Mobil Oil's research department, and he was a regular consultant. Dick was a dynamic person, somewhat heavyset, who constantly pushed up his horn-rimmed glasses. He never walked up a flight of stairs, but always leaped up two or three steps at a time. He would come to my office every month or two for an hour, and listen to my attempts to make mathematical models of the major oil refining processes, catalytic cracking and reforming. When I received my doctorate at MIT in 1955, the use of mathematics had not yet caught on in a big way, and the design of major processing equipment was mostly guided by empiricism and practical experience. That is to say, you built equipment and operated it in a manner that was far from optimal; then you made small changes in the process conditions, such as temperature and residence time, and observed changes in the process and the products. The ideal of the scientific approach is to learn as much as possible about the fundamentals through experiments and theories, and then to make a rational design with mathematical models and computers. My industrial mentor, Dwight Prater, and I had developed a model of the catalytic cracking unit based on the scientific and rational method. It was a lonely effort until Dick Wilhelm bounded into our office, and offered very shrewd observations and advice. When exposed to a problem, he was a superb idea person, and in rapid-fire he would suggest three to five ideas — and run out of breath in the process. Many of the ideas would not stand scrutiny, but some of them were full of insight and became the bases of future progress. He encouraged our efforts mightily and gave credibility to our work in front of our managers, as this was part of his mission to propagate the scientific method in engineering design.

He had started to make scientific studies on the fluidized bed, a reactor where a bed of fine powder is made to float like quicksand with the upflow of gases. The powder contains catalysts, such as finely divided platinum, which speeds up desired reactions. He made many fundamental discoveries which made this a useful tool in oil refining. But he gave up the effort after a while because it is notoriously difficult to "scale up" the fluidized bed, that is, to draw conclusions from studies in a three-inch diameter column, and to use the knowledge gained to predict accurately the flow in a twenty-foot diameter column. He liked to say, "we need to make mistakes on a small scale and profits on a large scale." He realized that an accurate study of the fluidized bed would require a column that would have been too large for the resources available at Princeton, and he turned his attention to the fixed bed, which is a bed of small pebbles that is much more amenable to the scientific method. He and his students built three-inch diameter columns, and injected tracers such as dyes and isotopes, and observed the tracers emerge at the exit. Then he developed a series of models, tested their validity and recommended their utility. His colleague Leon Lapidus developed a model in which each pebble in the fixed bed is treated like an element. It was not a practical model, however, as there are about a billion pebbles in a commercial reactor and so it would have taken too long to calculate something useful, especially with the lumbering computers then available. Dick's models of the fixed bed were much more practical, and became the standard in textbooks and in the industry. They also helped to establish the fixed bed as a predictable, low-risk reactor of choice.

Dick's models and methods were carried by his students to other universities and major companies, and through his own consulting to such companies as Mobil, Merck, and DuPont. Partly through his tireless efforts, the scientific method of reactor design and operations gradually caught on in industry, and became the core of the graduate curriculum.

One day, Dick was explaining his results to me in my office at Mobil when a phone call came in from John Quinn of the University of Illinois, asking if I would go to there next year as a visiting professor. I consulted with Dick about the wisdom of such a move, and he said "why don't you come to Princeton instead?" That is how I made my debut as a visiting professor at Princeton in the autumn of 1962, when the new Engineering Quadrangle had just opened. I met Bill Schowalter, a rising assistant professor, and, over cups of coffee, we discussed the people who had influenced our lives. It was clear that our role models were people who had educated the highest calibre students, who had done outstanding research, and who had led great departments — people like Dick Wilhelm. We also concluded that we did not know a single dean whose administrative career had inspired us, so it is ironic that, thirty years later, we would both become deans!

Dick was the unquestioned spiritual and temporal leader of the Chemical Engineering Department, greatly admired both for his scientific discoveries and for his organizational skill. He became chairman of the department in 1954, when Joe Elgin became dean of engineering, and he assembled a stellar faculty, five of whom would become members of the National Academy of

Engineering. Seven of the students who graduated under his tutelage also became members of the Academy. By then, Dick had won all the major awards from the American Institute of Chemical Engineers, and served as its director. He knew everyone at Princeton, too. When I walked with him through a national professional society meeting, or through the Princeton campus, we would be stopped constantly by people who wanted to have a word with him.

He handled departmental meetings with a great deal of authority. Faculty members were generally in awe of him, and some would slyly call him "Kaiser Wilhelm" behind his back. For all his stature, he remained a sensitive person. One day, I walked into his office half an hour before his talk at a seminar for graduate students, and found him pacing nervously. I was astonished at how seriously he took every audience, wanting to make sure that they received the best that he could deliver. He was very interested in the interaction between engineering and society, and in 1946 he directed Princeton's bicentennial conference, "Engineering and Human Affairs." He paid attention to his faculty, too. At the end of my year as a visiting professor at Princeton, he treated the entire departmental faculty and their wives to dinner at the Nassau Inn, and then took us all to McCarter Theater to see "Galileo" by Bertold Brecht.

Dick's first wife Rachel passed away in 1964, and he married Sarah Strayer in 1966. In 1968, Dick died suddenly from a heart attack while on vacation in Center Harbor, New Hampshire. In 1973, the American Institute of Chemical Engineers established in his honor the Richard Herman Wilhelm Award in Chemical Reaction Engineering "to recognize significant and new contributions in chemical reaction engineering." In 1974, the department that he helped to elevate to international leadership established in his honor the Richard Herman Wilhelm Lectureship. His greatest monument, however, is in the ideas that he inspired, which touched the lives of all his former students and colleagues.

READING LIST

With E. Singer: *Chemical Engineering Progress* 46 (1950): 343

With J. F. Wehner: "Boundary Conditions of a Flow Reactor," *Chemical Engineering Science* 6 (1956): 89

With F. A. Cleland: "Diffusion and Reaction in Viscous-Flow Tubular Reactors," *American Institute of Chemical Engineers Journal* 2 (1956): 489

With K. W. McHenry: "Axial Mixing of Binary Gas Mixtures in a Random Bed of Soheres," *American Institute of Chemical Engineers Journal* 3 (1957): 83

"Progress Towards the A Priori Design of Chemical Reactors," *Pure and Applied Chemistry* 5 (1962): 403

▾ CONTRIBUTORS ▾

William J. Baumol is Professor Emeritus and Senior Research Economist, Princeton University; and Professor of Economics and Director, C. V. Starr Center for Applied Economics, New York University. In recent years he has specialized in research on productivity growth and the role of scale economies in international trade. He continues to work in industrial organization and antitrust and regulatory policy. He also taught wood sculpture at Princeton University for more than ten years. His most recent book is *Entrepreneurship, Management, and the Structure of Chaos* (1995); the seventh edition of his *Economics: Principles and Policies*, a text with Alan Blinder, co-author, has just appeared.

Bernard Beck, who earned his Ph.D. from Princeton in 1963, is a sociologist at Northwestern University and Associate Chair of the Department of Sociology. He works in the areas of ideology, sociology of the arts, popular culture, and social problems. His research deals with the social organization of theater work, and he has had a long career as a professional actor in the Chicago area. He is the author of "Welfare as a Moral Category," *Social Problems* 4, no. 3 (1967): 258–277; "The Politics of Speaking in the Name of Society," *Social Problems* 25, no. 4 (1978): and "Reflections on Art and Inactivity," CIRA Monograph I (Center for Interdisciplinary Research in the Arts, Northwestern University, May 1988), based on his keynote address, "Art and Inactivity; or, Gee, Gang, This Old Theater Would Make a Swell Barn," Annual Conference on Social Theory and the Arts, April 1980 (unpublished).

one of the six Kodrati mentioned in the Menologion of the Greek Church he was meant to be. I suspect that it was Kodratos the Apostle, a very learned and wise man, for it was not only knowledge that Weitzmann shared with me, with us, with those who came near him. He passed on to us his firm belief in the value of scholarship and of art, and his belief in the world. This was his driving force, and this was the best lesson.

READING LIST

Illustrations in Roll and Codex. Studies in Manuscript Illumination, 2. Second edition with addenda (Princeton, 1970).

The Monastery of Saint Catherine at Mount Sinai. The Icons. Vol. 1: From the Sixth to the Tenth Century (Princeton, 1970).

With George Galavaris: *The Monastery of Saint Catherine at Mount Sinai. The Illuminated Greek Manuscripts. Vol. 1: From the Tenth to the Twelfth Century* (Princeton, 1990).

Sailing with Byzantium, from Europe to America. The Memoirs of an Art Historian (Munich, 1994).

David P. Billington, Class of 1950, is Professor of Civil Engineering and Operations Research and director of the Program in Architecture and Engineering at Princeton University. In 1995–1996, he was named by the Carnegie Foundation for the Advancement of Teaching as New Jersey State Professor of the Year, and has won many other awards for his teaching and research. He served as chairman of the American Society of Civil Engineering and the American Concrete Institute, and as a member of the executive council of the Society for the History of Technology. Among his many publications are *Thin-Shell Concrete Structures* (1982, 1989); *Robert Maillart's Bridges: The Art of Engineering* (1979, 1989), for which he won the Dexter Prize; *The Tower and the Bridge: The New Art of Structural Engineering* (1983, 1985); *Robert Maillart and the Art of Reinforced Concrete* (1990); and *The Innovators: The Engineering Pioneers Who Made America Modern* (1996).

John Tyler Bonner has been a Professor in the Biology Department since 1947; he became emeritus in 1990. Like Dr. Conklin, he is a developmental biologist, but instead of working on animal embryos he has concentrated on the development of slime molds. He has also written a number of books, including *Life Cycles* (1993) and the forthcoming *Sixty Years of Biology.*

Ellen Chances, Ph.D. 1972, is Professor of Russian Literature and Culture at Princeton University. Author of two books and well over two dozen articles, her specialties include the nineteenth- and twentieth-century Russian novel, contemporary Soviet and Russian literature, literature and cinema, literature and intellectual history, comparative contemporary Russian and American literature and culture, and literature and values. She has published articles on, among others, Dostoevski, Chekhov, poets Balmont and Mayakovsky, and the Soviet absurdist Kharms. Her most recent book, *Andrei Bitov: The Ecology of Inspiration*, is the first book in any language on Bitov, an important contemporary Russian writer. Chances is also a writer of poetry, fiction, and essays.

David R. Coffin, Class of 1940, received his Ph.D. from Princeton in 1954. He taught the history of Renaissance architecture and the history of gardening at Princeton until his retirement in 1988. Since 1970 he held the chair of the Howard Crosby Butler Memorial Professorship of the History of Architecture, first held by E. Baldwin Smith. Coffin has written three books on Renaissance Roman villas and gardens, and most recently a work entitled *The English Garden: Meditation and Memorial.*

Edward C. Cox, the Edwin Grant Conklin Professor of Biology and Professor of Molecular Biology, has been at Princeton since 1967. He was chairman of the Biology Department between 1977 and 1987. His papers on population biology referred to in the text were written with Tom Gibson, Class of 1970: E. C. Cox and T. C. Gibson, "Selection for High Mutation Rates in Chemostats," *Genetics* 77 (1974), p. 169; and T. C. Gibson, M. L. Scheppe, and E. C. Cox, "Fitness of an *Escherichia coli* Mutator Gene," *Science* 169 (1970), p. 686. Professor Cox's interests now lie in problems of development in simple organisms.

Vincent Davis received his Ph.D. from Princeton in 1961 and is presently the Patterson Chair Professor at the University of Kentucky. A former president of the International Studies Association, his books include *The Admirals' Lobby* (1967) and *Organizing for Defense* (1984).

Maurice A. East received his Ph.D. from Princeton in 1970 and is now Professor of International Affairs at the George Washington University. A former president of the International Studies Association, he has written *The Analysis of International Politics* (1972) and *Why Nations Act* (1978).

Val L. Fitch is the James S. McDonnell Distinguished University Professor of Physics, Emeritus. He taught at Princeton from 1954 until 1990 in courses ranging from freshman to graduate level. His research speciality has been in the area of elementary particles. He is a Fellow of the American Physical Society, a member of the National Academy of Sciences, the American Academy of Arts and Sciences, and the American Philosophical Society. In recognition of his research he has received the Research Corporation Award, the Lawrence Award, the Wetherill Medal, the Nobel Prize in Physics, and the National Medal of Science.

George Galavaris, art historian and painter, was born in Greece and educated in Europe and the United States. He earned his Ph.D. from Princeton in 1958, and is now Professor Emeritus of the History of Art at McGill University, Montreal. He is a Fellow of the Royal Society of Canada and a corresponding member of the Academy of Athens. He was co-author with Kurt Weitzmann of *The Monastery of St. Catherine at Mount Sinai: The Illuminated Greek Manuscripts. Volume I: From the Ninth to the Twelfth Century* (1990). His other books include *The Illustrations of the Liturgical Homilies of Gregory Nazianzenus* (1969); *Bread and the Liturgy* (1970); *The Illustrations of the Prefaces in Byzantine Gospels* (1979); and *The Icon in the Life of the Church* (1981). His most recent book, written in Greek, is *Byzantine Book Illumination* (1995).

Karl Galinsky is the Floyd Cailloux Centennial Professor of Classics at the University of Texas, Austin. He received tenure at the age of twenty-six and became a full professor at the age of thirty. He served for sixteen years as chairman of the Department of Classics at the University of Texas Austin, which he helped to build into the largest Classics department in the United States. Besides three awards for teaching excellence, he has received numerous awards for his scholarly work, including Guggenheim, ACLS, NEH, and Fulbright fellowships and a senior research award from the Alexander von Humboldt Foundation. His extensive professional activities include service as a regional director of the Mellon Fellowships in the Humanities under the guidance of Bob Goheen. Galinsky's many books include *Aeneas, Sicily, and Rome* (1960) and *Augustan Culture* (1996), both published by the Princeton University Press.

Daniel T. Gilbert received his Ph.D. from Princeton University in 1985 and is currently Professor of Psychology at the University of Texas at Austin. He has been a Fellow at the Center for Advanced Study in the Behavioral Sciences, a recipient of numerous grants and awards from the National Science Foundation and the National Institutes of Mental Health, and was the 1992 winner of the American Psychological Association's Distinguished Scientific Award for an Early Career Contribution to Psychology. His research interests include attributional processes, the psychology of belief, and affective forecasting. Among his recent publications are "How Mental Systems Believe" in *American Psychologist* 46 (1991), and with P. S. Malone, "The Correspondence Bias" in *Psychological Bulletin* 117 (1991). He is currently editing, with S. T. Fiske and G. Lindzey, the fourth edition of *The Handbook of Social Psychology*, to be published in 1997.

Irvin Glassman is the current Robert H. Goddard Professor in Princeton's Department of Mechanical and Aerospace Engineering. He received the Edgerton Gold Medal from the Combustion Institute for his research in the field of combustion, and the Roe Award from the American Society of Engineering Education for his teaching of engineering. He has advised more than forty Ph.D. students, most of whom are in academia. He has published more than 200 papers and written two books, *Combustion* and *The Performance of Chemical Propellants.*

Robert F. Goheen, Class of 1940, was president of Princeton University from 1957 to 1972. As an undergraduate he majored in Classics and the Special Program in the Humanities. Following World War II, he returned to Princeton and earned his Ph.D. in Classics in 1948, after which he served as an instructor and assistant professor of Classics until 1957. Along the way he held a Scribner Preceptorship, was a Senior Fellow in Classics at the American Academy in Rome, and for three years gave half-time to directing the National Woodrow Wilson Fellowship Program. As a classicist his principal scholarly interests were in Greek tragedy, literary criticism, and the history of ideas. These interests are reflected in his short book, *The Imagery of Sophocles' Antigone*, which constituted a novel application of the "New Criticism" to a classical text. Some of his reflections about the nature of liberal learning and its relevance in the contemporary world are included in another short book, *The Human Nature of a University*, as well as in various articles. On leaving Princeton's presidency, Dr. Goheen was for five years chairman and chief executive of the Council on Foundations and thereafter served as United States ambassador to India (1977–1980). From 1981 to 1992 he directed the Mellon Fellowships in the Humanities. Currently "retired," he continues to serve on a number of boards of worthy but impecunious cultural organizations while speaking and writing occasionally on South Asian affairs and issues relating to nuclear non-proliferation.

Suzanne Gossett is Professor of English at Loyola University Chicago, where she has taught since leaving Princeton. She writes on English Renaissance drama, as well as American literature. Her publications include articles on Shakespeare, Middleton, Beaumont and Fletcher, and Sarah Josepha Hale, as well as editions of play manuscripts from the English College, Rome, and the Folger Library for the Malone Society (*Collections XII* [1983] and *Collections XIV* [1988]); an edition of *Hierarchomachia* (1982); and a forthcoming edition of Thomas Middleton's *A Fair Quarrel* (Oxford, 1996). She is also the co-author (with Barbara Bardes) of *Declarations of Independence: Women and Political Power in Nineteenth-Century American Fiction* (1990).

Oleg Grabar received his Ph.D. from Princeton University in 1955. After thirty-seven years of teaching at the University of Michigan and at Harvard University, where he was the first Aga Khan Professor of Islamic Art, he joined the School of Historical Studies at the Institute for Advanced Study in Princeton. His latest book is *The Mediation of Ornament* (1992) and his *The Shape of the Holy,*

Early Islamic Jerusalem will be published by Princeton University Press in 1996.

William Happer, a Professor in the Department of Physics, Princeton University, is a specialist in modern optics, optical and radiofrequency spectroscopy of atoms and molecules, and spin-polarized atoms and nuclei. He received his B.S. degree in physics from the University of North Carolina in 1960 and the Ph.D. degree in physics from Princeton in 1964. From 1964 until 1980, when he joined the faculty at Princeton, he taught at Columbia University and served as Director of the Columbia Radiation Laboratory from 1976 to 1979. He was awarded the Class of 1909 Professorship of Physics at Princeton in 1988. In August 1991 he was appointed Director of Energy Research in the Department of Energy by President George Bush with the consent of the Senate. He was reappointed Professor of Physics at Princeton on 1 June 1993, and named Eugene Higgens Professor of Physics and Chairman of the University Research Board in 1995. He has served as a scientific consultant to numerous firms and government agencies, and has published more than a hundred scientific papers. He is a Fellow of the American Physical Society, the American Association for the Advancement of Science, and a member of the American Academy of Arts and Sciences and the National Academy of Sciences.

Marius B. Jansen, Class of 1944, is Professor of History and East Asian Studies, Emeritus, at Princeton University. He taught courses on Japanese History and is the author of *The Japanese and Sun Yat-sen* (1954); *Sakamoto Ryōma and the Meiji Restoration* (1961), which has recently been reissued as a paperback by Columbia University Press; *Japan and Its World: Two Centuries of Change* (1980 and 1996), and *China in the Tokugawa World* (1992).

Ernest F. Johnson is Professor of Chemical Engineering, Emeritus, at Princeton University. He was appointed to the Princeton faculty in 1948 after having spent two years in graduate school at the University of Pennsylvania and six years in the chemical industry. His research has focused on control theory, thermodynamic and transport properties of fluids, fusion power generation, and hazardous wastes management. In addition to teaching courses related to these research fields, he taught "Economy of Chemical Processes," the highly-rated capstone course for seniors. He has been a member of the board of Associated Universities, the corporation that operates the Brookhaven National Laboratory and the National Radio Astronomy Observatory, and its chairman for an unprecedented two terms. He has also served as Associate Dean of the Faculty, Clerk of the Faculty, as senior advisor to President Harold Shapiro, as chairman of the Long Range Planning Committee and the Conference Committee, and of the Judicial Committee and the Rights and Rules Committee of the Council of the Princeton University Community. He is an honorary member of the Class of 1962 and a Fellow of the American Association for the Advancement of Science, the American Institute of Chemical Engineers, and the American Institute of Chemists. In the autumn of 1995, an elegant new undergraduate lounge in the Engineering Quadrangle was dedicated in his honor, the gift of one of his former graduate students.

William Chester Jordan was a graduate student studying with Joseph Strayer at Princeton University from 1969 to 1973. He joined the faculty as an instructor in history in the fall of the latter year and has remained at Princeton ever since. His first book, a revision of his dissertation under Strayer, was *Louis IX and the Challenge of the Crusade: A Study in Rulership* (1979). Since then he has written on French serfdom, French royal policy towards the Jews in the Middle Ages, and a history of women and credit in pre-modern and developing societies. Most recently he has completed a study of *The Great Famine: Northern Europe in the Early Fourteenth Century*, which will appear in 1996. He is also the editor-in-chief of *The Middle Ages*, a four-volume abbreviation for middle-school aged children of Strayer's monumental *Dictionary of the Middle Ages.*

Walter J. Kauzmann, the David B. Jones Professor of Chemistry, Emeritus, received his Ph.D. from Princeton in 1940. His research has focused on the physical chemistry of proteins, a field that is now expanding rapidly. He is the author of several textbooks, including one on quantum mechanics, and a monograph on water (the properties of proteins depend very heavily on their interactions with water). During World War II, he spent two years at Los Alamos working on the atomic bomb. He has also made contributions to our understanding of the glassy state of matter. He is now working on problems in geochemistry.

Edmund L. Keeley, Class of 1948, is the Charles Barnwell Straut Class of 1923 Professor of English, Emeritus, at Princeton, where he served as director of the Creative Writing Program and director of the Program in Hellenic Studies. He is the author of seven novels, fourteen volumes of poetry in translation, and six volumes of non-fiction. His latest publications include *School for Pagan Lovers, The Essential Cavafy, Cavafy's Alexandria* (revised edition), and two books translated into Greek, *Some Wine for Remembrance* and *Albanian Journal: The Road to Elbasan.*

Daniel J. Kevles received his B.A. in physics and his Ph.D. in history from Princeton University and studied at Oxford University. In 1964, after a brief period on the White House Staff, he joined the faculty of the California Institute of Technology, where he is now the Koepfli Professor of Humanities and head of the Program in Science, Ethics, and Public Policy. He has written widely on the development of science and its relationship to American society past and present. His books include *In the Name of Eugenics: Genetics and the Uses of Human Heredity* (1985) and *The Physicists: The History of a Scientific Community in Modern America* (1978). He has published many articles and reviews in scholarly and general publications, including *The New York Review of Books, The Sciences, The New Republic, Harper's,* and *The New Yorker.* His works have earned a Page One Award and a National Historical Society Prize. He is a Fellow of the American

Association for the Advancement of Science and a member of the American Academy of Arts and Sciences and of the American Philosophical Society. He has held fellowships from the National Endowment for the Humanities and the Guggenheim Foundation.

Edmund L. King is the Walter S. Carpenter, Jr., Professor in the Language, Literature, and Civilization of Spain, Emeritus, and Professor of Romance Languages and Literatures, Emeritus, at Princeton University. He was born into a polyglot family of immigrants — German, French, and Russian — in 1914 and grew up in Austin, Texas, where, at the age of seven, he took his stepfather's surname. In school, he decided to learn Spanish, not one of the languages spoken at home, passing from a vaguely defined romantic attachment nurtured by frequent stays in Mexico to a more firmly structured interest in the civilization of Spain, thanks to his long association with Américo Castro. His publications include *Gustavo Adolfo Bécquer: From Painter to Poet*, the translation of *The Structure of Spanish History*, and an edition of Gabriel Miró's *El humo dormido*. He has published articles in the scholarly journals as well as in *Papeles de Son Armadans*, *The Hudson Review*, *The New Republic*, and *Encyclopedia Britannica* and several other reference works. For almost half a century he has been studying the life and works of Gabriel Miró (1879–1930), on which he is a recognized authority. He is married to the distinguished Hispanist Willard F. King.

Kenneth Levy, Princeton's Scheide Professor of Music History, Emeritus, is well known for contributions in the fields of medieval and early modern music history. During more than a quarter century he was lecturer in the University's introductory course for non-musician undergraduates, begun by the legendary Roy Welch. Levy's *Music: A Listener's Introduction* has been widely used.

John P. Lewis first spoke at Princeton in 1964 when, while he was a member of the U. S. President's Council of Economic Advisers, Arthur Lewis invited him to lecture to his development economics class. In 1969 John Lewis came to the Woodrow Wilson School as dean after five years as director of the USAID mission in India. After deaning he remained as professor of economics and international affairs until retiring in 1991, save for three years in Paris (1979–1981) as chairman of OECD's Development Assistance Committee. Among his books are (with Valeriana Kallab) *Development Strategies Reconsidered* (1985); *Strengthening the Poor* (1988); and *India's Political Economy: Governance and Reform* (1995). Currently he is working on an authorized history of the World Bank to be published by the Brookings Institution.

A. Walton Litz, Class of 1951, is Holmes Professor of Belles-Lettres and Professor of English, Emeritus, at Princeton University. He has edited (with Omar Pound) *Ezra Pound and Dorothy Shakespear, Their Letters: 1909–1914*, and recently published (with Lea Baechler) a new edition of *Personae: The Shorter Poems of Ezra Pound.*

Burton G. Malkiel received his Ph.D. from Princeton and is currently Chemical Bank Chairman's Professor of Economics at Princeton University. He studied with Machlup while in graduate school and served as Rapporteur for the Bellagio group that Machlup initiated in 1964. Malkiel specializes in financial economics and has written several books and many articles, including *The Term Structure of Interest Rates* (1964), *Expectations and the Structure of Share Prices* (1982), and *A Random Walk Down Wall Street* (sixth edition, 1995).

Gilbert Meilaender received his Ph.D. from Princeton University in 1976. He has taught in the Department of Religious Studies at the University of Virginia and the Department of Religion at Oberlin College. He has published widely in the field of Christian ethics. Among his most recent works are *Faith and Faithfulness: Basic Themes in Christian Ethics* (1991) and *Body, Soul, and Bioethics* (1995).

Walter F. Murphy joined Princeton's faculty in 1958 and served as chairman of the Department of Politics from 1966 to 1969. In

1968 he succeeded Alpheus Thomas Mason as McCormick Professor of Jurisprudence and held that chair until his retirement in 1995. Murphy's writings have dealt with constitutional politics in the United States and other nations. In addition, he has written three novels, *The Vicar of Christ* (1979), *The Roman Enigma* (1981), and *Upon This Rock* (1986). He is now living in the mountains near Albuquerque, New Mexico, finishing a scholarly book entitled *Constitutional Democracy* and writing a new novel.

Gary B. Nash, Class of 1955, received his Ph.D. from Princeton in 1964 and is a Professor of History at UCLA. As Associate Director and now Director of the National Center for History in the Schools, and as co-chair of the National History Standards Project, he has been deeply involved in the nationwide reform of the curriculum in American history. He has served as president of the Organization of American Historians and on the editorial boards of the *William and Mary Quarterly, American Indian Culture and Research Journal,* and other scholarly journals, and is the author of more than a hundred articles, reviews, and chapters in books. Among his most important books are *Quakers and Politics: Pennsylvania, 1681–1726* (1968, 1993); *Red, White, and Black: The Peoples of Early America* (1974, 1982, 1992); *The Urban Crucible: Social Change, Political Consciousness and the Origins of the American Revolution* (1979); *Forging Freedom: The Formation of Philadelphia's Black Community, 1720–1840* (1988); and *Race and Revolution: The Inaugural Merrill Jensen Lectures* (1990).

Alexander Nehamas is the Edmund N. Carpenter II Class of 1943 Professor in the Humanities, Professor of Philosophy, and Professor of Comparative Literature at Princeton University. He received his Ph.D. from Princeton in 1971, with a dissertation, directed by Gregory Vlastos, on Plato's philosophy of language. He has taught at the University of Pittsburgh, the University of Pennsylvania, and the University of California at Berkeley. He is the author of *Nietzsche: Life as Literature,* translator of Plato's *Symposium* and *Phaedrus,* and editor of *Aristotle's Rhetoric: Philosophi-*

cal Essays, and of the Greek edition of Vlastos' *Socrates: Ironist and Moral Philosopher.*

Robert L. Patten, who received his Ph.D. in 1965, wrote his dissertation on plot in Dickens's novels under the direction of Dudley Johnson. Subsequently he published a book on Dickens as a professional author and a two-volume critical biography of Dickens's first illustrator, *George Cruikshank's Life, Times, and Art.* Dr. Patten is professor of English at Rice University and editor of *SEL: Studies in English Literature 1500–1900.*

Franklin P. Peterson was a graduate student at Princeton from 1952 to 1955 and wrote his Ph.D. thesis under Norman Steenrod, who was one of Lefschetz's best students. From 1956 to 1958, he was Higgins Lecturer at Princeton. Since then, he has been on the faculty of the Massachusetts Institute of Technology. His field of research is algebraic topology.

Nicholas Moffett Pyle lives in Los Angeles, where he designs food-service facilities, as they are felicitously called. He received his A.B. from Harvard in 1964 and his M.Arch. from Princeton in 1971. After graduation he worked for Warren Platner Associates in New Haven. Upon arriving in Los Angeles he briefly taught and worked at UCLA with Charles W. Moore, M.F.A. 1956, Ph.D. 1957, with whom he edited *The Yale Mathematics Building Competition* (1974); that competition, by the way, was won by Robert Venturi. He has also taught at California State Polytechnic University, Pomona, and at Otis Art Institute in Los Angeles, and has worked in the design office of John Fellis and Associates.

George T. Reynolds, the Class of 1909 Professor of Physics, Emeritus, received his Ph.D. from Princeton in 1943. From May 1943 to May 1944 he worked for the National Defense Research Committee as a specialist in blast effects, and later participated in the Manhattan Project at Los Alamos. In September 1945 he went to Japan to do bomb damage analysis in Hiroshima and Nagasaki. During his tenure at Princeton, he served as Director of the High

Energy Physics Program, the Science in Human Affairs Program, and the Center for Environmental Studies, and as a member of the University Research Board.

Thomas P. Roche, Jr., Murray Professor of English Literature and Clerk of the Faculty at Princeton, is currently completing a study of the literary and visual iconography of the Muses from Hesiod through the Renaissance. He received his Ph.D. from Princeton in 1958 and is the author of many books and articles, among them *The Kindly Flame: A Study of the Third and Fourth Books of Spenser's The Faerie Queene* and *Petrarch and the English Sonnet Sequence.* Most recently, he has been entrusted to add another chapter to *The Princeton Graduate School: A History*, to bring Willard Thorp's story up to the present.

Ronald C. Rosbottom, Robert and Winifred Arms Professor in the Arts and Humanities at Amherst College, studied at Princeton in 1964–1967 and received his Ph.D. in 1969. He taught for six years at the University of Pennsylvania, sixteen at Ohio State University, and is beginning his seventh year as a professor of French and European Studies at Amherst, where he was Dean of the Faculty from 1989 to 1995. He is the author, among other things, of *Marivaux's Novels*, a book about one of Voltaire's more despised contemporaries.

James N. Rosenau received his Ph.D. from Princeton in 1957 and is University Professor of International Affairs at the George Washington University. A former president of the International Studies Association, his writings include *Turbulence in World Politics: A Theory of Change and Continuity* (1990), and *Thinking Theory Thoroughly: Coherent Approaches to an Incoherent World* (1995).

Teofilo F. Ruiz was a graduate student under Joseph Strayer at Princeton University from 1970 to 1973. He joined the faculty at Brooklyn College, History Department, in the fall of 1973, where he is now Professor of History. His most recent book, *Crisis and Continuity: Land and Town in Late Medieval Castile* (1994), was awarded the Premio del Rey by the American Historical Association as the best book in Spanish history before 1600. His area of research is the cultural and social history of Castile and Spain in the Middle Ages. In the spring of 1995 he was Visiting Professor of History at Princeton, where with fond memories and considerable trepidation he occupied Strayer's old office and taught his course, "Europe in the High Middle Ages."

Jerrold E. Seigel received his Ph.D. from Princeton in 1964, and taught European history there until 1988, when he moved to New York University, where he is William J. Kenan Professor of History. He is the author of *Rhetoric and Philosophy in Renaissance Humanism* (1968); *Marx's Fate: The Shape of a Life* (1978); *Bohemian Paris* (1986), which was a finalist for the National Book Critics Circle Award in Criticism; and most recently *The Private Worlds of Marcel Duchamp* (1995).

Martin Shubik, Ph.D. 1953, is the Seymour H. Knox Professor of Mathematical Institutional Economics at Yale University and has served as an economic consultant both in the United States and overseas. The author of more than 250 articles, he has also written or edited fourteen books, among them *Games for Society, Business and War* (1975); *Game Theory in the Social Sciences* (1982 and 1984); and *The Mathematics of Conflict* (1983). He edited *Risk, Organizations, and Society: Studies in Risk and Uncertainty* (1991) and *Essays in Mathematical Economics in Honor of Oskar Morgenstern* (1967).

Lyman Spitzer, Jr., born in 1914 in Toledo, Ohio, was an undergraduate at Yale, then came to Princeton for graduate study, receiving his Ph.D. in 1938. In 1947 he returned to Princeton as a Professor of Astronomy and also Director of the Observatory, a position he held for some thirty years. His professional work, following the example set by Henry Norris Russell, involved the use of physical laws to explain observations of stars, clouds, and galaxies. His research in plasma physics was helpful in the controlled fusion program, especially at the Princeton Plasma Physics Laboratory which he founded. He is best known for his association with the Hubble Space Telescope, which he proposed in 1946 and supported in many ways until 1994, when it finally operated successfully as planned. Among his many publications are "The Formation of Stars," in *Physics Today* 1 (1948); "On a Possible Interstellar Galactic Corona," in *Astrophysical Journal* 124 (1956); "The Stellarator Concept," in *Physics of Fluids* 1 (1958); "Astronomical Research with the Large Space Telescope," in *Science* 171 (1968); and *Physical Processes in the Interstellar Medium* (1968).

Lynn Staley is Harrington and Shirley Drake Professor in the Humanities at Colgate University, where she teaches in the English Department. She has written books on the *Gawain*-poet, on Edmund Spenser's *Shepheardes Calender*, and on *The Book of Margery Kempe.* Two more books are forthcoming, one an edition of *The Book of Margery Kempe*, the other, with David Aers of Duke University, *The Powers of the Holy: Religion, Politics and Gender in Late Medieval English Culture.*

Stanley J. Stein is the retired Walter Samuel Carpenter III Professor in Spanish Civilization and Culture, and Professor of History at Princeton. His publications include *Vassouras: A Brazilian Coffee County, 1850–1900* (1958); *The Brazilian Cotton Textile Manufacture: Textile Enterprise in an Underdeveloped Area, 1850–1950* (1957); and with Barbara Hadley Stein, *The Colonial Heritage of Latin America: Essays on Economic Dependence in Perspective* (1970). With Roberto Cortés Conde, he edited *Latin America: A Guide to Economic History, 1830–1930* (1977). He and Barbara Hadley Stein are currently completing a multi-volume study of the economic and political relations between Spain and Mexico, 1759–1810.

Robert Venturi is the partner responsible for architectural and urban design in the Philadelphia architectural firm of Venturi, Scott Brown and Associates, Inc., where he works closely with his wife Denise Scott Brown. Together, they have had decisive influence on architects and architectural design throughout the world.

Among his projects are the Sainsbury Wing of the National Gallery on Trafalgar Square in London; the Hôtel du Départment de la Haute-Garonne (a provincial capitol building) in Toulouse, France; and a resort complex in Japan. He has also done a great deal of work for Princeton University over the past twenty-five years, and this has given him special satisfaction. Besides his architectural practice, Mr. Venturi is highly regarded as a theorist. His book, *Complexity and Contradiction in Architecture*, is widely regarded as a milestone in architectural theory; published in 1966 and reissued in 1977, it has been translated and published in sixteen languages. His other books include one he wrote with Denise Scott Brown and Steven Izenour, *Learning from Las Vegas* (1972), and his latest book, *Iconography and Electronics Upon a Generic Architecture* (1966).

James Wei is professor of chemical engineering and Dean of Engineering and Applied Science at Princeton University. He received his doctorate from MIT in chemical engineering in 1955, and subsequently conducted research in catalysis and reaction engineering at Mobil Oil for fifteen years, including a year at Princeton as a visiting professor. He became a professor of chemical engineering at the University of Delaware, and later a department head of chemical engineering at MIT for fourteen years before coming to Princeton as dean in 1991. He has written more than 100 research papers on catalysis and reaction engineering, and a number of books. He was president of the American Institute of Chemical Engineers in 1988, and he has been a member of the National Academy of Engineering since 1978.

Arthur S. Wightman, Thomas D. Jones Professor of Mathematical Physics, Emeritus, Princeton University, has worked for five decades on the mathematical foundations of quantum field theory. The first stage of this work, in the 1950s, incorporated into quantum field theory the insights of Eugene P. Wigner on relativistic invariance in quantum mechanics. It involved the elaboration of what is sometimes called axiomatic quantum field theory. The second stage, now commonly called constructive quantum field theory, attracted a large and talented group of mathematical physicists in the decade-and-a-half after 1960. It involved the solution of a number of model quantum field theories in space-times of two and three dimensions. The last stage, which has continued to this day, extends the previous work in constructive field theory to quantum gauge field theories and to four-dimensional space-time.

Calhoun Winton received an A.B. degree from the University of the South, Sewanee, an M.A. from Vanderbilt University, and, in 1955, a Ph.D. from Princeton. He has taught at Dartmouth and the Universities of Delaware, Virginia, and South Carolina. Since 1975, he has taught at the University of Maryland, where he has served as department chairman and director of graduate studies. He has been awarded Guggenheim, Fulbright, and ACLS fellowships, and is the author of a two-volume biography of Sir Richard Steele, essayist and dramatist, as well as numerous articles and reviews. His latest book is *John Gay and the London Theatre* (1993). He is now working on the history of the book in America. He holds a commission in the United States Navy, Captain, USNR (Ret.). A loyal son of Princeton, he is a member of the Princeton Clubs of Washington and New York, and has served on the APGA board and as a fund raiser in the Washington area.

INDEX